Ethical Issues in Commun. Professions

Dynamic, rapid, and radical changes are transforming the communication professions, provoking major implications for ethics. Traditional boundaries blur as media converge; relentless competitive pressures cause some forms of communication to atrophy and permit others to explode; and technological advances occur daily. In this volume, a new generation of scholars takes a fresh look at the manner in which ethical issues manifest themselves in their areas of research and suggests new agendas for future research.

This book addresses a wide range of questions from a variety of communication professions. It raises issues such as how to define a journalist in an era when anyone can disseminate information to a global audience; how to use "advergames," crowdsourcing, and facial recognition technology in advertising responsibly; and how to respond ethically in situations of public crisis communication, among many others. This volume will be essential reading for scholars and professionals in media, communication, and digital arts, as well as philosophy, government, public policy, business, and law.

Minette E. Drumwright is Associate Professor in the Department of Advertising and Public Relations, College of Communication, University of Texas at Austin. Her research is in the area of ethics in advertising and public relations, corporate social responsibility, and communication for nonprofit organizations. Her work has been published in a variety of journals and books.

New Agendas in Communication
A Series from Routledge and the College of Communication at the University of Texas at Austin
Roderick Hart and Stephen Reese, Series Editors

This series brings together groups of emerging scholars to tackle important interdisciplinary themes that demand new scholarly attention and reach broadly across the communication field's existing courses. Each volume stakes out a key area, presents original findings, and considers the long-range implications of its "new agenda."

Global Communication
Edited by Karin Wilkins, Joe Straubhaar, and Shanti Kumar

Agenda Setting in a 2.0 World
Edited by Thomas J. Johnson

Identity and Communication
Edited by Dominic L. Lasorsa and America Rodriguez

Political Emotions
Edited by Janet Staiger, Ann Cvetkovich, and Ann Reynolds

Media Literacy
Edited by Kathleen Tyner

Communicating Science
Edited by LeeAnn Kahlor and Patricia Stout

Journalism and Citizenship
Edited by Zizi Papacharissi

The Interplay of Truth and Deception
Edited by Matthew S. McGlone and Mark L. Knapp

Ethical Issues in Communication Professions

New Agendas in Communication

Minette E. Drumwright

Routledge
Taylor & Francis Group

NEW YORK AND LONDON

First published 2014
by Routledge
711 Third Avenue, New York, NY 10017

Simultaneously published in the UK
by Routledge
2 Park Square, Milton Park, Abingdon, Oxon OX14 4RN

Routledge is an imprint of the Taylor & Francis Group, an informa business

Library of Congress Cataloging in Publication Data
Ethical issues in communication professions :
new agendas in communication / edited by Minette Drumwright.
    pages cm
    1. Mass media—Moral and ethical aspects. 2. Journalistic ethics.
    3. Advertising—Moral and ethical aspects. 4. Marketing—Moral and
    ethical aspects. I. Drumwright, Minette E., editor of compilation.
    P94.E755 2013
    302.23—dc23
    2013023332

ISBN: 978-0-415-86994-2 (Paperback)
ISBN: 978-0-415-86993-5 (Hardback)
ISBN: 978-0-203-79623-8 (eBook)

Typeset in Sabon
by Swales & Willis Ltd, Exeter, Devon

Contents

Figures

Contributors

Lucy Atkinson is an assistant professor in the Department of Advertising and Public Relations at the University of Texas at Austin. She earned her Ph.D. at the University of Wisconsin–Madison and her M.A. at New York University. Her primary area of research focuses on the intersection of politics and consumer behavior, particularly among young people. For example, she explores whether and to what degree socially conscious consumption, such as buying fair-trade coffee or hybrid cars, either helps or hinders conventional civic and political engagement, such as voting and volunteering. A second stream of research focuses on consumer socialization among children and teens, exploring how young children understand advertising and navigate consumer culture.

Vincent Cicchirillo is an assistant professor in the Department of Advertising and Public Relations at the University of Texas at Austin. His work focuses upon the study of media technologies—in particular, the influence of video game play features and contexts on post-game play outcomes. Of particular interest is the examination of character representations within video games (i.e., race and gender) and how that influences outcomes related to identification, positive and negative valence, as well as aggression. This research also examines the effect of stereotypical representations within violent video games. His work has appeared in *Human Communication Research*, *Journal of Broadcasting and Electronic Media*, *Journal of Social Psychology*, and *Journal of Advertising Research*.

Troy Elias is an assistant professor in the Department of Advertising in the College of Journalism and Communications at the University of Florida. He earned his Ph.D. at the Ohio State University. His research interest is in social influence, with an emphasis on race and ethnicity, information and communication technology, and Internet advertising. His research explores the impact of social identity and psychological distinctiveness on consumer attitudes in new media environments. He has taught courses in Social Influence in New Media Environments, Advertising Design and Graphics, Communication Technology, Visual Communication, and Persuasion. He has published in the *Journal of Advertising Research* and the *Journal of Interactive Advertising*. In 2008, he was awarded the Barrow Minority Doctoral Student scholarship.

W. Glenn Griffin is an associate professor at the University of Alabama (Tuscaloosa). He teaches courses in creativity and portfolio development and studies the creative process and social responsibility in advertising. In September 2010, his first book, *The Creative Process Illustrated: How Advertising's Big Ideas Are Born* (co-authored with Dr. Deborah Morrison), was published by HOW Books. His research on the creative process has been published in the *Journal of Advertising* and *Journal of Advertising Education*, and has been featured in the U.K.'s *Campaign* magazine, among other titles. His students' work has been featured in both national and international press, including *Advertising Age*, *Adweek*, *Archive*, and *CMYK* magazines, and has been recognized by the One Club for Art & Copy, the Art Directors Club of New York, the Clio Awards and the American Advertising Federation's NSAC and ADDY programs. He currently serves as secretary of the American Academy of Advertising (AAA). He completed his Ph.D. at the University of Texas at Austin in 2002.

Marie Guadagno is a current doctoral student in the Department of Advertising at the University of Texas at Austin. Her research focuses on health promotion to low health literate audiences and non-profit communication. In conjunction, she is also interested in the branding of social causes and direct response fundraising. Recent research has examined the role of appropriate health promotion campaigns and prenatal care among Hispanic women. Prior to the University of Texas at Austin, Marie worked for an agency that specialized in fundraising for national non-profit organizations.

Sara Kamal received her Ph.D. in Advertising at the University of Texas at Austin. She is an assistant professor of Marketing Communications at the American University in Dubai, United Arab Emirates. Her research interests include the economic effects of advertising, social media, cross-cultural consumer behavior, and advertising in emerging markets. Dr. Kamal's research has appeared in the *International Journal of Advertising* and *Journal of Interactive Advertising*, and is forthcoming in the *International Journal of Internet Marketing and Advertising*. Her research has also been published in books such as *Computer-Mediated Communication across Cultures: International Interactions in Online Environments* and *Handbook of Research in International*

Advertising: Special Issue on Emerging Markets and Advances in Advertising Research (vol. II). She regularly presents her work at various conferences, including the American Advertising Academy (AAA) and the Association for Education in Journalism and Mass Communication (AEJMC). Kamal teaches courses such as Principles of Integrated Marketing Communications, Integrated Marketing Communications Campaigns, Media Planning, and Integrated Marketing Communications Management.

Jenn Burleson Mackay is an assistant professor of Multimedia Journalism at Virginia Tech. Her primary research interest focuses on how journalistic ethics is constrained by various factors such as the profession, the news organization, technology, and the news medium. She is interested in how journalistic ethics are transforming as news organizations construct online identities and journalists acquire new technological skills and responsibilities. Her secondary research area centers on how technology influences journalism on a more general level. Mackay's research has been published in the *Journal of Mass Media Ethics*, *Journalism Practice*, *Newspaper Research Journal*, and *Journalism & Mass Communication Quarterly*. She is co-editor of the book *Media Bias: Finding It, Fixing It* and has contributed chapters in several other books. Mackay teaches courses related to multimedia journalism and communication ethics. Mackay earned her master's degree and her Ph.D. in Mass Communication from the University of Alabama. Before moving to Alabama, she earned a bachelor's degree in journalism from the University of North Carolina at Chapel Hill. She also worked at one television station and at several newspapers in Tennessee, North Carolina, and Virginia. Her last stop in the professional journalism world was at *The Roanoke Times* in Virginia.

Michael Mackert is an associate professor in the Department of Advertising at the University of Texas at Austin. His research focuses primarily on the strategies that can be used in traditional and new digital media to provide health education to low health literate audiences. Recent projects have looked at: health literacy issues in direct-to-consumer prescription drug advertising; health promotion including hand washing and prenatal care; training programs to improve how healthcare workers communicate with low health literate patients; and how e-health can improve quality of life for disabled cancer survivors. Mackert's research has recently appeared in *Health Communication*, *Patient Education and Counseling*, *Women & Health*, *Telemedicine and e-Health*, *Journal for Specialists in Pediatric Nursing*, *Fertility and Sterility*, *Journal of Computer-Mediated Communication*, *Journal of Technology in Human Services*, *Journal of School Health*, and *Journal of Telemedicine and Telecare*. He teaches classes in account planning, health communication, and integrated marketing communication management.

Danee Pye is a Ph.D. candidate in the Communication Studies Department at the University of Texas at Austin. Her research focuses on the intersections of rhetoric, feminism, and philosophy. Specifically, she is interested in the philosophy of Susanne K. Langer and its implications for political communication and rhetoric.

Karyn Riddle is an assistant professor in the School of Journalism and Mass Communication, University of Wisconsin, Madison. Her research focuses on the psychology of media effects with an emphasis on the effects of exposure to media violence. Most recently, she has been studying children's fear responses to media violence, including violence on the news. She earned her Ph.D. at the University of California, Santa Barbara.

Erin E. Schauster is an instructor of Advertising at Bradley University. She received a M.S. from Southern Illinois University Edwardsville and a B.S. from Southern Illinois University Carbondale, and is completing her Ph.D. at the Missouri School of Journalism. Her research follows an organizational approach for understanding the advertising industry and the many organizations therein. Her research examines advertising agency culture, ethics and decision-making by advertising executives, and higher education in advertising. Schauster's teaching philosophy incorporates real-world experience by sending students into the field of advertising and bringing her agency experiences back into the classroom. These experiences come from her research and her previous work as an account executive for five years in agencies in St. Louis and Nashville.

Jason M. Shepard is an assistant professor of Communications at California State University, Fullerton, where he teaches courses in journalism, media law, and media history. Shepard's primary research agenda has examined the law and ethics of journalists' confidential source protections. In 2011, LFB Scholarly Publishers published his first scholarly book, *Privileging the Press: Confidential Sources, Journalism Ethics and the First Amendment*. Shepard has published research in several scholarly journals and law reviews, including *Communication Law and Policy*, *Journal of Media Law & Ethics*, *Nexus Journal of Law and Policy*, and *Drake Law Review*. Recently, he served as an expert witness for the state of Maine in a campaign-finance case hinging on whether an Internet writer was considered a journalist for legal purposes. Shepard earned his Ph.D. from the University of Wisconsin–Madison in 2009, with an emphasis in media law. Previously, he spent 10 years as a newspaper reporter and is a former member of Teach for

America. Currently, Shepard is the head of the Gay, Lesbian, Bisexual and Transgender Interest Group of the Association of Education in Journalism and Mass Communication (AEJMC). He also served as the adviser of Cal State Fullerton's award-winning daily newspaper from 2009–2011.

Scott R. Stroud is an assistant professor in the Department of Communication Studies at the the University of Texas at Austin. He specializes in the intersection between rhetoric and philosophy. His current research concerns John Dewey's aesthetic theory and the insights it provides with respect to rhetorical experience. He is particularly interested in the connections between artful communication, individual flourishing, and democracy as explicated by the American pragmatists. His recent book, *John Dewey and the Artful Life* (Pennsylvania State University Press), engages these themes in detail. His work on rhetorical experience also extends to topics in comparative rhetoric, narrative theory, and communication ethics. His research has been published in venues such as *Rhetoric Society Quarterly*, *Philosophy & Rhetoric*, the *Journal of Communication and Religion*, the *Western Journal of Communication*, and the *Journal of Speculative Philosophy*.

Lina Svedin is an assistant professor of Political Science at the University of Utah. She is Swedish by origin and has worked both as a practitioner in government and as a researcher and training director at the Swedish national center for Crisis Research and Training. Her research focuses on governance challenges in crises. Recent publications include *Organizational Cooperation in Crises* (Ashgate Publishing), *Risk Regulation in the European Union and the United States* (Palgrave MacMillan), *Ethics and Crisis Management* (Information Age Publishing), and *Accountability in Crises and Public Trust in Governing Institutions* (Routledge). New research projects include ethics in crisis communication, managing health-related issues in response to the 2011 Japanese earthquake and tsunami, and crisis accountability mechanisms in American public administration. Svedin teaches core courses on administrative theory, policy analysis, ethics for public administrators, governance and the economy, as well as crisis management and conflict resolution within the U of U's Masters of Public Administration program.

Seung-Chul Yoo is an assistant professor of Digital Advertising in the School of Communication at Loyola University Chicago. He teaches Communication and New Media, Media Planning and new courses in digital advertising. Yoo is an expert on new media advertising and a consultant on digital media technologies and interactive advertising. In his many years as an advertising professional, he worked as a sales promotion media planner at Cheil Worldwide (In-House Agency of Samsung Group) and a senior account manager at W Brand Connection (WPP Communication Group). Also, he has been working as an international correspondent for Cheil Worldwide since 2008. Yoo's research explores marketing communication through new media technologies (e.g., 3D virtual reality, augmented reality, haptics, face recognition tools, and digital holograms) with a focus on persuasion design. He worked on advertising effectiveness measurement projects at several leading companies, such as CJ Media and Samsung Electronics. His more than one hundred marketing and new media columns have appeared in a variety of industry magazines and his academic articles have been published in the *Journal of Advertising Research* and *Cyberpsychology, Behavior, and Social Networking.* Yoo's recent digital media study about advertising in violent video games has been featured in many newspapers, magazines, and diverse online news outlets of several countries (e.g., U.S., U.K., France, Poland, Korea, Japan, and China.). He has also written a book titled *Digital Signage for Integrated Marketing Communication* (2011). He holds a Ph.D. and M.A. in Advertising from The University of Texas at Austin and a B.B.A. from Sungkyunkwan University.

Preface
Old and New Wine
Old and New Wineskins

Minette E. Drumwright

Dynamic, rapid, and radical changes are transforming the communication professions. Traditional boundaries blur as media converge; relentless competitive pressures cause some forms of communication to atrophy and permit others to explode; and technological advances occur daily. Everyone tweets, blogs, and sends messages via Facebook and YouTube, including companies, non-profits, and governmental agencies. The changes have vast implications for ethics. As one example, information about companies often was provided by traditional media and filtered by journalists; now it is often provided directly to consumers via company websites. Indeed, many of the new forms of communication, such as social media, often lack the ethical screens that communication professionals have traditionally provided, and some experts predict that firms will eventually be held responsible for what consumers say about their products through various forms of electronic media. The changes occurring are not simply a function of new technology. Changes in the political and legal environment are relevant. As a result of *Citizens United*, the Supreme Court case that deregulated political campaign contributions, an avalanche of corporate money has begun to flow into political communication with a growing inability to determine the source of the message. Ethical concerns abound. Globalization has important implications. Communication professionals have followed their multinational clients to far-flung places. Ethical issues are raised as cultures clash and business practices diverge. In short, in today's fast-changing environment, a renewed focus on ethics in communication professions is critical and timely. To be sure, many of the age-old questions persist, but they often have new twists. For example, the question regarding what constitutes responsible and ethical advertising to children is not new; but the entertaining and immersive experience of "advergames" on company websites is. This and other forms of persuasion that elicit heightened involvement from children present a multitude of perplexing new issues with ethical ramifications for advertisers. Wholly new questions also emerge. For example, in an era when anyone can disseminate information to a global audience, who is a journalist? Can journalism still be considered a pro-fession that can be defined by ethical frameworks? How is the Constitu-tional guarantee of a free press supposed to work in the Internet age? In short, some issues may be old wine in new wineskins; others may be new wine, but they all call for new thought.

If ever there were a time to inspire bright, young, scholarly minds to focus on ethics in communication professions, it is now. In March of 2012, a group of outstanding, young scholars who are "next generation thinkers" assembled for a two-day conference on ethics in communica-tion professions on the campus of the College of Communication at the University of Texas at Austin. Their assignment was to take a fresh look at the manner in which ethical issues manifest themselves in their areas of research and to suggest a new agenda for future research. At the confer-ence, each of the young scholars presented a paper that eventually became a chapter in this volume. Each paper was discussed and critiqued by an accomplished, senior scholar. I want to express my gratitude to these senior scholars, who added tremendously to the dialogue and discussion: Renita Coleman, Matthew Eastin, Kathleen Higgins, Robert Jensen, Wally Snyder, and Patricia Stout.

In her keynote address, renowned communication ethics scholar Ren-ita Coleman asserted that ethical issues are everywhere in communication professions, but scholars working in areas that are swirling with ethical issues often overlook them. She also noted that even some of the most commonly used theories in communication research, such as framing and agenda setting, raise ethical issues that are typically ignored. She urged the New Agenda scholars to view every communication research topic through ethical lenses, whether they write one paper on ethics or pursue an entire research stream. Coleman noted the potential usefulness of a wide variety of interdisciplinary theories in ethics research and empha-sized the importance of developing new theory to explain phenomena and guide professionals. She acknowledged that widely varied research methods, ranging from critical essays to qualitative methods to experi-mental design, could be productively employed in ethics research. Not-ing the practical usefulness of ethics research to professionals, Coleman emphasized the importance of focusing on solutions, not just criticism, and identifying and recommending best practices to guide professionals.

Distinguished business and government leader and now professor Wally Snyder brought important professional perspectives from his years as a Federal Trade Commission lawyer and as president of the Ameri-can Advertising Federation (AAF). He emphasized the importance of advertising being not only truthful but also fair. Truthful advertising is required by law in the U.S., but fair advertising goes beyond the law and requires ethical and responsible behavior by advertising professionals. He reminded the New Agenda scholars that advertising that is both truthful and fair plays a vital role in the marketplace and in the economic system by providing information to consumers and spurring product innovation. To increase the level of ethical behavior in the advertising profession, Snyder recently has led in establishing the Institute for Advertising Ethics, which is administered through the AAF in partnership with the Reynolds Journalism Institute and the Missouri School of Journalism. Its purpose is to inspire advertising, public relations, and marketing communications professionals to practice the highest personal ethics in the creation and dissemination of truthful and fair commercial information to consumers. One of its first contributions is to identify, explicate, and apply principles and practices for advertising ethics in the context of the explosion of changes in technology that are altering the domestic and international marketplace.

As someone who has wrestled with issues of communication ethics for more than 20 years, I am pleased to see key themes dealt with in ways that fill some of the voids in previous research. For example, research on communication ethics historically has taken a bi-polar approach—a micro-macro divide (Drumwright, 2007). The "macro" perspective focuses on communication's effects on society; the "micro" perspective focuses at an individual level—individual consumers, individual communication practitioners, individual ads or news stories, and specific advertising or journalism practices. In my research on communication ethics, I have proposed and focused on a third level—the "meso" level. The meso level, between the micro and macro-levels, is the level of the organization or groups of organizations—such as media, advertising agencies, or client companies—and it has largely been ignored in communication ethics research. I have argued that neglect of the meso level is particularly problematic because the organizational culture of media companies, advertising agencies, or advertisers has a strong influence on the moral sensitivity of individual communication professionals. Moreover, solutions to some macro-level ethical problems to which communication contributes require the collaborative efforts of organizations or groups of organizations. I am pleased that all three levels are addressed in this book and that the organizational level is given the attention that it is due in considering ethical issues in both persuasive and journalistic communication.

Merely identifying ethical issues has been a persistent problem in communication ethics, so I am pleased that chapters in this volume identify and examine a host of ethical issues. Patrick Murphy and I coined the term "moral myopia" for a distortion of moral vision in which ethical issues do not come clearly into focus for communication professionals (Drumwright & Murphy, 2004, 2009). Often "moral muteness," an unwillingness to talk about moral issues, contributes to moral myopia. Chapters in this volume identify ethical issues embedded in a variety of wide-ranging contexts—in the crowdsourcing of advertising messages on the Internet, in direct-to-consumer prescription drug advertising, in social blogging, in targeting certain market segments, in crisis communication, in television programming for children, in using facial recognition technology, and of course, in the newsroom and in the advertising agency, to name a few. The chapters also provide thought-provoking discussions of these issues, and they will certainly serve as catalysts for lively discussions.

Individuals can have the best ethical values in the world, but these values do not have the impact that they should if they are not put into action (Gentile, 2010). As such, individuals need to know how to translate their ethical values into action, how to give voice to their values and persuade others to follow their lead, and how to implement plans to live out their ethical values. I am pleased that some of the chapters in this volume deal with issues of this nature from the perspective of both communication professionals and consumers of communication.

The debates about some communication topics that are rife with ethical issues are so polarized and the rhetoric is so heated that the various parties are talking past each other or not talking at all (Drumwright & Williams, 2013). Witness the debate about food and beverage marketing to children and adolescents in light of the obesity crisis and the debate about direct-to-consumer marketing of prescription drugs and its effects on low literacy consumers. If progress is to be made in areas such as these, the discussions need to move past polarized debate to a more productive dialogue that brings together parties with very different perspectives— public health experts and advertisers, government officials and marketers, policy experts and professors. Chapters in this volume not only call for this type of productive dialogue, but also they clarify the issues, dispel common myths, provide policy recommendations, and present research agendas that will further collaborative solutions.

Some criticisms of communication ethics research and of communication research more generally have focused on its atheoretical nature (Drumwright, 2012; Thorson & Rogers, 2012). As Thorson and Rogers have argued, communication is a variable field that borrows theories from other fields and applies them to the unique contexts of communication. I am pleased that chapters in this volume draw on theory and conceptual models from a wide variety of disciplines, including philosophy, psychology, sociology, and organizational behavior, to name a few.

I cannot begin to do justice to the chapters in this book in this brief preface, but I will say a little about the topic of each chapter in an attempt to give a sense of the breadth of the book. Each chapter not only identifies and examines ethical issues but also, and perhaps most importantly, sets a future research agenda related to communication ethics.

Jason Shepard writes of the legal and ethical revolution that journalism is undergoing due to the Internet and addresses profound questions about the roles of ethics and law in a world characterized by the new, open, networked journalism. These questions go to the heart of who is a journalist, what is journalism, and what it means to be a professional, which must encompass ethical frameworks.

Jenn Burleson Mackay examines the plight of journalism ethics in light of external factors that influence and constrain a journalist's ethical decision making. Chief among these factors is new technology, which can both facilitate unethical behavior and, through nontraditional media, create a "fifth estate" to oversee established media. Other factors that affect a journalist's ethical decision making include professional routines, organizational influences, and characteristics of the various media themselves.

While some argue that blogging is a form of journalism, Scott Stroud and Danee Pye assert that it should be viewed as conversation. They demonstrate the power of normative ethics in analyzing contemporary media phenomena by applying Kantian analysis to social blogging. They focus on the manner in which blogging enables individuals to create anonymous, self-created identities online and consider whether or not this is a good thing based on Kant's view of conversation and his ideas on unsocial sociability (urges to both protect and express oneself in community with others).

Despite a flood of new media, television continues to be the most popular media activity of children aged eight to 18, even though the platforms on which they watch it have expanded. Karyn Riddle brings a renewed focus to the negative effects that stem from exposure of children to violence on television and examines the responsibilities of parents, the media industry, and media scholars.

Addressing the important question of children and media in another context, Vincent Cicchirillo focuses on "advergames," video games with branded content that are provided on company and even non-profit websites. He explores the ethical problems that stem from the confluence of the entertainment that advergames provide, the vulnerabilities of the youth they target, the lack of a rating system for advergames, and the absence of regulatory controls.

Lina Svedin examines ethical issues that emerge in the challenging and stressful context of public crisis communication—situations in which government managers communicate about crises that affect the public and public-governing institutions. She argues that researchers must focus not only on actions and decisions made but also on inaction and "decisions not made," and she demonstrates that responding appropriately to ethical issues is intimately intertwined with effectiveness in responding to public crises and with protecting democratic values and ideals.

When most people think of advertising ethics, they think of the criticisms or problems, but Erin Schauster argues that the focus should be on the causes and that, to understand the causes, one must understand what goes on inside an advertising agency. She sets the research agenda for an organizational approach to advertising ethics that calls for a keen understanding of both organizational culture and organizational communication and the manner in which they enable or constrain ethical decision making.

Consumers, the target of advertising, view advertising through the lenses of their ethical values, and some consumers view their purchasing as a venue for expressing their ethical values. Lucy Atkinson examines the manner in which ethically minded consumers interpret green advertising claims. She explores the "the attitude-behavior" or "word-deed gap"—the perplexing difference between what ethically minded consumers say that they intend to purchase (ethical products) and what they actually do purchase, which oftentimes is to the contrary.

W. Glenn Griffin examines ethical issues arising from two of the hottest topics in the creative function of advertising, which have been enabled and popularized through electronic media—crowdsourcing and co-creation. Crowdsourcing involves inviting a "crowd" of people outside the agency to create and submit commercials, typically as part of a contest, while co-creation involves inviting the "crowd" to submit ideas for commercials.

Troy Elias critically examines market segmentation—the most fundamental of marketing and advertising tools that involves separating a large, heterogeneous market into smaller, more homogeneous parts. He points to the deleterious effects it can have not only on racial minorities as it reinforces the stereotypes of the very groups that it seeks to attract, but also on society as it expands rifts in the social fabric. He highlights the manner in which this problem can be particularly acute for groups that represent "multiple minorities," such as Black homosexuals.

Michael Mackert and Marie Guadagno focus on the ethical issues related to direct-to-consumer (DTC) prescription drug advertising, a practice unique to the U.S. and New Zealand, but nonetheless a vast advertising expenditure and a practice surrounded by much debate. They discuss the potential harms and benefits of DTC advertising that advocates and critics have debated, but they push deeper to identify the underlying ethical questions and factors, such as low health literacy, that impact these questions and issues.

Seung-Chul Yoo focuses on the advertising applications of facial recognition technology, which provides advertisers a tool with which to analyze a human face to determine an individual's approximate age, gender, and race. While it enables the delivery of an advertising message that is likely to be relevant to an individual, it raises a host of ethical concerns related to consumer privacy and stereotyping.

Much of the advertising ethics research has been conducted in the context of developed markets in the West, but Sara Kamal points to the importance of focusing on advertising ethics in emerging markets in general and in the Middle East in particular. She points to a number of factors that can exacerbate ethical problems in advertising in emerging markets, including lack of regulation, youthful consumers with low literacy, a cadre of expatriate workers with short-term contracts and short-term perspectives, and socio-cultural factors such as the influence of Islam.

The pace of change in communication professions has rarely been greater or more revolutionary than in recent years. Given the dramatic changes, rarely has research related to communication ethics been as critically important as it is today. Professionals, academics, ethicists, social critics, and others may not agree concerning the state of communication ethics or what is ethical. Disagreement is not the problem; avoidance of the topic and/or failure to engage in a collaborative dialogue and fruitful, productive research is. My hope is that this volume has advanced the dialogue and contributed to setting the research agenda for the future of communication ethics.

References

Drumwright, M. E. (2007). Advertising ethics: A multi-level theory approach. In G. J. Tellis & T. Ambler (Eds.), *The Handbook of Advertising* (pp. 398–415). London: Sage Publications Ltd.

Drumwright, M. E. (2012). Ethics and advertising theory. In S. Rogers & E. Thorson (Eds.), *Advertising Theory* (pp. 473–479). New York: Routledge.

Drumwright, M. E., & Murphy, P.E. (2004). How advertising practitioners view ethics: Moral muteness, moral myopia, and moral imagination. *Journal of Advertising*, *33*(2), 7–24.

Drumwright, M. E., & Murphy, P. E. (2009). The current state of advertising ethics: Industry and academic perspectives. *Journal of Advertising*, *38*(1), 83–107.

Drumwright, M. E., & Williams, J. D. (2013) The role of ethics in food and beverage marketing to children. In D. Williams, K. E. Pasch, & C. Collins (Eds.), *Advances in Communication Research to Reduce Childhood Obesity*. New York: Springer, forthcoming.

Gentile, M. C. (2010). *Giving Voice to Values: How to Speak Your Mind When You Know What's Right* . New Haven: Yale University Press.

Thorson, E., & Rogers, S. (2012). What does "theories of advertising" mean? In S. Rogers & E. Thorson (Eds.), *Advertising Theory* (pp. 3–17). New York: Routledge.

Acknowledgments

This edited volume is the product of the conference "Ethical Issues in Communication Professions: New Agendas," hosted by the College of Communication at the University of Texas at Austin in March 2012. I would like to express my gratitude to the 15 young scholars who contributed their work to this volume for their keen insights and their diligence in meeting deadlines. They have demonstrated that they truly are talented scholars and "next generation" thinkers. I also want to thank the senior scholars who graciously served as discussants at the conference and added tremendously to the discussion: Renita Coleman, Matthew Eastin, Kathleen Higgins, Robert Jensen, Wally Snyder, and Patricia Stout. I want to thank my department chair, Isabella Cunningham, who has always been supportive of me and efforts to build the department and the college, and my departmental colleagues, who provide a stimulating work environment. The conference would not have been possible without the encouragement and support of my dean, Roderick Hart, who conceived of the New Agendas Series, and my associate dean, Stephen D. Reese, who is the editor of the New Agendas Series. I want to thank Candice Prose, Katherine Yerger, and Anne Reed for patiently and adeptly shepherding me through the process of planning, preparing, and hosting the conference. I also want to thank Mark Rogers and Larry Horovat for lending their amazing audio-visual and technical expertise to the conference. Finally, I want to thank my daughter, Lauren Perry, for her encouragement and patience, and my husband, H.W. Perry, Jr., for generously and selflessly supporting me in this endeavor as he has in every other important endeavor that I have undertaken.

Chapter 1

Freedom of the Press and Journalism Ethics in the Internet Age

Jason M. Shepard

After the website WikiLeaks disclosed thousands of classified United States military documents leaked by a soldier, Republican Vice Presidential candidate Sarah Palin called the site a terrorist organization, while a member of the Norwegian Parliament nominated it for a Nobel Peace Prize. In illuminating the threat of the Internet to the social-responsibility principles of journalism ethics in the U.S., the document disclosure torpedoed a bill pending in the U.S. Senate giving journalists a long-sought statutory journalist's privilege to protect confidential sources. But wasn't the website providing citizens with truthful information about public affairs and serving as a watchdog of government—precisely what we want from journalistic organizations? The dissemination of truth is a core value in American free-press theory and journalism ethics theory, but WikiLeaks and other recent examples underscore how the Internet age requires rethinking of traditional theories of freedom of the press and journalism ethics.

The Internet has revolutionized traditional media ecology, diminishing the news media's gatekeeping role and the role of journalists in mediating news. This technological shift has also reduced institutional barriers for individuals who want to disseminate information to the public. Matt Drudge's online scoop of President Bill Clinton's sexual dalliance with a White House intern in 1998 catapulted bloggers to the journalistic fore, and some bloggers quickly established their journalistic bona fides to openly compete with large, commercial media companies. Today, there is no longer the question of whether bloggers are journalists, but rather a question of what makes a blogger a journalist. Indeed, one wonders whether journalism itself is a profession and discipline that can sustain itself in the new media landscape. Professor Paul Starr in *The Creation of the Media* (2004) and Professor Elliot King in *Free for All: The Internet's Transformation of Journalism* (2010) demonstrate that the Internet is not the first technology to revolutionize the journalism profession. However, in *We're All Journalists Now* (2007), attorney Scott Gant argues that the Internet does indeed present a paradigm shift for the concept of journalism as a profession, arguing that journalism is better viewed as a process and product that can be done by anyone with a computer and modem.

This chapter explores the impact of the Internet age on the legal and ethical frameworks of traditional journalism. Can journalism, defined by ethical and legal frameworks, continue to be a distinct discourse in the Internet age? To what degree does adherence to traditional journalism ethical practices afford online communicators with legal protections as journalists? How should the law define who is a journalist in today's changing media landscape? Given the technological revolution, does it even make any sense to use ethical concepts to provide legal distinctions for journalism, and if so, how should traditional journalism's ethical principles evolve in light of new practices and legal problems raised by new technologies? After exploring these questions and concluding that journalism should remain a central component of normative free-press theory, I offer several suggestions on how future research can expand and apply free-press theory and journalism ethics to journalistic practices in the Internet age.

Journalism as a Preferred Press Freedom

As Supreme Court Justice Potter Stewart viewed it in 1974, the press clause of the First Amendment in the U.S. Constitution is a uniquely American structural provision that provides journalistic institutions—"the daily newspapers and other established news media"—with explicit constitutional rights in order to guarantee an independent "fourth estate" of government to provide "organized, expert scrutiny of government" (Stewart, 1975). In a seminal scholarly work, Professor Vince Blasi articulated a "checking value" theory of the First Amendment that positioned journalists as an archetype of First Amendment freedom fighters, professional experts whose ethical purpose was to advance democracy and improve government by serving as truth seekers acting in the public interest (Blasi, 1977). Professor David A. Anderson, in his treatise on the original intent of the press clause, concluded that this fourth estate model "seems so thoroughly supported by the legislative history that one may wonder why it has not been universally accepted" (Anderson, 1983). More recently, C. Edwin Baker has argued that the Supreme Court's free-press doctrine embraces this institutional, instrumental approach (Baker, 2007).

The idealistic, utilitarian vision of journalism as a constitutionally protected and imperative institution that Justice Stewart presented in 1974 is one normative model of modern free-press theory. But the theory is outdated when one considers the transformative effects of the Internet on journalism. The status and role of journalism has changed dramatically in recent years, with potentially transformative effects on free-press theory. For free-press and journalism-ethics scholars, a profound question is whether the Stewart–Blasi–Anderson view of journalism as a special dis-course—constitutionally protected and democratically important—is even worth rescuing in the Internet age. As Professor Randall D. Eliason has argued, laws specifically protecting journalism "may soon be considered a relic of a simpler era—a relic that now is neither workable or necessary" given the "rapid technological changes in both the nature and quantity of information regularly made available to the public" (Eliason, 2006).

This argument can be troubling to free-press and journalism-ethics scholars because it challenges theoretical frameworks and modern legal and ethical doctrines. Free-press theory as it has developed in American legal jurisprudence has emphasized normative claims about the role of journalism in a democratic society to justify special rights and responsi-bilities. Broadly speaking, the principle of freedom of the press forbids the government from censoring, punishing, or licensing the press except in extraordinary circumstances and under strict scrutiny of the judiciary, based on the justification that a free press is necessary for citizens to exercise their sovereignty over government. Indeed, one cannot read the U.S. Supreme Court's major press cases of the twentieth century without appreciating the Court's full embrace of the essential tenets of the free-press principle. This began in 1931 when, in *Near v. Minnesota*, the Court struck down a Minnesota law that allowed newspapers to be banned as a public nuisance. Five years later, in striking down a Louisiana law requir-ing the nine largest newspapers in the state to pay a 2% licensing tax, the Supreme Court wrote in *Grosjean v. American Press Co.* (1936), "A free press stands as one of the great interpreters between the government and the people. To allow it to be fettered is to fetter ourselves" (p. 250). The Supreme Court expanded its commitment to the free-press principle in ensuing decades. In the landmark 1964 decision *New York Times v. Sulli-van*, in which the Court overturned a $500,000 libel judgment against the *New York Times*, the Court wrote that "debate on public issues should be uninhibited, robust and wide open" (p. 270). Professor Lee Bollinger described the decision as the "fullest, richest articulation of the central image of freedom of the press" (Bollinger, 1991, p. 2), which he charac-terized as having a distrust of government, treating the citizen as sover-eign, emphasizing the importance of public debate, and viewing the press as the public's representative.

The special role of journalists in the free-press principle was the center-piece of the Court's ruling in *New York Times v. U.S* (1971). On a vote of 6–3, the Court rejected President Richard Nixon's attempt to halt pub-lication of the so-called Pentagon Papers—leaked, classified documents about the government's involvement in the Vietnam War. In separate opinions, several justices articulated visions of the institutional press and the journalism profession as noble crusaders of truth on behalf of the public. In an almost poetic opinion, Justice Hugo Black wrote

In the First Amendment the Founding Fathers gave the free press the protection it must have to fulfill its essential role in our democracy. The press was to serve the governed, not the governors. The Government's power to censor the press was abolished so that the press would remain forever free to censure the Government. The press was protected so that it could bare the secrets of government and inform the people. ... In revealing the workings of government that led to the Vietnam war, the newspapers nobly did precisely that which the Founders hoped and trusted they would do.

(p. 717)

Justice Black referred to the press as singular, referring clearly to the institution the public came to know as journalistic news organizations. Other justices in the case did the same. Justice Douglas cited *Near* in arguing that a "vigilant and courageous press" is needed to confront the "malfeasance and corruption of government officials in a vast bureaucracy" (p. 723). And Justice Stewart wrote that especially in regard to national defense and international affairs, "it is perhaps here that a press that is alert, aware and free most vitally serves the basic purpose of the First Amendment. For without an informed and free press there cannot be an enlightened people" (p. 728).

Despite this strong rhetoric of journalism as a special discourse that serves as the basis for free-press theory, a paradox exists in First Amendment jurisprudence. As Professor Anderson argued in the *Texas Law Review*, "as a matter of positive law, the Press Clause actually plays a minor role in protecting the freedom of the press. Most of the freedoms of the press the press receives from the First Amendment are no different from the freedom everyone enjoys under the Speech Clause" (Anderson, 2002, p. 429). As early as 1938, in *Lovell v. City of Griffin*, the Court emphasized an individual rather than institutional view of press freedom. "The liberty of the press is not confined to newspapers and periodicals. It necessarily embraces pamphlets and leaflets ... The press in its historic connotation comprehends every sort of publication which affords a vehicle of information and opinion" (p. 453). Indeed, while the Court has embraced the rhetoric of press freedom protecting journalistic institutions most fully, "The Court has not yet squarely resolved whether the Press Clause confers upon the 'institutional press' any freedom from government restraint not enjoyed by all others," Justice Burger wrote in *First National Bank v. Bellotti* in 1978 (p. 798). Burger made his view clear:

The very task of including some entities within the "institutional press" while excluding others, whether undertaken by legislature, court, or administrative agency, is reminiscent of the abhorred licensing system of Tudor and Stuart England—a system the First Amendment was intended to ban from this country.

(p. 801)

This legal approach views the press clause as generally impotent other than to emphasize an individual's right to disseminate information in print as well as verbally, analogous to legal protections under the speech clause of the First Amendment. On the other hand, Justice Stewart, in his 1974 speech "Or of the Press," said conclusively that the press clause "extends protection to an institution." He went on:

It is tempting to suggest that freedom of the press means only that newspaper publishers are guaranteed freedom of expression. They are guaranteed that freedom to be sure, but so are we all, because of the Free Speech Clause. If the Free Press guarantee meant no more than freedom of expression, it would be a constitutional redundancy ... By including both guarantees in the First Amendment, the Founders quite clearly recognized the distinction between the two.

(Stewart, 1975, p. 633)

Despite the seeming embrace of the individual rights model over the institutional model, the articulation of the free-press principle in the Supreme Court's jurisprudence often emphasizes the special role of journalism in a democratic system of government, and it has arisen in various contexts in which the press has sought to use the free-press principle both as a shield and as a sword. A free press serves two primary purposes, both of which can be viewed as utilitarian or instrumental: to inform citizens about public affairs to advance democracy and to check for abuses among those in power. The public-information theory of the First Amendment articulated by Alexander Meiklejohn (1948) and the checking-value theory of the First Amendment articulated by Vince Blasi (1977) both support the institutional view of journalism that has developed in modern Supreme Court jurisprudence. Journalists have been far more successful at using the First Amendment as a shield from government censorship and civil liability. The major foundations of press law doctrine establish judicial hostility toward prior restraints and higher burdens of liability based on First Amendment concerns. Thus far, the press has been less successful at convincing the Supreme Court that the free-press principle grants journalists broad special rights, such as an evidentiary privilege or access rights to jails and records. The press has had greater success in the lower courts and in state legislatures in securing special legal protections.

To be sure, the free-press principle is ripe for criticism in several respects. First, the principle generally prioritizes press freedom over other social interests, such as individuals' reputations and privacy, except in egregious cases. The press generally cannot be compelled to present multiple viewpoints, it can use sensationalism to distort, it can emphasize entertainment over public affairs, it can play to personal biases and prejudices, and it can fuel ignorance and pettiness. In addition to the market-based failings of journalism to live up to its ideals and the tensions between the institutional versus individual approach to the press clause, the Internet has raised profound questions about the premises and implications of the traditional free-press principle.

The Internet Revolution's Effects on Journalism

The development of the free-press principle into Supreme Court jurisprudence began in the 1930s and peaked in the 1970s. The legal doctrines are the creation of a media environment dominated by print journalism. However, this journalism-centric model of the free-press principle is ripe for alteration and rethinking because of the Internet revolution's effects on traditional journalism.

The journalism profession is in trouble. Between 2001 and 2010, American newspapers shed 25% of their newsroom employees. The title of Robert McChesney and Victor Pickard's 2011 book, *Will the Last Reporter Please Turn Out the Lights*, reflects the existential crisis for journalism. Due to changes in the production, dissemination, and consumption of news, traditional journalists no longer serve as citizens' primary gatekeepers and mediators of news. The business model for newspapers, the traditional core of the journalism profession, is being gutted by the irreversible loss of advertisers and declining circulation. Filling the void of traditional journalism is a cacophony of information disseminators and services. The Internet has created new models of information production, dissemination, and consumption that eliminate the monopoly newspapers had in gathering, sifting, and packaging news. The technologies associated with the new media—aggregation, search, hyperlinks, digital video and audio, smart phones, live blogs, forums and commenting, social media—mean that news dissemination occurs increasingly in an open information network. The Internet has also allowed for instant access to information, greater personalization, increased globalization, and low costs of entry to publishing. The technological changes have also erased the economic barriers for new journalism entities, and both organizations and individuals have used the new technologies to launch journalistic endeavors wholly on the web.

The flip side of the "journalism is dead" coin is that the Internet allows anyone with access to a computer and modem to publish information to a potentially worldwide audience. Histories of the blogosphere often point to Matt Drudge's exposé of the Clinton–Lewinsky affair as the birth of the blogger-as-journalist. Drudge was working as a gift-shop employee living in a $600-a-month basement apartment in Santa Monica, California, when he received a tip on January 17, 1998, that *Newsweek* magazine held a story alleging Clinton had an affair with a White House intern. The conventional wisdom suggested Drudge did little more than splash the tip onto his website, www.drudgereport.com, and sit back to watch American politics become embroiled in the most salacious political scandal of a generation, resulting in the impeachment of Bill Clinton. But Drudge was much more than simply a conduit of unconfirmed gossip. He worked the phones, tracked down multiple sources, and received subsequent tips based on his original reporting that furthered the story's developments. He wrote about the tips with background context and provided primary documentary material. Indeed, by reading post-scandal analyses, Drudge's own accounts and the original web postings, a clear picture emerges of Drudge as an aggressive reporter pushing the boundaries of a massive scandal. While one can lament the salaciousness of the content, Drudge unquestionably used many traditional investigative-reporting techniques to land him in the front of the line of those who broke news about a U.S. President's conduct in the White House (Drudge, 2000). In the debate over whether the work product of a blogger is similar to that of a traditional journalist, Matt Drudge became an important case study. Not only is Drudge's website one of the most well-read today because of his record to be right and first just often enough to establish a baseline of credibility, but his infamous rise to fame set the stage for today's political bloggers.

Drudge's performance in covering the Lewinsky story earned him scorn but also accolades. Andrew Sullivan, the former editor of the *New Republic* turned full-time blogger-journalist, said Drudge was a key player by "making history from his basement apartment with a Radio Shack computer and no journalistic training or institutional support against a White House almost as ruthless as Nixon's" (Sullivan, 2000). Today, the Drudge Report is one of the most visited news websites in the world. As newspaper readership continues to see record declines, Drudge continues to see record-high readership. On a random day in spring 2012, his website boasted of more than 29 million hits in the previous 24 hours. While Drudge operates in a new medium with somewhat different rules, he represents a possible new model of journalism, one in which anyone with motivation and a website can become a disseminator of news.

The emergence of blogs as an alternative to the mainstream press has been lauded as one of those transformative moments in American media history, as significant as the postal network or the telegraph. The early history of the blogosphere has revealed a complex relationship between bloggers and traditional journalists. Many journalists scoff at the suggestion that bloggers are one of them. Bloggers can be vapid, opinionated, self-absorbed, and deal in a currency that has nothing to do with facts, objectivity, and balance. But there is a segment of bloggers who write about current events and politics whose work habits, performance, and work product confound those who say what they do is not journalism. Many of these bloggers search for facts, dig through documents, and disseminate their findings for the world to read. Even some traditional journalists have left their stodgy confines in the mainstream media to create blogs of their own, bringing with them credentials and reputation. And perhaps most importantly, blogs have changed the mainstream media by serving as fact checkers, by providing a wealth of sources and background information for traditional reporters, and by pushing news organizations to cover stories they may not otherwise have covered. Bloggers may be ushering in a new marketplace for public debate while at the same time challenging the old one, and at least some of them are practicing journalism some of the time. Meanwhile, entire news organizations have developed successful business models online, including *Politico* and the *Huffington Post*. They are all part of this new, open, networked journalism.

Traditional Journalism: Legal and Ethical Frameworks

Two separate regulatory models of journalism have emerged in the legal and professional fields. The legal model emphasizes journalistic autonomy and embraces libertarian press theory that emphasizes negative liberty, or the absence of regulation. The ethics model embraces social responsibility theory and articulates frameworks and principles of responsible conduct, emphasizing the normative role the press plays in society and the utilitarian purposes of journalism. While law and ethics are often viewed as separate fields, they intersect in many important ways when it comes to the discussion of who and what is journalism. Because traditional free-press theory posits that journalism is a public good essential to democracy, using concepts and principles of journalistic ethics, a normative inquiry into the future of freedom of the press in the Internet age must consider the separate but related domains of legal doctrine and professional ethics.

One of the key features of the Internet era is the loss of journalistic identity through a diminution of journalistic institutions. For press law, the blurring of journalistic identity requires us to revisit the purposes of the First Amendment in thinking about how traditional legal doctrines might need to change based on the new problems presented by new technologies. For example, the law recognizes journalists as a special class of individuals in many contexts, including protection of confidential sources, exemptions from campaign finance laws, limited liability from libel suits through retraction statutes, and special access to government institutions such as press boxes in legislative chambers and courtrooms, to name a few.

For journalism ethics, the economic and technological changes require evaluation of the purposes and processes of journalism that are necessary and important for democratic self-government. Journalism ethics discourse needs to address the long-term sustainability of ethical journalism as well as whether different ethical doctrines describe and should guide the increasingly different domains of news production, dissemination, and consumption.

As Professor Hazel Dicken-Garcia has traced, journalism standards and principles developed with the rise of the occupation of a reporter in the late nineteenth century and were solidified by the development of journalism schools, professional organizations, and written codes of ethics in the early twentieth century (Dicken-Garcia, 1989). Modern free-press doctrine developed somewhat later, perhaps explaining why so much *dicta* in Supreme Court decisions embraces an understanding of the free-press clause that is based on the normative theory of journalism. As a result, journalism ethics helped create protective law. For example, journalists used ethical concepts of confidential-source protection to advocate for legal protections in legislatures and the courts, successfully turning an ethical principle into a legal principle (Shepard, 2011a).

One scholarly approach is to treat the law and ethics domains separately, recognizing that the general approach in law is egalitarian, where distinctions between journalist and non-journalist speakers are usually, but not always, problematic, while ethical discourse has emphasized an expert model that makes clear distinctions between journalists and non-journalists based on their adherence to ethical principles. Professors Erik Ugland and Jennifer Henderson (2007) used this dichotomy to create three categories of speakers based on adherence to ethical practices. "Top-level journalists" are those "who are not merely concerned with telling the truth but also with honoring the ethical canons of traditional American journalism, such as independence, proportionality, comprehensiveness, and accountability." Credentials such as training, education, and affiliation may help identify individuals as "top-tier" journalists, but their actions are ultimately what define them. Next, "second-tier" journalists are those who regularly engage in disseminating information to the public but do not adhere to professional standards and core values of ethics codes. Ugland and Henderson identify Arianna Huffington of the *Huffington Post*, Markos Moulitis of the *DailyKos*, the *Newsmax* website, magazines such as *The Progressive* and *The American Prospect*, and television programs such as *Countdown with Keith Olbermann* and *The Daily Show with Jon Stewart* as examples. Finally, they define "public communicators" as individuals who disseminate ideas or information occasionally and without a permanent media presence that enhances accountability.

> A college professor giving a public address, a witness to a terror-
> ist attack who posts a video on YouTube, or an aspiring film critic
> who sends reviews to others through a listserv would all fall into this
> category, as would professionals in advertising, public relations, or
> other fields whose communications are not designed to report on
> important events occurring in society.
>
> (Ugland & Henderson, 2007, p. 13)

In other words, Ugland and Henderson suggest that adherence to ethical
standards is a decisive factor in determining who is a journalist and what
is journalism.

Traditional ethical codes of conduct and practice, along with an institutional and organizational framework that encourages and enforces
responsibility, have helped identify journalism as a special discourse
that deserves special legal protection. The basis for these special laws
is under threat as lawmakers and judges increasingly worry about the
lack of gatekeepers and the corresponding potential for abuse. The First
Circuit Court of Appeals in 2011 seemed to agree, stating, "changes in
technology and society have made the lines between private citizen and
journalist exceedingly difficult to draw ... Such developments make clear
why the news-gathering protections of the First Amendment cannot turn
on professional credentials or status" (*Glik v. Cunniffe*, 1st Cir. 2011).
Given these new realities, can journalism, defined by ethical frameworks,
continue to be a preferred press freedom in the Internet age?

One of the foundations of traditional free-press theory is that journalists, in part because of their ethical frameworks, were able to fulfill their
fourth estate role. But it is worth asking whether we can continue to
expect traditional journalism to be able to serve its checking-value function. Additionally, new technologies have raised new problems for professionals, as well as old problems for new practitioners. What follows is
a discussion of a disparate set of new legal problems for both traditional
journalism and new media practitioners that highlight the complex relationship between law and ethics. All raise unresolved and difficult questions about the appropriate lines of rights and responsibilities for the
traditional press and their new media peers. Afterward, I offer a synthesis
of these problems in a discussion of where future scholarship could help
make sense of these legal and ethical issues.

New Legal and Ethical Problems in the Internet Age

Just as traditional print journalists have needed to learn new professional skills as a result of the Internet revolution—shooting and editing
audio and video, search engine optimization, basic web editing, to name

a few—traditional journalists have also had to think about new ways in which their new digital practices might get them into legal trouble in ways that did not happen before the Internet. Prior to the Internet, most publishing situations with legal risks had been satisfactorily resolved in traditional newsroom ethical decisionmaking. None is more obvious than in the realm of privacy law, where amorphous concepts of "public concern" and "newsworthiness" have made the law very deferential to journalists, in part because news organizations' ethics codes often instilled a responsibility in journalists to balance the public interests of their reporting with the harm it may cause, including the harm to persons' privacy. But traditional journalism has many new legal worries that carry related ethical dilemmas. Consider three examples.

Managing an Anonymous Public Forum

The Internet provides potential for deliberative discourse by removing barriers for public discussion that exist in other forms of mass communication. Online bulletin boards, forums, and commenting systems could embody the "marketplace of ideas" metaphor of the First Amendment unlike any other form of communication. However, in practice, news organizations have struggled with regulating their marketplaces of ideas, including, for example, commenting systems on their websites. Many newspaper websites want to draw as many "hits" as possible, and a "wild west" treatment of their comments pages can often draw hundreds of readers who regularly revisit pages and engage with others about news stories. On the one hand, this is a healthy new function for news organizations to provide an open forum for citizens to discuss the news of the day. The reality, of course, is that commenters can be obnoxious, racist, threatening, liars, or marketers and product promoters. News organizations have struggled with various systems to moderate, systems that have legal and ethical implications. If an individual posts something criminal or tortuous, under what circumstances is the newspaper required to provide the writer's identity to police or lawyers? Should the newspaper ever try to protect the identities of pseudo anonymous commenters as if they were confidential sources? What should a newspaper do when they themselves want to "out" a commenter because of the public interest in his or her identity and behavior?

The courts have developed varying tests to determine when an anonymous Internet writer must be identified, often through a subpoena to the web hosting service that tracks an individual's IP address, which usually then provides identifying information, such as a person's name, address, and telephone number. Generally, under section 230 of the federal Communications Decency Act, Internet websites are not legally liable for defamatory content posted by others, but the websites can be compelled through a subpoena to produce records identifying the posters. In an emerging judicial doctrine, lower courts have generally required the web service to notify the anonymous poster and give them an opportunity to intervene. Then, the plaintiff must make some level of a *prime facie* showing that the writer's actions were likely actionable (i.e., libelous or an invasion of privacy) before the court would unmask the writer's identity.

In some cases, newspapers have gone even further, entangling themselves in fighting for legal anonymity of people who posted on their websites by arguing that state shield laws protect commenters as if they were confidential sources. In a few cases, newspapers were allowed to argue in court on behalf of individuals who posted anonymous comments. This is a troubling development, as anonymous commenters do not often invoke the same characteristics as journalists who are protecting confidential sources. But perhaps sometimes the interests of protecting "whistleblower-like" commenters invokes the same interests as protecting traditional confidential sources, an area of underdeveloped judicial and scholarly articulation.

Alternatively, there have been cases in which newspapers have voluntarily unmasked commenters. In Wausau, Wis., after one commenter posted negative remarks about the *Daily Herald*'s selection of the local village administrator as person of the year in 2008, the mayor demanded to know the name of the disgruntled citizen. The newspaper's publisher gave the mayor the man's e-mail address, who then received a personal letter from the mayor. One high-profile and fascinating example occurred in 2010 when the *Cleveland Plain Dealer* "outed" one of its commenters as being that of a local judge—who was reportedly commenting on stories about cases appearing in her courtroom. The judge, Shirley Strickland Safford, sued the newspaper and its web host for breach of contract, fraud, invasion of privacy, and defamation, while denying she was the writer of the comments. The lawsuit was settled and its terms are not known, but the case reveals several ethical and legal dilemmas. Should a journalist expose a public official who is abusing her power by posting anonymously on a newspaper's website? Are newspapers legally vulnerable if they voluntarily unmask the anonymity of a poster?

These examples suggest that news organizations need to discuss and develop appropriate policies for policing the public forums on their websites in ways that encourage openness and also reasonableness, in ways that take into account both the ethical and the legal implications of this new technology. News organizations want to build stronger relationships with readers, and comment sections can sometimes be the most interesting corners of a website. Comment sections also further a news organization's function in providing citizens with new tools to scrutinize government and encourage the expression of unpopular ideas, which is facilitated by anonymity. The costs and benefits of anonymity should continue to be the source of dialogue for practitioners and scholars. Some newspapers have moved away from a completely open forum by requiring posters to register, and sometimes use their real names publicly, in an effort to increase responsibility. Others heavily moderate the forums, which requires resources and potentially increases liability. The risk is that registration will significantly restrict the quantity of posts and might inhibit people from speaking their minds. Newspaper policies need to be debated for the right calibration of openness and responsibility. They also need to be transparent in what protections are afforded to users.

Erasing the Past

Given the permanence and wide access of the Internet, do journalists have new ethical obligations to make corrections, follow-ups, and deletions because of the effects of their stories? In a pre-Internet era, an individual was far less likely to be haunted by old news stories that existed only in hard copy in newsroom morgues and microfilm. Today, a Google search can quickly lead to old, incomplete, and sometimes erroneous stories about a person's criminal record, making statutory expungement laws powerless in aiding individuals from escaping a criminal paper trail. Journalists are supposed to seek and report truth while mitigating harm. The permanence of the Internet makes this task more complicated when every possible old story might have multiple or new truths that individuals want told in order to the minimize the harms they have suffered as a result of that publication. Others want news stories on the Internet to disappear altogether, including those whose criminal records have been expunged in the courts but remain available for all to see on the Internet.

Courts have just begun to wade into this problem of privacy and permanence, including a Pennsylvania judge who ordered two newspapers to delete stories about individuals who sought to get their criminal records expunged. The judge reversed himself after the newspapers objected. It would take a dramatic and dangerous shift in First Amendment doctrine for the courts to mandate that news websites remove truthful stories about past crimes. Rather, Professor Clay Calvert argues that journalists have an ethical duty to follow up on stories involving crimes, to report not just an arrest but the ultimate adjudication. This would place new responsibilities on journalists to focus on the follow-up, when journalists are more likely to conduct reporting on crime at the beginning—the crime, the arrest, and the charging stage (Calvert & Bruno, 2010).

The data trail of an arrest is but one of many examples in which the content of websites can haunt individuals. For example, the website Best Gore, among others, published the gruesome crime scene photos of the traffic death of 18-year-old Nikki Catsouras, whose decapitated body was so disfigured that the coroner refused to allow the parents to identify their daughter's body. The family identified the leak of the photos as two California Highway Patrol officers, who lost a privacy lawsuit brought by the family. It is not far-fetched to envision the website coming under legal threat. Could the judge, after a legal finding of invasion of privacy, provide as a remedy a permanent injunction prohibiting the publication of the photograph? In the pre-Internet days, it would be hard to imagine a news organization publishing a photo of a decapitated teenage girl who died in a car accident. It is less inconceivable to think that websites of all sorts might post, or link to, similar photos under some circumstances. Professor Calvert notes:

> It thus may be here where the judicial or legislative intervention is needed the most—targeting non-journalism organizations and, in the case of Catsouras, the downstream distributors of her images after they left the hands of the members of the California Highway Patrol.
>
> Calvert suggests that broadening the ability of individuals to recover damages through tort law is a "legal nudge to an ethical result"
>
> (Calvert, 2010).

As Professor Calvert suggests, some argue that the law should treat "non-journalism" organizations differently in some contexts. Where ethics constrains traditional journalists from publishing the gruesome crime scene photographs of a teenage girl, the law likely does not. A website dedicated to gory crime scene photos is but one of the new publications on the web that suggest traditional journalism ethics are not able to enforce responsibility through informal regulatory schemes.

There are troubling aspects to the proposition that the law should treat journalistic and non-journalistic entities differently, but the law already does so in a number of contexts. In campaign finance law, for example, individuals are limited in using money to speak about political preferences in particular contexts, but these laws specifically exempt media organizations.

Protecting Confidential Sources

The questions of who is a journalist and what is journalism have been most explored in the legal scholarship in the context of a journalist's right to protect confidential sources. Bloggers have increasingly sought protection as journalists for purposes of privilege protection, and judicial interpretations of state and federal laws have provided a framework for developing models of when individuals are and are not sufficiently similar to traditional journalists to warrant privilege protection.

Notably, case law provides a number of useful analogies in the pre-Internet era. Journalists have argued for a legal right to protect confidential sources dating back to the mid-1800s, and by the early 1900s, states began passing statutory protections for journalists. Today, all but one state provide some legal rights for journalists to protect confidential sources and other newsgathering information. A more ambiguous right exists under federal law, based on a mix of constitutional law, common law, and administrative rules. As a result of this long history, precedents existed before bloggers were created to test the boundaries of who and what is journalism. Generally, courts have extended privilege protection to individuals whose work purposes, processes, and products were sufficiently similar to those of traditional journalists (Shepard, 2011a). So, a documentary film maker and investigative book author were found by federal appellate courts to be deserving of journalistic privilege protection even if they were not working for traditional news organizations. However, federal appellate courts rejected privilege claims by an aggrieved mistress and a professional wrestling commentator, ruling that their purposes, processes, and product were not journalistic in nature and thus were not deserving of protection. The general rule to emerge from these cases is whether a person has an intent at the beginning of a newsgathering process to disseminate information to the public. In 2006, bloggers who regularly covered Apple Computer products were sued by Apple, which wanted the names of individuals who leaked information about yet-to-be-released Apple products. A California appeals court found no distinctions in the purpose, process, or product between the bloggers and traditional journalists. The court noted:

> [W]e can see no sustainable basis to distinguish petitioners from the reporters, editors, and publishers who provide news to the public through traditional print and broadcast media. It is established without contradiction that they gather, select, and prepare, for purposes of publication to a mass audience, information about current events of interest and concern to that audience ... If their activities and social function differ at all from those of traditional print and broadcast journalists, the distinctions are minute, subtle, and constitutionally immaterial.
>
> While the court did not expressly define its analysis in journalism ethics discourse, among the criteria used were a commitment to accuracy, editorial oversight, transparency, authority, readership, intent, and past publication record
>
> (*O'Grady v. Superior Court*, 2006).

Ethical principles will likely continue to emerge in judicial doctrines as more and more Internet writers make claims to be journalists. The functional analysis to emerge from the federal case law, which I have expanded as a "comprehensive functional analysis" in *Privileging the Press: Confidential Sources, Journalism Ethics and the First Amendment* (2011a), requires a case-by-case assessment of the individual's journalistic characteristics. For example, this comprehensive functional analysis supports the conclusion that blogger Crystal Cox was not a journalist for legal purposes in a 2011 defamation lawsuit filed by a bankruptcy trustee who became the target of a number of websites created by Cox. A federal judge refused to define Cox as a journalist or media defendant based on her failure to demonstrate adherence to basic journalism ethical standards. In rejecting Cox's claim as being a "media" defendant or a "journalist," the judge used seven relevant criteria:

> Defendant fails to bring forth any evidence suggestive of her status as a journalist. For example, there is no evidence of (1) any education in journalism; (2) any credentials or proof of any affiliation with any recognized news entity; (3) proof of adherence to journalistic standards such as editing, fact-checking, or disclosures of conflicts of interest; (4) keeping notes of conversations and interviews conducted; (5) mutual understanding or agreement of confidentiality between the defendant and his/her sources; (6) creation of an independent product rather than assembling writings and postings of others; or (7) contacting "the other side" to get both sides of a story. Without evidence of this nature, defendant is not "media."
>
> (*Obsidian Finance Group v. Crystal Cox*, 2011)

Using these standards to legally define a journalist may be problematic, but some standards are necessary if we are to determine that who is a journalist is important in journalist's privilege law. Making a distinction between journalist and non-journalist speakers is also important in the context of campaign finance laws. Federal laws limiting electioneering speech, as well as their state counterparts, generally exempt press entities from regulation, so as not to chill journalists from covering politics and elections. Under the two-part analytical framework developed by the Federal Elections Commission (FEC) and the federal courts over the interpretation of the "press exemption," an individual or organization must first be a "qualifying press entity," defined as a broadcast or cable television, newspaper, magazine, or other periodical publication that must ordinarily derive revenue from advertisements or subscriptions, and appears at regular intervals. Second, the entity must be engaged in a "proper press function," and it must not be controlled by a political party, committee, or candidate. The two-prong model has been used by the FEC and the courts to rule that some press entities that engage in activities outside of their proper functions have run afoul of the FEC, including one political advocacy group that created a special publication, beyond its regular newsletter, to expressly advocate for and against candidates. However, the FEC has ruled that regularly updated Internet websites with political commentary were legitimate press entities serving legitimate press functions. The diminution of media institutions, the new uses of the Internet, and the variety of political communications make the FEC framework of continuing importance for evaluating claims by web writers and websites that they fall under the press exemption (Shepard, 2011b).

WikiLeaks: A New Paradigm?

The website WikiLeaks presents perhaps the most fascinating and challenging case study for the future of journalism law and ethics. Depending on who is asked, WikiLeaks is a stateless terrorist organization (Sarah Palin and Joe Biden) or an important new form of networked journalism that will advance self-government and democracy by exposing government and corporate secrets outside the legal jurisdiction of any state and deserving of a Nobel Peace Prize (founder Julian Assange and a Norwegian MP). To a large degree, the WikiLeaks phenomenon is the result of a single document leak from a U.S. soldier. It is, however, apparently the largest leak of classified information in world history. That a start-up website run outside the jurisdiction of any country and by a larger-than-life eccentric could come into possession of this material is perhaps a historical anomaly. But the case points to the promises and perils of rogue, stateless websites apparently unconstrained by traditional law or ethics.

On the one hand, as Charlie Beckett points out in *WikiLeaks: News in the Networked Era* (2012), WikiLeaks demonstrates how new forms of investigative journalism and political communication can be unleashed by new technologies, challenging the paradigm of corporate media accountable to government. WikiLeaks founder Julian Assange used the language of free-press theory and journalism ethics to argue for journalistic credibility and autonomy. In holding governments accountable by disclosing their secrets, the website was simply a new model of journalism. Its features were different. It was independent of a state or corporation. Its mission was to publish everything and protect its sources. Raw data was its central content.

On the other hand, WikiLeaks challenges some fundamental legal and ethical principles. By wholesale disclosure of thousands of classified documents, the website may have violated the Espionage Act, and a federal grand jury was empanelled to pursue possible criminal charges. Several U.S. corporations shut down modes of access to the website in an unprecedented display of private–public censorship. Journalism ethicists criticized the website for failing to articulate what ethical standards it was using to reduce the potential harm from disclosure. That one man could

unilaterally publish thousands of government secrets without accountability in law or ethical frameworks is indeed a troubling and fascinating
development for free-press and journalism ethics scholars.

Implications for Future Research

In many ways, the Internet's transformative nature raises profound questions about the appropriate role of ethics and law in moderating and
regulating mass communication. For scholars interested in the future
of journalism, studying the ways in which the Internet is changing the
domains of journalistic production, dissemination, and consumption may
lead to new models for practitioners that will help economically sustain
the kinds of journalism that scholars believe are necessary components
of democratic self-governance. For media law and ethics scholars, these
domains are particularly relevant in determining whether, or under what
circumstances, journalism as a special discourse should be treated differently than other forms of communication. A fundamental concern for
scholars should be whether law or ethics should dictate the norms and
boundaries of journalism. If, as I believe, journalism should remain a
distinct and special discourse in the Internet era, scholars should situate
research agendas that help explain why.

First, scholars should focus on developing standards and models of
journalism that can inform practitioners, lawmakers, and the courts. If
we cannot adequately explain what journalism is and what it is not, we
cannot expect the law to provide special status to journalism. Ugland
and Henderson's (2007) three tiers of communicators framework uses
ethical standards to discriminate among speakers, but it does not easily
translate into legal rules, which are arguably more important as a practical matter in several areas of communication law. One approach I have
examined elsewhere (Shepard, 2011a), and that has broad support in case
precedents, is a comprehensive functional analysis that examines whether
a person's purposes, process, and products are like that of a traditional
journalist. Further refinement of these standards, drawing from ethical
frameworks and professional practices, may be useful. Historical research
examining different types of journalism in a historical context may help
support normative frameworks to apply to online communicators.

Second, scholars should focus on legislative efforts that expand freedom of information laws, protect the journalist's privilege, and approve
policies that support journalistic institutions. While most scholarship
focuses on constitutional theory and judicial doctrines, legislative efforts
can have as much, if not more, impact on press freedom. State legislatures
often tinker with public records and public meeting laws, and openness
advocacy can help legislative lobbying. At the federal level, legislative
advocacy is necessary for access to government information, as well as

continued efforts in passing a federal shield law giving journalists a legislative right to protect confidential sources. Finally, legislation that supports journalism institutions is not often examined, but some legislation
significantly influences journalism organizations. For example, many
states require notices of government actions to be published in advertisements in newspapers, which until recently were a stable and sizeable slice
of revenue for news organizations.

Third, scholars need to explain why the Internet's easy and permanent
access to data should not justify new limits on government information
and public records. In this area, scholars should pay particular attention
to the text and interpretations of public records laws, which are under
threat in some jurisdictions as lawmakers and judges worry about the
consequences of the Internet on disclosure. The physical limitations of
records access that existed before the development of the Internet helped
reduce abuse of information while providing journalists in particular
with necessary information. But paradoxically, the low access costs of the
Internet are causing some to recalibrate the harms of some public records.
The examples of the criminal records and crime scene photos discussed
earlier in this chapter are but a few examples that may lead to increasing
limits on public records.

Fourth, scholars need to better articulate the constitutional standards
of "public interest" and "public concern" that courts use in many First
Amendment cases. Whether speech is about matters of "public concern"
or in the "public interest" is central to many media law doctrines. For
example, in libel law, whether the allegedly defamatory statement is about
a matter of public concern significantly restricts plaintiffs in recovering
damages in the absence of a showing of actual malice, and assertions
must be proven false in order to recover any damages if the statement was
about a matter of public concern. Additionally, in order to win an invasion
of privacy public disclosure of private facts suit, a plaintiff must establish
that the disclosed information was not of public concern or newsworthy.
States with anti-SLAPP (strategic lawsuit against public participation)
statutes often allow frivolous lawsuits to be dismissed when individuals
are legitimately exercising their speech rights on matters of public concern. And in assessing whether public employees can be disciplined for
pure speech acts, courts assess whether the statements are about matters
of public concern. In journalist's privilege law, many courts have also
evaluated the public interest in assessing whether the privilege should
give way to other interests. Most courts apply a case-by-case balancing
of interests, assessing whether the public has a "legitimate" interest in the
information and whether the information is "newsworthy." While courts
have traditionally deferred to news organizations for these definitions,
the Internet era makes this deference increasingly unlikely and irrelevant.
Stronger scholarly articulations of the purpose of the public concern and

public interest doctrines, drawn from a wider range of theory than the legal case law provides, can help advocates better defend their positions. What is a legitimate vs. non legitimate public concern? Can newsworthiness be defined any better than simply being whatever deliberative news organizations decide to publish? This normative approach should also draw on the foundations of journalism ethical standards and practices, as journalists have long discussed the difficulties in assessing what and when to publish as a matter of ethical duty.

And fifth, scholars need to ask how, or maybe whether, journalism can continue to carry out its responsibility to hold power to account. This is clearly a big endeavor, but journalism as a distinct discourse risks being crowded out in the Internet marketplace of ideas. It is necessary to develop ways in which the law and ethics can help sustain the types of journalism important to democratic self-government. John Nichols and Robert McChesney's proposals for taxes on broadcast spectrum and Internet service providers are a starting point for direct intervention by the government to support journalism organizations (McChesney & Nichols, 2010, p. 209–211). The decline in news organizations has broader implications than content. For example, Professor RonNell Andersen Jones has recently drawn attention to what she calls the impending "critical lapse in legal efforts to demand accountability and accessibility to government" with the diminution of access lawsuits filed by news organizations (Jones, 2011, p. 561). In the last century, newspaper plaintiffs established some of the most important constitutional precedents that exist in the Supreme Court's free-press doctrine, not to mention access issues at the state level. But in 2011, nearly 80% of media lawyers said access to information litigation has declined, while 60% said litigation had "fallen dramatically" (Jones, 2011, p. 595). Because litigation is required for the courts to weigh on constitutional and policy questions, two sobering questions present themselves: Who will take the place of news media litigators in the twenty-first century, and what are the consequences to the public's right to know if nobody does? Professor Jones suggests that universities, non-profit foundations and advocacy organizations, and publicly funded solutions help fill the void. All are ripe for further exploration by scholars interested in the causes and effects of access litigation and accountability journalism.

Conclusion

In the midst of a technological and economic revolution sparked by the Internet, journalism is undergoing a legal and ethical revolution as well. Ethics scholars need to examine how journalism's core principles and ideals can remain relevant and viable on the Internet even as its gatekeeping and agenda-setting roles increasingly diminish in a crowded Internet marketplace. By extension, ethical principles and practices for online journalism may help preserve and possibly extend legal protections for journalism that embody the public-information and checking-value theories of the First Amendment's press clause.

References

Anderson, D. (1983). The origins of the press clause. *UCLA Law Review, 30,* 455–541.

Anderson, D. (2002). Freedom of the press. *Texas Law Review, 80,* 429–530.

Baker, C.E. (2007). The independent significance of the press clause under existing law. *Hofstra Law Review, 35,* 955–1026.

Beckett, C. (2012). *WikiLeaks: News in the Networked World.* Cambridge, UK: Polity Press.

Blasi, V. (1977). The checking value in first amendment theory. *American Bar Foundation Research Journal, 2*(3), 521–649.

Bollinger, L. (1991). *Images of a Free Press.* Chicago: The University of Chicago Press.

Calvert, C. (2010). Salvaging privacy and tranquility from the wreckage: Images of death, emotions of distress and remedies of tort in the age of the Internet. *Michigan State Law Review, 2010,* 311–340.

Calvert, C.& Bruno, J. (2010). When cleansing criminal history clashes with the first amendment and online journalism: Are expungement statutes irrelevant in the Digital Age? *CommLaw Conspectus, 19,* 123–147.

Dicken-Garcia, H. (1989). *Journalistic Standards in Nineteenth-century America.* Madison: University of Wisconsin Press.

Drudge, M. (2000). *Drudge Manifesto.* New York: Penguin.

Eliason, R. (2006). Leakers, bloggers, and fourth estate inmates: The misguided pursuit of a reporter's privilege. *Cardoza Arts and Entertainment Law Review, 24,* 385–446.

Gant, S. (2007). *We're All Journalists Now: The Transformation of the Press and Reshaping of the Law in the Internet Age.* New York: Free Press.

Jones, R.A. (2011). Litigation, legislation and democracy in a post-newspaper America. *Washington & Lee Law Review, 68,* 557–637.

King, E. (2010). *Free For All: The Internet's Transformation of Journalism.* Evanston, Ill.: Northwestern University Press.

McChesney, R., & Nichols, J. (2010). *The Death and Life of American Journalism: The Media Revolution That Will Begin the World Again.* Philadelphia: Nation Books.

McChesney, R., & Pickard, V. (2011). *Will the Last Reporter Please Turn Out the Lights: The Collapse of Journalism and What Can Be Done to Fix It.* New York: Free Press.

Meiklejohn, A. (1948). *Free Speech and its Relation to Self Government.* New York: Harper Bro. Publishers.

Shepard, J.M. (2011a). *Privileging the Press: Confidential Sources, Journalism Ethics and the First Amendment.* El Paso, TX: LFB Scholarly Publishing.

Shepard, J.M. (2011b). Campaigning as the press: *Citizens United* and the problems of press exemptions in law. *Nexus: Chapman's Journal of Law and Policy, 16*, 137–152.

Starr, P. (2004). *The Creation of the Media: Political Origins of Modern Communications*. New York: Basic Books.

Stewart, P. (1975). Or of the press. *Hastings Law Journal, 26*, 631–637.

Sullivan, A. (2000, October 30). Scoop. *The New Republic*, 10–12.

Ugland, E., & Henderson, J. (2007). Who is a journalist and why does it matter? Disentangling legal and ethical arguments. *Journal of Mass Media Ethics, 22*(4), 241–261.

Cases

First National Bank of Boston v. Bellotti, 435 U.S. 765 (1978).

Glik v. Cunniffe, 655 F. 3d 78 (1st Cir. 2011).

Grosjean v. American Press Co., 297 U.S. 233 (1936).

Lovell v. City of Griffin, 303 U.S. 444 (1938).

Near v. Minnesota, 283 U.S. 697 (1931).

New York Times Co. v. Sullivan, 376 U.S. 254 (1964).

New York Times Co. v. U.S., 403 U.S. 713 (1971).

Obsidian Finance Group v. Crystal Cox, 2011 WL 5999334 (D.Or. 2011).

O'Grady v. Superior Court, 44 Cal. Rptr. 3d 72 (Cal. Ct. App. 2006).

Chapter 2

The Plight for Journalistic Ethics Amid Technological Innovation and Exterior Forces

Jenn Burleson Mackay

Journalists juggle social networking accounts, smart phones, and an assortment of cameras and recording devices as they communicate with an audience that sometimes adores and sometimes loathes them. They remember the roles and responsibilities of the profession that echoed through the halls of their journalism schools. They take mental notes of the unspoken rules and traditions of their news organizations and strive to identify with a particular type of news medium in a world where the media are rapidly shifting into a single platform.

A variety of scholarship suggests that journalists are surrounded by forces that shape their decisions (Dimmick & Coit, 1982; Shoemaker & Reese, 1996; Shoemaker & Vos, 2009; McQuail, 2005). Many scholars have looked at how individual-level constraints, such as an individual's background and socioeconomic status, affect journalistic ethical decisions (White & Pearce, 1991; White & Singletary, 1993; Valenti, 1998; Plaisance & Skewes, 2003; Coleman & Wilkins, 2004; Plaisance & Deppa, 2009). What fewer scholars have considered, however, is how constraints outside the individual journalist's control may mold or perhaps taint journalistic ethical decisions. How might pressure from the news organization shape an individual journalist's approach to an ethical quandary on a tight deadline? Even less emphasis has been placed on whether different types of new media influence journalistic ethical choices. Another question to ponder is how technology intersects with other constraints and shapes ethical choices.

Technology plays a critical role in journalism. Technology can determine how journalists collect, edit, display, and distribute information. Audiences may select how they consume media on the basis of technological access or skill. I argue that technology plays a major role in journalistic ethics by enhancing and defining the influence of forces that constrain journalists. I will begin my argument by explaining and extrapolating from Josh Meyrowitz's information system theory. Meyrowitz argues that media have different attributes that influence the social roles of society in divergent ways. These different attributes evolve from the technological aspects of the media (Meyrowitz, 1994). This paper will consider the implications of information system theory for journalism ethics through the lens of journalistic constraints. First, information system theory will be described. Then, the ethical dimensions of individual, professional, organizational, and medium-level constraints will be extrapolated. The effect of technology on those various constraints will be described utilizing information system theory. The chapter will conclude with a discussion of a new agenda for research in journalistic ethics.

Information System Theory

Meyrowitz describes his theory as an extension of Marshall McLuhan's medium theory (Meyrowitz, 1985). Classic medium theory suggests that the medium that delivers content is more important than the message itself. McLuhan (2004) argues that some media have more information than other types of media. Some media encourage more audience involvement than other media. As a result of those differences, people will be affected differently by various types of media. Meyrowitz approaches the concept by viewing media such as books and television as separate types of information systems (Meyrowitz, 1994). He says that media affect audiences differently because they give them varying ways to access information. Differences exist among people because they have access to different types of media.

Meyrowitz focuses on three types of roles that are affected by the media: group identity, socialization, and hierarchy. Group identity is concerned with how one identifies with a particular group, such as how African Americans identify with other members of the African American community; how Caucasians identify with other Caucasians; how journalists identify with other journalists, etc. Socialization concerns how one is socialized from one social role to another, such as how one is socialized from being a lawyer to becoming a judge, or how one is socialized to become a journalist. Hierarchy focuses on how social roles are distributed on a social ladder, such as why some people, such as company vice presidents, are higher in the social hierarchy than others, such as elementary school teachers. Electronic media allow those social role differences to vanish because they provide people a common way to access information. In other words, people who once had access to different information systems suddenly have access to the same information system (Meyrowitz, 1994).

Meyrowitz expands on those concepts by utilizing the work of situationist Erving Goffman (Meyrowitz, 1994). Goffman describes how people have different patterns of behavior that they utilize depending on the type of audience they face. People deploy "front stage" behavior when they feel that they are in front of an audience. For example, a corporate executive behaves differently when he/she is in front of colleagues. "Backstage" behavior is utilized when the corporate executive is in a more private setting (Goffman, 1973).

Meyrowitz added a "middle region," or "sidestage," to Goffman's work (Meyrowitz, 1994). During this stage, audiences receive a ticket into the private lives of people. Meyrowitz argues that technology gave birth to this new stage by changing the way that people's lives are presented. A television camera might take the viewer into the personal home of a source, allowing the audience to see a mesh of front-stage behavior that was intended for the audience along with the more personal backstage behavior, such as the source interacting with a spouse. Once individuals cannot protect the secrecy of their backstage behavior, they lose some of the power that may have allowed them to sustain a particular position in the social hierarchy. Once again, the boundaries between the social roles blur, allowing people to find common ground despite their different individual characteristics. A clear example of sidestage behavior occurred on September 11, 2001. Journalists knew they were on camera, but they were unable to keep themselves from crying and gasping as the twin towers collapsed in New York City. That moment allowed audiences to see a journalistic behavior that is normally private.

While information system theory originally was designed to look at the effects of the media on society, the theory can be extended to consider the effects of technology on news media practitioners (Mackay, 2009; Mackay, unpublished). For example, one might consider how traditional journalists rank above bloggers in the journalism hierarchy, but new technology gives bloggers the opportunity to compete to publish information before traditional journalists, thus improving their rank in the hierarchy. As another example, one could consider how social networking and television cameras allow the sidestage behavior of journalists to seep into public view. This extension of information system theory onto journalists allows one to consider how technology affects journalists' group identity, hierarchy, socialization, and the revelation of sidestage behavior.

Journalistic Constraints

Journalistic constraints typically are analyzed on one of two levels: the microlevel or the macrolevel. The microlevel considers influences that come from or directly affect an individual journalist. Exterior influences that are beyond the direct control of an individual journalist represent macrolevel influences. They might come from the culture that surrounds the journalist, the organization that employs him/her, or a variety of other areas (Shoemaker & Reese, 1996).

Individual Influences

The characteristics of the individual are one way to approach individual-level influences. The background of the journalist, such as education, gender, socioeconomic status, and race, can influence journalistic decisions (Shoemaker & Vos, 2009; Shoemaker & Reese, 1996). As of 2002, 67% of American journalists were male, compared to 33% female. Few journalists classified themselves as African American (12.7%) or Hispanic (13.4%), and even fewer considered themselves to be of other minority races. Most journalists reported that their religious preference was Protestant Christian or Catholic, while far fewer considered themselves affiliated with Jewish, Islamic, or other religious traditions. Most journalists considered themselves to be either Democrat or Independent, while fewer identified with Republican or other political parties (Weaver, Beam, Brownlee, Voates, & Wilhoit, 2007).

Research has shown that individual characteristics can affect journalistic ethics. Journalists have a tendency to discuss ethics by describing their own personal values. They cite their background and previous experience as influencing their work (Plaisance & Deppa, 2009). Professional experience and confidence also appear to play a role in ethical choices (Berkowitz & Limor, 2003). Moral development research suggests that education also is a factor. Moral development tools often are used to gauge individuals' ability to use higher levels of moral reasoning when they face ethical dilemmas. Studies show journalists who have more education tend to score higher on moral development instruments than those with less education. Journalists with a propensity for fundamental Christian beliefs tend to score lower on moral development instruments than those with other religious convictions (Coleman & Wilkins, 2002, 2004). Individuals with strong fundamental beliefs may opt to defer to a higher power when facing ethical issues (Rest, Bebeau, & Volker, 1986). Other research has indicated that journalists believe that their own religion plays a role in their ethical choices (Steele, 1987).

An individual's experience with technology is highly personal. Individuals who obtain journalism and mass communication degrees will be introduced to technology and software that are relevant to their field, whereas individuals who get their college training in other areas may have less exposure to that relevant technology. Just as an individual's background can influence his/her ability to use technology, that technology can have a direct influence on the individual. As such, technology and the individual-level constraint have a reciprocal relationship with individual characteristics influencing technological use and technology affecting individual behavior.

Consider the role that education plays in the use of technology. On one hand, education influences one's ability to use technology. For example, someone who has taken broadcast-style courses will be more comfortable using professional television equipment than someone who has not had the same training. Information system theory would suggest that these individuals have been socialized to use the technology for their profession. Those individuals also would have a better understanding of how to use microphones and other devices specific to the television media. Software training is similarly important. Individuals who have taken digital photography classes are more likely to know how to use the various tools in Photoshop than individuals who have not had the same training. That training gives individuals the ability to use technology for both ethical and unethical behavior. The trained photographer can easily use Photoshop to manipulate the content of a given photograph.

Consider the work of former *Toledo Blade* photographer Allan Detrich. The award-winning photographer, who was a Pulitzer Prize finalist, routinely removed objects from his photographs to create a more pleasing image. The staff of the *Blade* found that Detrich had removed everything from legs to light switches from his photographs. In other cases, he added objects to his photos, such as branches or basketballs. He later explained that he adjusted the photos because the technology was so easy to use (Ricchiardi, 2007).

One might interpret Detrich's actions as an attempt to maintain a high position in the journalistic hierarchy. A photographer who turns in weak photos is less likely to maintain a high degree of respect. The ease of using software such as Photoshop makes it easy for everyone to have good photos. In essence, the technology provides a way to erase the hierarchical boundaries between less skilled and more highly skilled photographers. While other people may use the technology to try to destroy hierarchical boundaries, the same technology may be used unethically to help others maintain or raise their own position in the hierarchy.

Ambition might be viewed as an attempt to improve or maintain one's hierarchical position. Tech-savvy staff members may be the most likely journalists to maintain a job as the weak economy leaves newsrooms struggling for survival. As each year passes, news organizations increasingly post job advertisements for employees with multimedia and social networking expertise (Wenger & Owens, 2012). Newsrooms and universities are transforming and utilizing training techniques to ensure that employees are ready to meet the technological demand (Deuze, 2010; Blom & Davenport, 2012).

Individual characteristics also came into play for Mike Gallagher of the *Cincinnati Enquirer*. Gallagher and a colleague produced an 18-page series which accused Chiquita Brands International of various misdeeds in Central America, including the use of pesticides that were dangerous to employees. The report acknowledged that voice mails, which were allegedly obtained by a source at Chiquita, were used for the report. Less than two months after the stories were published, the *Enquirer* ran a front-page apology to Chiquita for the reports. The paper agreed to pay Chiquita $10 million because they believed that Gallagher had illegally obtained voice mails that were used in his research (Shepard, 1998). Gallagher later pled guilty to two felony voice mail thefts and agreed to reveal the names of sources who were involved in the theft (Lyman, 1999).

Gallagher chose to access the voice mails himself. There may be many reasons as to why Gallagher chose to use the technology. He may have felt that a great injustice needed to be addressed and that the technology was the only way to establish that wrongdoing. Journalists are trained or perhaps socialized that their role is to expose injustices. As a member of the journalism group, Gallagher was compelled to find a way to unmask potential wrongs. He may also have viewed this investigative report as an opportunity to potentially move up the journalistic hierarchy. This package may have given Gallagher a chance to win the Pulitzer Prize. That certainly would have raised his status in the profession.

The actions of Detrich and Gallagher were made available to people who read the newspaper or viewed content online. As that information was released, some of the backstage behavior of both journalists was revealed to the world—to an extent. No one can know everything that the journalists may have done or all of the thoughts that were involved in their choices. Thus, the sidestage behavior of both journalists was revealed rather than their true backstage. For example, Gallagher chose what information he presented to the court when he was on trial for voice mail theft. Nobody can be sure if he told the whole story, except Gallagher.

Technology and individual attributes can interact to create a playground for unethical behavior. The ambition that drives a journalist to want to be part of an elite group or the raw desire for success in the journalism hierarchy can lead to questionable behavior. Journalists are often socialized in journalism schools as to proper behavior, yet individual characteristics may override that training, leading the journalist to rely on his or her own background and technological skill when ethical questions arise.

Professional Routines

Models of journalistic constraints often place the individual at the bottom of a hierarchy of pressures. In the case of those models, macro-level influences, such as professional routines, are viewed as more powerful forces in the decision-making process than the individual. Scholars have suggested that routines are more important to determining journalistic coverage than individual-level influences (Shoemaker, Eichholz, Kim, & Wrigley, 2001; Shoemaker & Reese, 1996; Shoemaker & Vos,

2009). Routines can explain why journalists in different newsrooms may approach the same story with the same writing style. They ensure that news stories are covered (Tuchman, 1997). Routines help journalists avoid offending audiences, and they help the news organization to determine what stories can and should be covered (Shoemaker & Reese, 1996). The shared understanding of what constitutes news extends to the professional level. Students may adopt these routines when they attend journalism schools (Voakes, 1997). Journalistic ethical routines also are learned during media ethics and law courses (Mackay, 2004). One might think of routines as journalistic norms that extend across the media, regardless of medium.

In terms of information system theory, journalists identify with other journalists. They belong to the same group. The shared routines help them to identify who is a member of the group and who is not. Bloggers, for example, can pose a challenge to traditional journalism. Bloggers typically do not follow traditional journalistic procedures. Many post commentary to stories without conducting interviews or using traditional reporting techniques.

One routine that has beleaguered the profession is the need to break a story before other news organizations. Nothing illustrated this better than the Clinton/Lewinsky debacle. After Matt Drudge, who is renowned for his love of rumor, released the scoop on his blog, news organizations rushed to catch up. One author described the frantic speed with which the news media rushed out stories as creating news "cycles within cycles" (Shafer, 1998, p. 24). News organizations such as *The Wall Street Journal* and *The Dallas Morning News* published stories online that were quickly taken back down when journalists realized that additional reporting and fact-checking were needed (Shafer, 1998).

Drudge used technology to force journalists to play catch-up. He challenged the established boundary that existed between traditional journalists and bloggers, or new media journalists, and weakened the ability for traditional journalists to segregate themselves from non-traditional journalists. He also challenged the journalistic hierarchy. Respected news organizations, including *The Wall Street Journal*, were shifted from their previous position of power at the top of the hierarchy as a non-traditional journalist beat them to the story without making a mistake.

The speedy news cycle and the spirit of professional competition have challenged the profession on other stories as well. Consider the rapid spread of false reports claiming that former Penn State football coach Joe Paterno had died. That inaccurate report first was revealed on a student publication's website and a radio station near State College, PA. Then CBS Sports published a story on its own website without providing clear attribution (Sonderman, 2012). Social networking sprang to attention with post after post clamoring about the coach's death.

The rumor was allowed to spread feverishly due to the technology available to both journalists and social networking users. The hierarchy that once might have ensured that only trained journalists were able to spread the information through the electronic media was nonexistent. The technology leveled the playing ground to the point of allowing everyone to circulate "news." That same technology also pressured professional journalists to make quick announcements without checking their facts. The profession competed to maintain its prominent position at the top of the journalistic hierarchy at a time when anyone could spread information for him or herself. It seems clear that journalists across the profession jumped on the story before they double-checked the facts with Paterno's family.

One also might view the Paterno fiasco as a demonstration of sidestage behavior. On one hand, technology allowed the private life of Paterno to become national news in an instant—even before he died. Without new technology, that information could not have spread so rapidly. Traditionally, one would think of the death of a celebrity as being a private event, or backstage behavior, until the family was prepared to release the information. This time, backstage behavior leaped into cyberspace. On the other hand, this event also allowed the public to see the sidestage behavior of journalists. Audiences watched as journalists and people on social networking sites announced the coach's death and then corrected the error. Reporters had more time to double-check their sources and to ensure that the facts were in order before new technology threatened the hierarchy and forced journalists to compete not only with other journalists, but also with their audiences. Instead of following that pattern, the journalists jumped to release inaccurate information. Audiences were able to see, to some extent, how the reporting process was conducted. They saw journalists reporting information without providing attribution. Then they watched as the journalists corrected their all-too-public mistakes.

The profession has struggled to adapt to both the threat and the promise that new technology brings to the field. New technology has blurred, if not destroyed, the wall that once stood between journalists and their audiences as a publishing free-for-all unfolds in cyberspace. In terms of information system theory, one might view journalists as struggling to preserve their group identity. News organizations have attempted to absorb bloggers into their websites and their news routines as a method for preserving their occupation (Lowrey & Mackay, 2008). Another way to preserve that separation between journalist and audience may be for journalists to commit the profession to social responsibility, thus allowing journalists to help audiences recognize what information is important to society (Singer, 2010). For now, however, technology is posing a host of ethical challenges to the profession.

Medium Pressures

Journalistic pressures associated with the news medium traditionally have received limited attention from scholars, although they have been acknowledged periodically (McQuail, 2005; Mackay, unpublished). Each medium affects people differently because different technology is utilized (Meyrowitz, 1985; Croteau & Hoynes, 2003; Mackay, 2007). The medium model of journalistic ethics suggests that journalists are trained to work for a specific type of news media. They develop techniques and priorities that are dependent on that specific news medium (Mackay, unpublished).

Scholars have acknowledged that technology is a two-way process, rather than a mere tool for the journalist. Both the audience and the journalist play a role in technological use. On one hand, the degree to which the audience attends to a medium can vary. Radio sends only audible messages, whereas television sends both auditory and visual content. Those differences lead television to require more attention than radio (Croteau & Hoynes, 2003). The relationship that the journalist has with the audience plays a role in how he or she makes professional ethical choices (Mackay, unpublished). Audiences have a different relationship in regards to how they interact with different types of media. The power of the audience is clearly felt by television producers, who carefully watch ratings. As a result of ratings power, the television journalist may weigh audience opinion as he/she chooses how to behave. An unethical decision might be easier to make if it is likely to increase ratings (Mackay, 2007).

While new media technology has changed the way the news media do their jobs, different media outlets continue to have different technological needs and expectations. Television journalists need visual and audio content for nearly every story. The journalist also might face multiple deadlines for newscasts throughout the day while also filing online posts. The daily newspaper journalist, on the other hand, utilizes some video, but is not required to support every story with visual or audible content. The daily newspaper journalist is likely to be responsible for posting online stories in addition to print content. Weekly newspaper journalists, however, have very different deadline expectations. They may file stories once or twice per week, but they are not likely expected to post frequent online updates and have limited video/audio requirements (Mackay, 2007). Studies also have suggested that journalists working for different media have different perspectives on their jobs. Television, weekly newspaper, and radio journalists suggest that audience response affects whether an event is deemed newsworthy. Television journalists also value an ample audience more than other types of journalists (Weaver et al., 2007).

Research has indicated newspaper reporters are at the top of the journalistic hierarchy—at least in the eyes of journalists. The flash and appearance that are important elements to the television industry leads journalists who work for other media to have less respect for television journalists (Meltzer, 2009). The medium-based hierarchy may be extended onto new media as well. Consider the organization of material on *The New York Times* website. The site masters acknowledge blogs as a type of content, but blogs are separated from the other material on the website. They are acknowledged, but they are not likely to be positioned as the most important content on the home page of the site. That position is reserved for more traditional news content. This hierarchy could lead journalists who work for media that are lower in the hierarchy to make questionable ethical decisions in order to potentially raise their position in the hierarchy. On the other hand, journalists working for established media may make questionable ethical choices if they feel threatened by another medium.

WikiLeaks represents a hierarchical challenge to the medium hierarchy. The site can be viewed as both a challenge to the profession and an illustration of medium-level influence on journalistic ethics. The WikiLeaks website managers are devoted to using the site as a place for citizens to publicize documents that were never meant for public eyes. The site has published hundreds of classified documents, and the site master promotes WikiLeaks as a type of non-profit journalism. The site leaped into the limelight after a video depicting an American military helicopter attack on 12 people was uploaded to the site. The video was deemed classified by the U.S. military, but it was leaked to WikiLeaks allegedly by U.S. Army Private Bradley Manning. While some have hailed Manning as a hero, many have questioned the ethics of publishing such material and whether WikiLeaks can be prosecuted under the Espionage Act (Peterson, 2011). The man behind the site, Julian Assange, purports to protect individuals who leak documents to the website by allowing them to upload documents securely or by organizing an in-person exchange of information. Many journalists have used the site as a reporting tool that provides them with information that they might never obtain through other means (Lynch, 2010).

WikiLeaks demonstrates not only how technology can allow questionable journalistic ethical choices to be made, but also how it can influence the journalist's ability to obtain information. High-profile leaks can help Assange to position himself on a higher rung in the journalism hierarchy from more traditional journalists, particularly as news organizations cover information that is accessible only through WikiLeaks. In this sense, the new media site not only provides material that may be ethically questionable, but the high-profile status of the site pressures journalists working for more traditional media to further publicize questionable material.

The website is riddled with sidestage behavior. First, individuals are allowed and encouraged to post classified or private documents to

WikiLeaks. This opportunity gives individuals the ability to expose the backstage behavior of various people, agencies, and organizations. Audiences are not able to see all of the background that surrounds the documents or how they were developed, yet information that was never meant for the public circulates rapidly through the site. Once agencies are aware that their information has been published, they engage in sidestage behavior, investigating the leaks, explaining why decisions were made, etc. After their documents have been published, individuals recognize that backstage behavior has been revealed. As a result, they can never completely hide it again. They recognize that they are in the public view, and they make public statements and decisions with that thought in mind. The website also allows the journalists to reveal their own sidestage behavior. When journalists write stories about documents or videos that have been leaked to the site, they reveal to the public how they do their reporting. The public also is free to view the documents for themselves rather than waiting for journalists to interpret the information for them. This blurs the boundary between those who are journalists and those who are audience members.

Medium-level influences do not have a strictly negative effect on the media, however. Sidestage behavior can have positive consequences. Consider the concept of transparency. The term is commonly associated with a movement across the profession to provide audiences with a greater understanding as to how decisions are made in the newsroom. It was bloggers who called for transparency from Dan Rather and CBS News after a story aired questioning the military career of George W. Bush. The story was based partially on questionable documents. By the next day, bloggers were questioning whether a document could have been produced on a typewriter during the time frame when it was supposedly written. One day later, mainstream media outlets began questioning the authenticity of the documents, too (Kurtz, Dobbs, & Grimaldi, 2004). Shortly following the scandal, CBS acknowledged that it could not prove the legitimacy of the documents used in the story, and Rather announced that he was retiring (Rutenberg & Steinberg, 2004).

The very essence of transparency demands that journalistic sidestage behavior is revealed. It calls for journalists to show how they do their jobs and asks them to explain how decisions were made. In the case of CBS's military story, two types of media were at odds. In this case, however, the non-traditional media acted as a "fifth estate" overseeing the established media. New media played a card that potentially could raise the status of bloggers on the media hierarchy.

Different news media have different technological needs and responsibilities. Those differences could lead to different ethical questions across the media. Research has suggested that television journalists are not only more willing to use deceptive techniques, but their desire for images could lead them to use hidden cameras and other questionable practices for a story (Lee, 2005). ABC News producers not only hid their identities to attain jobs at Food Lion, but they used hidden cameras for an exposé that showed the questionable practices that grocery chain employees used. Among other things, their footage depicted Food Lion employees re-dating meat, extending the expiration date (Kirtley, 2000). The news staff's desire to show footage from those hidden cameras left the journalists revealing sidestage behavior. Audiences were free to see how the story evolved. It is quite likely that the journalists expected that the investigative piece would raise their prestige in the medium hierarchy. The revelation of that sidestage behavior, however, resulted in years of legal battles against the grocery chain, who proclaimed that the ABC employees were un-loyal to Food Lion when they brought hidden cameras into the store.

While journalists have a shared understanding of the values of their field at the professional level, journalists have different roles and expectations depending on which medium employs them. They rely on different technologies or at the very least different intensities of various technologies. They face different deadlines and their placement on a medium-level hierarchy can leave journalists jockeying to raise their status.

Organizational Influences

Pressures from the organizational level have been described by multiple scholars. These are pressures that radiate from within the specific news organization that employs the journalist. Employers make rules that staff members follow even if the staff is never officially informed of the policies (Breed, 1955). There is a hierarchy within the organization that must be enforced. At this level, one considers how people interact with one another within the newsroom (Reese, 2010). A deeper connection to professional values leads journalists to be less supportive of their organizations (Berkowitz & Limor, 2003). It has been suggested that journalists should strive to uphold professional values rather than deferring to organizational needs (Borden, 2000).

A journalist who defers to the needs of the organization might avoid writing stories that would frame his or her own news organization in a negative light. Likewise, organizational pressure would dictate that a journalist should not publicize a negative story about a company that is a major advertiser for the news organization. In short, the journalist who responds to organizational pressure chooses to make decisions that will enhance the organization's status. In a television market with three stations, one wants his or her organization to attain the highest ratings, or the highest point on the organizational hierarchy.

One might view the tense relationship between organizational influences and technology by considering the ethical lapses at the now defunct British tabloid *News of the World*. An ever-increasing number of employees from the organization have been arrested and accused of a host of illegal activities, such as secretly receiving private voice mail messages that were intended for celebrities, crime victims, and other people (Burns, 2012). Numerous staff members also have been accused of paying police officers for information. One of the peaks in the saga of Rupert Murdoch's sinking newspaper was when *The Guardian* published a story accusing their competitor of hacking the mobile phone owned by a murdered teenager. Murdoch closed the *News of the World* after the story was published (Low, 2011). Out-of-court settlements were made to several alleged phone hacking victims. Murdoch has denied any knowledge of the payments and has denied any suggestion that he covered up the phone hacking scandal (Beattie, 2011). As this chapter was being written, the story was continuing to evolve.

The employees of *News of the World* identify themselves as being part of a group. As described by Meyrowitz (1985), group members are socialized to the expectations of their group. If group members were led to believe that phone hacking and paying public officials for information was an accepted practice within the organization, then it stands to reason that other members of that group would have engaged in the same behavior. The need to be part of the group may have led multiple people to participate in the illegal activities. Technology gave the staff the capability to allegedly hack mobile phones. Journalists may have felt that the ability to hack into phones would lead them to get better information for stories. That information could have helped the organization to move up the organizational hierarchy, placing their newsroom above competing publications. As the authorities continue to release details about how the *News of the World* journalists may have collected information for stories, audiences are given a potential view into the backstage behavior of the journalists. Readers are given the opportunity to see how the reporting process worked for these journalists. If the journalists respond to those accusations and explain their reporting techniques or provide evidence of their reporting techniques, their sidestage behavior will be revealed. At that time, audiences will see some combination of the back and front stages of the journalists.

At the organizational level, the effects of technology are rooted in how a specific newsroom chooses to use technology. The influence can be caused by which technology journalists utilize in that newsroom, but it also can be determined by how the newsroom community chooses to use the technology. Group dynamics and organizational leadership are important factors in organizational culture.

New Agenda for Journalistic Ethics Research

Technology spins an intricate and sometimes treacherous web around journalists who already are encapsulated by constraining forces (Figure 2.1). The influence of technology may be directed at specific journalists

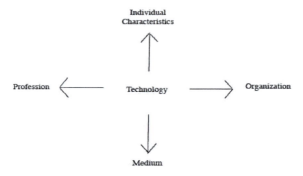

Figure 2.1 Technological Influences on Journalistic Ethics

who have varying education and experiences, but it also can shape professional, organizational, and medium expectations and responsibilities. The effects of this complex relationship on journalism need to be investigated further. The over-arching influence that technology has on the industry cannot be ignored.

Long before the Internet rippled change through journalism, Meyrowitz's information system theory dissected the differences among media. His theory considered the hierarchical, group, and socialization differences that are associated with different media and the ability that electronic media has to break down barriers within the society (Meyrowitz, 1985). The social roles that transform audiences as they use the media also can be applied to the media practitioners who create media content. Those social roles and the dramatic power of technology have significant implications for journalistic ethics.

Some scholarship already has touched on medium, organizational, and professional constraints and their implications for journalism. Limited scholarship has sought to thoroughly understand the ethical ramifications of these constraints, however. For example, how are ethical choices influenced at the medium level as journalists compete to survive in a world where audiences demand free content—a world where audiences challenge the established medium hierarchy by practicing their own forms of journalism? From the professional perspective, how will journalists maintain high ethical standards as pundits and other politically biased media giants continue to flood the profession? At the organizational level, how will online non-profit news entities balance the financial needs of their organization against their own ethical standards? As we begin to understand the complex relationship between constraining forces and technology, we will be better prepared to educate future journalism students on the ethical challenges that they will face in the real world.

The individual-level constraint has frequently been studied in regards to ethics, but that scholarship needs to expand. We must have a better descriptive understanding of why and how ethical choices are made and what influence rapidly changing technology has on journalists before we can hope that our normative arguments will have success in the real world. Once we have expanded our knowledge base of these issues, we will be better equipped to help practicing journalists and our students to recognize the complex factors that influence their own ethical choices.

New research approaches and instruments may be needed to advance this research agenda. The best place to begin developing this area of research may be interviews with journalists. Scholars need to tap into where journalists view themselves within the journalism hierarchy, how they identify with groups, and how they perceive their own sidestage behavior. In addition to those factors, the journalists also must be encouraged to discuss individual, organizational, professional, and medium-level pressures that may affect their ethical decisions. Those conversations should be followed by analyses of how organizations have dealt with specific ethical challenges. An ethical case could be studied at multiple levels. For example, consider the public suicide of Pennsylvania State Treasurer Bud Dwyer. The official shot himself directly in front of several journalists. News organizations had to choose whether they would show the footage of the suicide. This case could be studied at the individual level by asking a single reporter how he/she chose to cover the case; at the organizational level by looking at how a single newsroom covered the case; at the professional level by considering how the profession as a whole chose to cover the case; and then by evaluating the role the news medium played in how the case was covered. Once those data have been collected, new dilemma-based instruments and scales can be designed to examine how hierarchy, group identity, and socialization influence ethical choices at the individual, organizational, medium, and professional levels. Some dilemma-based work has already been done testing influences at the organizational and professional levels (Mackay, 2007). Ethnographies might also be useful as they could provide a more detailed understanding as to how ethical choices are made over time.

This paper has touched on a few of the constraining forces that are shaped by technology. There are additional factors, such as ideology and government regulations, which also intertwine with technology and may shape journalistic ethical choices. For example, ideology may determine which technology is available to audiences and journalists. How might that technological access influence ethical choices? As journalists sit in newsrooms debating how frequently they should update microblogging sites such as Twitter or whether they should friend their sources on social networking sites such as Facebook, perhaps we also should begin considering software and social networking as additional factors that influence journalistic ethics. How often do journalists use this technology to access personal information about potential news sources? Are journalists more inclined to mask their identities as they communicate with potential news sources now that this technology is available? Future research should consider the ethical implications of those forces as well.

Technological advances will continue to raise perplexing ethical issues at the individual, organizational, medium, and professional levels. It is incumbent upon both scholars and professionals to focus on understanding and responding to these issues. Once we have a better understanding of these forces, journalists will be better prepared to tackle the challenging ethical quandaries that they will face in the years to come.

References

Beattie, J. (2011, July 20). "They caught us with dirty hands": Murdoch empire in crisis the grilling. *The Mirror*, 4, 5.

Berkowitz, D., & Limor, Y. (2003). Professional confidence and situational ethics: Assessing the social-professional dialectic in journalistic ethics decisions. *Journalism & Mass Communication Quarterly*, 80, 783–801.

Blom, R., & Davenport, L. D. (2012). Searching for the core of journalism education: Program directors disagree on curriculum priorities. *Journalism & Mass Communication Educator*, 67, 70–86.

Borden, S. (2000). A model for evaluating journalist resistance to business constraints. *Journal of Mass Media Ethics*, 15, 149–166.

Breed, W. (1955). Social control in the newsroom: A functional analysis. *Social Forces*, 33, 236–335.

Burns, J. F. (2012, January 8). Latest hacking scandal arrest suggests focus on cover-up. *The New York Times*, 6.

Coleman, R., & Wilkins, L. (2002). Searching for the ethical journalist: An exploratory study of the moral development of news workers. *Journal of Mass Media Ethics*, 17, 209–225.

Coleman, R., & Wilkins, L. (2004). The moral development of journalists: A comparison with other professions and a model for predicting high quality ethical reasoning. *Journalism & Mass Communication Quarterly*, 81, 511–527.

Croteau, D. R. & Hoynes, C. (2003). *Media/Society: Industries, Images, and Audiences*. Thousand Oaks, CA: Sage Publications.

Deuze, M. (2010). What is journalism? Professional identity and ideology of journalists reconsidered. In D. Berkowitz (Ed.), *Cultural Meanings of News: A Text Reader* (pp. 17–47). Thousand Oaks, CA: Sage Publications.

Dimmick, J., & Coit, P. (1982). Levels of analysis in mass media decision making: A taxonomy, research strategy, and illustrative data analysis. *Communication Research*, 9, 3–32.

Goffman, E. (1973). *Presentation of Self in Everyday Life*. Woodstock, NY: Overlook Press.

Kirtley, J. (2000). Don't pop that cork. *American Journalism Review*, January/February. Retrieved March 7, 2012 from www.ajr.org/article.asp?id=3132.

Kurtz, H., Dobbs, M., & Grimaldi, J.V. (2004, September, 19). In rush to air,

CBS quashed memo worries. *The Washington Post*, A01. Retrieved March 7, 2012 from www.washingtonpost.com/wp-dyn/articles/A31727-2004Sep18.html.

Lee, S. T. (2005). Predicting tolerance of journalistic deception. *Journal of Mass Media Ethics, 20*(1), 22–42.

Low, V. (2011, July 18). She wanted to be a lightning rod. Now she really is at the heart of a storm. *The (London) Times*, 6, 7.

Lowrey, W., & Mackay, J. B. (2008). Journalism and blogging: A test of a model of occupational competition. *Journalism Practice, 2*, 64–81.

Lyman, B. (1999). More bad banana. *Columbia Journalism Review, 38*, 14–15.

Lynch, L. (2010). "We're going to crack the world open": WikiLeaks and the future of investigative reporting. *Journalism Practice, 4*, 309–318.

Mackay, J. B. (2004, August). The media ethics necessity: Do journalism students need to study ethics? Paper presented at the 87th annual conference of the Association for Education in Journalism and Mass Communication, Toronto, Canada.

Mackay, J. B. (2007, August). The suffocating ethicist: A model of journalistic ethical constraints. Paper presented at the 90th annual conference of the Association for Education in Journalism and Mass Communication, Washington, DC.

Mackay, J. B. (2009, August). Journalistic constraints: Weighing the pressures that surround the modern media. Paper presented at the 92nd annual conference of the Association for Education in Journalism and Mass Communication, Boston, MA.

Mackay, J. B. (unpublished). *The Medium Model of Journalistic Ethical Constraints*.

McLuhan, M. (2004). *Understanding Media: The Extensions of Man*. London: Routledge.

McQuail, D. (2005). *McQuail's Mass Communication Theory*. Oxford: The AldenPress.

Meltzer, K. (2009). The hierarchy of journalistic cultural authority. *Journalism Practice, 3*, 59–74.

Meyrowitz, J. (1985). *No Sense of Place: The Impact of Electronic Media on Social Behavior*. New York: Oxford University Press.

Meyrowitz, J. (1994). Medium theory. In D. Crowley & D. Mitchell (Eds.), *Communication Theory Today* (pp. 50–77). Stanford, CA: Stanford University Press.

Peterson, E. (2011). WikiLeaks and the Espionage Act of 1917. *News Media & The Law, 35*, 9–11.

Plaisance, P. L., & Deppa, J. A. (2009). Perceptions and manifestations of autonomy, transparency, and harm among U.S. newspaper journalists. *Journalism & Communication Monographs, 10*, 327–386.

Plaisance, P. L., & Skewes, E. A. (2003). Personal and professional dimensions of news works: Exploring the link between journalists' values and roles. *Journalism & Mass Communication Quarterly, 80*, 833–848.

Reese, S. D. (2010). Understanding the global journalist: A hierarchy-of-influences approach. In D. Berkowitz (Ed.), *Cultural Meanings of News: A Text Reader* (pp. 53–66). Thousand Oaks, CA: Sage Publications.

Rest, J. R., Bebeau, M., & Volker, J. (1986). An overview of the psychology of morality. In J. R. Rest (Ed.). *Moral Development Advances in Research and Theory* (pp. 1–39). New York: Praeger Publishers.

Ricchiardi, S. (2007). Distorted picture. *American Journalism Review, 29,* 36–43.

Rutenberg, J., & Steinberg, J. (2004, November 24). A reporter-anchor who blazed a trail of his own. *The New York Times.* Retrieved March 7, 2012 from www.nytimes.com/2004/11/24/business/media/24dprofile.html.

Shafer, J. (1998, February 15). "The web made me do it." *The New York Times Magazine,* 24.

Shepard, A. C. (1998). Bitter fruit. *American Journalism Review, 20,* 32.

Shoemaker, P., & Reese, S. D. (1996). *Mediating the Message: Theories of Influences on Mass Media Content.* White Plains, NY: Longman.

Shoemaker, P. J., & Vos, T. P. (2009). *Gatekeeping Theory.* New York: Routledge.

Shoemaker, P. J., Eichholz, M., Kim, E., & Wrigley, B. (2001). Individual and routine forces in gatekeeping. *Journalism and Mass Communication Quarterly, 78,* 233–246.

Singer, J. B. (2010). The socially responsible existentialist. In D. Berkowitz (Ed.), *Cultural Meanings of News: A Text Reader* (pp. 53–66). Thousand Oaks, CA: Sage Publications.

Sonderman, J. (2012, January 21). How false reports of Joe Paterno's death were spread and debunked. *Poynter.* Retrieved March 7, 2012 from www.poynter. org/latest-news/mediawire/160270/how-false-reports-of-joe-paternos-death-were-spread-and-debunked/.

Steele, R. M. (1987). Video ethics: the dilemma of value balancing. *Journal of Mass Media Ethics, 2,* 7–17.

Tuchman, G. (1997). Making news by doing work. In D. Berkowitz (Ed.), *Social-Meaning of News: A Text Reader* (pp. 173–192). Thousand Oaks, CA: Sage Publications.

Valenti, J. M. (1998). Ethical decision making in environmental communication. *Journal of Mass Media Ethics, 13,* 219–231.

Voakes, P. S. (1997). Public perceptions of journalists' ethical motivations. *Journalism and Mass Communication Quarterly, 74,* 23–38.

Weaver, D. H., Beam, R. A., Brownlee, B. J., Voakes, P. S., & Wilhoit, G. C. (2007). *The American Journalist in the 21st Century: U.S. News People at the Dawn of a New Millennium.* Mahwah, NJ: Lawrence Erlbaum.

Wenger, D. H., & Owens, L. C. (2012). Help Wanted 2010: An examination of new media skills required by top U.S. news companies. *Journalism & Mass Communication Educator, 67,* 9–25.

White, H. A., & Pearce, R. C. (1991). Validating an ethical motivations scale: Convergence and predictive ability. *Journalism Quarterly, 68,* 455–464.

White, H. A., & Singletary, M. W. (1993). Internal work motivation: Predictor of using ethical heuristics and motivations. *Journalism Quarterly, 70,* 381–392.

Chapter 3

Kant on Unsocial Sociability and the Ethics of Social Blogging

Scott R. Stroud and Danee Pye

The social activity of blogging seems innocent enough not to provoke much commotion in the rapidly diversifying world of online thought-sharing. Yet two recent cases illustrate the opposite. First is the instance in September of 2006 when a blog titled "Wal-Marting Across America" (sponsored by "Working Families for Wal-Mart") caused quite a stir. Jim and Laura, the two individuals running the on-going weblog, used the platform to recount their travels in an RV across America. Along the way, they parked their RV in many Wal-Mart parking lots and talked with local employees. They recounted multitudes of uplifting stories about Wal-Mart and its treatment of its workers. All of this seemed like normal—if not boring—web content that might go unnoticed by anyone turning to the Internet for breaking news. What critics of Wal-Mart soon discovered, however, was that Jim and Laura were far from the "normal people" they seemed to be. Jim was revealed to be a professional photographer and Laura was a freelance writer for the Treasury Department (Gogoi, 2006). None of this background information was revealed in the blog set-up, nor was the fact that Wal-Mart had hired the high-power public relations firm Edelman to create "Working Families for Wal-Mart." As David Craig (2007) put it, "the blog, which appeared to be unaffiliated with Wal-Mart, was actually backed by the company and was part of Edelman's public relations efforts on its behalf" (p. 216).

This publicity campaign generated outrage from the blogging community, as other "bloggers felt betrayed and feared guilt by association" (Boynton, 2007, p. 218). The issue that underlies this case is that of identity and blogging ethics. Both bloggers and scholars of communication ethics are reacting to the impact that Jim and Laura's real identity (including their connection to Wal-Mart) has on those evaluating the content and persuasiveness of their blog (Baker, 2007). Authenticity and transparency of identity seem important elsewhere, so why should they not be important in the blogosphere? In reference to the Jim and Laura blog, Sherry Baker (2007) argues that "The lack of authenticity causes readers in retrospect to question everything that was posted" (p. 224).

Yet the possibility remains that these stories are true, even if they are not representative of the whole range of possible stories (Pauly, 2007). The challenging issue of *occluded identity* and its relation to truth and virtue in the blogosphere only grows stronger with consideration of complex cases like this.

A second case involves a more sinister string of events occurring in Mexico. Amidst a drug war that has cost nearly 43,000 their lives, Mexican drug cartels warring with government forces have found that information control and force are helpful assets (CNN, 2011). Yet a new problem has appeared for the cartels. Having shut down traditional media with kidnappings and assassinations of journalists, the concerned public has moved to a news source more difficult to pin down through violence—social media such as blogs and "micro-blogging" (i.e., Twitter). Such blogs allow individuals to post information about suspicious vehicles, drug activity, and violent events. They also allow bloggers to speak out against cartels such as the "Zetas" who typically punish unfavorable speech. Such blogs are more difficult for the cartels to influence due to their diffuse and largely anonymous nature. Some cracks in the anonymity provided by online identities have appeared, and the cartels have taken brutal advantage of those lapses. Recently, two dead bodies were found hanging from an overpass in Nuevo Laredo displaying signs of torture. They were accompanied by signs that indicated that they were killed for posting information against cartels online, that mentioned two sites by name (Al Rojo Vivo and Blog del Narco), and that warned others not to "post funny things on the Internet." This killing was widely attributed to the Zeta cartel (Castillo, 2011). Another victim, Maria Elizabeth Macias, was also killed for her activities in running "Neuvo Laredo en Vivo," a website that expresses views hostile to the cartels and allows for the sharing of information related to drug activity. Macias' decapitated head was found "next to a keyboard, computer mouse, headphones, and speakers... [this killing was] intended not just to get rid of the victim, but to graphically display the extent of the Zetas' power" (Stone, 2011). A fourth victim was later found in Nuevo Laredo, with signs indicating he had been slain because of chat room activity (Pachico, 2011). Clearly, the expressions of outrage and information against the cartels provoked the cartels to try to identify their online critics.

This case is fascinating because of what it displays concerning the tenuous state of online anonymity. Clearly, the activities of some bloggers were not totally anonymous, as four of them had their online identity "fixed" to a real-life identity, allowing the cartels to do what they do best—use pain, mutilation, and death as a visible deterrent to others. But it also shows the *limitations* to such pursuits—not all of the identities of those using blogs and online forums to post anti-cartel views could be tracked down using IP addresses, cookie information, and so forth. This case shows the tragic limitations to online identity *in some cases*, but it shows the encouraging amount of anonymity that comes with mass adoption of semi-anonymous means of blogging activity. Thousands continued blogging despite the "examples" the cartels made out of those four bloggers, and it is unclear whether all of them will be tracked down offline in a similar fashion. Indeed, they may have been "innocent" slip-ups in securing their identity (such as using a consistent Internet "handle" across domains or not using America-based webhosts) that led to cartel hackers fixing their real-life identities. Clearly, nothing online is totally anonymous and disconnected from our "real-life" activities, but there is a sense of *practical anonymity* that the thousands of unharmed anti-cartel bloggers and posters share in Mexico. Add in technological countermoves such as proxy servers and such a de facto anonymity could potentially be increased. Yet what this admittedly extreme case of online and real-life identity highlights is not the *descriptive* question of whether online identity can be totally compartmentalized from our "real" identity or be truly anonymous. As the case of the anti-cartel bloggers shows us, there is a sense in which people are protected by a sort of practical anonymity that comes from mass action. The question that is highlighted by this case, as well as the former case involving the Wal-Mart blog, is a *normative* question: Is online anonymity or occluded identity a morally *good* thing? If we have the chance to *increase* and *enable* anonymous, self-created online identities, *should* we? Such a question focuses on the ethics of blogging, a realm of interest that is distinct from the descriptive realms of what is possible given certain technologies of the present and the future, or certain contingent uses (such as that of the cartels). Ethically, is malleable or occluded online identity a *good* thing?

Instead of descriptive approaches that draw upon what bloggers already value (e.g., Kuhn, 2007; Perlmutter & Schoen, 2007), we return to the powerful normative theory of Immanuel Kant (1724–1803) to clarify what virtuous blogging might look like. J. B. Schneewind (2002) points out that Kant's ethical thought is "one of the two or three most important contributions that modern moral philosophers have made to our culture ... Kantian views of morality are a central topic of contemporary moral philosophy" (p. 83). It is therefore worth some interpretive effort to ask what Kant—a philosopher with no knowledge of blogging or the Internet— *might* have to say concerning the ethics of this evolving, technologically mediated communicative activity. Such an account will do justice to the rhetorical and structural potentials of blogging involving malleable identities and full self-expression. Kant's value to rhetoric and communication ethics has been explored in regard to general issues of community and religion (Gehrke, 2002; Hove, 2009; Stroud, 2005), yet more must be said on his relevance to contemporary practices of communication. If blogging activity seems to involve some amount of occluded identity, self-expression, and possible deception, what clarity can Kantian ethics bring to this realm of rhetorical activity? Clearly, Kant did not write on this topic, nor is it valuable to look for *exact* analogues in his thought to blogging in all its particular details (or Kant's thought would be *prima facie* irrelevant to all modern technology of which he was unaware). What can be done is to constructively engage themes and ideas in Kant's writings on moral philosophy in a useful fashion—a fashion that will result in us seeing blogging and the ideal ways it can be pursued that we may have overlooked.

To hone our normative account of ideal blogging behaviors, we will focus on what we define as "social blogging," or the use of websites to enable and encourage the sharing and exchanging of non-expert opinions on matters of interest to a wide audience. This would include sites about celebrities, political opinion blogs, the blogs enabling sharing anti-cartel views among Mexican citizens, as well as blogs about individuals' experience with certain corporations. There are many types and permutations of blogs, but such diversity (and the consequent lack of necessary and sufficient conditions for defining "blogging" exhaustively) should not preclude or paralyze discussion of certain ideals for blogging interaction. Acknowledging these caveats to our subject matter and approach, we make the case that Kant would advocate certain guiding maxims for social blogging that stem from his rich concept of autonomy. Others may continue to advance discussion of blogging ethics by bringing in other ethical systems or definitions of "blogging." Yet we hope to show that this concept of autonomy represents an interesting chance to ethically justify the multiple senses of identity that the online world often enables. Our argument will proceed in the following manner: (1) We begin by explaining Kant's important (and often overlooked) grounding for his ethics—the complex notions of autonomy and human "unsocial sociability" taken from Kant's lesser-known works, especially his lectures on anthropology and ethics. (2) Using this rich notion of autonomy, we argue that a Kantian approach would conceive of social blogging less as *journalism* and more as *conversation*. Kant's thoughts on conversational ethics then allow us to show ways in which the opacity of online identity further human autonomy. (3) We conclude with some general maxims for virtuous social blogging that can be extracted from Kant's moral and anthropological thought.

Kant and the Ideal of Autonomy

Many of the core issues of blogging ethics revolve around the notion of autonomy, a particularly valuable quality of human moral agents. Privacy concerns implicate the autonomy of the one potentially revealing information about herself, whereas issues with openness, interactivity, and authenticity all point to concerns about the autonomous activities and self-direction of an active blogger. Even concerns about multiple online selves are grounded on autonomy—is such a complex "self" more or less autonomous than a unified, direct self that we often see over the course of everyday interaction? The argument of this study will be that the normative ethical theory of Immanuel Kant can provide guidance in these troubled matters of online identity, particularly through his rich notion of autonomy.

The standard view of Kant on autonomy comes from his *Groundwork of the Metaphysics of Morals* (1785/1996). It is in this text that Kant develops his central concepts of what comprises moral worth—an agent actively willing certain action-guiding maxims from a respect for duty. This respect is composed of a consciousness of the moral law, which Kant proceeds to give in alternative (but putatively equivalent) formulations. He famously states the "Formula of Universal Law" (FUL): "act only in accordance with that maxim through which you can at the same time will that it become a universal law" (4:421). One can also formulate the moral law in terms of how one treats other moral agents. The "Formula of Humanity as an End in Itself" (FHE) commands: "so act that you use humanity, whether in your own person or in the person of any other, always at the same time as an end, never merely as a means" (4:429). The line of thought in both formulations—encompassing both universalizable form and the content of treating others as ends—culminates in Kant's notion of autonomy. In the *Groundwork*, Kant gives a straightforward definition of the often-ambiguous term "autonomy." He claims it is "the property of the will by which it is a law to itself (independent of any property of the objects of volition)" (4:440). We are autonomous when we will maxims of action that apply equally and consistently to all rational agents—including ourselves and others. Paul Guyer (2005) points out that this notion of autonomy is really a notion of "self-governance by universal law" that focuses on "independence of the choices and actions of a person not only from domination by other persons, but also from domination by his own inclinations" (p. 116). Maxims that are universalizable can be willed by any agent, and thereby oppress no particular agent. One is fully autonomous when her guiding maxims are free from the influence of contingent, particular desires or powerful other agents.

This is one common reading of Kant on autonomy. Yet it leaves out the "impure" side to Kant's ethics that Robert Louden (2000) argues is still "a well-kept secret, even among Kant scholars" (p. vii). Louden's account of Kant's "impure ethics" highlights the role that "anthropological" pursuits contribute to his analysis of morality and moral development. Extending this sort of treatment of Kant's ethics, we believe it is profitable to look at the rich context of Kant on human sociability and autonomy, as both our independence from and community with others underlie many of the ethical issues associated with online identity. Autonomy is more than the universalizable willing of maxims. It encompasses those features of human nature that undergird this operation of moral judgment, as well as the features that mitigate against it. It is our argument that Kant's contribution to blogging ethics can best be understood through a rich notion of autonomy, one that properly grounds our willful use of rational agency in our social setting.

For Kant, autonomy was always connected to our social situation as human beings. Right before the rather rigoristic reading of moral worth provided in the *Groundwork*, Kant emphasized the role that our peculiar sort of sociability plays in our personhood in his essay "Idea for a Universal History from a Cosmopolitan Point of View" (Kant, 1784/1963). Kant argues that one can "discover a natural purpose in this idiotic course of things human" (8:18). Of course, Kant is using purpose in a regulative sense—it is a useful principle to guide us in how we think about nature and its operations. Of particular interest to this project is his invocation of a natural antagonism among humans. By humans' natural "unsocial sociability," Kant refers to "their propensity to enter into society, bound together with a mutual opposition which constantly threatens to break up the society" (8:20). Nature has endowed humans with a variety of inclinations, but Kant notices two important urges humans feel:

> Man has an inclination to associate with others, because in society he feels himself to be more than man, i.e., as more than the developed form of his natural capacities. But he also has a strong propensity to isolate himself from others, because he finds in himself at the same time the unsocial characteristic of wishing to have everything go according to his own wish.
>
> (8:20–21)

For Kant's way of thinking, these conflicting inclinations must eventually align to bring about the development of all of humanity's capacities. In other words, they exist because they indirectly further the cause of human autonomy—our freedom from ways of willing and acting that are not systemically consistent or sustainable. We see the draw of socializing with others, yet we also see that their powers of choice (their freedom, in short) put a de facto limit to what we desire. There are needs to socialize, yet we constantly want to draw back into unsocial ways of privileging our own projects and will. How can autonomy come out of such a challenging contradiction?

In Kant's analysis, this unsocial sociability does not result in paralysis or arbitrary choice. It conditions our social commitment to others in a unique fashion. We engage with others, but we expect opposition to our will and projects. This "opposition" is the force that "awakens all his powers, brings him to conquer his inclination to laziness and, propelled by vainglory, lust for power, and avarice, to achieve a rank among his fellows whom he cannot tolerate but from whom he cannot withdraw" (8:21). Thus, humans take their first collective step from "barbarism to culture" (8:21). The social opposition that is created by human freedom ends up being a spur to the development of individual talents, since the individual realizes that others will not automatically assist her in her projects. Humans want concord, Kant says, but instead nature "wills discord" (8:21). Whether Kant is right about this being nature's "intention," his regulative point is clear—there is a way to see the human urges to associate with others and to privilege idiosyncratic needs and wishes as going together purposively. Their purpose suits the overall project of furthering human autonomy, and it serves as a way we can hope to make progress down such treacherous paths.

Notice that Kant's grounding of morality on an "impure" human foregrounds the complex social aspects of our existence. We argue that this means that communication is a vital element to what it means to be a human moral agent—a view similar to contemporary views positing the importance of language in constructing the human sense of self (e.g., Benveniste, 1971). In dealing with our social unsociability, humans necessarily must make a variety of communicative decisions on how to interact with other agents. These decisions are vital because they not only reveal our autonomy, but they also reveal our self. Indeed, for Kant, our spontaneity of choice was a central element to who "we" are (Kant, 1793/1996). It is the tension between self and other that allows for such a spontaneity, a fact acknowledged in Kant's notion of unsocial sociability and modern approaches to "face" in communication. For instance, Brown and Levinson's (1987) analysis of "face" breaks down into "negative face" and "positive face." The former concerns "freedom of action and freedom from imposition," whereas the latter acknowledges "the positive consistent self-image or 'personality' (crucially including the desire that this self-image be appreciated and approved of) claimed by interactants" (p. 61). Such notions of face, while not the main focus of this excursus in Kantian ethics, do dovetail nicely with the competing urges in humans to be valued by others and to be held apart from others. Like Kant, such an approach to face has been criticized for a strongly individuated, western notion of self at its core (e.g., Bargiela-Chiappini, 2003; Werkhofer, 1992). But the Kantian point is that an individual's autonomy must involve both of these factors, and the online realm would seem to offer promise in promoting both aspects through some amount of malleable identity. The question becomes: Would Kant's perspective on ethics merely judge such altering or occlusion of "who one is" in online venues as "unethical?"

Unsocial Sociability and the Virtuous Blogger

The contemporary trend is to see blogging as a category of journalistic expression, since it shares the rhetorical feature of disseminating information and opinions to a wide audience in a one-to-many fashion. Kuhn (2007) notes this tendency, while still acknowledging that blogs have many non-journalistic functions. Yet Kuhn (and others) seems to emphasize a value that, if not unique to journalism, is clearly foregrounded in journalism—transparency. Kuhn specifically links transparency with a non-opaque identity—"Transparency with regard to identity is important in building trust, an essential ingredient in building human relationships" (p. 23). He later explicates the notion of trust and argues that *normatively* bloggers should choose to be more transparent in their identity:

> Trust depends largely on the degree to which the identity of a communicator is known to the recipient of the communication. Bloggers are able to choose how much of their identity to reveal. To maximize transparency during interactions with others is to move discourse toward a more authentic communicative model.
>
> (p. 24)

This connection of transparency, authenticity, and trust makes perfect sense if one sees blogging as journalism. Journalism can be conceptualized as the utterance of important, factual claims about the real world, and thus concerns about accuracy, bias, and effect enter into the ethical discussion of it. In other words, "Journalism's challenge, according to its standard epistemology, is to perceive the world correctly and then represent perceptions correctly through language" (McGill, Iggers, & Cline, 2007, p. 296). If this sort of charge is taken to be the starting point, a Kantian approach may recommend transparency of identity in such areas of media activity, as Plaisance (2007) does in arguing for Kantian reasons behind "full disclosure" and "upholding transparency" in communication (p. 189). Transparency allows us to know who uttered what, which in turn is important for holding that person accountable for false declarations. Kuhn (2007) writes, "The authenticity of communication is enhanced to the extent that the receiver of a message comprehends 'who' is sending the message" (p. 23). If we know who is sending a particular message, the idea is that we are then empowered to critically consider sources of bias and prejudice underlying that message (and its supporting evidence). We might also be able to see how that source has an interest in saying that particular message. Kuhn's point is that "Identity, transparency, and accountability are linked" (p. 23). Transparency of identity would be a normatively important value to protect and promote whenever we can.

Blogging, however, adds elements that journalism typically lacks—interactivity, enhanced expressiveness, and the ability to construct one's identity through rhetorical means. Kuhn (2007) points out that an essential part of human communication is interaction, extending Christians' (1989) emphasis on the "human" in determining the moral worth of technology. Indeed, it is claimed that it is the interactive nature of blogging that makes it an exemplar of technologically mediated forms of communication: "The interactive form of blogs creates a potential to halt this progression away from the 'human.' A blog's rhetorical form serves to foster self-definition, one-to-one dialogue (while simultaneously maintaining a one-to-many) and community building" (p. 26). How does such interactivity interact with human autonomy? What the previous section has shown us is that a Kantian picture of autonomy—often the stated rationale for communicative disclosure and transparency (e.g., Plaisance, 2007)—is more complicated than typically realized. It stands to reason, then, that transparency and its value might differ if one conceives of blogging in a different sense than merely as journalism. How should we normatively navigate the values of changing one's identity to encourage self-definition and expression and the value of accountability through transparency?

While Kant did not discuss blogging per se, he did talk about something close to it—conversation. Of course, blogging and conversation are not identical; yet this comparison can serve as the nearest entry point for bringing Kant's ethics to bear on the modern activities and technologies of blogging. It is our contention that the rhetorical form of blogging is better conceived as *conversation*, and that this shift in conception will yield ethical guidance for blogging behaviors. Kant's main discussion of communication as conversation comes in his published anthropology lectures, *Anthropology from a Pragmatic Point of View* (1800/2006). In this text, Kant discusses an unusual topic—how to hold an "appropriate" dinner party. This was an important issue for Kant, as he often held social engagements with prominent friends that featured stimulating discussion (Kuehn, 2001; Melville, 2002). Such social situations also come closest to mirroring the unique communicative qualities of modern social blogging, having echoes of both one-to-one and one-to-many interactions among the guests. Kant (1800/2006) lists the three main stages of conversation at a multi-course meal: "1) narration, 2) arguing [*Räsonniren*], and 3) jesting" (7:280). He then proceeds to describe each stage in detail:

A. The first stage concerns the news of the day, first domestic, then foreign, that has flowed in from personal letters and newspapers. B. When this first appetite has been satisfied, the party becomes even livelier, for in subtle reasoning [*Vernünfteln*] it is difficult to avoid diversity of judgment over one and the same object that has been brought up, and since no one exactly has the lowest opinion of his own judgment, a dispute arises which stirs up the appetite ... C. But because arguing is always a kind of work and exertion of one's powers, it eventually becomes tiresome as a result of engaging in it while eating rather copiously: thus the conversation sinks naturally to the mere play of wit ...

(7:280–281)

While not all dinner parties proceed like this, one sees the *ideal* of free conversation in social settings. Such conversation is not the sort of communicative activity that is featured in a court of law, say, where a definite decision must be reached. Instead, Kant's notion of dinner conversation as social interaction focuses on *how* we interact and what sort of *character* this creates. No immediate decision or impact rides on the outcome of this particular period of conversation. Serious topics are broached, but one can also lighten the mood with jesting. One could end the conversation at dinner with violent actions or words, but Kant sees the best outcomes for a human afflicted with social unsociability in the *mix* of argument and frivolity. This is the Kantian model of *conversation*, taken in a different sense than "serious" communication aimed at reaching time-sensitive decisions in judicial or legislative arenas.

Despite differences in the details, blogging can be taken normatively as conversation on this account. Like our dinner party, our blogging interactions are driven by our innate inclinations toward unsocial sociability. We want to engage a topic or blogger, yet we are worried about total self-disclosure. This is a benefit of online interaction that Turkle (1995) points out—the Internet allows individuals to "try out" various identities in various online venues in a safe manner. Only in the extreme and largely unlikely cases, such as the identified anti-cartel bloggers, is this de facto autonomy compromised; instead, the activity of blogging allows most the practical chance to shape and mold their online identity with little chance of it being "fixed" to an actual person. Yet, if an individual were to take certain discursive risks at the dinner party, they may risk social sanctions from taboo and expectancy violations (Bargh, McKenna, & Fitzsimons, 2002). One could easily ask the host or a table mate, "Who is that person?" Normal discursive means would be available to fix such a face-to-face identity, whereas fixing online identity requires special initiative and extra-ordinary resources. Unlike the dinner party, blog interaction (in many cases) is *practically anonymous* —both the original poster and the commentators can and do project various images of who is doing the posting. The blogger can provide a detailed profile, or none at all. Many comments on blogs are only identified by a created name (often "verified" by a created email account) that does not clearly identify the poster. Such anonymity insulates the poster or blogger, thus accommodating their "unsocial" needs for protection from the other interactants. On the other hand, this protection and freedom allow them the power to post thoughts in a creative way in the first place. Blogs thus seem ideally suited for beings driven by unsocial sociability.

The normative question, assuming some amount of practical anonymity is available, is whether such anonymity or malleable identity is a good thing. Is the projection of an identity that is not really "you" deception? Should Kant's arguments for honesty translate to reasons to be transparent online, regardless of the cost? We see at least three reasons why blogging, if conceived of as conversation, would avoid such rigid judgments.

1. The utterances on blogs often lack imputable consequences, whereas Kant is concerned in the strict case with lying as consequential. Thus, Kant (2001) distinguishes an untruth from a lie by noting that the latter "is uttered with an associated intention to injure the other by the untruth" (27:700). This is an unjust use of one's external freedom. Most utterances (or omissions) in online venues do not fit this description—most are fairly non-consequential. The ones that do cause direct harm or abridgement of freedom can be easily dealt with (such as a fake doctor intentionally dispensing misleading advice), yet the problematic cases that drive the central questions of blogging ethics and identity are not these cases. They are more likely to be cases of unknown or inaccurate identity, such as would be the case if an individual posts comments on a blog that insinuate that they are female (when they really are a male). Is the practical opacity of online identity the same as a deliberate falsehood that harms others? We would claim it is not.

2. Of course, Kant still ethically condemns lies or "deliberate untruths," even if they do not harm others (e.g., Kant, 2001, 27:701). Like his complex personal negotiations of what constitutes a lie (e.g., McCormick, 2005), Kant's theoretical account of lying is far from simple. But if one looks at Kant's reading of human anthropology, one sees that he has some sensitivity to context. In his lectures on ethics, he notes that "the telling of tall stories" or bragging "can only pass as a jest if the judgment of others about the content of their truth cannot be in doubt" (27:700). Thus, if one is in a context that would lead others to recognize putative limits to what one is claiming, then such a non-transparent use of language is allowable. If they will take you as absolutely serious and base their actions on such an utterance, it will make a difference if one is knowingly deceptive. If one's interlocutors anticipate certain kinds of utterance or hyperbole due to the context of interaction, then one cannot be taken as fulfilling the conditions of telling a deliberate untruth. It simply is not taken as a "truth" in the same sense as Kant's examples of lying in the case of

contract are. The context there points toward the honesty of all parties, and the lying party gains an advantage over the other by violating that context. In the case of blogging, it is far from certain that the context dictates expectations of transparent identity—one can and often does post effectively on blogs without revealing such matters. Conversation still proceeds, facilitated by the fact that (a) the context and (b) the effects do not necessitate certain knowledge of one's identity. If one was buying a car or adopting a child, party identity and location would be important. The legal context and the magnitude of the effects dictate that each party should know certain things about the other party. Another case might be "mixed-mode relationships" (Ellison, Heino, & Gibbs, 2006). Giving (or failing to correct) a radically inaccurate online identity will obviously have practical consequences once one's relationship moves from the online world to the "real world." In the case of social blogging, however, nothing much rides on the outcomes of any given opinion-laden post or comment, and the online forum comes with no expectation of absolute veracity of identity. One is protected by the medium to a certain extent, and in the cases where one reveals one's self, one realizes the other's own self-disclosures will be hard to verify. The conversational context of blogging leads one to see ambiguous or uncertain identity as not the same as the lying or deception that Kant highlights as a violation of one's humanity.

3. There are Kantian reasons why the concealment of online identity in social blogging would serve a morally significant purpose. Like human social unsociability, our specific worries over identity couple with our need for self-expression in a useful way. We want to express who we are and to express various thoughts we have. Yet we do not want to express *all* of our thoughts. Kant (1800/2006) considers the case of a species of rational beings on another planet that cannot think anything without saying it out loud. Discussing this seemingly open and transparent situation, he claims that "Unless they were all *pure as angels*, it is inconceivable how they could live in peace together, how anyone could have any respect at all for anyone else, and how they could get on well together" (7:332). Such transparency would do nothing for the goal of true community among humans. It would only engender conflict, according to Kant. Instead, we must count it as fortunate that "it already belongs to the original composition of a human creature ... to explore the thoughts of others but to withhold one's own" (7:332). Such social pretense or dissimulation—the donning of social images or identities—is a recognized part of humanity for Kant. It *can* lead us to immoral actions (such as deliberate untruths in contexts that lead to truthful expectations), yet it also leads us to cautiously engage others in a tentative attempt to form com-

munity. All the while, one's own self is protected and one's freedom to act in future situations is preserved. Community can easily turn into manipulation for *either party* if one does not approach unknown others with caution. Kant's notion of autonomy not only recognizes the ideal of law-like universality of one's maxims, but it also recognizes the necessary protection of one's own agency. Descriptively, this is our characteristic unsocial sociability; normatively, this is the equation of our will and agency with that of all other rational beings. Concealment of identity in online contexts does not clearly violate the freedom of other online denizens, and it does uphold the freedom of one's self by not revealing too much. Thus, it is in line with Kant's reading of autonomy in impure human action. It even can serve a teleological function—that of allowing us to challenge our thoughts and ideas with interaction. This is an important theme in Kant's cosmopolitanism, and one sees free interaction on blogs as an even safer forum in which to pursue this. Indeed, Bargh et al. (2002) argue that it is the relative anonymity and consequence-free nature of online interaction that allow for it to greatly "facilitate self-expression" (p. 35). This self-expression, of course, is not done in solitude. It will be undertaken in response to the utterances of others, and others will have their hand in reacting to our expression of self.

Kantian Guidance for the Virtuous Social Blogger

What sort of ethical guidance might Kant provide for those engaged in blogging? Kuhn (2007) provides a provocative reading of what he calls the "categorical blogging imperative": "Bloggers have a duty to sustain the discourse on blogs" (p. 31). While useful, we believe this use of Kant should not take attention away from Kant's formulations of the categorical imperative. Kant argues that the categorical imperative cannot be limited to specific areas of content, or it would cease to be universally binding and necessary. The spirit of Kuhn's imperative, though, is important. Interactivity, free expression, and the human element are all important. Yet Kuhn also places strong commands to "strive for factual truth" and to "be as transparent as possible" in his code of ethics (p. 34). As we have demonstrated, there are clear Kantian reasons why these latter two pronouncements should be tempered. In certain *contexts* (viz., conversation, jesting, etc.), one does not expect or need absolute self-disclosure of self or fact through utterance. We argue that social blogging, if approached from the context of informal conversation similar to that of the dinner party, can acceptably feature uses of ambiguity and uncertainty around such vital topics as the identity of one's interlocutors. But what might Kant specifically recommend for those actively blogging? To begin such a discussion, we turn to the "rules" for Kant's (1800/2006) dinner party:

a) to choose topics for conversation that interest everyone and always provide someone with the opportunity to add something appropriate, b) not to allow deadly silences to set in, but only momentary pauses in the conversation, c) not to change the topic unnecessarily or jump from one subject to another: for at the end of the feast, as at the end of a drama (and the entire life of a reasonable human being, when completed, is also a drama), the mind inevitably occupies itself with reminiscing on various phases of the conversation ... d) not to let *dogmatism* [*Rechthaberei*] arise or persist, either in oneself or in one's companions in the group; rather since this conversation should not be business but merely play, one should avert such seriousness by means of a skillful and suitable jest, e) in a serious conflict that nevertheless cannot be avoided, carefully to maintain discipline over oneself and one's affects, so that mutual respect and benevolence always shine forth.

(7:281)

These are not only rules for dinner parties, but also "laws of refined humanity" (7:282). They clearly apply to cases of interaction that can be classed as conversational, as opposed to "serious" or "business" uses of communication (viz., judicial, legislative, or scientific uses). These "laws" can provide us with some normative maxims that can guide virtuous social blogging.

I. Discuss Topics of Interest and Importance to your Audience; Allow All to Add to the Conversation

When one blogs about opinionated topics, one should look at this as a chance for conversation. If one sees this as simply journalism, it anticipates a one-way flow of information from the informed to the uninformed. Seeing social blogging as conversation means seeing it as interactive, and as involving autonomous agents who possess equal value. Thus, one should establish topics of interest to their audience. One may assume a certain kind of audience—for instance, a political blogger assumes certain kinds of people will be interested in reading what she writes about certain political arenas. Since these topics both apply to some audiences and are important to their lifeworld, a Kantian view of social blogging as conversation would insist that one allow interested individuals "the opportunity to add something appropriate" (Kant, 1800/2006, 7:281). In social blogging, this would mean that one should always allow one's audience to interact with the blogger and other commentators (viz., those who post comments) in a public fashion. This most likely will occur through the posting of comments. Each should be allowed her say, since the topic at hand was broached because of its relevance and importance to the audience. A Kantian approach would indicate that respecting the audience as conversational equals means allowing them their say. Of course, sometimes what they have to say is not in line with what one believes or finds favorable. This issue is dealt with in the next two maxims.

2. Do Not Stop Conversation on your Blog

This guideline can be operationalized in a variety of ways. The most important sense, adapted to blogging from Kant's view on conversation, would concern actively stopping conversation. This might occur through "locking" a thread of replies to a post, by deleting comment(s), or by forbidding posts from certain commentators. All of these actions evaluate the content of replies and judge them quite harshly with conversation-stopping force. Kuhn's (2007) code of blogging ethics gets at this point under the rubric of "promoting free expression" (p. 33), but a Kantian justification would emphasize the equal value of each individual to post on a topic of concern. The autonomy of each should be equal—when that freedom to undertake certain actions infringes on the ability of others to act, then one can coercively adjust the offending actions. Kant's (1797/1996) *Metaphysics of Morals* points out this justification behind coercively enforcing a state of equal external action (physical action), and his work on virtue and autonomy deals with internal universalizability in willing. It is not clear that the maxim that allows one to post her thoughts on some issue gives one the justification to judge and evaluate the posts of others on that material. Off-topic posts (such as "spam" or advertisements) do not advance *this* conversation on topic x because of their generic nature; on the contrary, the large numbers of such spam posts could even preclude or stymie the valuable interaction of on-topic commentators. Deleting such off-topic posts would not contravene Kant's normative value of conversation.

Indeed, equal agents should be allowed to post as long as the freedom of one does not curtail the freedom of others. The fact that one runs a blog should not provide justification to override this idea, as it is primarily an *ethical* concern, not one over what one is *legally* or *actually* able to do with her blog. The virtuous social blogger on this Kantian scheme would only reluctantly moderate comments and surely would not eliminate the posting of others' opinions because she does not agree with their content or tone. Another way that one could stop discussion would be through the chilling effect of requiring a commentator to "fix" her identity prior to airing her thoughts. Requiring an identifiable email address (such as one affiliated with an institution or company) or a verifiable name to be posted with one's comment is not necessary to ensure "interesting" comments, and it may very well chill expression by individuals fearing real-world identification. Even requiring that some or all of one's offline identity be revealed only to the blogger (acting as a moderator) would place an unequal share of power in the hands of the blogger. They would be able to know who posted the comment, leaving that individual exposed to a variety of reactions. If Kant's notion of unsocial sociability shows us anything, it is that we have urges to both protect and express our self in community with others. Notice, however, that "loose" verification systems that largely serve to avoid advertising programs to post "spam" on comment threads are allowable—they do not "fix" offline identity to a specific expression of content; they merely raise the bar for posting any comment in an attempt to make sure only humans leave their mark on the blog comment thread. Allowing anyone to post relevant comments, even offensive ones (as judged by the blogger), would be the preferable way to respect the autonomy of all involved on an issue of common importance to schemes that privilege the blogger's autonomy and power over the expression of the thoughts of others. From Kant's perspective, if one does not want to risk hearing the thoughts of others, one should not engage in conversation.

3. Do Not Change the Subject Unnecessarily

Social bloggers and commentators should not randomly change the subject. In many cases, this is more of a risk for those who post comments. The blogger broached that subject, so all should post on that subject. Other topics can be reserved for other threads or other conversations. While the blogging format holds no theoretical limit to discussion space, it has a practical limit—one can only join a conversation by reading over so many pages of previous comments. While the cost of deleting or forbidding "hostile" or "unfavorable" comments has a cost to autonomy that Kant would find too high, the cost of requiring comments to have some direct link to the original topic is not too demanding. It saves time and energy in focusing the discussion, both for those present and those who may join at a later time. "Spam" messages denigrate topic focus and can therefore be permissibly deleted. More difficult is the case of "trolling," or posting intentionally inflammatory—but often topical—comments in an effort to provoke heated reactions. As will be discussed in the following maxim, the Kantian concern is the infringement of autonomy without clearly determining when a post is "trolling" or simply expressing an opinion not shared by the blogger or other commentators.

4. Resist Dogmatism in Self and Others

One of the fundamental insights of Kant's moral system is that our autonomy and value is integrally tied up in the activities and capabilities of others. One is a rational agent, but she is not alone. She is among other rational agents, in thought or reality. This motivates Kant's formulations of the moral law in the *Groundwork*, and it continues to operate in his anthropological notions of unsocial sociability. We want to be around others, but we also want to preserve our "self." In the often opaque online environment, this issue becomes more complex, but it does not disappear. The uncertainty and ambiguity surrounding online identity does not negate the fact that certain identities can be correlated with an excessive focus on self *or* other. Kant's concern with the dinner party guests evincing an attitude of " *Rechthaberei*" is a vital moral point. This term can be translated as "dogmatism," or as a "know-it-all-attitude" or "self-opinionated." One sees that the common factor is an over-emphasis on what *that person* thinks is right. This tends to exclude the contributions others make to that conversation. Thus, discourse becomes more like a lecture between a teacher and a disciple than a conversation among equals. In both his *Anthropology* (1800/2006) and his *Critique of the Power of Judgment* (1790/2000), Kant provides three rules for use of human reason. In his *Anthropology*, he puts them in a form that emphasizes their communicative import: "1) To think *for oneself*. 2) To think oneself (in communication with human beings) into the place of every *other person*. 3) Always think *consistently* with *oneself*" (7:228). Notice that dogmatism or "egoism" as he paints it at the beginning of the *Anthropology* (e.g., 7:128–129) is diametrically opposed to the second rule. Thinking from the position of others involves a devaluing of one's putatively perfect conclusions, and this is valuable for learning from and interacting with other humans. Our unsocial sociability, with its disproportionate valuing of the self, makes following this rule difficult.

In social blogging, it is fairly easy to think *for* oneself. It is more difficult to understand (and allow) the expression of contrary opinions. But the virtuous blogger must do so if he or she wants to respect the autonomy of self and others. This tendency toward self-focus should always give us pause when we move to censor an opinion we clearly judge as "trolling." How do we know these are "trolls," an interactant not worthy of being heard, opposed to a non-friendly opinion voiced by a morally equal other? Kant would err on the side of honoring the cognitive flexibility and openness connected to thinking "in the position of everyone else" (Kant, 1790/2000, 5:294) that is a vital part to showing a "reciprocal recognition of freedom among moral agents" (Rossi, 2005, p. 153). Social blogging is not solely about the "dear self" of the blogger. Self-expression and identity creation play *a* role, but not the *only* role. One is discussing issues he or she believes will be of interest to some audience. That audience is like the blogger in that they are moral agents with autonomy and drives toward community and cautious separation. Ideally, one should protect her self *while* fully interacting with others in conversation. For Kant, this means the topic of the conversation is the focus of the discussion, not any individual's self. If the blog is about bolstering one's reputation, airing one's ideas as final or solely illuminating, or an attempt to simply get confirmation from an audience, the Kantian position would find this approach problematic.

The normatively better use of social blogging, like dinner conversation, is to instantiate a sense of interactive community *there* and *then*. While the blogging scenario has a more complex aura of identity surrounding it, it shares the same dialectic drives toward communing with others and being cautiously reserved. The virtuous social blogger is one that realizes that he or she could be wrong and others—even if initially judged off-base or as "trolls"—could be right. Seeing the blog as conversation, and not as vitally important business, allows one the freedom to explore topics regardless of the identities and expertise of the others involved. This would necessarily foreclose taking comments too seriously, personally, or as importantly wrong enough to forbid. It would also distract a blogger from "fixing" the identity of some poster in a way to make her "accountable" for her comments. In this way, virtuous social blogging resembles play more than journalism or legal argument. Like conversation, its primary concern ought to be to instantiate a certain kind of free, interactive exchange between online identities.

5. Enter and Leave a Discussion with Mutual Respect

Ideally, the virtuous social blogger would enter and leave a discussion over any topic with mutual respect among the interactants. Like the former maxim, this is a difficult guideline to negotiate in practice. But if we take Kant seriously, we see that there is no prima facie reason to take our lengthy or brief comments as more serious, less personal, more charitable, etc. than the comments of others. Yet this is often the temptation when we fail to think in the place of the ambiguous online other who is challenging our position. We might dismiss her wholesale as a "troll" or as a pawn to some interest, as was done in the case of the Wal-Mart bloggers. As Kant reminds the dinner party guests, bloggers should attempt to control their tone and affect. If others provoke strong emotions in a blogger, a quick recourse to threats, insults, moderated action, and so on will not display the charitable respect of the online other that Kant's take on conversation seems to demand. Perhaps the blogger can change the subject, agree to disagree, or try to see the logic in a seemingly hostile or irrational point.

But as a virtuous online agent, the social blogger should not treat her autonomy as trumping that of the poster—even if the former has the de facto power to delete comments or forbid the posting from certain commentators. The effects of such posting are minimal and do not clearly impact the freedom of the original blogger, so such a use of freedom is the privileging of self that Kant believes we should avoid. Indeed, it is an unbalanced way of dealing with our unsocial sociability—one treats herself as so certain that she can easily silence another's opinion. Kant's ethics not only privileges the autonomy of equal agents, but also connects autonomy to the freedom of expression. For instance, in his *Anthropology* (1800/2006), he notes that censoring opinions opposed to our own only deprives us "of a great means of testing the correctness of our own judgment" (7:129). Both the virtuous blogger and his or her audience are driven by unsocial sociability; both parties should honor the parallel drives toward engagement with others and a cautious protection of identity in their actions. Obviously, topics of importance to all involved should be discussed and argued. Yet the blogger and commentators should not take the process or themselves so seriously that they leave the conversation lacking mutual respect. Such an outcome can be avoided by taking the interaction in the right way.

New Agendas for Kantian Media Ethics

To approach blogging interactions on opinionated topics as conversation entails a change in the perspective of both the blogger and the audience. Yet it seems to do more justice to the rhetorical form of blogging and its features of rhetorically changeable identity, enhanced expressivity, and communicative interactivity. Our argument is that the various issues surrounding ambiguous and plastic online identity can be rendered understandable if one views blogging as closer to conversation than to journalism. As problematized in the Wal-Mart and anti-cartel blogging cases, anonymity and a lack of information about a speaker's identity can often enhance expression in morally laudable ways. At the very least, these tough cases attune our sensitivity to our own autonomy in relations with incompletely-known others. Valuable normative guidance for social blogging can be gained by taking the ethical ideals associated with Kant's views on conversation seriously. Such a creative reframing highlights the uniquely Kantian mix of malleable identity, expression, and protected autonomy that might be furthered in the ever-evolving world of online interaction.

This Kantian approach does not exhaust all of the important normative questions to be asked and answered in regard to the activities of social blogging. The agenda for future research, however, must avoid two pitfalls on this account. First, *descriptive* approaches to the ethics of blogging get us only so far. Ascertaining what people (including bloggers) *do* value does not necessarily equate to determining what they *should* value. Perhaps the surrounding society has so skewed the values involved that describing the ethics of practice leaves our normative aspirations and critiques empty. Future approaches should continue to take descriptive features—such as the capacities of technology and the existing values and practices of concrete humans—into account, but they should also recognize that the power of normative ethics lies primarily in its independence for the realm of "what is." Normative ethics, such as the system explicated by Kant's philosophy, allow us the grounds to criticize and meliorate any given existing practice. Of course, such criticism will take place in the realm of imperfect and uncertain debate, but such is the nature of ethical inquiry. It rarely proceeds as social science does. The second direction for future work on the ethics of social blogging concerns the role of meta-ethical reflection. Simply discussing technology and its effects does not settle much in ethics; the *value* of effects, respect being shown, and the preserved capacities of freedom also might matter depending on your system of ethics. The study of blogging and other related fields must never forget that "results," conclusions, or judgments will be radically different depending on different starting points. Starting with the meta-ethical backdrop of materialism and utilitarianism will result in a radically different context for ethical evaluation than starting with Kant's deontological system. Combining such systems into a larger framework is not without its theoretical problems—what is one to do in the situations that could allow her to either maximize pleasure for the majority or to respect the rights of the minority? Achieving desired effects concerning happiness and showing a certain amount of respect due to humans—regardless of the effects—are clear spaces of conflict between the ethical theories that are so often bandied about in unison.

Blogging is an ever-evolving realm, so future work in Kantian approaches to media ethics will take into account the variety of forms "blogging" takes. Just as there are many forms of conversation, blogging's diversity also demands further scrutiny. As illustrated in this study, identity issues and autonomy will likely play a role in all of these domains. For instance, more reflection is needed in the various forms of "microblogging," such as posting on Facebook and Twitter. These arenas for personal expression and identity formation are interestingly different, and Kantian explications of more or less virtuous activities in them will be of great interest to an increasingly interconnected public. Facebook policies and user powers tend to mitigate against fake accounts, whereas Twitter allows a wide range of "fake" accounts. Further research can delve into the relative autonomy, empowerment, or disempowerment of these different levels of identity formation. Of interest to such studies might be the dynamic of *richness* of identity in each arena—Facebook tends to implicate some face-to-face relationships among some of one's network, whereas Twitter-based microblogging can be largely one-directional. How does autonomy fit into both types of conversational interaction in such venues? A third realm of application for future research might be comment threads, a ubiquitous feature of many news and opinion sites, as well as Internet forums. How is autonomy preserved and promoted through identity manipulation in such activity, especially given the depth and range of such commenting activity (ranging from one post to an online forum "identity")? In all of these arenas, the model of communication we must assume in our ethical investigations is not merely one of truth-conveyance. As this inquiry has demonstrated, there are other, more playful ways of thinking of the values and dimensions of communication, and one such way—conversation—seems to fit the often hypothetical and quickly changing nature of Internet interaction. Kant's ethical system gives us a powerful way to normatively evaluate such conversational activities to make sure that they preserve and promote human autonomy and more or less virtuous ways of communicating.

A final issue that future research must continue to examine is the complicated realm of autonomy in online interaction involving advertising or public relations interests. One of the immediate responses to the "Wal-Marting Across America" case that started this chapter was to demur about the virtue of the bloggers since they were paid by Wal-Mart. Yet this assumes a radically simplistic view of human will. Pay people, and they *must* be inclined in your favor. In Kant's terms, the provision of material incentive is seen to necessitate certain motives and actions, and thus can be used to judge with certainty the fact of some action. This view of human decision making and its susceptibility to being necessitated by such incentives is what Kant decried as the "freedom of the turnspit." Human choice is not truly autonomous—it is merely a vacillation between certain inclinations. The sense of autonomy developed in this chapter has the richer form that Kant attributed to human beings, creatures who are able (sometimes) to choose against the largest of material incentives (life, death, pleasure, earthly gain, etc.) to protect their dignity and to uphold the dignity of others. Future research can more completely examine the nature of coercive incentives, such as the issue of how much financial support of an endeavor prima facie impugns the truth of what is said. How often do individuals in the world of blogging choose *against* incentives that naturally predispose them to do something (say, in their self-interest)? We ought to also continue to use Kant's concept of autonomy and human value to analyze what appeals advertisers in online arenas make to an audience and how that preserves or harms the autonomy of that audience. Such a normative framework seems invaluable in demarcating "manipulative" or "dehumanizing" techniques or appeals, in online advertising and beyond. If Kant's ethics is anything, it is wide-ranging and effectively universal in the realms that it wants to protect and promote human autonomy.

This chapter has attempted to show what an in-depth commitment to Kant's way of valuing humans and spelling out the activities of moral judgment would result in. Not all future inquiry into blogging ethics will be Kantian, of course, but it should be clear about the *system* of values that underlies it and the reasons justifying the use of that system instead of others. Future work should also be clear that research in normative ethics requires commitment to mutually exclusive value systems, and that we should not picture ethical research as comprehensively "solving" a problem for all possible observers involved. At best, it involves scholars taking an educated stand and clarifying issues from that standpoint of argument. The ethics of communication technologies and practices is an exciting domain of inquiry, primarily because it implicates massive swaths of our everyday existence. Yet we must not fall prey to the false hope that focused attention can solve many of these issues. Like all issues in ethics, they are pressing and vital because they involve opposing stances that stem from contrary intuitions and argumentative systems that can be taken by a variety of partisans. What we ought to hope for from systems like Kant's moral theory is a new way of looking at such problems in communication, a new agenda for how we *might* try approaching them. Ethical inquiry focuses our future judgments and actions with certain ways of reasoning, even if they are not ultimately final or certain.

References

Baker, S. (2007). A case of covert persuasion. *Journal of Mass Media Ethics, 27,* 221–225.

Bargh, J. A., McKenna, K. Y. A., & Fitzsimons, G. M. (2002). Can you see the real me? Activation and expression of the "true self" on the internet. *Journal of Social Issues, 58,* 33–48.

Bargiela-Chiappini, F. (2003). Face and politeness: New (insights) for old (concepts). *Journal of Pragmatics, 35,* 1453–1469.

Benveniste, E. (1971). Subjectivity in language. In Mary Elizabeth Meek (Trans.), *Problems in General Linguistics* (pp. 223–230). Miami: University of Miami Press.

Boynton, L. A. (2007). This PR firm should have known better. *Journal of Mass Media Ethics, 27,* 218–221.

Brown, P., & Levinson, S. C. (1987). *Politeness: Some Universals in Language Usage.* Cambridge: Cambridge University Press.

Castillo, M. (2011, September 15). Bodies hanging from bridge in Mexico are warning to social media users. *CNN.com.* Retrieved from http://articles.cnn.com/2011-09-14/world/mexico.violence_1_zetas-cartel-social-media-users-nuevo-laredo.

Christians, C. G. (1989). A theory of normative technology. In Paul T. Durbin (Ed.), *Technological Transformation: Contextual and Conceptual Implications* (pp. 123–139). Dordrecht, Netherlands: Kluwer Academic.

CNN. (2011, October 29). At least 14 shot dead in western Mexico. *CNN.com.* Retrieved from http://edition.cnn.com/2011/10/28/world/americas/mexico-violence.

Craig, D. A. (2007). Wal-mart public relations in the blogosphere. *Journal of Mass Media Ethics, 22,* 215–218.

Ellison, N., Heino, R., & Gibbs, J. (2006). Managing impressions online: Self-presentation processes in the online dating environment. *Journal of Computer-Mediated Communication, 11*, 415–441.

Gehrke, P. J. (2002). Turning Kant against the priority of autonomy: Communication ethics and the duty to community. *Philosophy and Rhetoric, 3*, 1–22.

Gogoi, P. (2006, October, 9). *Walmart's Jim and Laura: The Real Story.* Retrieved April 23, 2013 from www.businessweek.com/stories/2006-10-09/wal-marts-jim-and-laura-the-real-storybusinessweek-business-news-stock-market-and-financial-advice.

Guyer, P. (2005). *Kant's System of Nature and Freedom.* Oxford: Clarendon Press.

Hove, T. (2009) Communicative implications of Kant's aesthetic theory. *Philosophy and Rhetoric, 42*, 103–114.

Kant, I. (1784/1963). Idea for a universal history from a cosmopolitan point of view. In L.W. Beck (Ed.), *On History* (pp. 11–26). Indianapolis: Bobbs-Merrill.

Kant, I. (1785/1996). Groundwork of the metaphysics of morals. In M. J. Gregor (Trans.), *Practical Philosophy* (pp. 37–108). Cambridge: Cambridge University Press.

Kant, I. (1790/2000). *Critique of the Power of Judgment.* P. Guyer & E. Matthews (Trans.). Cambridge: Cambridge University Press.

Kant, I. (1793/1996). Religion within the boundaries of mere reason. In A. W. Wood & G. Di Giovanni (Trans.), *Religion and Rational Theology* (pp. 39–216). Cambridge: Cambridge University Press.

Kant, I. (1797/1996). Metaphysics of morals. In M. J. Gregor (Trans.), *Practical Philosophy* (pp. 353–604). Cambridge: Cambridge University Press.

Kant, I. (1800/2006). *Anthropology from a Pragmatic Point of View.* Robert B. Louden (Trans.). Cambridge: Cambridge University Press.

Kant, I. (2001). *Lectures on Ethics.* P. L. Heath & J. B. Schneewind (Trans.). Cambridge Cambridge University Press.

Kuehn, M. (2001). *Kant: A Biography.* Cambridge: Cambridge University Press.

Kuhn, M. (2007). Interactivity and prioritizing the human: A code of blogging ethics. *Journal of Mass Media Ethics, 22* (1), 18–36.

Louden, R. (2000). *Kant's Impure Ethics: From Rational Beings to Human Beings.* New York: Oxford University Press.

McCormick, S. (2005). The artistry of obedience: From Kant to kingship. *Philosophy and Rhetoric, 38* (4), 302–327.

McGill, D., Iggers, J., & Cline, A. R. (2007). Death in Gambella: What many heard, what one blogger saw, and why the professional news media ignored it. *Journal of Mass Media Ethics, 22* (4), 280–299.

Melville, P. (2002). Kant's dinner party: Anthropology from a Foucauldian point of view. *Mosaic, 35*, 93–109.

Pachico, E. (2011, November 11). "Twitter Manifesto" confronts gang threats to Mexico bloggers. *InSightCrime.org.* Retrieved from www.insightcrime.org/news-analysis/twitter-manifesto-confronts-gang-threats-to-mexico-bloggers.

Pauly, J. J. (2007). We have all been here before. *Journal of Mass Media Ethics, 27*, 225–228.

Perlmutter, D. D., & Schoen, M. (2007). "If I break a rule, what do I do, fire myself?" Ethics codes of independent blogs. *Journal of Mass Media Ethics, 22* (1), 37–48.

Plaisance, P. L. (2007). Transparency: An assessment of the Kantian roots of a key element in media ethics practice. *Journal of Mass Media Ethics, 22,* 187–207.

Rossi, P. J. (2005). *The Social Authority of Reason: Kant's Critique, Radical Evil, and the Destiny of Humankind.* Albany, NY: State University of New York.

Schneewind, J. B. (2002). Why study Kant's ethics? In A. W. Wood (Ed./Trans.), *Groundwork for the Metaphysics of Morals: Immanuel Kant* (pp. 83–91). New Haven, CT: Yale University Press.

Stone, H. (2011, September 28). The Zetas' biggest rival: social networks. *InSightCrime.org.* Retrieved from www.insightcrime.org/news-analysis/the-zetas-biggest-rival-social-networks.

Stroud, S. R. (2005). Rhetoric and moral progress in Kant's ethical community. *Philosophy and Rhetoric, 38,* 328–354.

Turkle, S. (1995). *Life on the Screen: Identity in the Age of the Internet.* New York: Simon & Schuster.

Werkhofer, K. (1992). Traditional and modern views: The social construction and the power of politeness. In R.J. Watts & K. Erlich (Eds.), *Politeness in Language: Studies in Its History, Theory and Practice* (pp. 155–199). Berlin: Mouton de Gruyter.

Chapter 4

The Case of Media Violence

Who is Responsible for Protecting Children from Harm?

Karyn Riddle

Media effects scholars have spent decades documenting the negative short- and long-term effects that can occur when children and adults are exposed to media violence. Some even consider it a public health issue, with meta-analyses suggesting that media violence has a small yet substantial impact on public health (Browne & Hamilton-Giachritsis, 2005). Despite a relative consensus among media scholars about the possible harms that can result due to media violence exposure, violent content still pervades our media landscape, and children are exposed to violent content on a fairly regular basis. Media violence became a hot topic in the 1990s among the public and legislators alike, but it appears to have fallen back to a low-priority status. In this chapter, I will make the case that the public should still be concerned about the possible negative effects that stem from exposure to mediated violence. Moreover, I will argue in this paper that three groups of people have an ethical responsibility to do a better job protecting children, in particular, from these possible negative effects. Those three groups are parents, the media industry, and media scholars.

Although children can experience violent content on a variety of platforms (e.g., video games, movies, the Internet), the focus of this paper is going to be violence that appears on television. Despite our changing media landscape, television still dominates children's leisure time. A recent study by the Kaiser Family Foundation found that the amount of time children spend watching television content increased by 22% in 2009 compared to 2004 (Rideout, Foehr, & Roberts, 2010). Furthermore, watching television was still the most popular media activity for children aged 8–18 in 2009, eclipsing the amount of time they spend playing video games, using the computer, and listening to music. What *is* changing in terms of children's relationships with television is the platform on which they view television content. Children appear to be spending more time than ever streaming television content online, watching it on a DVD, or using DVRs to watch programs after their original air time. However, these new platforms do not change the fact that children still love television programs, and their leisure time is still dominated by television programming. Young children, in particular, rely heavily on television, as they may not yet own mobile devices or have the ability to read and type. Thus, although protecting children from violent content that appears in video games and online is of course important, this chapter will focus specifically on the topic of television violence.

In the first section of this chapter, I will review content analyses that demonstrate the level of violence in television programming seen by children. After that, I will briefly review the research demonstrating negative effects of exposure to such violence. Next, I will debate the central issue of this paper: the groups that have an ethical responsibility to protect children from harm. In that section, I will focus on the three key groups listed above: parents, the media industry, and media scholars. I will review what these groups are currently doing to protect children from harm, and I will make suggestions for future action.

Children's Television: A Violent Landscape

A number of content analyses have documented the prevalence of violence on television. Perhaps the most commonly cited content analysis is the National Television Violence Study, conducted in the mid-1990s (NTVS, 1997). The NTVS study was an ambitious, large-scale content analysis of thousands of hours of television programming spanning three television seasons. The NTVS study coded programming on the major broadcast networks as well as on the largest cable networks, including children's networks such as Nickelodeon and the Disney Channel. The findings of the NTVS study revealed that 60% of television programs include at least one act of violence, and children's programs were rated as one of the most violent genres on TV. The nature of the violence on children's programming, however, differed from violence found in other television genres. For example, the violence in children's programming tended to be humorous, and it tended to be presented in unrealistic ways. Thus, we see Teenage Mutant Ninja Turtles battling criminals, or Tom and Jerry fighting each other.

The NTVS research study is one of the most comprehensive content analyses of violence on television, but because so many years have passed since its completion, a more recent account of the amount of violence on television must be considered. Due to the tremendous costs associated with conducting a content analysis of that scale, however, we have not seen a content analysis of the magnitude of the NTVS study since it was published. Still, smaller-scale content analyses have been conducted in the meantime, and many of them have expanded scholars' definitions of the word "violence." Whereas the NTVS study focused only on physical violence, for example, more recent studies are starting to include depictions of verbal aggression. For example, Glascock (2008) conducted a content analysis of primetime programming on the broadcast networks during the 2005 season. In this study, programming was coded for the presence of physical aggression (i.e., hitting, kicking, shooting) as well as verbal aggression (i.e., insults, yelling, threats, taunts). The findings revealed that verbal aggression is the most prevalent type of aggression on television, with 38 acts of verbal aggression occurring every hour. In fact, across this study's sample, 95.5% of all shows had at least one act of verbal aggression. In terms of physical aggression, this study found 13 acts of physical aggression per hour during primetime. Furthermore, 71% of shows had at least one act of physical aggression.

Television networks such as the Disney Channel and ABC often show Disney movies, and thus recent content analyses documenting the prevalence of violence in Disney films are relevant here. Aust and Everhart (2007), for example, analyzed 24 G-rated Disney films released between 1937 and 2000. They found 464 incidents of violence in these films, committed using 564 weapons, and the amount of violence in these films was increasing over time. Coyne and Whitehead (2008) analyzed 47 animated Disney films and found 584 acts of indirect aggression, such as social exclusion, malicious humor, and plotting to harm characters. In their study, they found a total of 9.2 acts of indirect aggression per hour.

Research also suggests that the television news is quite violent. Many people believe journalists adhere to a principle of "if it bleeds, it leads," and content analyses would appear to support this idea. For example, almost half of all news stories covered in news magazine programs such as "Dateline NBC" are on the topic of crime (Graber, 1996). Furthermore, the amount of "sensationalistic" stories on network newscasts is on the rise, defined as stories dealing primarily with violence, crime, accidents, and disasters (Slattery, Doremus, & Marcus, 2001). More recently, journalists have come under fire for airing especially gruesome content, such as photographs of Saddam Hussein's dead sons (Romano, 2003) or the killing of U.S. contractors in Iraq (Perlmutter & Major, 2004).

Thus, whether watching children's cartoon programs, Disney movies, or network news reports, television presents ample opportunities for children to see violent content and images, either deliberately or accidentally. In the next section, I will detail some of the effects of exposure to this type of content.

The Negative Effects of Exposure to Violence

Decades of research on media violence effects have documented a variety of negative outcomes that can result from exposure to media violence (for a review, see Kirsh, 2012; Potter, 1999). In this section, I will highlight some of the findings of this research. First, I will describe the research documenting negative effects that can occur when children are exposed to fictional media violence. Next, I will detail the findings on exposure to violence in the news.

Effects of Exposure to Fictional Violence

A plethora of studies has demonstrated behavioral effects of watching media violence, such as imitation, behavioral modeling, and aggressive actions. Research working under a social cognitive theory framework (Bandura, 1986), for example, demonstrates how children often model violent actions seen in the media, especially when the violence is rewarded or when it seems justified. Script theory research (Huesmann, 1986) suggests children can develop aggressive scripts, or schema, after having direct or mediated experience with situations. These scripts help children decide how to behave in various situations. The general aggression model (GAM, Anderson & Bushman, 2002) posits that input variables such as violent media have an impact on viewers' affect, cognitions, and arousal. These internal states in turn determine the types of action a child will take after exposure to media violence. It is important to note that media violence can still lead to outcomes such as imitation and behavioral modeling even when it is humorous, unrealistic, and sanitized (for a review, see Potter, 1999).

Other research focuses on media violence effects that are more cognitive in nature, such as people's beliefs and thoughts. Research falling under a cultivation framework, for example, shows how prolonged exposure to media violence is related to an exaggerated view of the amount of crime and violence that exists in the real world (for a review, see Shanahan & Morgan, 1999). Thus, people who watch a lot of television violence tend to believe there is more real-world violence than do people who are lighter television viewers.

A separate line of research documents how children can become desensitized to violence over time. In these studies, repeated exposure to media violence over multiple days leads to less emotional and physiological arousal on the part of children (Thomas, Horton, Lippencott, & Drabman, 1977). Perhaps most alarmingly, children who have just viewed media violence may react more slowly when they see real-life violence. In one study, for example, children who watched a violent film were slower to report a fight they witnessed than children who had not watched a violent movie (Drabman & Thomas, 1974). Thus, exposure to media violence has been shown to lessen the degree to which children react to real-world violence immediately after viewing.

Finally, research also demonstrates the prevalence and intensity of children's fright reactions to media violence (see Cantor, 2009). In this line of research, studies have documented a variety of symptoms related to children's fear, such as problems sleeping, crying, shaking, and obsessive thinking about disturbing things seen in the media. Perhaps most disturbingly, research suggests these reactions are often long-lasting. Harrison and Cantor (1999), for example, found that over 90% of young adults could remember watching something in a television program or movie in the past that caused a fear reaction that lasted after exposure ended. They described post-viewing symptoms such as sleep disturbances, eating problems, and avoidance of depicted events (e.g., avoiding clowns or swimming pools). Amazingly, 26% of the young adult participants indicated that their feelings of fear and worry still continued "to this day."

Thus, the accumulated research exploring media violence effects demonstrates that watching fictional media violence can frighten children, it can desensitize them to real-world violence, it can affect their perceptions about how violent the real world is, and it can lead to imitation and behavioral modeling. It is important to note, however, that there are a number of individual difference variables that matter in the media violence literature. That is, certain types of children are more susceptible to these effects than others (e.g., children from low SES, children already high in terms of trait aggression). Nonetheless, the prevalence of negative effects due to media violence exposure suggests that it is an issue of serious public concern.

Effects of Exposure to Violence on the News

Research focusing on children's reactions to disturbing news reports is in its infancy compared to studies on fictional violence. The research on news effects tends to focus on fear reactions, and the mounting research suggests children experience fright reactions—often of severe intensity and duration—during and after viewing televised news reports. Some readers may be surprised to learn that children watch the news, but studies suggest they do (Children Now, 1994), with exposure to the news increasing as children age (e.g., Smith & Moyer-Gusé, 2006; Walma van der Molen, Valkenburg, & Peeters, 2002). Perhaps not surprisingly, most of children's exposure to the news is accidental (Cantor & Nathanson, 1996; Riddle, 2012).

It has been well documented that children became frightened after watching news reports of major crises such as the 9/11 terrorist attacks (Saylor, Cowart, Lipovsky, Jackson, & Finch Jr., 2003; Smith, Moyer, Boyson, & Pieper, 2002), the space shuttle Challenger explosion (Terr et al., 1999), the first Gulf War (Cantor, Mares, & Oliver, 1993), and the recent Iraq War (Smith & Moyer-Gusé, 2006; Walma van der Molen & Konijn, 2007). Even in the absence of a major crisis, however, children become frightened when watching "everyday" news reports (Cantor & Nathanson, 1996; Smith & Wilson, 2002; Walma van der Molen et al.,

2002). These studies document a range of symptoms children experience during and shortly after exposure to disturbing news stories, such as sadness (Buijzen, Walma van der Molen, & Sondij, 2007), fear (Smith & Wilson, 2002; Cantor & Nathanson, 1996), anxiety-related behaviors (Smith & Moyer-Gusé, 2006), and even post-traumatic stress disorder (Saylor et al., 2003), to name a few.

Taken together, these studies suggest that many children experience both short- and long-term fear responses as a result of exposure to the news. In an era of around-the-clock news coverage through broadcasting, cable, and Internet news outlets, opportunities for children to be deliberately or accidentally exposed to disturbing content on the news is ever-increasing.

Who is Responsible for Preventing Harm?

As Plaisance (2009a) notes, media producers and practitioners tend to be mindful when it comes to preventing harm to media audiences. What constitutes as "harm," however, is often a matter of great debate. Many philosophers and ethicists cite the work of Joel Feinberg (1984), in which he defined harm as an act or state that "sets back" the interests of someone else. For example, if somebody takes an action that sets back or impedes a person's career or health, this constitutes harm according to Feinberg. By this definition, therefore, any media content that has been demonstrated to "set back" the interests of the audience could be seen as having "harmed" the audience. As Plaisance (2009b) argues, the media effects literature has demonstrated many situations in which media violence clearly "sets back" the interests of audience members. For example, if a television program prevents a child from being able to sleep for weeks on end, the interests of that child have clearly been set back. If a violent program causes a child to imitate a violent action, the program has certainly led to harm, based on Feinberg's definition.

Plaisance (2009b) notes, however, that there are situations where the degree to which violent media effects constitute "harm" is less clear. For example, cultivation research suggests that prolonged exposure to media violence may render violent constructs easily accessible in memory on a chronic basis (Shrum, 1999). And although this increased accessibility may in turn affect people's beliefs and attitudes about the world, the degree to which chronic accessibility on its own "sets back" one's interests may not be readily apparent. Similarly, if a person thinks the world is a mean and violent place due to media violence, would this constitute "harm" as defined by Feinberg? Most parents would probably prefer that their children not be constantly thinking violent thoughts, or thinking of the world as a mean and violent place. But these thoughts would have to actually "set back" their child's interests somehow in order to constitute "harm" from an ethical perspective. As a result, Plaisance (2009b) suggests we may need to reconceptualize what constitutes "harm" in the case of media violence effects. I would argue, in particular, that we need to consider that less "visible" media effects, such as cognitive or emotional outcomes, still can constitute harm. That is, even if a person does not rearrange his life due to violent media exposure (e.g., refusing to go outdoors after dark, taking self-defense classes), he has still experienced "harm" if he is constantly thinking about the possibility of being victimized, or worrying about the amount of violence in the world.

Finally, Plaisance argues that ethics theory can help us "delineate responsibility" in the case of media violence. That is, ethics can be used to determine the parties responsible for protecting audiences—especially children—from harm. The need to delineate responsibility is a common refrain from ethics scholars, yet very few provide concrete examples of what should be done. This is perhaps due to the fact that it is very difficult to answer the question "who is responsible?" To be certain, there are numerous parties who have the potential to protect children from harm: parents, the government, the industry itself, and our school system, to name a few. In this chapter, I will focus on the three parties I feel are most critical in terms of protecting children. First, I will focus on the parents themselves, as they have the closest access to the children needing protection. Second, I will focus on the industry, as it has the closest access to the content that might cause harm. And third, I will focus on scholars, as they have the closest access to the knowledge and information that is desperately needed by all parties.

The Responsibilities of Parents

Without question, parents have an ethical responsibility to protect their children from harm. Fortunately, studies suggest many parents work hard to try to prevent any potential harm that might result from exposure to media. One set of strategies that parents currently undertake is referred to by scholars as *restrictive mediation strategies* (Nathanson, 1999; Valkenburg, Krcmar, Peeters, & Marseille, 1999), which are rules limiting children's media use. In the case of television, almost half of children between the ages of 8 and 18 (46%) live in households that have rules dictating the type of television content they can watch, and 28% come from households in which their time with television is limited by their parents in some way (Rideout et al., 2010). Although we do not know from this data what it is that parents are trying to prevent (e.g., exposure to violence, sex, advertising, or time spent in front of a screen in general), these statistics suggest many parents are mindful of their children's television use and try to restrict their children from having unlimited exposure.

Research on the effectiveness of restrictive mediation strategies, however, provides mixed results. On the one hand, parents who have rules limiting their children's media exposure do tend to have children who use media less often than parents who do not have rules (Rideout et al., 2010). But does this mean their children have the tools to protect themselves when they do see disturbing media content? The research suggests they may not. One study, for example, found children who came from households using restrictive mediation strategies during a crisis that was reported heavily in the broadcast news had more intense fright reactions when they did happen to see news reports of the crisis. The researchers suggested that is possible that restrictive mediation strategies enhanced negative expectations and vigilance about the particular news situation, leading to even greater anxiety and worry among children who did eventually have exposure to the news event. Other studies have found similar findings, with children who experience severely restricted television viewing exhibiting more severe reactions when they do have exposure (for a review, see Nathanson, 2002). Thus, reducing children's exposure to media violence might help reduce their exposure to disturbing content, but may not necessarily equip them with the tools they need when they do, inevitably, see violent content in the media. Furthermore, we often see a forbidden-fruit effect, with some youth and adolescents seeking out content that is restricted by their parents when they are with their friends (Nathanson, 2002).

The practice of restrictive mediation is especially problematic in the case of media violence because research shows that parents are possibly concerned about—and thus restricting—the wrong kinds of media violence. Numerous studies suggest that, when it comes to violence, the public is overwhelmingly concerned about violent portrayals that are graphic and explicit in nature (Potter, 1999; Riddle, Eyal, Mahood, & Potter, 2006). The types of violent programming that tend to upset parents are those that are bloody, are filmed using close-up shots, and include graphic depictions of guts and gore. The public tends to be less concerned about media violence when it is sanitized, non-graphic, humorous, and presented in a fantasy format. This is in stark contrast to the types of violent media portrayals that concern media researchers. Media researchers know that violent content can have negative effects even when it is sanitized, humorous, and presented in a fantasy format (for a review, see Potter, 1999). Thus, if parents who engage in restrictive mediation only prevent their children from seeing graphic, bloody violence, their children may still be exposed to large amounts of media violence.

The use of restrictive mediation might be especially unsuccessful at preventing children from seeing violence and mayhem on the news. As discussed above, most of children's exposure to the news is accidental—they view it because it interrupts their programming, or because their parents are watching it at home in the background (Cantor & Nathanson, 1996;

Riddle, 2012). As a result, household rules limiting a child's television-viewing habits in general may have no impact on his or her television news exposure. Furthermore, parents may not know they need to be concerned about their own viewing of the news as background noise, as they may assume that children are not interested in or able to comprehend content seen on adult news programs. Finally, parents may also view the news as being "educational," and may therefore not have household rules limiting their children's exposure to it. Therefore, even children in households with strict rules about television exposure levels may still have high exposure to violent content in the news.

Because restrictive mediation strategies may be limited in terms of how well they can protect children from harm, many parents also engage in *active mediation strategies* (Nathanson, 1999; Valkenburg et al., 1999). Active mediation strategies occur when parents not only co-view media with their child, but also talk to their child about things they have seen in the media. For example, a parent can tell a child that a scene in a scary movie is "only make believe," or can admonish a character who engages in an act of violence.

Once again, the big question is whether or not active mediation strategies are successful at reducing negative media effects. Unfortunately, the research also produces mixed results in terms of the success of the mediation strategies undertaken by parents. On the one hand, active mediation strategies have been shown to lead to a number of positive outcomes (Corder-Bolz, 1980; Nathanson, 1999; Nathanson & Cantor, 2000). In one study, for example, children watched a cartoon in which one character was attacking another. When an adult asked children to focus on the victim and how he must feel, it reduced aggressive tendencies in boys who viewed the cartoon (Nathanson & Cantor, 2000). In other studies, however, it has been found that the comments made by parents can boomerang and actually increase negative effects. One study had children watch a violent television program, and afterward the researchers gave the children factual information about the violence they had seen (Nathanson, 2004). For example, the children were told that the characters were simply actors playing a part. The findings of the study revealed that children who heard this message had greater aggressive tendencies after viewing the program than those who did not hear the message. Children who heard a different type of message that focused more on evaluations (e.g., "What that character did was very mean") exhibited lower aggressive tendencies after viewing.

Thus, the research on active mediation strongly suggests that *what* parents say to children matters. Some messages given to children during or after exposure to media violence might reduce negative effects, but some might actually increase them. The difficult problem for parents, however, is that it might be difficult to know, intuitively, what are the "right" and the "wrong" things to say to children. We see a similar issue in research on children's fright reactions to media violence. Sometimes, when parents engage in active mediation during a frightening movie or television program, the words they say can decrease their children's fright reactions. For example, telling an older child (e.g., 8 and older) that a fictional movie is "just pretend" has been shown to decrease their feelings of fear (Cantor & Wilson, 1984). On the other hand, young children (i.e., kindergartners and first-graders) who viewed a frightening scene involving snakes in *Raiders of the Lost Ark* became *more* frightened when they heard information beforehand telling them that most snakes are not poisonous (Wilson & Cantor, 1987). This finding was not expected by the researchers, and suggests that what parents *think* might help their children may actually make the situation worse.

Suggestions for Parents

The research reviewed above suggests that many parents do make efforts to try to prevent negative media effects. At the same time, however, many strategies that parents undertake can boomerang and lead to increased negative effects. Thus, the key for parents is education, education, and more education! As the above review demonstrates, the strategies and tactics that parents may feel intuitively are the appropriate steps to take to minimize negative media effects may often fail or even boomerang. Thus, it is important for parents not to rely on their intuition, and instead rely on the research.

Most parents work hard to educate themselves on a variety of topics when they become a new parent. The *What to Expect When You're Expecting* book and other parent manuals have become indispensable handbooks for new and impending mothers, and thus many parents are clearly willing to do their homework when it comes to rearing children. Parents clearly need to also do their homework on the topic of mass media—indeed, they have an ethical responsibility to educate themselves on the topic of the mass media so that they can make household policies and decisions in an informed way. Children today spend close to eight hours per day using media, as much time as they spend sleeping and at school (Rideout et al., 2010). Parents need to be significantly more informed about an activity that absorbs so much of their children's lives. Therefore, parents should be encouraged to head to their local bookstore to check out the "Parenting" section to find books that address the issue of media use and effects. Scholars such as Joanne Cantor and Jim Potter, for example, have written books for the general public on the topics of media in general and disturbing media in particular.

This advice is of course easier said than done. Some low-income parents may not have the time or resources to devote themselves to learning about the mass media. Even parents from higher SES may have trouble accessing literature on the topic of media effects. Therefore, a second resource for parents is their child's pediatrician. When parents meet with their child's pediatrician on a yearly basis to address the child's overall health, a discussion about media use needs to be a part of these discussions. Media use can affect a child's physical and psychological well-being, and thus parents should turn to pediatricians for advice regarding appropriate practices and procedures. Indeed, many pediatricians are starting to distribute literature on the topic of media effects, and should be encouraged to continue doing so.

To echo the advice years ago from the National Television Violence Studies (1997), parents also need to know what their children are watching when they are watching television. This is absolutely the first step that has to take place before parents can enact any type of in-home policies regarding media use: They have to know what their children are doing when they are using media. Therefore, television and media use should take place in open spaces, such as living rooms or family rooms. The amount of media in a child's bedroom should be minimized—which would be a dramatic change versus current practices, given that 71% of children aged 8–18 have a television set in their bedroom (Rideout et al., 2010). In addition, parents need to monitor their children's use of mobile media and the household computer. This is an increasingly complex problem, as children's ability to access media content via mobile devices is ever-expanding. Still, this only increases the need for parents to be vigilant in terms of monitoring their children's media use.

Finally, parents should model good media use habits for their children. They should not have television sets in their own bedrooms. They should not spend their days attached to computers or mobile devices. They should turn the television off—the recent Kaiser Family Foundation study found that 45% of children between the ages of 8 and 18 have the television set turned on "all or most of the time" in their households, even if nobody is watching it. Thus, parents need to turn the television sets off and stop relying on them as background noise. Finally, parents should model positive media literacy habits by questioning, criticizing, and analyzing media messages.

The Responsibilities of the Media Industry

In the section prior, I argued that parents have an ethical responsibility to do a better job protecting their children from the possible harms of media violence. The research demonstrates, however, that parents are somewhat ill-equipped to do an adequate job achieving that goal. For one thing, the research is mixed in terms of what are the "right" strategies to take to reduce the negative effects of exposure to violence. Furthermore, even when the literature does conclusively point to strategies that can work, most parents are not aware of the strategies.

Thus, parents need some partners in the fight against media violence effects. Certainly, the partner with the greatest power to reduce the amount of violence in the media is the media industry itself. Of course, the First Amendment provides media producers with free speech rights, and depictions of graphic violence are examples of speech protected by the First Amendment. Thus, the media industry is not legally obligated to reduce or change the violent content they portray. Rather, as media ethics scholars before have argued (e.g., Plaisance, 2009b), the media industry has an ethical and moral responsibility to prevent harm from occurring. This is particularly important, argues Plaisance, in the case of media violence effects, which are often unknown to the audience member who has been affected. That is, because audience members often have no control over media effects processes, this robs them of their free will. This is especially the case when we are looking at children as audience members—they often lack the cognitive and emotional skills necessary to prevent negative media effects. As such, the industry has a moral obligation to take steps to minimize harm to children.

What is the industry currently doing to minimize or prevent harm? One strategy currently being used is the V-chip technology and accompanying program rating system. The V-chip legislation of the 1990s dictates that all broadcast television programs (minus sports and news) must be rated based on content and age appropriateness. Violent programming receives a "V" rating, for example, and fantasy violence receives an "FV" rating. The purpose of these ratings is to provide information to parents, so that parents can decide whether or not they want to prevent their children from seeing certain types of programming. Therefore, if parents object to violence, they can prevent their children from seeing programs with "V" or "FV" ratings.

Unfortunately, research suggests the television rating system is fraught with problems (for a review, see Greenberg & Rampoldi-Hnilo, 2001). The first problem is that programs tend to be under-rated. Because there is no advisory board that decides on each program's rating, the networks provide the ratings themselves. A study by Kunkel and colleagues (1998) found that a large number of shows with violence and sex in them (as defined by scholars) were not labeled as such. A second problem regarding ratings is that parents simply are not aware of the rating system or cannot interpret the ratings. For example, a Kaiser Family Foundation study in 1998 found that 18% of parents were unaware of the television rating system altogether (Foehr, Rideout, & Miller, 2000). Still other studies suggest that parents do not know what the rating labels such as "L" and "FV" mean (Rampoldi-Hnilo & Greenberg, 2000).

In addition to using ratings, television networks will often put a disclaimer before the start of a show if it has an excessive amount of graphic violence. These messages often appear on a black screen at the start of a show or after each commercial break. These types of disclaimers are voluntary actions taken by the networks to inform viewers of upcoming scenes that might be "extra" violent. Thus, there is no standard for what types of violence might warrant a special disclaimer on the part of each network.

Finally, journalists also have an ethical responsibility to their audience to prevent harm. Most newspapers and broadcasters have a code of ethics that dictates the guidelines that dictate the decisions they make as journalists. Keith and colleagues (Keith, Schwalbe, & Silcock, 2006) conducted a content analysis of 47 U.S. journalism ethics codes and found that only nine codes address the issue of how to treat images of tragedy and violence. Some of these codes warn journalists to take care when displaying "graphic footage of dead bodies" (p. 253). The codes tend to warn journalists to think carefully before showing graphic scenes of violence, but they do not instruct them not to display such images. Thus, very few U.S. journalists are working under codes of conduct that explicitly ask them to consider harm to audiences when making decisions about graphic images. Furthermore, television news reports are not rated, and thus parents typically do not receive warnings that violent content is going to be shown.

To be fair, however, journalists are not intending to write for an audience that includes children. Thus, to expect that journalists must take extra care to consider the children in their audience when they make decisions regarding violent and graphic content may be unrealistic.

Suggestions for the Media Industry

In the section prior, I argue that producers of media content are not currently doing enough to protect children from the possible harms that may occur due to media violence exposure. There are several things the industry could be doing, however, in order to do a better job. I will first start with suggestions for producers of fictional television programming, and I will conclude with suggestions for journalists who produce news programs.

First, the television industry should mimic the movie rating system. Whereas research suggests the television rating system is under-utilized by parents, the movie rating system, in stark contrast, is quite popular among parents. A vast majority of parents report that they regularly use movie ratings when they are giving their children permission to attend a movie. And although the movie rating system is not without some problems, its popularity among parents suggests that rating systems *can* be successful at giving parents information. Thus, we should consider what it is about the nature of movie ratings that makes them so useful and apply those principles to the television industry.

For example, every time a movie is advertised, its rating is displayed (it is typically displayed as the last piece of information at the end of a television advertisement, and it is printed in print advertisements). The television industry should do the same: every time it advertises episodes for an upcoming show, it should be required to devote screen time to the rating of the show. When television programs are advertised in magazines, the show's rating should be listed prominently. When television programs are listed in various types of television guides, the ratings should always be listed.

This first suggestion might make a television program's rating more prominent, but it still does not overcome the issue of confusion. That is, most parents still do not know what ratings such as "FV" and "D" mean. Thus, my second suggestion is that the television industry include a black-screen warning at the beginning of any children's show rated "V" or "FV" that more clearly explains that violent content is about to be shown. As stated above, networks already adopt this approach for programs that have extensive amounts of violence. For example, the AMC program "The Walking Dead" starts every program with a black screen and a disclaimer message warning viewers of the intense violence they are about to see. Currently, these disclaimers are only reserved for programs that are deemed by media producers as being especially graphic. I suggest the networks adopt this strategy for any children's program containing violence. If the show contains fantasy violence, for example, the black-screen message can spell out for viewers that the program their child is about to watch contains fantasy violence (FV).

This suggestion, however, is only useful if a parent is co-viewing with his or her child, and both research and intuition tell us that that is not always the case. Thus, we need some solutions that can be successful even when a parent is not sitting down to watch television with a child. Thus, a third suggestion is for all television networks that provide children's programming to provide "Violence Free" blocks of television time during time periods in which children are likely to be watching (e.g., early morning or after school on weekdays, weekend mornings, etc.). If parents can be confident that certain time periods are free of violence and aggression, they may feel more comfortable allowing their child to watch without having to co-view.

As mentioned above, it may be unrealistic to expect journalists to consider children who might be in their eventual audience when they are making decisions about which news stories to present, and how to present them. At the same time, however, the reality is that children are watching the news, and they are becoming frightened by what they see. My suggestion for television news programs, therefore, is that they provide ratings in the same way fictional programs provide ratings. Currently, the V-chip legislation does not require that television news programs have to provide content or age-based ratings. Given the prevalence of children exposed to the news, news programs should be rated using strategies I described above.

The Responsibilities of Media Scholars

Finally, media researchers also have an ethical responsibility to do a better job of using their research to protect children from harm. To be fair, media researchers have spent decades exploring, documenting, and reporting what happens when audiences are exposed to violent content in the media. Where media researchers have failed, unfortunately, is in sharing this information with the public that needs it. Most media researchers publish their findings in academic journals or books that tend to be read by other academics. We present our findings at academic conferences attended by our fellow academics. Although a handful of media scholars have written books aimed at the general public—scholars like Joanne Cantor and Jim Potter, for example—most of what has been discovered by media scholars tends to be shared with media scholars only.

Suggestions for Media Scholars

My suggestions for media scholars are twofold. First, more media effects scholars need to focus their research on projects that can ultimately be used to protect children. This can include research projects that develop strategies for parents, or research projects that could communicate information to the industry. For example, the following provides a list of new agendas for research in this area:

1. More scholars should be developing and testing active mediation strategies designed to reduce the negative effects of media violence. We know that strategies such as fictional identification (Nathanson & Cantor, 2000) and evaluative mediation (Nathanson, 2004) can successfully reduce negative effects, but there are certainly more strategies parents can undertake to reduce the negative effects of violent media.
2. Scholars should develop and test different ways of communicating to parents whether or not a television show is violent. For example, do parents know what the television ratings "V" and "FV" mean? Are there better ways of communicating violent content to parents? Do parents pay attention to disclaimers that appear prior to programs?
3. Scholars should also focus their efforts on restrictive mediation strategies. As stated above, modern families have a variety of rules regarding media use. Some families restrict the amount of *time* their children can use media, whereas others have rules restricting certain

types of *content* (e.g., guns, sex, swearing, etc.). Other families have rules dictating the times of day at which media are not allowed (e.g., no television during dinner, no television until homework is finished). And still other families have no rules at all. Scholars should look more closely at all of these strategies to see which are related to positive and negative media outcomes. For example, are families with a certain type of restrictive strategy more likely to have children that experience sleep disturbances? Are families with a different type of restrictive strategy likely to have children who approach media with a critical, questioning eye?

4. Scholars should conduct more research that might demonstrate the economic disadvantages of violent media content. For example, Weaver and Wilson (2009) conducted an experiment that found viewers enjoyed nonviolent versions of television programs more than the violent versions. Of even greater concern to the media industry, Bushman and colleagues have shown that memory for advertisements is lower when the ads are embedded within violent programming (Bushman, 1998; Bushman & Phillips, 2001). These findings, if communicated to the media industry, could give media producers a financial incentive for reducing the amount of violence in the media. Therefore, more research along these lines should be conducted.

My second suggestion for media scholars is that they need to do a better job communicating their findings to the public, especially parents. The following provides a list of suggestions for scholars to follow:

1. Scholars need to write more books targeted at the general public. When parents approach the "Parenting" section of their local bookstore, it should contain a multitude of resources written by qualified professionals to help them make decisions regarding mass media. As others have argued (Bushman & Anderson, 2001), educating the public needs to be a cornerstone of the media researcher's job.

2. Scholars need to connect with the medical community in general and pediatricians in particular. Pediatricians need to approach this issue as a public health problem, and they need to be aware of the research findings in order to communicate advice and strategies to parents of their patients. Media scholars should be applying for grants that would allow them the funds needed to develop a strategic communication campaign in conjunction with pediatricians.

Conclusion

As a civilized society, we have an ethical obligation to educate, nurture, and support the youngest members of our society. In a contemporary world, there are a number of issues related to raising children that concern parents, educators, and the public at large: protecting children from predators, the effectiveness of our nation's public school system, bullying, the growing childhood obesity epidemic, and online privacy issues, to name a few. It would be naïve to assume that the problem of media violence might all of a sudden jump to the forefront of the public conscience and occupy a significant portion of people's time and energy. Nonetheless, the purpose of this paper is to serve as a reminder of the ongoing concerns associated with children's exposure to mediated violence, especially that which occurs on television.

References

Anderson, C. A., & Bushman, B. J. (2002). Human aggression. *Annual Review of Psychology, 53*, 27–51.

Aust, P. J., & Everhart, K. (2007). *What Is Your Child Watching?: A Content Analysis of Violence in Disney Animated Films: Scene 1*. Paper presented at the annual conference of the International Communication Association, San Francisco, CA.

Bandura, A. (1986). *Social Foundations of Thought and Action: A Social Cognitive Theory*. Englewood Cliffs, NJ: Prentice-Hall.

Browne, K. D., & Hamilton-Giachritsis, C. (2005). The influence of violent media on children and adolescents: A public-health approach. *Lancet, 365*, 702–710.

Buijzen, M., Walma van der Molen, J. H., & Sondij, P. (2007). Parental mediation of children's emotional responses to a violent news event. *Communication Research, 34*, 212–230.

Bushman, B. J. (1998). Effects of television violence on memory of commercial messages. *Journal of Experimental Psychology: Applied, 4*, 291–307.

Bushman, B. J., & Anderson, C. A. (2001). Media violence and the American public: Scientific fact versus media misinformation. *American Psychologist, 56*, 477–489.

Bushman, B. J., & Phillips, C. M. (2001). If the television program bleeds, memory for the advertisement recedes. *Current Directions in Psychological Science, 10*, 44–47.

Cantor, J. (2009). Fright reactions to mass media. In J. Bryant & D. Zillmann (Eds.), *Media Effects: Advances in Theory and Research, 3rd Edition* (pp. 287–303). Mahwah, NJ: Erlbaum.

Cantor, J., Mares, M. L., & Oliver, M. B. (1993). Parents' and children's emotional reactions to TV coverage of the Gulf War. In B. S. Greenberg & W. Gantz (Eds.), *Desert Storm and the Mass Media* (pp. 325–340). Cresskill, NJ: Hampton Press.

Cantor, J., & Nathanson, A. I. (1996). Children's fright reactions to television news. *Journal of Communication, 46*, 139–152.

Cantor, J., & Wilson, B. J. (1984). Modifying fear responses to mass media in preschool and elementary school children. *Journal of Broadcasting & Electronic Media, 28*, 431–443.

Children Now. (1994). *Tuned In or Tuned Out? America's Children Speak Out on the News Media*. A Children Now Poll conducted by Fairbank, Maslin, Maullin, & Associates. Retrieved from www.childrennow.org/index.php.

Corder-Bolz, C. R. (1980). Mediation: The role of significant others. *Journal of Communication, 30*, 106–118.

Coyne, S. M., & Whitehead, E. (2008). Indirect aggression in animated Disney films. *Journal of Communication, 58*, 382–395.

Drabman, R. S., & Thomas, M. H. (1974). Does media violence increase children's tolerance for real-life aggression? *Developmental Psychology, 10*, 418–421.

Feinberg, J. (1984). *Harm to Others: The Moral Limits of the Criminal Law*. New York: Oxford University Press.

Foehr, U. G., Rideout, V., & Miller, C. (2000). Parents and the TV ratings system: National study. In B. S. Greenberg, L. Rampoldi-Hnilo, & D. Mastro (Eds.), *The Alphabet Soup of Television Program Ratings* (pp. 195–216). Cresskill, NJ: Hampton Press.

Glascock, J. (2008). Direct and indirect aggression on prime-time network television. *Journal of Broadcasting & Electronic Media, 52*, 268–281.

Graber, D. A. (1996). "Say it with pictures." *Annals of the American Academy of Political and Social Science, 546*, 85–96.

Greenberg, B. S., & Rampoldi-Hnilo, L. (2001). Child and parent responses to the age-based and content-based television ratings. In D. G. Singer & J. L. Singer (Eds.), *Handbook of Children and the Media* (pp. 621–634). Thousand Oaks, CA: Sage.

Harrison, K., & Cantor, J. (1999). Tales from the screen: Enduring fright reactions to scary media. *Media Psychology, 1*, 97–116.

Huesmann, L. R. (1986). Psychological processes promoting the relation between exposure to media violence and aggressive behavior by the viewer. *Journal of Social Issues, 42*, 125–139.

Keith, S., Schwalbe, C. B., & Silcock, B. W. (2006). Images in ethics codes in an era of violence and tragedy. *Journal of Mass Media Ethics, 21*(4), 245–264.

Kirsh, S. J. (2012). *Children, Adolescents and Media Violence: A Critical Look at the Research*. Los Angeles, CA: Sage.

Kunkel, D., Farinola, W. J. M., Cope, K., Donnerstein, E., Biely, E., & Zwarun, L. (1998). *Rating the TV Ratings: An Assessment of the Television Industry's Use of the V-chip Ratings*. Menlo Park, CA: Kaiser Family Foundation.

Nathanson, A. I. (1999). Identifying and explaining the relationship between parental mediation and children's aggression. *Communication Research, 26*, 124–143.

Nathanson, A. I. (2002). The unintended effects of parental mediation of television on adolescents. *Media Psychology, 4*, 207–230.

Nathanson, A. I. (2004). Factual and evaluative approaches to modifying children's responses to violent television. *Journal of Communication, 54*, 321–336.

Nathanson, A. I., & Cantor, J. (2000). Reducing the aggression-promoting effect of violent cartoons by increasing children's fictional involvement with the victim: A study of active mediation. *Journal of Broadcasting & Electronic Media, 44*, 125–142.

NTVS (1997) *National Television Violence Study* (Vol. 1). Thousand Oaks, CA: Sage.

Perlmutter, D. D., & Major, L. H. (2004). Images of horror from Fallujah. *Nieman Reports*, *58*, 71–74.

Plaisance, P. L. (2009a). *Media Ethics: Key Principles for Responsible Practice*. Thousand Oaks, CA: Sage.

Plaisance, P. L. (2009b). Violence. In L. Wilkins & C. G. Christians (Eds.), *The Handbook of Mass Media Ethics* (pp. 162–176). New York: Routledge.

Potter, W. J. (1999). *On Media Violence*. Thousand Oaks, CA: Sage.

Rampoldi-Hnilo, L., & Greenberg, B. S. (2000). A poll of Latina and Caucasian mothers with 6–10 year old children. In B. S. Greenberg, L. Rampoldi-Hnilo, & D. Mastro (Eds.), *The Alphabet Soup of Television Program Ratings* (pp. 177–194). Cresskill, NJ: Hampton Press.

Riddle, K. (2012). Young adults' autobiographical memories of seeing frightening news stories on the news. *Communication Research*, *39*(6), 738–756.

Riddle, K., Eyal, K., Mahood, C., & Potter, W. J. (2006). Judging the degree of violence in media portrayals: A cross genre comparison. *Journal of Broadcasting & Electronic Media*, *50*, 270–286.

Rideout, V. J., Foehr, U. G., & Roberts, D. F. (2010). *Generation M²: Media in the Lives of 8- to 18-year-olds*. Menlo Park, CA: Kaiser Family Foundation.

Romano, A. (2003, July 28). News execs defend their use of gruesome images. *Broadcasting & Cable*, 9.

Saylor, C. F., Cowart, B. L., Lipovsky, J. A., Jackson, C., & Finch Jr., A. J. (2003). Media exposure to September 11: Elementary school students' experiences and posttraumatic symptoms. *American Behavioral Scientist*, *46*, 1622–1642.

Shanahan, J., & Morgan, M. (1999). *Television and its Viewers: Cultivation Theory and Research*. Cambridge, UK: Cambridge University Press.

Shrum, L. J. (1999). Television and persuasion: Effects of the programs between the ads. *Psychology & Marketing*, *16*, 119–140.

Slattery, K., Doremus, M., & Marcus, L. (2001). Shifts in public affairs reporting on the network evening news: A move toward the sensational. *Journal of Broadcasting & Electronic Media*, *45*, 290–302.

Smith, S. L., & Moyer-Gusé, E. (2006). Children and the War in Iraq: Developmental differences in fear responses to television news coverage. *Media Psychology*, *8*, 213–237.

Smith, S. L., & Wilson, B. J. (2002). Children's comprehension of and fear reactions to television news. *Media Psychology*, *4*, 1–26.

Smith, S. L., Moyer, E. J., Boyson, A. R., & Pieper, K. M. (2002). Parents' perceptions of their child's fear reactions to TV news coverage of the terrorists' attacks. In B. S. Greenberg (Ed.), *Communication and Terrorism: Public and Media Responses to 9/11* (pp. 193–209). Cresskill, NJ: Hampton Press Inc.

Terr, L. C., Bloch, D. A., Michel, B. A., Shi, H., Reinhardt, J. A., & Metayer, S. (1999). Children's symptoms in the wake of Challenger: A field study of distant-traumatic effects and an outline of related conditions. *American Journal of Psychiatry*, *156*, 1536–1544.

Thomas, M. H., Horton, R. W., Lippencott E. C., & Drabman, R. S. (1977). Desensitization to portrayals of real-life aggression as a function of exposure to television violence. *Journal of Personality and Social Psychology*, *35*, 450–458.

Valkenburg, P. M., Krcmar, M., Peeters, A. L., & Marseille, N. M. (1999). Developing a scale to assess three styles of television mediation: "Instructive mediation," "Restrictive mediation," and "Social coviewing." *Journal of Broadcasting & Electronic Media*, 43, 52–66.

Walma van der Molen, J. H., & Konijn, E. A. (2007). Dutch children's emotional reactions to news about the war in Iraq: Influence of media exposure, identification, and empathy. In D. Lemish & M. Gotz (Eds.), *Children and Media in Times of War and Conflict* (pp. 74–97). Cresskill, NJ: Hampton Press Inc.

Walma van der Molen, J. H., Valkenburg, P. M., & Peeters, A. L. (2002). Television news and fear: A child survey. *Communications*, 27, 303–317.

Weaver, A. J., & Wilson, B. J. (2009). The role of graphic and sanitized violence in the enjoyment of television dramas. *Human Communication Research*, 35, 442–463.

Wilson, B. J., & Cantor, J. (1987). Reducing children's fear reactions to mass media: Effects of visual exposure and verbal explanation. In M. McLaughlin (Ed.), *Communication Yearbook* (Vol. 10, pp. 553–573). Beverly Hills, CA: Sage.

Chapter 5

Ethics and Advergaming
Concerns of Marketing to Youth

Vincent Cicchirillo

On average, American youths spend an average of an hour-and-a-half every day using the computer outside of school work. Social networking, game playing, and web surfing are among their primary online activities (Rideout, Foehr, & Roberts, 2010). The Internet is an increasing part of the media diet of children and adolescents, and the prevalence of home Internet access and the ongoing proliferation of online information have facilitated their increased consumption of data. Furthermore, children's media environment is filled with a glut of advertising, both offline and online; in fact, advertising permeates every aspect of our society and culture. This advertising clutter has led consumers to develop cognitive ad-avoidance strategies (Rumbo, 2002). Because of this over-saturation, agencies and companies have had to re-define their messages as entertainment. By creating unique entertaining experiences, advertisers have found new ways to cut through clutter and provide something that consumers will cognitively process.

Advergaming, video games with branded products or images, is one of the newest weapons through which marketers and advertisers have been creating entertaining experiences for children, adolescents, and young adults. Many companies' websites now feature some form of interactive advergame (Radd, 2007), and non-profit organizations also use advergames on their websites to promote their issues and related products and services. Lee and Youn (2008) content-analyzed the use of advergames on leading advertisers' websites. The results of this research showed that, out of 100 websites, only 26 incorporated advergames; however, those 26 companies provided a total of 294 advergames (Lee & Youn, 2008). Thus, even though a relatively small number of companies used advergames, they resulted in an overwhelming majority of the actual number of advergames that were developed as a promotional tool. In addition, a majority of the food and beverage industry is incorporating advergames on their websites (Cai, 2008). Clearly, advergames are becoming a staple in the marketer's tool box.

Despite the growing popularity of advergaming, little research and discussion have focused on the ethical considerations of using digital games as an advertising venue. A focus on ethics seems particularly important given that adolescents and children are among the biggest target segments for advergames (Hernandez & Chapa, 2010; Mallinckrodt & Mizerski, 2007; Moore, 2006). In addition, online content and online advertising have been slow to gain government oversight and regulation, which makes ethical, responsible behavior on the part of advertisers even more important.

The purpose of this chapter is to focus on ethical issues related to advergaming. After discussing the definition of advergames, this chapter examines research related to the content and effects of advergames. It then identifies potential ethical considerations and recommends guidelines for self-regulation. It concludes with a discussion of directions for future research.

Advergame Content

Unlike in-game advertising, advergames are specifically designed with the intent of promoting and marketing a brand, product, or food item. Thus, the brand or product is the reason for the game, and the game's content centers around the best positioning and promotion of that brand. Furthermore, there are levels of brand promotion within an advergame. Chen and Ringel (2001) noted that a product or brand integration can occur at an associative, illustrative, or demonstrative level. The extent to which a brand is integrated into the game increases at each level. Thus, at the associative level, the lowest level of brand integration, the brand is often incorporated only as a background object or billboard. The illustrative level, the second highest level, integrates the product's spokesperson or personality as a main character within the gaming environment (Huang & Dinu, 2010). Finally, at the demonstrative level, the highest level of integration, the product is an integral part of the game play. In this regard, demonstrative advergames ask that participants learn about and use the products within the game in order to advance to further levels within that game (Huang & Dinu, 2010).

Some research has been conducted to examine the content of advergames marketed toward children (Dahl, Eagle, & Báez, 2009; Lee, Choi, Quilliam, & Cole, 2009; Moore, 2006). Lee and Youn (2008) content-analyzed advergames to examine the extent to which they are used by leading national advertisers. Although this research was not explicitly analyzing advergame elements in terms of ethical considerations, the results did point to some concerns. The results showed that advergames often incorporated brands as a major part of the gaming content and were single-player type games, and about a third of the advergames sampled asked users to pass along the game to friends (Lee & Youn, 2008). Thus, the advergames that were sampled were likely to incorporate demonstrative integration and ask the users to become viral marketers, passing them along to friends. This brings up concerns regarding both the processing of content and privacy as marketers are incorporating viral marketing tactics to spread game play.

Advergames exist for multiple types of children's products; however, one of the most popular categories for advergame usage is that of the food and beverage industry (Lee & Youn, 2008; Moore, 2006; Weber, Story, & Harnack, 2006; Cicchirillo & Lin, 2011). Lee et al. (2009) conducted a content analysis of food advergames marketed toward children and examined the context and content of the brand messages that were integrated within them. The results of this study showed that a majority of the advergames marketed low-nutrient food items and often incorporated products as active game components (Lee et al., 2009). Active components are any objects (tools or equipment) that players interact with during game play. It is clear that advergames will often incorporate some form of branded product as an interactive component to the game. Interactivity is likely to influence efficacy and attitudes toward that content and the products themselves.

Moore (2006) content-analyzed leading food marketers' usage of advergames, examining elements that might appeal to children. The results of Moore's (2006) research showed that advertisers integrate features that help to stimulate extended play through encouragement (positive feedback) and challenging players to advance further within that advergame. It was also noted that the most common genres of advergames were arcade, sports, and adventure games (Moore, 2006). Advergames often incorporate elements that help to keep children and adolescents playing for extended periods. The length of play can extend upward of 10 to 15 minutes, much longer than any television commercial. Weber et al. (2006) conducted a content analysis of food and beverage websites' marketing tactics with a particular emphasis on child and adolescent audiences. The results showed that half of the websites incorporated some form of advergame. More importantly, the advergames that were featured on those websites were likely to include tie-ins to children's cartoons and movies (Weber et al., 2006). Although not specifically examined within this study, these tie-ins could indicate instances of host-selling. Host-selling is when the spokescharacter for a given show or program also appears during the commercial breaks selling products or services. An example of host-selling would be when a child watching *Sesame Street* on television sees an advertisement for Big Bird cereal (a regular character on *Sesame Street*) during a regularly structured advertising break. This practice is problematic because it interferes with children's abilities to differentiate between program content and advertising (Hoy, Young, & Mowen, 1986).

The Federal Communications Commission (FCC) has set rules and guidelines against host-selling with television commercial content (FCC, 2012a). The Children's Television Act (FCC.gov) prohibits the use of host-selling during television commercials because of children's vulnerability to its effects. No such guidelines or rules exist for online websites.

However, the FCC did amend the Children's Television Act (CTA) in 2004 to try to restrict host-selling in online environments through limiting the display of a show's website during the program. Thus, websites that do engage in host-selling are prohibited from being displayed during the airing of a television program. While host-selling is limited on television, extant research suggests that it is virtually unlimited in online spaces. Advertisers and marketers are using advergames with branded spokescharacters and personalities in these virtual spaces. For instance, Bucy, Kim, and Park (2011) content-analyzed children's websites and advergames for their usage of brand-product characters for the purpose of advertising (i.e., host-selling). The results showed that the usage of spokescharacters within product-based advergames increased by 13% from 2003 to 2009, with over half of advergames including a brand persona within that content by 2009 (Bucy et al., 2011). The distinction here is something that should be of concern. In television contexts, host-selling is strictly prohibited, while in online contexts marketers and advertisers seem to be pushing the boundaries between content and advertising.

What about potential content differences between non-profit and for-profit advergames? Cai (2008) did find evidence of differences between for-profit and non-profit websites' usage of advertising that targeted children. One could assume that for-profit online content is geared toward best positioning a brand or product, while a non-profit's usage of online content is geared toward promoting an issue, cause, or problem. The research has shown that for-profit websites for children were more likely to host advertising and collect personal information from children than non-profit websites (Cai, 2008). More specifically related to advergames, Cicchirillo and Lin (2011) content-analyzed for-profit and non-profit food-related advergames in order to improve the ways in which they market socially responsible eating habits to children. Non-profits exist to advance public interest often in the areas of health and social responsibility, while for-profits' main goal is to maximize communication and sales objectives. Although goals related to such things as awareness and sales or donations may seem similar, the routes that each type of organization takes to get to their goals are often very different. The results did show significant differences; non-profit advergames were more likely to use quiz and word games, while for-profit advergames incorporated more genres related to action and role-playing (Cicchirillo & Lin, 2011). Furthermore, for-profit advergames were more likely to:

- Focus upon promoting a product or service over healthy eating behaviors.
- Incorporate human representations of self in the advergames.
- Give negative feedback for failure to meet objectives during advergame play.

The results of this research pointed to differences in how for-profit advergames were more effective than non-profit advergames in positioning themselves and their brands in the context of gaming. For-profit advergames were able to incorporate representations of self through character representations that may impact perceptions of identification. For-profit advergames also provided better opportunities for social learning and reinforcement through repeated game play. However, non-profit advergames were also likely to offer performance-based feedback during game play. The overall difference was that for-profit advergames used more negative feedback strategies, while non-profits used more positive feedback strategies (Cicchirillo & Lin, 2011). This could be because for-profits focus more upon using the brand or product in a correct way during game play. Thus for-profits maybe more concerned with getting repeated visits so that the individual will use the brand in the proper way during game play (i.e., using the brand to advance levels within the game).

The Effects of Advergaming

Although, the content of advergames is worthy of discussion, there is research that specifically examines the impact of playing advergames upon an individual's responses. The incorporation of a branded product within an advergame offers an engaging experience that may influence a child's or an adolescent's preference for that product. Mallinckrodt and Mizerski (2007) conducted an experiment in which children played a cereal advergame (*Fruit Loops*). Following exposure, their responses and preferences for that cereal compared to various food products and other cereals were examined. The results showed that children who played the *Fruit Loops* advergame were more likely to prefer that brand to other cereals and food options (cheeseburger, fruit salad, sandwich) and were more likely to report that they would request that brand in the future (Mallinckrodt & Mizerski, 2007). The enjoyment and engagement that was created by playing the advergame influenced children's preferences for the branded product that appeared in the advergame.

Hernandez and Chapa (2010) examined how adolescents' memory and product affect via advergame play impacted their cognitions and snack choices. The researchers used advergames that incorporated well-known brands from Nabisco (i.e., Ritz Bits, Oreo, Fun Fruits, and Chips Ahoy!). It was predicted that positive attitudes toward advergames, positive affect toward the products, and repeated media usage (video games and television) would impact brand recognition (Hernandez & Chapa, 2010). These factors would increase the overall recall of the branded products shown in the advergames. The hypotheses make sense as positive advergame attitudes overall should impact recognition of the brands incorporated in advergames. Furthermore, familiarity with a brand through various other media sources should also impact recognition of branded products in advergames. If adolescents have seen a product before, then the likelihood of them recognizing it in other contexts should increase. The results supported the hypotheses; positive affect toward both advergames and the product itself positively increased brand recognition (Hernandez & Chapa, 2010). Furthermore, the research showed that brands placed in the advergames were more likely to be chosen as snacks in a post-test measure after game play. The results of this research indicated that emotional evaluations can impact adolescents' memories and preferences for brands in advergames. Although, the positive effects of this research were highly touted, they should create some very serious concern. Adolescents are not as able to control their own emotions as are older individuals and, therefore, any type of appeal that engages affective evaluations to influence memory warrants caution.

Some research has even gone further to examine the impact that advergames have upon beliefs and intentions. Waiguny, Nelson, and Terlutter (2010) examined children's understanding of the persuasive nature of advergames and the effects those games have upon brand beliefs, brand attitudes, and purchase intentions. The understanding of persuasion and its use in advertising targeted at younger audiences has been a major concern among scholars, parents, non-profits, and government organizations. For instance, research has shown that some children by the ages of 8 and 10 years of age have an understanding of the tactics used in advertising (Rozendaal, Buijzen, & Valkenburg, 2011). However, advergames offer a uniquely new perspective and form of engaging and entertaining experience that makes it harder for children to disentangle entertainment from persuasion. The results of Waiguny et al. (2010) showed some interesting findings based upon children's identification of the commercial and persuasive nature of advergaming content. Children who identified the advergame as a persuasive form of communication were more likely to hold negative attitudes toward that game and were less likely to believe the message that the brand was healthy. However, when positive affect toward the advergame was high, the negative effects of persuasive knowledge became non-significant and positively related to beliefs that the brand was healthy (Waiguny et al., 2010). Emotions are often a construct that children have less experience mitigating in their decision making than older individuals. It should be noted though that, while emotions still may impact adults' decision making, it is to a lesser extent than children. Zillman's (1991) excitation transfer theory accounts for instances when positive emotions from one stimuli or manipulation can contribute to the emotional reactions that occur after being exposed to subsequent situations and stimuli. Thus, positive emotions from playing the advergame can be transferred to the valence of the product or brand incorporated in that advergame.

Huang and Dinu (2010) specifically examined the impact that the different types of brand integration and the presence of spokescharacters have upon outcomes related to recall, attitudes, and purchase intentions. As mentioned previously, there are three different categories of advergames that differ from high to low in the level of brand integration, and host-selling is a serious concern among academics and organizations for the protection of young consumers. The results of this research showed that the incorporation of a spokescharacter in an advergame had positive effects upon brand recall, attitudes toward the game itself, and purchase intentions (Huang & Dinu, 2010). The results of brand integration showed no significant differences between the different advergame categories. These results were elicited with a sample of college students rather than children or adolescents, so interpretation warrants caution. However, if spokescharacters can impact young adults, then it should stand to reason that these effects could be extended to younger audiences. Concerns are warranted given the effects that host-selling may have in advergames that target children and young adolescents. The results of this research have shown that a brand character incorporated in an advergame can impact individuals' cognitions, emotions, and behavioral intentions (Huang & Dinu, 2010).

Cauberghe and De Pelsmacker (2010) examined the effects of brand exposure strength and game play repetition with a diverse older sample ranging from 15 to 40 years of age. The results showed that brand integration did not positively or negatively impact brand attitudes; this effect is similar to the previously mentioned study (Huang & Dinu, 2010). One interesting effect of this research was that brand repetition negatively impacted brand attitudes (Cauberghe & De Pelsmacker, 2010). This may have been because of simple wear-out effects of repeated exposure to the same game. The researchers suggested that, to combat these advergame wear-out effects, managers should create more complex advergames and build variations into the gaming world (Cauberghe & De Pelsmacker, 2010), presumably to keep them fresh. The managerial implications section of the Cauberghe and De Pelsmacker (2010) article indicated that there are also some ethical concerns from academic research. Researchers need to be more aware of the audience of advergames before suggesting potential improvements to make advergames more persuasive.

In summary, advergames have been shown to be used by a wide variety of industries; however, food marketers are often the most likely to use them. Furthermore, for-profits are more likely to use advergames than non-profits, and their games often contain different genres of gaming and use different types of learning objectives related to the content of the game that are likely to make them more effective in achieving persuasive goals. In terms of effects, there is a wide variety of outcomes that can be achieved through different advergame tactics. It is clear from the research that advergame marketing tactics can include:

- Different levels of product integration that impact brand recall.
- Spokescharacter integration that influences brand recall and recognition.
- Spokescharacter integration that influences brand and advergame attitudes.
- Feedback and performance systems that encourage repeated game play.
- Affective appeals that can counteract a young player's understanding of the persuasive intent of advergames.
- Feedback systems that socialize children to spread the advergame to other children (viral marketing).
- Feedback systems that teach children about how to use the product.
- Feedback systems that teach children about the healthiness of the product.

Advergame marketers have a variety of features they can manipulate in order to influence the brands' effects upon consumers. Much like traditional advertising objectives, these games are often created to influence:

- Attitudes toward the brand featured during game play.
- Cognitions and beliefs about the brand featured during game play.
- Memory, recall, and recognition of the brand featured during game play.
- Positive word-of-mouth about the advergame itself.
- Attitudes toward the advergame.
- Preferences and behavioral intentions toward the brand featured in the advergame.

With a multitude of tactics and effects for impacting the player, a discussion of the ethical concerns is highly warranted.

Ethical Concerns of Advergames and Children

This section will identify and discuss ethical issues related to video game ratings, children's persuasive knowledge, children's vulnerabilities to persuasion, and childhood obesity.

Ratings

Since advergames are a form of video game, first and foremost, a discussion of how video games are rated is needed because ratings enable parents to make informed decisions about the appropriateness of game content and whether or not their children should play those video games. According to the Entertainment Software Association (ESA, 2012), video games have positive impacts upon artistic design and education, increase interactions between parents and children, benefit the economy, help promote healthy behaviors through motion-sensing technology, and bring awareness to social issues. The ESA created the Entertainment Software Ratings Board (ESRB) as a self-regulatory body that rates video games so individuals can make informed decisions about whether games contain content that is appropriate for certain audiences. The ratings system developed by ESRB is structured simply based upon content. The current system rates games as (E) for Everyone, (T) for Teen, (M) for Mature, or (AO) for Adults Only (ESRB, 2012). However, these ratings also contain content descriptors (www.esrb.org/ratings/ratings_guide.jsp); examples range from mild violence, intense violence, blood and gore, drug use, sexual themes, and strong sexual violence. It seems somewhat contradictory for the ESA to tout the positive effects of video games, while also acknowledging the strong need for ratings systems that include content description such as strong sexual violence. Another concern lies in the ratings system itself. The ratings are not actually based upon extended game play. That is, reviewers for the ESRB do not actually play the games themselves, but rather they watch video footage of game play and then make decisions on a game's rating (Davison, 2004). Accordingly, the ESRB notes that actually playing the video games would take too much time and is prohibitive. Some research even shows that, while parents agree with the ratings for content that is inappropriate for children, some parents consider the industry ratings to be too lenient for what is considered appropriate (Walsh & Gentile, 2001). A former insider at the ESRB asserted that the ratings system needs to be overhauled and updated and reported that often a consensus vote on a rating for a game was overturned without any reason (Bonner, 2008). Thus, as research and industry professionals have suggested, there are questions about the reliability and validity of the ESRB ratings.

While advergames are considered a form of video game, they are not subject to the same ratings system as video games. Thus, advergames are not rated for content or appropriateness based upon the ESRB system. This means that advergames, regardless of genre (i.e., strategy, puzzle, action, adventure, and fighter), are not rated based upon any type of content descriptors. Given that self-regulation is often implored by the advertising industry, this is somewhat odd. However, this does not mean that online content geared toward children is totally unregulated.

Regulation of online content related to children often focuses upon issues regarding the collection of personal information. Marketers and advertisers should follow strict government guidelines about the collection of personal information from children. In 1999, the Federal Trade Commission (FTC) issued the Children's Online Privacy Protection Act (COPPA), which established rules for collecting information from children under 13 years old online and for establishing parents' rights and access to that information (Neeley, 2007). Under COPPA (www.ftc.gov/privacy/coppafaqs.shtm), websites that collect information from children must adhere to the following:

1. Post a clear and comprehensive privacy policy on the website describing the information practices for children's personal information.
2. Provide direct notice to parents and obtain verifiable parental consent, with limited exceptions, before collecting personal information from children.
3. Give parents the choice of consenting to the operator's collection and internal use of a child's information, but prohibiting the operator from disclosing that information to third parties.
4. Provide parents access to their child's personal information to review and/or opportunity to have the information deleted.
5. Give parents the opportunity to prevent further use or online collection of a child's personal information.
6. Maintain the confidentiality, security, and integrity of information collected from children.

Thus, COPPA establishes that advertisers must provide disclosure about the information that they access from children, give access to that information to parents, and allow parents the right to remove or delete any information collected from their children. Another act passed by Congress is the Children's Internet Protection Act (CIPA; see FCC, 2012b), which allows for filtering software on public Internet terminals to block material and websites that may be deemed to be harmful or inappropriate for children (Strauss & Frost, 2012). This is one of the few acts that have been passed that actually restricts content from minors. However, the biggest concern still remains that advergames that are not deemed to be inappropriate for children frequently target children, and their content is not rated for appropriateness based upon age level. A ratings system similar to the ESRB's would be a good suggestion for marketers. This form of self-regulation would help to quell concerns that government intervention may be needed for the regulation of children's advergames.

Children and Persuasive Knowledge

According to Synder (2011), one of the greatest concerns that must be addressed is how marketers need to make clear distinctions between entertainment and advertising. This is an even greater concern for younger audiences. Children at younger ages do not have the same cognitive abilities to process and interpret information as do older audiences (Neeley,

2007). Children go through multiple stages of development during early childhood, and at each stage, they increase in proficiency to process information (Piaget, 1971). Thus, children at younger ages are less cognitively developed, and they must go through a growth process in order to develop abilities related to encoding, storage, and retrieval of information. Kunkel (2001; 2010) has shown that, until the ages of 7 or 8, children cannot separate television advertising from show content. The FCC strictly advocates the usage of ad-breakers and indicators, so that children understand when something is content and when something is advertising. Television programs include structured advertising breaks that help to make the distinction between the two. However, online advertising (banner ads, pop-ups, etc.) often appears alongside website content, making it difficult for content differentiation. For instance, Weber et al. (2006) found that few of the websites they content-analyzed included any type of ad-break warnings. Thus, the structure of online information furthers the difficulties and concerns of children's processing of advertising online.

Eastin, Yang, and Nathanson (2006) examined how children between the ages of 8 and 11 years evaluated online sources of information when dynamic advertising (animation) was also present on the webpage. This research takes into consideration the limitations of individuals to process multiple forms of information. In this regard, Eastin et al. (2006) based their research on Lang's (2000) Limited Capacity Model (LCM), which states that individuals are information processors who actively engage in encoding, storing, and retrieval of information. Individuals thus cognitively process information; however, the extent to which that information is processed is limited. According to Lang (2000), "You can think about one thing, or two, or maybe even seven, at the same time, but eventually all your resources are being used, and the system cannot think yet another thing without letting a previous thought go" (p. 47). The LCM was originally designed to understand the effects of television on information processing; however, Eastin et al. (2006) applied the same reasoning to children's processing of online content on dynamic webpages. Thus, webpages that incorporate multiple different elements and advertising would make it difficult for the children to process all of the incoming information. The results suggested that children have problems recalling information when presented with dynamism and advertising on a website (Eastin et al., 2006). Furthermore, children were also likely to misidentify the advertisement as the source of the website when no other source information could be found. This research shows that children are susceptible to rich media advertising and dynamic features on websites, so much so that they cannot reasonably identify a source and that the information influences what they deem to be credible.

It should be noted that some research does suggest that by ages 10 and up children are able to identify the persuasive tactics of marketers and advertisers. Children around the ages of 8 to10 years of age can identify the persuasive intent of peer popularity appeals, premiums (free give-aways), and advertising repetition (Rozendaal et al., 2011). However, one should be cautious in interpreting this research; just because children might be able to identify tactics of advertising does not mean they are any less vulnerable to those messages. This is especially true when advergames incorporate multiple dynamic features and incorporate elements that require higher levels of involvement and offer opportunities for repeated exposure.

Vulnerability to Advertising Messages

According to Livingstone (2009), there are two concerns related to targeting advertising toward children. First, as mentioned previously, children do not necessarily have the cognitive abilities to identify the persuasive nature of advertising. The second concern is that children are uniquely susceptible to advertising messages because of their developing cognitive abilities (Livingstone, 2009). The age distinction often comes into play when children hit 8 or 10 years of age, which is when it is assumed that they develop cognitive defense strategies against advertising. Moore (2004) notes that this is established, but children at younger ages (7 and under) are more likely to believe advertisers' claims and have more positive attitudes toward advertising. Even as children progress cognitively, they are not necessarily completely free of the influence of advertisers. For instance, most industry and academic researchers would argue that advertising can influence the most cognitively adept adult. And just because a child or adolescent has developed an understanding of advertising and a dubious attitude toward it does not mean that she will use them when presented with such messages (Moore, 2004).

Advergames seem to take advantage of these factors when targeting adolescents. "Advergames do not look like other, more familiar types of Internet advertisements (e.g., pop-ups or banners), nor are the ads separated from the content spatially or temporally as commonly occurs in traditional media like television or magazines" (Stern & An, 2009, p. 5). Thus, advergame strategies seem to circumvent features that would allow a child or an adolescent to apply understandings or skeptical attitudes about the purpose of the game. The commercial content and messages built into advergames may not be readily identifiable to children or even adolescents. As mentioned previously, advergames have the ability to impact children's and young adults' preferences for the featured brand (Mallinckrodt & Mizerski, 2007), brand recognition (Hernandez & Chapa, 2010), brand beliefs (Waiguny et al., 2010), and brand attitudes (Huang & Dinu, 2010). Clearly, advergames offer enjoyable and entertaining experiences. Overall, individuals play online games for enjoyment purposes; the main difference is *what* those individuals find enjoyable. Thus, when trying to pick out certain elements that gain users' attention, differences in motivations often affect what is recalled. Children and adolescents most often use the Internet for socialization, entertainment, and game playing (Neeley, 2007; Subrahmanyam, Kraut, Greenfield, & Gross, 2001). Marketers use advergames to target children and adolescents because this type of content is directly in line with the types of content that appeal to younger audiences. The commercial message may get lost in what the child or adolescent finds to be an enjoyable and engaging experience. Furthermore, these types of games are often played online without the direction of parents (Neeley, 2007). Therefore, no one is there to help young game players understand the meaning behind some of the advergames in regards to persuasive content.

Recall and recognition for brands (see Hernandez & Chapa, 2010) in advergames may be elicited through repetition in game play and a lack of understanding of advertiser tactics. One unique aspect of advergames is their ability to facilitate repeated game play. For instance, Choi and Kim (2004) examined features of online game play that contribute to an optimal experience and customer loyalty. Choi and Kim (2004) did so by constructing a conceptual model composed of social and personal interactions that may combine to influence an experience of flow, which then influences customer loyalty and repeated exposure. The researchers invoked flow as the operationalization of an optimal experience. Flow can be attributed to the work of Csikszentmihalyi, who characterized flow as experience that resulted from immersion in one's actions (as cited in Sherry, 2004). According to Sherry (2004), "video games possess ideal characteristics to create and maintain flow experiences in that the flow experience of video games is brought on when the skills of the player match the difficulty of the game" (p. 340). Thus, flow relies heavily on an interaction between an individual's ability and how difficult the video game is to that person. Once flow has been established, children may be challenged to keep playing and they may lose sense of time. Thus, they are less likely to recall how long they have been playing, contributing to potentially longer game play sessions. Also, it has been noted that repeated exposure has been encouraged through positive and negative feedback (Cicchirillo & Lin, 2011), as well as through the ability to post high scores (socialization/competition) and personalize or customize the environment or character (Moore, 2006). It should also be noted that some advergames build in options and persuasive appeals for children to pass along or "share" these games with their friends. Viral marketing aspects of advergames encourage children to pass along those games to their friends, and this is a repeated request from advertisers on certain websites (Dahl et al., 2009). Viral marketing through children may be especially problematic because it can further cause misattributions of identification of the source of the website or advergame. Children may be less likely to try to identify the source, or they may be less concerned about the persuasive nature of that content if it comes from a friend or acquaintance.

Childhood Obesity and Advergames

One special kind of effect that needs to be addressed is that of unhealthy eating behaviors and a potential link to advergames. As mentioned, food marketers are most likely to use advergames to promote their brands (Cicchirillo & Lin, 2011; Lee & Youn, 2008). Childhood obesity is a great concern in the United States. One of the most controversial debates focuses on the impact that food marketing strategies have upon younger audiences (Bakir & Vitell, 2010). Some research even suggests a potential link between advertising and marketing of certain food products and unhealthy eating behaviors (Story & French, 2004). According to Kunkel (2001), one unintended effect of television advertising is its influence on the eating habits of children. Recently, these trends of targeting children have moved to online venues. A recent report published by the Institute of Medicine (IOM) (2006) showed that food marketers have used a multi-variate media strategy (television, magazines, and the Internet) to impact and influence younger audiences. Furthermore, the results showed that these efforts have impacted short-term consumption patterns and preferences that put children at risk. Content analyses have shown that advergames are likely to market low-nutrient food items and offer little educational value about the nutrition levels of the brands featured in those advergames (Lee et al., 2009). Furthermore, they are likely to incorporate host-selling and viral marketing, and promote consumption of the brands featured in the advergames or on the websites (Weber et al., 2006).

Research on the effects of advergames further supports a potential link between game play and food preferences and brand beliefs. For instance, as discussed earlier, Mallinckrodt and Mizerski (2007) showed that exposure to an advergame influenced children's responses and preferences for a cereal (*Fruit Loops*) over other food options. Hernandez and Chapa (2010) showed that advergames influenced children's brand recognition and their requests for the brand featured in the game in a post-test measure. Thus, children were more likely to ask for the brand promoted in the advergame. This result supports contentions that advergames can impact short-term consumption patterns. Finally, Waiguny et al. (2010) showed that the positive affect of playing an advergame can impact perceptions and beliefs about the nutritional value of a brand. This effect can occur regardless of whether the brand is actually healthy or not. The evidence suggests that advergames can impact children's preferences and requests for food products, their recognition of those brands, their attitudes toward those products, and their beliefs about the nutritional value of those brands. The overall results of advergame effects have potential implications for the misidentification and misunderstanding of advertising content as entertainment, the vulnerability and over-exposure of persuasive messaging, and a potential link to unhealthy eating behaviors. It is important that industry regulators understand these effects and put into place rules and guidelines for appropriately incorporating advergames into their marketing mix.

Self-Regulation of Advergames

It is important to note that self-regulation and adherence to rules and regulations might be the easiest path to ethical and socially responsible marketing and advertising online. Advertising professionals often see the need for ethics and social responsibility in advertising to reduce the need for government intervention and regulation in the industry. However, according to Dahl, Eagle, and Baéz (2009), marketers and advertisers seem to be unconcerned with the guidelines that apply to traditional media contexts when their efforts move to online formats. For instance, the separation or identification of advertising content from entertainment content seems to be lacking. Furthermore, the inclusion of nutritional information or the promotion of moderation in consumption of food products in advergames is relatively non-existent. Moreover, advergames offer instances where the application of normal guidelines is not possible. For instance, the limitations of host-selling on television are easily applied as advertising on television can structure in advertising breaks and restrict shows from advertising during their own programs. However, advergames can be placed on the show's website, which markets and sells the DVDs and toys associated with that show. Although the FTC has tried to limit host-selling in online contexts by restricting the posting of website addresses during the program, more self-regulatory practices need to be initiated.

The first recommendation is that marketers go beyond advertising and content separators often outlined through self-regulation. It has been noted by Quilliam, Lee, Cole, and Kim (2011) that content separators themselves have proven to be somewhat invalid in their efficacy. Evidence shows that ad-breaks and separators do not currently work to accomplish their intended cause (Moore, 2004). This also must be addressed as advergames cannot easily separate the brand from the gaming experience. In order for marketers to ethically promote their brands in advergames, they must clearly identify those advergames as advertising and let children know in language understandable to their age group the persuasive intent of that advergame. Synder (2011) echoed this sentiment that children need to understand the persuasive nature of the games that they are playing online in order to be treated fairly as consumers. Furthermore, marketers should develop a ratings system for advergames similar to the one that has been established by the ESRB. This will allow parents to make more informed decisions about the types of advergames that children play online. The system should include identification about the genre of game (strategy, puzzle, fighting, etc.) and content descriptors related to violence, language, and adult content, and finally, a ratings system should incorporate a description of the type of brand integration the advergame incorporates (illustrative, associative, or demonstrative). This would allow parents and children to understand the content and the overall level of brand placement in an advergame.

The second recommendation is that marketers curb the tactics used in advergames to influence children's preferences, cognitions, and attitudes. Viral marketing is one such tactic used with advergames that subverts the ability of young audiences to identify the nature of the message. Viral marketing blurs the line between advertising and editorial content (Synder, 2011). This effect may further be exacerbated by children's cognitive limitations. Therefore, marketers must limit their usage of this tactic when targeting children or include identification of the sponsor or advertiser so the user knows the source of the advergame. Also, advergames incorporate feedback systems, challenges, and customization aspects that encourage repeated exposure. Some research has even shown that emotional appeals in advergames impact children's understanding and attitudes about those products (Hernandez & Chapa, 2010), which can impact repeated exposure and influence unrealistic beliefs about the brand. This is not to say that marketers cannot use advergames for promotional purposes, but they must do so with caution, and the games should limit the number of features that encourage repeated exposure, especially to younger audiences. Advergames should offer feedback to users that discourages over-consumption of the product featured in the advergame. Thus, the advergame can incorporate the brand, but it should depict over-usage as hindering advancement in the game. This will help curb potential increases in preference requests. To limit over-exposure, advergames should incorporate restrictions that limit the overall amount an individual can play in one session. Therefore, software features should be used that identify to the user how long he has been playing in a single session. This system will help combat potential flow effects.

The final recommendation is that marketers and advertisers must encourage more socially responsible content in order to aid in developing healthy eating behaviors. Promoters of public health efforts need to advance the techniques that they use to the level of those used by commercial entities (Jain, 2010). For instance, Cicchirillo and Lin (2011) noted that, while non-profit advergames focused upon positive performance feedback to help improve potential self-efficacy in engaging in healthy eating behaviors, those same advergames lacked in content that might be deemed to be entertaining and encourage repeat exposure. Thus, non-profits that promote healthy behaviors should take a page from for-profit advergames and incorporate features that enhance engagement and involvement. As mentioned previously, advergames should also preach moderation in consumption of snacks that appear in advergames and that are identified as low in nutritional value. Advergames should promote a more balanced diet to encourage a variety of food products that meet nutritional standards outlined by non-profit and government organizations.

Finally, advertisers and marketers, both for-profit and non-profit, should encourage media and eHealth literacy skills. According to Bodie and Dutta (2008) "eHealth literacy consists of skills related to health literacy such as actively processing and being able to use health information to make informed decisions and computer and Web navigation skills" (p. 187). Thus, individuals who have high eHealth literacy skills should show a proficiency in finding and understanding health information online. A study conducted by Hove, Paek, and Isaacson (2011) showed that the implementation of an eHealth literacy program can improve skills of finding and navigating health information online. Improved eHealth skills also increased the chances that individuals identified commercial websites as the least reliable source of information (Hove et al., 2011). It should be noted that these results were found with groups of sixth-, seventh-, and eighth-graders. Similar programs should be employed to teach children about reliability and trustworthiness of commercial advergames. Advergame education programs should be tested in schools to teach children about the purpose of advergames and, more importantly, to recognize and identify which types of advergames are reliable sources of health information.

Future Directions for Research

This chapter has shown that advergames are a common type of marketing practice used to target younger audiences. Many companies now incorporate advergames on their websites (Radd, 2007), and a majority of food marketers use advergames to promote their brands (Lee & Youn, 2008). Furthermore, these types of games are relatively easy to play and are distributed via websites, email, or viral marketing (Cauberghe & De Pelsmacker, 2010). The content of these advergames can range from various genres and use various levels of brand integration. Advergames have multiple kinds of effects impacting children's preferences, beliefs, and attitudes toward branded products featured in the games. Ethical and socially responsible efforts need to be employed to combat the potential negative effects of advergame play. For instance, advergames exacerbate the difficulties children have distinguishing advertising content from entertainment and editorial content. The features of advergames also exploit the vulnerabilities of children to such types of messages, and advergames can lead to over-consumption and preferences for sugary snacks and products that have little nutritional value. In order to combat these effects, involvement from both advertising practitioners and government organizations is needed through the promotion of self-regulation strategies. Marketers must include identification and ratings systems to help parents and children recognize the persuasive nature and the content of advergames. Furthermore, tactics that marketers use to promote repeated exposure and long playing sessions must be inhibited through software limitations and warnings. Finally, eHealth literacy must be promoted by both non-profit and commercial entities in order to promote moderation and improve self-efficacy in children to find appropriate health and media information in advergames and on websites. Only through self-regulation and improved communication between researchers and advertising practitioners can more ethically and socially responsible advertising and marketing strategies be enacted.

Future directions in research should be established to examine the extent to which aspects related to product category (food, beverage, entertainment, music, etc.), product integration (associative, illustrative, demonstrative), and genre (strategy, puzzle, action, etc.) interact with one another to predict outcomes related to cognitions, attitudes, and behaviors. For instance, how might a brand featured at the associative level in a fighting game impact children's perceptions of that product compared to a brand featured in a fighting game at the demonstrative level? We could also extend this research to examine potential effects of violence in advergames. Experimental research should be conducted to examine whether violence in an advergame impacts children's aggressive cognitions and attitudes. This could be conducted while examining perceptions of the brands featured in those "violent" advergames. Product category effects also need to be examined to see if congruity between a category and genre of game elicits differences in responses among children. For instance, including an advertisement for a cell phone in a *Transformers* game would be a congruent brand and genre type of gaming experience. Given that children are developing cognitively, how might congruity or incongruity impact their processing of message content?

We know from the research cited that advergames can impact preferences and requests (see Mallinckrodt & Mizerski, 2007), but to what extent do these games influence behaviors related to consumption and exercising? Although short-term exposure can garner significant results, longitudinal research with children needs to be conducted to examine the impact of digital game playing on a host of factors related to eating and exercising. While children are a primary concern, we must extend this research to older samples of adolescents and young adults. Adolescents are known to be impulsive and often subject to peer pressure. This fact may compound the effects of brands featured in advergames. Furthermore, we should extend research to examine the potential influence of augmented reality and three-dimensionality (3-D) on children's and adolescents' cognitions and attitudes. Advertisers are starting to use these new media technologies to grab user attention. How might these options impact children's and adolescents' views of advertising within a virtual context? Does this format offer better opportunities for brand reinforcement, especially if the virtual environment elicits a sense of presence among users?

Finally, we must go beyond computer-mediated online game playing and examine new directions involving mobile applications to understand how this access may or may not be impacting child consumers. Games are a popular form of mobile application (Mintel, 2011) that often appeals to children. Since mobile games and applications are becoming incredibly popular among children and adolescents, we must understand how they might impact information processing among these groups. This information will then allow us to better understand the negative and positive effects associated with mobile gaming. It may also enable non-profit organizations to construct better messages to influence pro-social behaviors. Only through extending advergaming research to encompass ethical issues can we come to understand how the intersection of gaming and advertising impacts the youth of America and offers practitioners ethically sound methods of promoting their brands and products.

References

Bakir, A., & Vitell, S. J. (2010). The ethics of food advertising targeted toward children: Parental viewpoint. *Journal of Business Ethics*, 91, 299–311.

Bodie, G. D., & Dutta, M. J. (2008). Understanding health literacy for strategic health marketing: eHealth literacy, health disparities, and the digital divide. *Health Marketing Quarterly*, 25, 175–203.

Bonner, J. (2008). How to fix the ratings system. *Electronic Gaming Monthly*, 227, 30–32.

Bucy, E. P., Kim, S. C., & Park, M. C. (2011). Host selling in cyberspace: Product personalities and character advertising on popular children's websites. *New Media & Society*, 13(8), 1245–1264.

Cai, X. (2008). Advertisements and privacy: Comparing for-profit and non-profit web sites for children. *Communication Research Reports*, 25(1), 67–75.

Cauberghe, V., & De Pelsmacker, P. (2010). Advergames: The impact of brand prominence and game repetition on brand responses. *Journal of Advertising*, 39(1), 5–18.

Chen, J., & Ringel, M. (2001) *Can Advergaming Be the Future of Interactive Advertising?* New York.

Choi, D., & Kim, J. (2004). Why people continue to play online games: In search of critical design factors to increase customer loyalty to online contents. *Cyber Psychology & Behavior, 7*, 11–24.

Cicchirillo, V., & Lin, J. (2011). Stop playing with your food: A comparison of for-profit and non-profit food related advergames. *Journal of Advertising Research, 51*(3), 484–498.

Dahl, S., Eagle, L., & Báez, C. (2009). Analyzing advergames: Active diversions or actually deception. An exploratory study of online advergames content. *Young Consumers, 10*(1), 46–59.

Davison, J. (2004). The ratings game. *Computer Gaming World, 242,* 31.

Eastin, M. S., Yang, M. S., &, Nathanson, A. I. (2006). Children of the net: An empirical exploration into the evaluation of internet content. *Journal of Broadcasting & Electronic Media, 50*(2), 211–230.

ESA, Entertainment Software Association (2012). *Games: Improving what Matters.* Retrieved from www.theesa.com/games-improving-what-matters/index.asp.

ESRB, Entertainment Software Ratings Board (2012). *ESRB Game Ratings.* Retrieved from www.esrb.org/ratings/index.jsp.

FCC, Federal Communications Commission (2012). *Children's Educational Television-Rules and Orders.* Retrieved from www.fcc.gov/encyclopedia/childrens-educational-television-rules-and-orders.

FCC, Federal Communications Commission (2012). *Children's Internet Protection Act (CIPA).* Retrieved from www.fcc.gov/guides/childrens-internet-protection-act.

Hernandez, M. D., & Chapa, S. (2010). Adolescents, advergames and snack foods: Effects of positive affect and experience on memory and choice. *Journal of Marketing Communications, 16,* 59–68.

Hove, T., Paek, H., & Isaacson, T. (2011). Using adolescent eHealth literacy to weigh trust in commercial web sites: The more children know, the tougher they are to persuade. *Journal of Advertising Research, 51*(3), 524–537.

Hoy, G. M., Young, E. C., & Mowen, J. C. (1986). Animated host-selling advertisements: Their impact on young children's recognition, attitudes, and behavior. *Journal of Public Policy, 5,* 171–184.

Huang, S., & Dinu, L. F. (2010). *More than an Advergame: Effects of Advergame Type and Presence of Spokes-characters on Advergame Effectiveness.* Paper presented at the American Academy of Advertising annual conference, Minneapolis.

IOM, Institute of Medicine (2006). *Food Marketing to Children and Youth: Threat or Opportunity?* Retrieved from www.iom.edu/Reports/2005/Food-Marketing-to-Children-and-Youth-Threat-or-Opportunity.aspx.

Jain, A. (2010). Temptations in cyberspace: New battlefields in childhood obesity. *Health Affairs, 29*(3), 425–429.

Kunkel, D. (2001). Children and television advertising. In D. Singer & J. Singer (Eds.), *Handbook of Children and Media* (pp. 375–393). Thousand Oaks, CA: Sage.

Kunkel, D. (2010). Mismeasurement of children's understanding of the persuasive intent of advertising. *Journal of Children and Media, 4*(1), 109–117.

Lang, A. (2000). The limited capacity model of mediated message processing. *Journal of Communication, 50,* 46–70.

Lee, M., & Youn, S. (2008). Leading national advertisers' uses of advergames. *Journal of Current Issues and Research in Advertising, 30*(2), 1–13.

Lee, M., Choi, Y., Quilliam, E., & Cole, R. (2009). Playing with food: Content analysis of food advergames. *The Journal of Consumer Affairs, 43* (1), 129–154.

Livingstone, S. (2009). Debating children's susceptibility to persuasion—where does fairness come in? A commentary on the Narin and Fine versus Ambler debate. *International Journal of Advertising, 28,* 170–174.

Mallinckrodt, V., & Mizerski, D. (2007). The effects of playing an advergame on young children's perceptions, preferences, and requests. *Journal of Advertising, 36,* 87–100.

Mintel. (2011). *Mobile Gaming—US—May 2011.* New York: Mintel.

Moore, E. S. (2004). Children and the changing world of advergaming. *Journal of Business Ethics, 52,* 161–167.

Moore, E. S. (2006). Real brands in imaginary worlds: Investigating players' experiences of brand placement in digital games. *Journal of Consumer Behavior, 5,* 354–366.

Neeley, S. M. (2007). Internet advertising and children. In D. W. Schumann & Thorson, E. (Eds.), *Internet Advertising: Theory and Research* (pp. 343–362). Mahwah, NJ: Lawrence Erlbaum Associates.

Piaget, J. (1971). The theory of stages in cognitive development (S. Opper, Trans.). In D. R. Green, M. P. Ford, & G. B. Flamer (Eds.), *Measurement and Piaget* (pp. 1–11). New York: McGraw Hill.

Quilliam, E. T., Lee, M. L., Cole, R. T., & Kim, M. (2011). The impetus for (and limited power of) business self-regulation: The example of advergames. *The Journal of Consumer Affairs, 45*(2), 224–247.

Radd, D. (2007, May 23). The secrets of advergaming. *Bloomberg Businessweek.* Retrieved August 10, 2010 from www.businessweek.com/innovate/content/may2007/id20070523_844955.htm.

Rideout, V. J., Foehr, U. G., & Roberts, D. F. (2010, January). *Generation M[2]: Media in the lives of 8–18-year-olds.* Retrieved March 11, 2011, from www.kff.org/entmedia/upload/8010.pdf.

Rozendaal, E., Buijzen, M., & Valkenburg, P. (2011). Children's understanding of advertisers' persuasive tactics. *International Journal of Advertising, 30*(2), 329–350.

Rumbo, J. D. (2002). Consumer resistance in a world of advertising clutter: The case of *Adbusters. Psychology & Marketing, 19*(2), 127–148.

Sherry, J. L. (2004). Flow and media enjoyment. *Communication Theory, 14*(4), 328–347.

Stern, S., & An, S. (2009). *Increasing Children's Understanding of Advergames' Commercial Nature: Does an Advertising Literacy Lesson or Ad Break Make a Difference?* Paper presented to the National Communication Association Annual Conference.

Story, M., & French, S. (2004). Food advertising and marketing directed at children and adolescents in the US. *International Journal of Behavioral Nutrition and Physical Activity, 1,* 3.

Strauss, J., & Frost, R. (2012). *E-Marketing* (6th Ed.). Upper Saddle River, NJ: Prentice Hall.

Subrahmanyam, K., Kraut, R., Greenfield, P., & Gross, E. (2001). New forms of electronic media: The impact of interactive games and the internet on cognition, socialization, and behavior. In D. G. Singer & J. L. Singer (Eds.), *Handbook of Children and the Media* (pp. 73–99). Thousand Oaks, CA: Sage.

Synder, W. (2011). Making the case for enhanced advertising ethics: How a new way of thinking about advertising ethics may build consumer trust. *Journal of Advertising Research*, 51(3), 477–483.

Waiguny, M., Nelson, M. R., & Terlutter, R. (2010). *Persuading Playfully? The Effects of Persuasion Knowledge and Positive Affect on Children's Attitudes, Brand Beliefs and Behaviors*. Paper presented at the American Academy of Advertising annual conference, Minneapolis.

Walsh, D. A., & Gentile, D. A. (2001). A validity test of movie, television, and video-game ratings. *Pediatrics*, 107(6), 1302–1308.

Weber, K., Story, M., & Harnack, L. (2006). Internet food marketing strategies aimed at children and adolescents: A content analysis of food and beverage brand websites. *Journal of the American Dietetic Association*, 106(9), 1463–1466.

Zillman, D. (1991). Television viewing and physiological arousal. In J. Bryant & D. Zillman (Eds.), *Responding to the Screen: Reception and Reaction Processes* (pp. 103–133). Hillsdale, NJ: Erlbaum.

Chapter 6

Ethics in Crisis Communication

Persistent Challenges and Emerging Issues

Lina Svedin

Public crisis communication aims to fill and solve very practical crisis management related tasks and issues, but also to uphold core democratic ideas and values.[1] The topic of this chapter, ethical crisis communication, centers on how information and communication are used to facilitate good crisis management and to support democratic functions and ideas under difficult circumstances. The actors considered are public managers, political and administrative, as they set out to manage and communicate about crises that affect the public and public governing institutions. A crisis for the purposes of this discussion is an event or development that is perceived by stakeholders or decision makers as posing a threat to core values, under conditions of considerable uncertainty and with a heightened sense of urgency.[2]

The empirical discussion takes long-standing challenges of crisis communication identified in prior crisis research as its springboard into identifying emerging issues raised by very nascent scholarship on ethics and public crisis management (see Capelos & Wurzer, 2009; Svedin, 2011, 2012; Vinten, 1993). In addition to published research, the reflections provided in this chapter are based on the author's experience researching and teaching crisis cases, training policy-makers in crisis management, supervising graduate research on crises and crisis management across the world, but also on experience working as an administrator with expertise in crisis management at the national level of Swedish government.

The research questions outlined in this chapter are both meta-ethical and normative in nature. They allow us, hopefully, to reflect on the assumptions we make about what is good crisis management and good crisis communication, as well as putting us on a path toward what the author views as good, or better, crisis management and crisis communication.

Persistent Challenges

There are some inherent characteristics of crises that make it difficult to plan for and execute effective crisis communication. First of all, crises are not objective events but rather have to be experienced and identified as such by those affected, regardless of whether they are victims or the actors charged with managing these events. Some disaster events seem almost synonymous with crisis, such as earthquakes, airplane crashes, and large-scale social disruptions. In these cases, it may seem more apparent to everyone involved that communication of critical information and values is needed, and this task is more readily assumed by those in charge. However, these events and other types of crises are largely a product of perceptions, and what constitutes a crisis ultimately rests in the eye of the beholder (Allison, 1971; Vertzberger, 1990). There is, therefore, almost instantaneously a battle of perceptions when surprising, urgent, and uncertain events take place that seem to threaten stakeholders' core values. This battle centers around establishing a dominant narrative about what happened, who is responsible, what should be done for the victims (see Schneider & Ingram, 1993), and how to make sure these things never happen again.

> Sensemaking is not about truth and getting it right. Instead it is about continued redrafting of an emerging story so that it becomes more comprehensive, incorporates more of the observed data, and is more resilient in the face of criticism.
>
> (Weick, Sutcliffe, & Obstfeld, 2005, p. 415)

A key to shaping the perceptions of other stakeholders and winning the battle of narratives is communication (see Brändström & Kuipers, 2003; Rochefort & Cobb, 1994).

Second, in cases where people experience urgency, uncertainty, and threat to core values, powerful psychological coping mechanisms are triggered that make them less willing and able to take in and process new and complex information (see, for instance, C. Hermann, Stein, Sundelius, & Walker, 2001; M. Hermann, Preston, Korany, & Shaw, 2001; M. G. Hermann, 1979). This is particularly the case with information that in some way diverges from or contradicts an individual's already-held beliefs and conceptions (see Hemmer, 1999; Khong, 1992). These mechanisms make it harder for people in crisis situations to accurately process and understand what got them to this unexpected, unwanted, and unfair situation. In the best of circumstances, when those in charge of managing a crisis are actually able to accurately assess the situation, it is still hard for them to communicate a complex message about what people are supposed to do, why the situation is the way it is, who is in charge, and what might happen next to a stressed set of audiences. The public, while needing and wanting information about these things, has even less tolerance for details like jurisdictional complexities, bureaucratic procedures, contingent forecasts, and timetables than under normal circumstances.

People want to hear messages that give them clear guidance and certainty and that promise a rapid return to normalcy. As a cognitive activity, crisis communication is therefore fundamentally challenging for both senders and receivers.

Third, crises trigger an intense and active search for information. Information is sought by victims, managers, the public, and the media in order to eliminate uncertainty and to protect themselves from the perceived threat.[3] If this information search is not met with an active supply of information (on behalf of those the media and the public turn to for information), the media will fill the void with whatever they want or can. In other words, if competing crisis narratives are not presented by actors in charge, the media will write its own narrative nonetheless. It is the nature of what the media do—present narratives—and crises present almost irresistible situations of *things being out of control* that the media thrive on (Deppa, Russell, Hayes, & Flocke, 1994). The point here is not whether or not this is an appropriate mode for the media to operate in, but rather that there is a massive search for information at the outset of crises that needs to be met by those in charge.

Looking at these adverse circumstances and inherent challenges, is it worth investing public funds in research on public crisis communication and forcing those charged with managing crises to plan for and to train for communication in crises? The answer to these questions seems to be yes. Media training for bureaucrats and political decision makers who do not regularly stand in front of cameras has proven helpful. It can make them clearer and more consistent in their messaging, and it can help them avoid credibility traps during stress and when they have to be the carrier of bad news. It can also help them deliver their message in a way and with a timeliness that makes it possible for the media to better relay their message. Having greater understanding of and experience with putting different people of organizations in front of cameras has also helped organizations make better choices about who is chosen to speak for the organization in a crisis communication setting.

Next, we turn to the essence of messaging; what is it public managers and public organizations need and want to communicate in crises? This is where our focus on ethics comes in because ethics is about what is right and what is wrong. Public crisis management, despite its seemingly unique and sometimes frightening circumstance, is in its essence decisions about and administration of public policy. It is about the authoritative allocation of values and the distribution of resources in society. By placing focus on the structures and people in charge of citizens' affairs, crises also provide an opportunity for public managers to reaffirm the legitimacy of the system in place, our governing institutions.

One of the things public managers want to communicate in crises is reassurance. They want to convey a sense of control in chaos and show that governing intuitions are in charge and on top of managing the crisis. Part of the reassurance is conveying that those in charge are doing all they can, which propels individual decision makers, particularly politicians, to want to show they are actively doing something rather than just sitting around collecting more information and analyzing the situation (even when that may be the more appropriate action). They also want reassurance to build societal trust and support of the people and structures in place. This sometimes leads them to downplay some chaotic situations by stating that this is not a "crisis" and rebrand it as a critical or severe situation, or to play up threatening situations with calls for national unity and the need to come together to overcome some external threat.

Public managers also want to define whose crisis it is and allocate blame, usually away from themselves and the institutions they represent. The media are quick to allocate the dramatic roles in crises: the hero, the villain, the victim, and in some instances a neutral observer. The narrative of what has happened and what or who is to blame for the crisis is a pressing issue, and the battle of perceptions and their real consequences leave public managers little choice (and time) but to engage in communication about these issues. At times, they try to diffuse blame by pitching the situation as the result of a system failure (too large for any one individual to be held responsible for) or by focusing on one or a few individuals who serve as scapegoats (a few rotten apples). If they are favorably positioned, they may also seize the opportunity to defend organizational turf (areas of responsibility and resources) or even to gain turf. If the situation is perceived as a political crisis, they make choices about how to best protect senior political and administrative managers and the integrity of the system in place.

Finally, public crisis managers also want to promote more general values promoting and supporting governance structures. The values are put forth in how senior political and administrative officials frame what the crisis is about and what the appropriate roles of government and the individual are in this situation. The promotion of values is central in efforts to convey that the crisis is managed by a caring government, or alternatively that this crisis is being managed competently, i.e., business as usual, by professional, street-level public servants like police and fire departments, or expert search-and-rescue personnel. At its pinnacle, the communication of values for public managers centers on what values ought to be prioritized, what behavior is appropriate, and identifying people who are deserving of help or rescue, which is the very same authoritative allocation of values that we see in any other policy setting.

The next section of this chapter explores the horizon of challenges public officials face as they try to convey these messages in an evolving administrative setting and the challenge of pursuing crisis communication ethically.

Emerging Issues

There are a number of things that remain challenging for public managers with regard to successful crisis communication—that is, communication that at least achieves what the sender was hoping it would accomplish regardless of what specific evaluating criteria the sender holds. Then there is the issue of ethics, of doing what is right and avoiding what is wrong from a moral point of view. Successful, ethical crisis communication becomes infinitely harder to do and to analyze since it implies that one or more values, held by government and the governed, is set up as the criterion on which to evaluate the success of any communication. At a minimum, in order to be ethical, communication in crises needs to make it possible for stakeholders to evaluate and judge who analyzed the information and situation in government, what decisions and actions the governing institutions took or did not take, and why they argue they did what they did. This enables the governed and collaborating organizations to evaluate, judge, and ultimately sanction poor performances, to redress perceived injustices, and to reject unacceptable management and policy outcomes.

With this in mind, public organizations communicating in crises should strive for providing a consistency of message (inside and outside governing organizations, by different representatives of the same organization or management team), being transparent in order to enable accountability, and publically outlining the rationales for decisions and actions so that the public can assess the fairness and reasonableness of the use of power and the allocation of resources. In the sections below, I outline some anecdotal evidence of how well public managers seem to do on these parameters and, where appropriate, I suggest how we as communication scholars may help managers become better at ethical crisis communication by further exploring these issues in theory building and case research.

Internal and External Messaging

Because of the quick establishment of the battle of narratives and the drive of media attention, crisis managers often focus their crisis communication efforts externally outside their own organization. Their efforts to establish their view of what has happened, who is responsible, and what should be expected of individuals and the governing institutions involved tend to focus on the media as a platform for communication, sometimes to the detriment of internal communication of this narrative.[4] The internal organization and the public servants who are expected to reflect and implement senior managers' points of view and policy decisions are often left with considerably less guidance and information than external stakeholders.

Naturally, this can cause problems of consistency of messaging by personnel in the line organization toward individual citizens, which is an ethical concern when it comes to the fair and effective administration of policy. It may also, however, leave this staff with a sense of leadership abandonment in a situation where they themselves may be victims of the crisis or in a situation where they are expected to be in the know about what the organization is doing. In the first instance, they are inadvertently treated as a second-class, or not prioritized, group of citizen victims. In the second instance, they may face the wrath of citizens who turn to them for help or may have their actions publically scrutinized and criticized by the media in a situation where they really have not been given adequate information to perform their duties well. In an extreme case of this latter scenario, public administrators in the line organization may face *aporatic* situations (see Boin & Nieuwenburg, 2011) where, due to a lack of communication about priorities and an ordering of values to protect, lower-level administrators are forced to make decisions about real and tragic circumstances that they really are not prepared for and that are essentially political decisions.

In an effort to improve crisis communication as it pertains to external and internal messaging, we should look more closely at the following research questions:

- How are line organizations affected by a lack of internal information about how to perform their tasks and duties and how do they deal with it?
- How do line organizations deal with their responsibilities to communicate with citizens when they lack the information that they need?
- How common is the experience of leadership abandonment in line organizations, and what effects does it have on lower-level administrators' use of discretion and on their emotional states?
- When and how do aporatic situations occur as a result of a lack of communication of values and policy priorities, and what are the ethical implications of line organizations being forced to deal with aporatic situations?
- What is the effect on performance, morale, and organizational culture when bureaucrats are forced to manage crises and make decisions that are political and inherently value-laden (aporatic situations)?
- What are the effects of bureaucrats being forced to manage crises and make decisions that are political and inherently value-laden on accountability and democratic decision making?

Accounting for Action and In-Action

It is a significant challenge for the governed to hold public managers, political and administrative, accountable in crises, especially with regard to what they *did not* do and the responsibility they *did not* assume. Oftentimes the information and communication about managers' omissions and in-action are by their very nature missing. Other times, competing groups within the managing institutions realize that drawn-out turf battles in crises can contribute to public fiascos that they ultimately have to explain (Sundelius, Stern, & Bynander, 1997).[5] In this situation, they create vague, ambiguous, and ad hoc decision and management arrangements in an effort to prevent conflicts from becoming public and disturbing elements of public debate in the management of the crisis. This has happened many times in the Swedish experience of crises, but the executive body at the national level managing the stranding of the Soviet U-137 submarine in the Swedish archipelago in 1981 is one example of this purposely vaguely defined decision unit.

In order to get a picture of and judge where those in charge missed important information and failed to act on signals or situational imperatives, the public needs to establish a counter-narrative that challenges the established perception among public managers about what the situation was like, what they experienced, and what they decided was a reasonable thing to do or way to proceed. Efforts to construct a counter-narrative that can shed light on shortcomings are made more difficult when ministries and agencies fail to appropriately document the process leading up to decisions and actions (Konstitutionsutskottet, 2005). A Swedish parliamentary investigation[6] into the Swedish government's management of the 2004 tsunami disaster pointed to this problem in what may very well be an intentional circumvention of accountability mechanisms in Swedish crisis management (Svedin, 2012). In the Swedish tsunami case, the commission pointed out "the added value of documenting the management of crises while they are happening to promote transparency in post crisis evaluations" (Wockelberg, 2011, p. 170) and expressed regret that the commission was not able to fulfill many of its tasks due to this lack of documentation. This is a real ethical problem in terms of crisis communication when outside stakeholders need this information to accurately evaluate, judge, and sanction the actions and decisions of public managers. Frequently notes of when information was received, passed on, and to whom are not properly documented, and relying on the memory of those involved after the fact, when the stress of a crisis is over, is often a less reliable source.

As crisis communication scholars, we are going to have to put on a new pair of glasses as well in order to contribute constructively to the analysis of communication around actions and in-action, especially when considering ethical issues. Crisis research tends to be very action-oriented, i.e., it strives to assess what happened and how and why the actors did what they did. This research has gravitated toward action and decisions made, rather than in-action and decisions not taken. To discuss the ethics surrounding omission and failures to act will require researchers to look for in-action and opportunities for decisions not taken (so-called decision situations). Just as it is harder for the governed to establish a counter-narrative to the espoused narrative held by public managers, it is going to be harder for researchers to document and establish this kind of missing-in-action problem than it would be to point to wrongful judgments made and actions taken.

Formal and Informal Communication

Formal leaders of organizations and political parties tend to have great influence over the management of crises. However, how actively or passively a leader chooses to exercise her influence is a matter of leadership style and situational characteristics, but both cases carry important consequences for the ability of other stakeholders to assess the ethical aspects of leadership. In crises, there is often a strong imperative to do something, to act decisively, even if it means dispensing with formal procedure and chains of communication that could slow down urgent decisions and pressing actions. Many times citizens and the media are urging senior managers to be fast, flexible, effective, and coordinated in crises, which further pushes crisis managers to rely on informal decision making and communication, at least until things simmer down a bit and there is time to put things down on paper. Decision authority is frequently delegated and pushed down the line in fast-moving stressful crises. There are many practical advantages to this management strategy. Even intensely hierarchical organizations like the military see the advantage of delegating authority to smaller, more flexible units with stronger observation of conditions on the ground in particularly dynamic conflicts (Pigeau & McCann, 2000). However, there are also drawbacks that are not practical as much as they are ethical in nature. In public organizations, this kind of delegation of tasks and responsibilities in the face of a crisis is often communicated informally to speed up the process with, or without, a promise of formal sanctioning of this delegation at a later point.

Olsson (Beckman, Olsson, & Wockelberg, 2003) sheds additional light on the conundrum that a lack of recordkeeping and not following standard operating procedures can imply for effectiveness in crisis management. He states that discretion and decisiveness cannot guarantee effectiveness and both can actually hinder organizations from effectively reaching their goals. However, he states both recordkeeping and standard operating procedures were developed to alleviate the very real risk of decision makers, under stress and with imperfect information, making terrible mistakes. In light of the challenges crises pose for key decision makers, "it is rather natural to establish routines for decision making. The routines create consistency and help decision makers avoid simple cognitive mistakes that are easily made under chaotic conditions" (Beckman et al., 2003, p. 31). Drawing a parallel to journal keeping at hospitals, Olsson shows how key standardized information collection and transformation can be in pressing and complex situations.

> When a patient is received at an emergency room in a hospital, a journal is immediately established, even though doctors and nurses are fully occupied with trying to save the patient's life. Establishing the journal obviously takes time and effort away from other things that may seem more pertinent and pressing. Prioritizing this issue might therefore seem unnecessary when so much is at stake. However, the journal is of vital importance to the further treatment of the patient. The ER doctor only manages the patient for a short period of time. From there on the patient is sent to another hospital unit where another doctor takes over and assumes responsibility for the patient's welfare. This doctor has to be able to discern what measures have been taken up to that point with regard to the patient's condition; for example, what pain killers has the patient been given? If the doctor cannot determine this, his or her efforts to help the patient may kill rather than save the patient. The journal, a "limiting" routine, does not undermine effectiveness but rather is a fundamental precondition for successful goal achievement.
>
> (Beckman et al., 2003, p. 31)

There is a fundamental ethical challenge in the practice of informally communicating the delegation of power in public crisis management and in leaving considerable discretionary room to implementing agencies when making crisis policy decisions. When decisions do not specify how a policy should be implemented and when senior public managers cannot or will not steer the executing agency's implementation, then a lack of accountability materializes. The decrease in accountability can be to lower administrators' advantage or it can end up biting them in the rear when accountability is exerted after the crisis. Either way, the public loses out in its ability to make ethical judgments about individuals' and organizations' performance. At best, the lack of specificity regarding implementation and how to prioritize values in the new policy is a way for senior managers to affirm administrative discretion and a way to decentralize policy-making in fast-moving crises to those most familiar with local conditions. At worst, however, the lack of specificity turns into a tool for not assuming responsibility, i.e., for avoiding making politically costly decisions and avoiding exercising the kind of normative leadership that enables effective crisis management (Boin, 2005; Boin & Nieuwenburg, 2011).

It is not only the case that informal communication that raises ethical dilemmas comes from the top down in public organizations. Often lower levels of the implementing structure seek informal clarification or sanctioning of important crisis decisions from higher levels. In some administrative systems, like Great Britain's or the Netherlands', the minister who is heading a department also has responsibility to Parliament for decisions made and actions taken by independent agencies that are under that particular ministry. However, in other systems like the Swedish one, ministers are not allowed to steer implementation by individual agencies other than through highly formalized annual instructions and regulations. Informal, rather than formal, communication seeking sanctioning at the ministerial level can make accountability for decisions and actions harder to exert in the aftermath of a crisis in both types of administrative systems. In systems like Sweden's, it is technically illegal.

The Swedish experience of crisis management at the national level has shown that the prime minister often plays a key role. Other authorized decision makers, however, often seek political mandate or assurances from the prime minister before making critical decisions. The desire to anchor decisions with the prime minister seems to increase as the potential impact of the decisions grows (Sundelius et al., 1997). In fact, the desire to get political buy-in and a blessing from the national political leadership often trumps the desire for individual recognition among other ministers or agency heads (Sundelius et al., 1997, p. 158). One of the reasons this informal blessing is sought is that whoever takes initiative in a crisis, such as a ministry or independent agency, often ends up footing the bill for costs incurred through these actions. The fear of assuming leadership and making potentially costly decisions in crises has at times been a real stumbling block to administrative action even, when it is clearly needed.[7] Informal sanctioning of decisions is the only way for agencies to try to ensure that they alone will not bear the brunt of the cost since a formal sanctioning is technically illegal. These kinds of budgetary concerns will have to be sorted out through the regular appropriations process, after the fact, but it leaves agencies anxious and fearing political reprimand in that process if their decisions and actions were not in line with the perceptions and desires of the political powers. While politically convenient and possibly administratively savvy, this type of informal communication about decisions and action in crises actually undermines the governing principles set in place to guarantee Swedish agencies and administrators considerable independence of political influence.

A different version of how ethical dilemmas play out in informal as opposed to formal communication about crisis decisions was exemplified during Sweden's management of the 2004 tsunami disaster. During this disaster, as pictures and frantic reports were coming in about people affected by the tsunami, informal rules of operation within the Swedish Government Offices (the national level ministries) steered public servants' response to the information they were getting about the disaster. In this case, the ability to grasp the nature and scope of the disaster and its implications for Swedish government "was severely hampered by a reluctance [among key public servants] to bother top-level officials" (Daléus & Hansén, 2011, p. 27). The way the informal rules shaped the response to the disaster was:

> [l]ike Chinese Whispers, the alarming messages from the bottom of the administrative hierarchy transformed beyond recognition, to look quite harmless, before they reached upper echelons. The reasons for this transformation can be found in the pressure to respect hierarchy and in a fear on behalf of the middle management of overreacting in the eyes of political officeholders; that is, interrupting their vacations without a true cause.
>
> (Daléus & Hansén, 2011, p. 27)

This illustration reinforces what we have already stated about the importance of a consistent internal and external message. You cannot ethically communicate a message that states that the Ministry for Foreign Affairs will deal with crises involving Swedes abroad externally, and internally communicate that the minister should not be informed about any events or developments involving Swedes abroad unless they constitute war. In this case, the informal message that the minister did not want to know about or be drawn into the management of a crisis directly contradicted the responsibility that the ministry held, but the informal communication was effective enough to keep inconvenient and unwanted information down in the line organization, placing lower-level bureaucrats in an extremely difficult situation and ultimately aggravating the effects of the crisis.[8]

In order to get a better sense of the ethical implications of the use of formal and informal crisis communication, we need to look at things like:

- How is crisis management effectiveness impacted by the choice of utilizing either formal or informal communication modes?
- How does formal and informal communication affect how we perceive crises, how we frame the situation or problem at hand, how and when we are triggered into action, the use of discretion or standard operating procedures, the likelihood of implementation slippage with regard to policy intent or implementation timing, the up-scaling/centralization and down-scaling/decentralization of a crisis response, the ability to maintain a unified message in communication, and post-crisis evaluation processes? The sections above indicate that problem framing, our perceived need to act, how and when we act, as well as the evaluation of that action or in-action are affected by how (formally or informally) pertinent information was disseminated and received.

- What are the ethical implications of a priority on speedy decisions and consensus-building that informal communication facilitates?
- What are the ethical implications of using broad and informal delegation of tasks and responsibilities that facilitates adaptation to changing circumstances and thereby potentially increases effectiveness and efficiency versus more narrowly defined and formal divisions of responsibilities that garner clarity and enable greater accountability?
- Why do accountability actors choose informal accountability mechanisms and communication instead of using the full force and power of a formal exchange? When do they use formal accountability communication? And why, when they choose to use the formal exchanges, do they choose to do so in a way that, in particular, makes tangible consequences for those held accountable least likely? What is the effect of these choices on public trust in governing institutions in crises and during politics and administration as usual?

The Blurred Boundary between Politics and Administration

Bureaucracy as an organizational form, while it is detested by many, is designed as "an institutional method for applying general rules to specific cases, thereby making the actions of government fair and predictable" (Wilson, quoted in Daléus & Hansén, 2011, p. 22). The role of the administrative public manager is to analyze cases objectively and consistently and to fit these cases into a policy guided by law in crises as well as normal circumstances.

> The way in which bureaucracy in general is construed can hence be seen as an answer to some of the inherent ethical challenges implied in public decision making over resource allocation and issue priority. ... At the top, there is a political rationality that guides action in ethically tricky situations, which does not necessarily heed Weberian ideals of fairness and predictability. As long as the politics-administration dichotomy is preserved, ethical challenges inherent in the nature of bureaucracy are unlikely to manifest, even in times of crises.
> (Daléus & Hansén, 2011, p. 22–23)

Sweden, like many other states, has seen an increasing blurring of these boundaries of what is considered appropriately within the sphere of political influence and what is seen as purely administrative activities. This blurring of boundaries manifests in crises and carries important implications for communication and the possibility of holding either administrators or politicians responsible after a crisis. Sweden, while not alone in this by any stretch, also has an affinity for small-group decision making and setting up ad hoc intra-agency working groups when faced with a difficult situation. The actual, as opposed to formal, decision-making group in crises often ends up being a mix of elected politicians and public servants. As a consequence, it is hard to discern whether political or administrative professionals were the primary decision makers in these groups. "These complex and largely hidden interaction processes were characterized by a two-way interactive influence. As such, the division of formal authority and responsibility between decision-maker and advisor became very diffuse in these crises" (Sundelius et al., 1997, p. 140). Political responsibility and power, which need to ultimately supersede bureaucratic power and authority (Goodnow, 1900), become anonymous in this kind of crisis management. As a result, when policy and decisions are communicated in crises, it is unclear for whom this small-group is speaking and who can be held accountable for what has been decided and disseminated.

Symbolism

Perception management in crises is like walking a tightrope for those in charge. Nobody wants to be managed, particularly not in terms of having their minds manipulated, and the power decision makers have naturally makes this kind of manipulation suspect. If successful, the act of managing perceptions in crises can help diffuse crises, bring about closure, and avert latent societal conflicts from emerging. However, if perception management is done unskillfully and the manipulation is uncovered, it often adds a feeling of righteous indignation with the public, produces justified man-hunts in the media, and instills distrust in the relationship between the government and the governed. Furthermore, how a message is received depends not only on the message itself but also on how one chooses to communicate it. As Olsson (2011) has shown, the way one communicates, as well as when and how one engages stakeholders affected by the crisis (both as receivers of communication, reference point or information shaping, and as a feedback loop on the messaging), are critical to the perceived legitimacy of the response and the ability to diffuse a social crisis.

Symbolic acts and communications, if managed well, can generate important signaling effects like diffusing conflict, uniting stakeholders, bringing about a sense of closure, and expressing deep societal feelings of grief or injustice in crises ('t Hart, 1993). Important lessons to be learned about symbolic communication in crises include the importance of saying and doing the same thing for coherent messaging. If there is a discrepancy between the symbolic act and the message communicated, these kinds of perception management efforts can backfire dramatically. One example was provided by the British minister of the interior who, in an effort to convey that British beef was safe to eat at the outset of the

Mad Cow crisis, showed his four-year-old daughter eating a hamburger in front of the media in 1990 (BBC News, 2000). Shortly after, more scientific evidence came forward confirming the connection between eating Mad Cow-infected meat and Creutzfeldt–Jakob disease in humans, and the symbolic act instead was seen as a callous attempt by a politician to control a situation even at the expense of his own child (Grönvall, 2000). Another example can be drawn from the Swedish government's experience of wanting to communicate caring government by walking the grounds of a burned-out building where 65 teenagers had been killed before the police had finished combing through the rubble. When it was found out days later that the body of another girl was still to be found in the rubble the prime minister had walked on, the symbolic act was perceived as disrespectful and opportunistic behavior by national politicians that interrupted the routines of rescue workers and investigative staff (Hagström & Sundelius, 2001).

These kinds of unintended effects of symbolic communication can also be directly related to the crisis management actions and decisions pursued to try to deal with the acute crisis. One example of when actions in crises communicate the wrong message can be drawn from the U.S. government's response to the 2008 Wall Street financial crisis and its related bankruptcies and defaults. Leadership and leaders' communication play a key role in setting the tone and in creating and disseminating an ethical or unethical culture of organizations (Sims & Brinkmann, 2003). In the same way that leaders set this tone in organizations, the U.S. government's decisions and behaviors prior to the 2008 financial crisis set the tone for American citizens' and corporations' relationship to ethics and helped bring the financial crisis into fruition.[9] The way the U.S. government acted during the 2008 financial crisis further communicated to citizens and corporations that the government could be counted on to support, and possibly fix, the poor or unethical decisions individuals and corporations had made. Furthermore, the government's rescue efforts and failure to pursue legal recourse sent the message that corporations could get away with unethical behavior seemingly without repercussions (Svedin, 2011).

Governing institutions dictate rules and serve as role models that tell society what values and behaviors are acceptable in crises. Governing institutions' response also tells people and organizations something about what values are prioritized and what actions are rewarded or negatively sanctioned. The government's approach to managing the 2008 Wall Street crisis is likely to perpetuate unethical behavior and make similar crises likely to occur again in the future.

The British decision to go to war in Iraq serves as another example of this direct but unintended effect of symbolic nature. When it became apparent that the British government had not spoken honestly about its reasons for going to war and that the reasons communicated had little to no support, the whole war policy quickly unraveled (Bynander, 2011). It became clear to the audiences that the value of teaching Iraq a lesson rather than any weapons of mass destruction likely drove the justification for the decision to go to war. Similarly in the U.S., public support of the Bush administration and the wars in Afghanistan and Iraq as well as public perceptions of torture allegations changed dramatically as the claim to moral grounds for the wars unraveled (see Bynander, 2011; Kuipers, Kochańska, & Brändström, 2011).

There are many directions that future research on the ethical implications of symbolism in crisis communication could take. Some important and pressing questions are:

- How do we achieve worthy closure (management/governance task) to a crisis through communication? How do we achieve closure without closing the wound too quickly and thereby covering up important but painful lessons and preventing voices of discontent from being heard? How can public officials use symbolism to bring closure without becoming too ceremonial or trite?
- Should top-ranking officials or political managers visit the site of a disaster to signal the official recognition and end of the disaster?
- What happens to public trust in governing institutions and governance when information and information restrictions in crises are used unethically? The sections above indicate that bad decisions and untenable justification strategies can create massive and cascading political fallout, as well as larger national perceptions and policy repercussions for years to come.
- Can we bring about a worthy and ethical closure to crises in which the post-crisis process prioritizes fact-finding and *evaluation* and refrains from *judgment* and *sanctioning*? Can we bring worthy and ethical closure to crises without judgment and sanctioning of perceived good and bad performance? The democratic values involved in public accountability and public service performance evaluation seem to stand in opposition here to need and desire for societal unity and emotional closure.

Assuming and Avoiding Public Responsibility

In light of their responsibilities and how they are held accountable in the aftermath of crises, it would seem reasonable for public managers to be quite open to and embrace the fact that crises are fraught with uncertainty, especially in the early phase of a developing situation. By contrast, public managers, political and administrative, tend instead to uphold and communicate an image of professionalism and technical competence that can lead to a public undervaluing of the uncertainty of assessments and forecasts. The communication of excessive optimism and confidence may be the result of wanting to convey reassurance, to avoid panic, or the result of personal stress of trying to mitigate the hardship the victims are actually facing. However, the communication of exaggerated certainty and confidence may also stem from rigid perceptions that risks will decrease or be eliminated as the crisis progresses. Strong assertions and rigid perceptions can create credibility gaps for public managers if it turns out, as the crisis progresses, that previous statements were not true or were incomplete (Newlove, Stern, & Svedin, 2003; Stern, 1999; Stern & Sundelius, 1998). To regain or maintain public trust and a fair hearing by the media once they are in that kind of credibility trap becomes very difficult (Sundelius et al., 1997, p. 205).

The importance politicians attach to being seen as the one solving the crisis is reflected in the critique and counter-attacks during crises between the government and members of the opposition in the media (Löfgren, 1998, p. 157). Quick and authoritative assertions of leadership very early on in crises, such as publically assuming responsibility, are not likely to be challenged (Brändström, 2001; Newlove et al., 2003). A forceful display of leadership and being in charge establishes a situational narrative and frame that can become strongly path-dependent (Pierson, 1993). In some instances, initial assessments and decisions shape all subsequent actions and analyses by other actors to a point where they do not question the rationale behind the first assertion (Vertzberger, 1990).

Displaying being in charge or assuming responsibility, through actions and words, early on in a crisis can be an effective way of avoiding being blamed in post-crisis evaluations.[10] The media has often been the strategic tool of choice for political and administrative managers that want to assume responsibility in crises. As way of example, in the 1993 Stockholm JAS fighter crash (Brändström, 2001), which was a demonstration flight over downtown Stockholm that received a great deal of media coverage, two information officers determined a few minutes after the crash that the accident fell under the jurisdiction of the Air Force and that the Air Force was the chief responsible party. "This decision was not contested and the Air [F]orce assumed ... ultimate responsibility even though the [responsibility] situation was very complicated" (Brändström, 2001, p. 33, footnote 25). The political managers in this case did not enter the crisis management until the day after the crash, but quickly expressed symbolic support, but also concern, for the fighter plane production project. A formal accountability process was initiated soon after the crisis (Brändström, 2001, p. 75), and showing responsibility early in the crisis proved to be an effective way for elected managers to avoid blame.[11]

Crises that become perceived as large-scale public failures require political damage control (Bynander, 2003, p. 152). Managing perceptions in policy fiascos or crises gone badly awry is a precarious strategy for political managers, however. Any crisis-induced consensus that has at first tied political parties together is easily ripped apart when managers feel the political need for damage control. Differences are more likely to become solidified rather than resolved at this point, and taking responsibility is turned to a public blame game. During the two currency crises that Sweden experienced in 1992 (Stern & Sundelius, 1997, 1998), for example, the political opposition first opted to assume responsibility by publically supporting and advocating for the political compromise it made with the government. They even advocated that not participating and watching the crisis ravage the country would have been irresponsible. During the second crisis, however, the opposition stalled, was not forthcoming, and ultimately failed to compromise before the market de facto forced the government to abandon its monetary policy. The opposition avoided assuming responsibility and the political costs of a new political compromise, and in this case, they avoided being directly linked to the negative turn of events in the crisis (Sundelius et al., 1997, p. 174). The costs to the country as the result of the opposition's effort at domestic political damage control, in real monetary terms and in terms of lost market confidence, were substantial.

Whereas researching the ethics of assuming and avoiding responsibility in and through crisis communication could go in many directions, one key question that seems worthy of consideration is:

- How do we communicate in a way that supports trust, in each other as citizens of a collective (maintaining social capital and bringing about collective action for the common good), and in the governing institutions (that hold the power in these frightening times)? The first aspect highlights a lot of needs in the practical management of crises, whereas the second aspect highlights democratic values at stake and the long-term health of governance.

Implications for Public Managers

In an effort to help public managers communicate ethically and make decisions that support ethical conduct in crises, a preliminary check-list can be compiled based on the issues and challenges identified above. Organizations striving for ethical crisis communication should attempt to do the following:

Communicate Honest and Forthcoming Situational Assessments and Consistent Messages

✓ Be honest and forthcoming about what you know and what you do not know. Provide your honest assessment of the situation and what is likely to happen in light of what you know and the resources available.

✓ Strive for consistency of organizational message toward the audiences both inside and outside the organization. Make an effort to keep the internal organization as updated on policy-relevant information as possible and provide supporting information to internal representatives as they may be victims of the crisis as well.

Identify Competing Values and Make the Trade-Offs

✓ Make value trade-offs and communicate in what order values and stakeholder groups should be prioritized by the organization internally so that lower-level decisionmakers and representatives on the ground are not forced to make these decisions.

✓ Support transparency in order to enable internal and external organizational accountability. Record and talk about actions taken and not taken, values that were considered as competing or conflicting, and how these value trade-offs were resolved (which value was prioritized and which were not in individual decisions).

✓ Consider the societal costs and benefits of using symbolic acts to achieve a policy goal, given the likelihood that these acts may be misinterpreted by diverse stakeholders or undermined by developments in the crisis.

Assume Responsibility and Grant Others the Benefit of the Doubt

✓ Utilize formal communication channels and procedures for allocating authority as much as possible. When informal channels and procedures are deemed necessary for a speedy response, designate someone the function of following up with a formal communication and formal sanctioning mirroring that informal communication as quickly as possible.

✓ If a communication or decision is called into question because it was not formalized, assume responsibility on behalf of lower levels of the organization for their questioned actions. In the case that it involves another organization, assume that the other organization acted in good faith rather than throwing them under the bus and avoiding assuming responsibility.

Outline Your Reasoning for Others to Assess and Judge

✓ Publically outline the rationales for decisions and actions so that the public can assess the fairness and reasonableness of the use of power and the allocation of resources.

✓ Pursue public accountability processes after the fact and use them to their fullest extent rather than shirking the public allocation of responsibility and performance evaluation. Support these processes by being cooperative and forthcoming.

Conclusions: Ethical Communication in Crises

Crises test the performance of governing institutions and our commitment to democracy. The social contract that underlies government power includes the stipulation that the government should protect its citizens from harm. Crises, by their very existence, suggest that government has failed in its preventative function, and the continued trust in government now hangs in the balance of mitigation and a rapid return to normalcy, and a worthy and earnest closure to a tragic episode. Communication is one of the tasks of crisis management that public managers spend a large amount of time doing. Whether it is external or internal communication, or intra-organizational to facilitate coordination, crisis communication is difficult and time-consuming. It is demanded of managers at a point when time and certainty are in short supply and great values are at stake. What they say, how they say it, what platform they use to communicate it, the consistency of message, as well as their intended and unintended messages have real consequences and ethical implications. How do we communicate earnestly in crises, without creating further harm? How do public crisis managers communicate with the public interest(s) in mind and without the intent to deceive, without intentional omissions to protect their self-interest, and without wrongfully attributing causes or claiming management success when serendipity should be credited?

There is a conflict between the need, on the one hand, for access to credible and reliable information in the aftermath of crises so that problems can be addressed and the need, on the other hand, for public accountability (Brändström, 2001, p. 55). The first need is seen as most effectively accomplished "[b]y ensuring that a specific individual will not be personally held accountable for his or her actions" (Brändström, 2001, p. 55) thereby, theoretically, facilitating honest testimony in hearings. In Sweden, this approach to individual accountability has been prevalent, and formal inquiry commissions often, like truth commissions, forego the possibility of public judgment and sanctioning of poor crisis performance in favor of evaluation and fact-finding.

In situations where a trust-gap has started developing between the public and those in charge of managing a crisis, an inability to exert accountability can have a magnifying effect. In other words, in crises where those making decisions become isolated from feedback on public perceptions and public opinion related to the decisions and actions that they take, an inability to discern who bears responsibility for making these decisions can aggravate the distrustful relationship between the governed and the governing institutions. In addition to public frustration and criticism, these circumstances have the potential to contribute to a steady erosion of trust in government and a public despondence. The public is less likely to rally around what politicians see as important issues (key political fights and elections) if politicians do not communicate that they care about public opinion when it matters a lot to the public (in crises) and do not want to own their part in unpopular or even catastrophic decisions made on behalf of citizens when they are most vulnerable (in crises).

Only a limited amount of trust can be (re)built through formal accountability mechanisms. The relationship between the governed and the governing institutions is carefully crafted over time through consistency, transparency, and argumentation. The Swedish government is often quick to point out that "openness is the foundation of the public's trust in democracy" (Beckman, 2004, p. 19; my translation). However

> [t]he point to "understandable" exercise of government power is not solely to promote trustful relations between the government and those governed. The purpose must also be to respect certain principles that we think should guide a just state. Openness thereby becomes a part of the legitimacy of the just state.
>
> (Beckman, 2004, p. 19; my translation)

Crisis communication constitutes a critical test of these democratic principles and can be done ethically. Our commitment as researchers should be to facilitate this growth through honest investigation and careful analysis that can give crisis managers normative guidance.

Notes

1 The reason for distinguishing crisis management and crisis communication here as public is that there is a wide body of research pertaining to corporate crisis management that this chapter does not address at all and that may generate other ethical considerations that are not accounted for in this discussion (see, for example, numerous publications by Mitroff et al. (1988, 1993, 2001).

2 This perceptual definition of crisis is broadly based on definitions proposed by Rosenthal, Charles, and 't Hart (1989), Sundelius, Stern, and Bynander (1997), and Boin (2004). These definitions are widely used in research on public sector crisis management (see numerous volumes of publications by CRISMART, www.crismart.org, case studies produced within the Transboundary Crisis Management project at Syracuse University, www.maxwell.syr.edu/moynihan/tss/Crisis_Management/, and case studies conducted at the COT, Leiden University, www.cot.nl).

3 Media outlets' search for information in these situations may not primarily be to eliminate uncertainty (it may in fact be to capitalize on it) or to protect

themselves from threat but rather may be to convey information about something their audience perceives as out of control or threatening.

4 There is also a distinct tendency among externally focused crisis managers to be reactive rather than pro-active in their messaging. They tend to respond primarily to the questions and topics the media confronts them with, allowing the media discourse to shape what they talk about and when they address these issues. It is possible to imagine that a more pro-active approach would allow public managers more freedom in what issues their narrative addresses and how they frame the story of what happened and what is right in a way that better suits the values they themselves want to promote. In Sweden, this propensity to let what the media is focused on drive public managers' narratives in crisis communication has over time gone so far that these managers do not think a situation is a crisis or something that warrants their attention *unless* the media reports on it. This extreme reliance on the media, both the alarm to alert public managers to crises that need managing and as a crisis framer to which public managers simply react rather than try to proactively meet, caused considerable public criticism in relation to the 2004 tsunami disaster (Konstitutionsutskottet, 2005) and served as an administrative turning point with regard to the Swedish government's approach to event monitoring and crisis identification (Svedin, 2012, p. 141).

5 The public wants and expects organizations and leaders to come together in a time of crisis and cooperate to solve difficult situations. The ordinary differences, conflicts of interest, and competition these groups have do not magically disappear when a crisis hits, however. They tend to just play out in a slightly different way. Organizations still fight, negotiate, and manipulate in decision situations, and they pursue mixed strategies of cooperative and conflictive behavior across whole crises (Svedin, 2009).

6 The investigation was conducted by the Parliamentary Committee on the Constitution and documented in Konstitutionsutskottet (2005).

7 It also seems, in looking at bureaucrats' responses to uncertainty, that fear of saying too much or taking initiative would lead to getting stuck with the costs of necessary actions, or being reprimanded for being hysterical or out of order can prevent a great deal of internal and interdepartmental communication that can lead to a more timely and effective response (Daléus & Hansén, 2011).

8 Boin and Nieuwenburg (2011) and Daléus and Hansén (2011) illustrate how informal communication and a lack of communication and cross-hierarchical deliberation of important value decisions can leave street-level bureaucrats in an *aporatic* paralysis or lead them to poor decisions.

9 The fact that the U.S. government did not pay attention to questionable behavior by corporations and the signals that the regulatory protection was not adequate prior to the crisis communicated that ethics and regulation were not important.

10 When it comes to administrative managers assuming responsibility in crises, a recipe for success seems to be to clearly uphold an operational tone and focus.

11 This crisis was also handled by a professional organization, the Air Force, which. like other professional organizations such as the Police and Fire Department, is a favorite organization for decision makers to point at when they want to communicate reassurance, that a crisis is under control, and it is being handled by professionals.

References

Allison, G. (1971). *Essence of Decision: Explaining the Cuban Missile Crisis.* Boston: Little, Brown.

BBC News (Producer). (2000, October 11). *John Gummer: Beef Eater.* BBC News World Edition. Retrieved on 9 July, 2012 from http://news.bbc.co.uk/2/hi/uk_news/369625.stm.

Beckman, L. (2004). Krishantering och legitimitet: Den legitima krishanteringen—inte enbarteffektiv ochförtroendeskapande. *Politologen*, Spring (Separate print), 15–24.

Beckman, L., Olsson, S., & Wockelberg, H. (2003). Demokratin och mordet på Anna Lindh. *KBM:s Temaserie*, 6. Stockholm: Krisberedskapsmyndigheten.

Boin, A. (2004). The forum: Lessons from crisis research. *International Studies Review*, 6(1), 165–194.

Boin, A. (2005). Att utforma effektiva krishanteringsstrukturer: En diskussion av kända fällor, mönsterlösningar och kritiska parametrar i utformningen. *Sverige och tsunamin: granskning och förslag* (pp. 339–358). Stockholm: 2005 års katastrofkommission.

Boin, A., & Nieuwenburg, P. (2011). Drowning in discretion: crisis management ethics and the problem of aporia. In L. Svedin (Ed.), *Ethics and Crisis Management* (pp. 75–95). Charlotte, NC: Information Age Publishing.

Brändström, A. (2001). *Coping with Credibility Crisis: The Stockholm JAS Fighter Plane Crash* (Vol. 13). Stockholm: Ateljé/Faktor AB.

Brändström, A., & Kuipers, S. (2003). From "Normal Incidents" to Political Crises: Understanding the Selective Politicization of Policy Failures. *Government and Opposition*, 38(3), 279–305.

Bynander, F. (2003). *The Rise and Fall of the Submarine Threat: Securitization of Underwater Intrusions in Sweden 1980–2002.* Ph.D., Uppsala Universitet, Uppsala, Sweden.

Bynander, F. (2011). Value conflicts in foreign policy crises: How the United States and the U.K. wrestled with the ethical dilemma of going to war in Iraq. In L. Svedin (Ed.), *Ethics and Crisis Management* (pp. 37–56). Charlotte, NC: Information Age Publishing.

Capelos, T., & Wurzer, J. (2009). United front: Blame management and scandal response tactics of the United Nations. *Journal of Contingencies & Crisis Management*, 17(2), 75–94. doi: 10.1111/j.1468-5973.2009.00567.x

Daléus, P., & Hansén, D. (2011). Inherent ethical challenges in bureaucratic crisis management: The Swedish experience with the 2004 tsunami disaster. In L. Svedin (Ed.), *Ethics and Crisis Management* (pp. 21–36). Charlotte, NC: Information Age Publishing.

Deppa, J., Russell, M., Hayes, D., & Flocke, E. (1994). *The Media and Disasters: Pan AM 103.* New York: NYU Press.

Goodnow, F. (1900). *Politics and Administration: A Study in Government.* New York: Russel & Russell.

Grönvall, J. (2000). *Managing Crisis in the European Union: The Commission and "Mad Cow" Disease* (Vol. 10). Stockholm: Ateljé/Faktor AB.

Hagström, A.-Z., & Sundelius, B. (2001). *Krishantering på göteborska: En studie av brandkatastrofen den 29–30 oktober 1998* (Vol. 15). Stockholm: Ateljé/Faktor AB.

Hemmer, C. (1999). Historical analogies and the definition of interests: The Iranian hostage crisis and Ronald Reagan's policy towards the hostages in Lebanon. *Political Psychology, 2*, 267–289.

Hermann, C., Stein, J. G., Sundelius, B., & Walker, S. G. (2001). Resolve, accept, or avoid: Effects of group conflict on foreign policy decisions. *International Studies Review, 3*(2), 133–168.

Hermann, M., Preston, T., Korany, B., & Shaw, T. (2001). Who leads matters: The effects of powerful individuals. *International Studies Review, 3*(2), 83–132.

Hermann, M. G. (1979). Indicators of stress in policymakers during foreign policy crises. *Political Psychology, 1*, 27–46.

Khong, Y. F. (1992). *Analogies at War*. Princeton: Princeton University Press.

Konstitutionsutskottet. (2005). *Konstitutionsutskottets betänkande KU8 (2005/2006). Regeringens krisberedskap och krishantering i samband med flodvågskatastrofen 2004*. Stockholm: Konstitutionsutskottet.

Kuipers, S., Kochańska, K., & Brändström, A. (2011). Chasing evil, defending atrocities: Blame, avoidance and prisoner abuse during the war in Iraq. In L. Svedin (Ed.), *Ethics and Crisis Management* (pp. 119–140). Charlotte, NC: Information Age Publishing.

Löfgren, U. (1998). Svenska offentliga aktörers agerande vid gisslankriser utomlands. In E. Stern & F. Bynander (Eds.), *Crisis and Internationalization: Eight Crises Studied from a Cognitive-Institutional Perspective* (pp. 134–162). Stockholm: The Swedish Agency for Civil Emergency Planning.

Mitroff, I. I., & Anagnos, G. (2001). *Managing Crises Before They Happen: What Every Executive and Manager Needs to Know about Crisis Management*. New York: AMACOM.

Mitroff, I. I., & Pearson, C. M. (1993). *Crisis Management: A Diagnostic Guide for Improving Your Organization's Crisis-Preparedness*. San Francisco: Jossey-Bass Publishers.

Mitroff, I. I., Pauchant, T. C., & Shrivastava, P. (1988). Conceptual and empirical issues in the development of a general theory of crisis management. *Technological Forecasting and Social Change, 33*, 83–107.

Newlove, L., Stern, E., & Svedin, L. (2003). *Auckland Unplugged: Coping with Critical Infrastructure Failure*. Lanham, Boulder, New York, Oxford: Lexington Books.

Olsson, E.-K. (2011). Communication in crises of public diplomacy: The quest for ethical capital. In L. Svedin (Ed.), *Ethics and Crisis Management* (pp. 141–162). Charlotte, NC: Information Age Publishing.

Pierson, P. (1993). When effect becomes cause: Policy feedback and political change. *World Politics, 45*(4), 594–628.

Pigeau, R., & McCann, C. (2000). *The Human in Command: Exploring the Modern Military Experience*. New York: Kluwer Academic/Plenum Publishers.

Rochefort, D. A., & Cobb, R. W. (1994). Problem definition: An emerging perspective. In D. A. Rochefort & R. W. Cobb (Eds.), *The Politics of Problem Definition: Shaping the Policy Agenda* (pp. 1–31). Kansas: University Press of Kansas.

Rosenthal, U., Charles, M. T., & 't Hart, P. (1989). *Coping with Crises: The Management of Disasters, Riots, and Terrorism*. Springfield, IL: C. C. Thomas.

Schneider, A., & Ingram, H. (1993). Social construction of target populations: Implications for politics and policy. *American Political Science Review*, 87(2), 334–347.

Sims, R. R., & Brinkmann, J. (2003). Enron ethics (or: Culture matters more than codes). *Journal of Business Ethics*, 45(3), 243–256.

Stern, E. (1999). *Crisis Decisionmaking: A Cognitive Institutional Approach* (Vol. 6). Stockholm: The Swedish National Defense College.

Stern, E., & Sundelius, B. (1997). Sweden's twin monetary crises of 1992: Rigidity and learning in crisis decision making. *Journal of Contingencies and Crisis Management*, 5(1), 32–48.

Stern, E., & Sundelius, B. (1998). In defense of the Swedish crown: From triumph to tragedy and back? In P. Gray & P. 't Hart (Eds.), *Public Policy Disasters in Western Europe* (pp. 135–152). London: Routledge.

Sundelius, B., Stern, E., & Bynander, F. (1997). *Krishantering på svenska:* Teori och praktik (Vol. 1). Stockholm: Nerenius och Santérus Förlag.

Svedin, L. M. (2009). *Organizational Cooperation in Crises*. Burlington, VA: Ashgate Publishing Company.

Svedin, L. M. (2011). The ethical dilemmas of straddling the public–private divide in economic crises. In L. M. Svedin (Ed.), *Ethics and Crisis Management* (pp. 97–118). Charlotte, NC: Information Age Publishing.

Svedin, L. M. (2012). *Accountability in Crises and Public Trust in Governing Institutions*. Oxford: Routledge.

't Hart, P. (1993). Symbols, rituals and power: The lost dimensions of crisis management. *Journal of Contingencies and Crisis Management*, 1(2), 36–50.

Vertzberger, Y. (1990). *The World in their Minds: Information Processing, Cognition, and Perception in Foreign Policy Decisionmaking*. Stanford, CA: Stanford University Press.

Vinten, G. (1993). Whistleblowing on crises and disasters. *Journal of Contingencies & Crisis Management*, 1 (2), 101.

Weick, K. E., Sutcliffe, K. M., & Obstfeld, D. (2005). Organizing and the process of sensemaking. *Organization Science*, 16(4), 409–421.

Wockelberg, H. (2011). The politics–administration dichotomy and the failure of symmetrical responsibility doctrines. In L. Svedin (Ed.), *Ethics and Crisis Management* (pp. 163–182). Charlotte, NC: Information Age Publishing.

Chapter 7

Putting Problems into Context

An Organizational Approach to Advertising Ethics

Erin E. Schauster

> Most criticism of advertising is written in ignorance of what actually happens inside these agencies.
> (Michael Schudson, *Advertising, The Uneasy Persuasion*, 1984)

We need to understand what happens inside advertising agencies to understand advertising ethics. The events and tasks occurring within an advertising agency include planning for and creating paid announcements by members internal to the agency, which is influenced by members external to the agency. Internal members are the creative, account, and media executives who plan for and create advertising for multiple clients who are in need of solving communication problems. Clients are the marketers representing a multitude of products and services, from financial to beverage industries, who are trying to reach audiences of business owners and consumers. And their problems range from the simple to the complex, such as tapping into a new target segment with new and innovative forms of tailored messaging. What happens inside an advertising agency is multifaceted and complex.

Organizational culture provides a perspective for understanding what goes on within the environment of an advertising agency. Culture is the theory of shared beliefs and feelings, held by internal organizational members and influenced by external members. Organizational culture goes beyond the superficial and gets at a deeper meaning of shared values, assumptions, and feelings (Schein, 1990), which allows organizational members to make sense of their environment (Gabriel, 2000). Organizational culture acknowledges both the internal members involved in holding a shared sense of meaning and the external influences. So, for example, at an advertising agency, internal members include account executives, copywriters, and art directors, and external members include clients and media representatives, to name a few partners that agencies work with, as well as the audiences advertising is intended to reach.

Culture is learned by the internal members of an organization as a result of solving organizational problems. When one considers the complexity of work done in an advertising agency, it is reasonable to expect that problems arise. Problems in advertising include things such as keeping up with new technology, creating strategic messages that resonate with their targeted audiences, and maintaining client partnerships. When the problems that arise in advertising involve ethics, they can be categorized as business or message ethics (Drumwright & Murphy, 2009). Business ethics focuses on the processes involved in running an advertising agency (Drumwright & Murphy, 2009). Problems include how to handle accurate billing, as well as treating clients, employees, vendors, and other agencies fairly. Message ethics is related to creating and delivering the advertisement and encompasses the content and messages within an advertisement and the media placement. Problems categorized as message ethics include using stereotypes, targeting vulnerable audiences including the elderly and children, and advertising specific goods and services, such as tobacco (Drumwright, 2007).

The organizational culture of an advertising agency is a context for the problems that arise in advertising. Furthermore, this cultural context is in a relationship with the problems that arise, therefore having an influence on the ways in which these problems are acknowledged and resolved by the members working within this environment. The process for acknowledging problems related to ethics is advertising ethics.

Advertising ethics has previously been defined as "what is right or good in the conduct of the advertising function. It is concerned with questions of what ought to be done, not just with what legally must be done" (Cunningham, 1999, p. 500). As a normative process, advertising ethics begins with an awareness of problems in terms of good and/or bad, proceeds with a discussion of problems in terms of what ought to be done, and ends on the decisions made. By further acknowledging advertising ethics as a process situated within a complex organizational environment, a new agenda for advertising ethics research is proposed. A new agenda for advertising ethics research acknowledges three interrelated factors, including: 1) the process of awareness, articulation, and decision-making in response to problems that might have an ethical dimension; 2) the context of an organizational environment; and 3) the dynamic relationship between process and context.

An organizational approach to advertising ethics situates the process within an environment where advertising work takes place to show the relationship this environment has with and the impact it has on decision-making. In the proceeding sections of this chapter, advertising ethics is presented as a process, and normative theory is discussed. Problems faced in advertising are reviewed as the cues for awareness and decision-making. Following is a discussion of theories of organization, organizational culture, and organizational communication. It should be noted that the theory of organizational culture provides the impetus behind and the foundation for the proposed new agenda for advertising ethics research. Baker and Martinson (2001) suggested that problems in advertising ethics still exist because emphasis is awarded to the problems that are faced as opposed to the causes. The authors further suggested that the issues and problems of advertising are part of a larger culture that advertising professionals occupy. The new agenda addresses their proposed challenge to emphasize the causes. Finally, as part of this new agenda, research questions for future studies will be presented, along with challenges and implications for research, practice, and education.

Advertising Ethics

Problems faced, the controversial issues raised by advertising, and criticisms of advertising are often the topics that come to mind when thinking about advertising ethics. While these concerns are important, advertising ethics cannot be reduced down to the problems faced. Advertising ethics is a process that occurs in response to the problems that advertising practitioners face, but it is not limited to them. Normativity is integral to this process. The philosophy of normativity, which will be elaborated upon below, is concerned with what ought to be done, what is right versus wrong, what is good versus bad. When the steps of awareness, articulation and decision-making are grounded in normativity, the process becomes ethical.

Solving dilemmas is the business of ethics, which, as a process, provides the necessary tools for problem-solving (Patterson & Wilkins, 2008). From Aristotle (1998) on finding happiness, to Bok (1983) on secrecy, and Baker (2008) on the virtuous advertising practitioner, awareness for problems as moral dilemmas is understood as the first step in ethics. The moral, philosophical theory of normativity is action-guiding. Advertising ethics, approached from a normative perspective, assumes that ethical issues do arise, and when they do, it is best if they are acknowledged and are dealt with in an ethical way (Drumwright & Murphy, 2004). Therefore, to deal with the problems that arise, advertising practitioners must first be aware of the problems that exist and then have a process for determining what ought to be done.

Moral normative theories are concerned with the duty to act, consequences of action, values, and moral virtues such as honesty and respect for others (Hill, 2006), to name a few. Under the perspective of normative theory, one would ask, "How should I act because it is my duty?" or "What ought to be done because of the consequences that will follow?" Regarding the latter, consequentialism is the normative theory that states that the consequences of one's actions are the ultimate criteria for determining rightness. Falling from the normative theory of consequentialism is utilitarianism, which is a balance of good over bad consequences for all those affected by an action (Shafer-Landau, 2010). In determining rightness, utilitarianism maximizes the good for all interested parties by considering the ratio of happiness to unhappiness, short-term versus long-term effects, predictability of consequences, individual pleasure, and that all circumstances are at one point in time morally right (Shaw & Barry, 1995).

When consequences are acknowledged, the related question becomes consequences for whom? Therefore, normative theory emphasizes the moral importance and consideration for others, including fairness, respect, and dignity. Kant's principle of humanity is to always treat humans as ends, with the respect they deserve, versus means, which helps one achieve one's own goals (Shafer-Landau, 2010). Acknowledging the diversity of humanity, Christians and Cooper (2009) proposed the sacredness of life as the one universal presupposition that could be applied to a universal media ethic. For there to be further moral principles such as truth, freedom, respect, etc., there must first be an existence of life and an ethics committed to preserving it (Christians & Cooper, 2009).

Pertaining to advertising specifically, the consideration of others would include agency employees, clients, and service partners, as well as consumers. Baker and Martinson (2001) called special attention to the advertising consumer. According to the authors, respect for humans is the relative end or moral end that centers on respect for the consumer when creating persuasive messages.

Determining what ought to be done cannot occur without an awareness of problems in terms of rightness or in relationship to values. Carroll (1987) argues that organizational ethics is the capacity of an organization to reflect on values during decision-making. This reflection is led by organizational leaders, who play a vital role in creating and maintaining an ethical organization. The elements essential to creating an ethical organization include the ethical orientation of leadership, support from top management, and an established corporate ethics policy (Carlson, Perrewe, & Pamela, 1995).

Actions of rightness might be self-guided or guided by other people who have and who promote ethical awareness, such as organizational leaders. Aristotle's virtue ethics, similar to Baker's (2008) virtuous role model, acknowledges that an individual must first know what he/she is doing (Patterson & Wilkins, 2008) or have ethical awareness. Ethical awareness enables advertising practitioners to see an issue for its ethical implications. For example, role models in advertising with virtues of humility, truth, transparency, respect, care, authenticity, equity, and social responsibility can navigate dilemmas and guide other advertising practitioners on how to act (Baker, 2008). Role models may be the leaders of an advertising agency. For example, a Catholic CEO of an advertising agency set the example for his employees to contribute to a greater good by setting the agency's philosophy toward advertising which encouraged creating socially responsible messages in all advertisements (Krueger, 1999).

Ethical decision-making does not stop at awareness but extends into the articulation of problems faced and, ideally, a discussion. Habermas's (1984) theory of communicative action presents the idea that an ethic should maximize the participation of all competing voices in a dialogue. Speech contains claims of truth, rightness, and sincerity, and speech is often judged by its recipients for these elements (Habermas, 1984). Drumwright and Murphy (2004) found that an agency with a seeing, talking moral environment embraced ethical discussions in which advertising practitioners felt obligated to talk with their clients about potential ethical issues and implications of their work. In a moral seeing and talking agency, for example, an account executive might inform her client that the costs associated with a project have increased since the original estimate was agreed upon, and speak to the internal team on opportunities, and to the agency's vendors on cost alternatives before sending the invoice. In Drumwright and Murphy's (2004) study, a seeing, talking agency's culture was expressed through widely held norms on ethical behavior and the clear articulation of these norms among agency members.

Awareness may be not only for the problems that are faced but also for the tools available for decision-making. For example, a code of ethics set by an organization, especially a code of ethics that is enforced, provides employees with the awareness to process problems when they occur and to choose a more ethical alternative for action (Singhapakdi & Vitell, 1990). Industries also have codes of ethics. To guide behavior, as opposed to enforce regulations, the Public Relations Society of America has set the following codes: advocacy (serving the public by acting as responsible advocates for the corporation), honesty, expertise (continued professional development), independence (providing counsel and being responsible for action—as opposed to saying, "The client/corporation made me do it"), loyalty (relates to advocacy), and fairness (respecting various opinions) (Wilcox, Cameron, Reber, & Shin, 2011). The American Association of Advertising Agencies issues Standards of Practice that offer guidelines that address the responsibility of working with clients and competing agencies, the priority of recruiting employees, and the ethical standards for creating honest advertising messages (The American Association of Advertising Agencies, 1924).

While Nwachukwu and Vitell (1997) agree that a corporate code of ethics can influence decision-making, their study found no significant difference in the perception of advertising as less ethical between those organizations with a code of ethics versus those without one. While some would disregard this finding due to its lack of significance, it sheds light on the advertising ethics process. It is important because neither ethics nor organizational culture can be reduced down to a code of ethics.

As will be discussed later, a corporate code of ethics, as for any organizational artifact, does not stand in isolation but within an organizational environment influenced by and influencing internal and external members. Murphy (2005) suggested that, as products must be promoted to consumers and other stakeholders, corporate ethical statements must be shared. Between 1992 and 2003, Murphy (2005) found that the sharing of ethical statements, including value statements, corporate credos, codes of ethics, and Internet privacy policies, has increased with both internal and external audiences as opposed to sharing codes with only internal audiences.

Once an ethical problem has been identified, articulated, and shared with others, decision-making must follow. Normative models have been proposed to guide decision-making. Bush, Harris, and Bush (1997) based their model for decision-making on three criteria: 1) if the performance of the agency is consistent with the client's expectations of the agency; 2) if the morals of the agency parallel the moral character of the client; and 3) if ethical boundaries have been installed to help deal with consequences. This model for decision-making and determining the rightness of actions in the advertising function are responses to the problems that practitioners face. These problems will be reviewed in more detail below.

Ethical Problems in Advertising

The ethical problems in advertising are the same issues for which advertising is criticized. For example, a problem faced by practitioners is what it means to create honest advertising and how to create it. On the flip side, consumers criticize advertising for being misleading and deceptive. Advertising, the process and message, has been criticized for being one-sided, supporting a cause in accordance with the advertiser, seeking out the individual rather than the individual seeking advertising, affecting media content and scheduling, being rewarded for buying media space, and creating opportunities for differing interpretations (Christians, Rotzoll, & Fackler, 1991). In addition, audiences hold the advertising industry responsible for taking advantage of helpless consumers and for encouraging harmful behaviors (Kirkpatrick, 1994). As a result, advertising practitioners have been ranked by consumers just above car salesmen on the degree to which they are trusted (O'Toole, 1980; Steel, 1998; O'Barr, 2005).

For simplicity and best fit for an organizational approach, this section will review these issues as the problems faced in advertising by referring back to Drumwright and Murphy's (2009) message ethics and business ethics. Message ethics, Drumwright and Murphy (2009) proposed, has changed through the years based upon new technology and new communication platforms, such as mobile devices and social media websites. So while honesty and what makes for an honest message are still problems faced in creating advertising today, issues of privacy and transparency on the Internet, for example, create similar but new problems in placing advertising. Note that prominent advertising executives have insisted that they are not out to "get" people or intentionally mislead client or consumer audiences. Advertising executives are both professionals and consumers themselves. Leo Burnett, famous adman and founder of Leo Burnett Company in Chicago, said it best: "Anyone who thinks that people can be fooled or pushed around has an inaccurate and pretty low estimate of people—and he won't do very well in advertising" and "Regardless of the moral issue, dishonesty in advertising has proved very unprofitable" (Burnett, 2012).

Business ethics, as mentioned earlier, is concerned with what goes on in an advertising agency. These day-to-day procedural problems have not changed in type but in degree, in part due to 1) media holding companies taking over agencies and demanding a profit and 2) pressure to participate in corporate social responsibility, which includes recruiting and employing underrepresented segments and participating in pro bono work (Drumwright & Murphy, 2009). Social responsibility can be thought of as the concern for a wider public interest and common good, not merely self-interest, or profit (Baker & Martinson, 2001). And, as noted in message ethics, technology plays a role in business ethics as well. As technology advances and the advertising industry keeps pace, each new technology has the capability to transform society and, as a result, may have unintended consequences that need to be addressed ethically (Christians & Cooper, 2009). From an advertising agency's perspective, technology affects the cost of doing business as well as communication with the client.

Problems in advertising do not stand in isolation from one another, which means that business practices have an effect on the messages that are produced. Furthermore, business practices involve many people, who have an influence on the processes. An honest or dishonest message is produced by an agency, which is an agency of individuals working with a client, media organizations, and vendors to create the message; these individuals are working with other clients to maintain the success of the agency; and they are working within a marketplace or industry of other agencies, clients, media organizations, and vendors. When asked which ethical problems are most difficult, advertising practitioners reported treating clients fairly (28%), creating honest ads (24%), treating employees fairly (5%), and treating other agencies fairly (2%) (Hunt & Chonko, 1987).

Problems that are faced in advertising are influenced by a myriad of factors, including, but not limited to, ethics. When asked what influences decision-making, advertising practitioners first indicated legality (48%), then ethics (28%), and finally business matters (15%) or the consequences of the decision on the agency's or client's business (Davis, 1994). It is important to note that ethics is one factor of decision-making and is oftentimes used interchangeably with legality. However, advertising ethics should not be reduced to what is merely legal (Cunningham, 1999; Drumwright, 2007; Preston, 2010). If advertising ethics is reduced down to the problems that are faced or to what is merely legal, the complexity of the process is lost.

A New Approach for Advertising Ethics

Advertising ethics is a process situated within an organizational environment. As a result, advertising ethics affects and is affected by the organizational environment in which the process takes place. An organizational perspective acknowledges the various dimensions of advertising, including: 1) an industry made up of businesses and organizations with internal and external members; 2) the process of preparing paid announcements on behalf of an advertiser to share with an audience; and 3) the outcome of this process, which is a message executed as television commercials, radio spots, Internet banner ads, and billboards, to name a few. The new agenda focuses on the first two dimensions. In the following section, organizational culture is presented as a perspective for understanding the context of the process and the people involved, as well as for understanding the relationship that the organizational context has with ethical decision-making.

Advertising Ethics in Context

A new agenda for advertising ethics research acknowledges ethics as a process situated within an organizational context. While there are many organizations that contribute to the advertising industry, an advertising agency has primarily provided the services of planning for and creating advertisements. Therefore, an advertising agency is an ideal, although not the only, site for an organizational approach to advertising ethics. The first advertising agency started in the early 1840s (Applegate, 2008; Burt, 1940; Holland, 1976; McDonald & Scott, 2007; Vos, 2010). Advertising agencies first served as liaisons between media companies and advertisers by offering discounted rates on media space and time and later provided expertise on how to do advertising by incorporating a consumer's perspective. This transition led to the full-service advertising agency, which is "an organization of professionals who provide a creative and business service to clients related to planning, preparing and placing advertisements" (O'Guinn, Allen,& Semenik, 1998, p. 39; 2009, p. 55).

Organizational culture tells us several things about the environment where the preparation of paid announcements takes place. First, organizational culture tells us what it means to be an organization or to engage in the act of organizing. Second, organizational culture tells us who is involved in and who influences these acts of organizing. Third, organizational culture gets below the surface to expose a deeper meaning behind acts of organizing, which includes shared perceptions, values, and assumptions.

An organization is "a dynamic system of organizational members, influenced by external stakeholders, who communicate within and across organizational structures in a purposeful and ordered way to achieve a superordinate goal" (Keyton, 2005, p. 10). A superordinate goal is something so time-consuming and so complex that no one person can achieve it on his or her own (Keyton, 2005). The superordinate goal of an advertising agency is preparing paid advertisements for distribution to an audience on behalf of an advertiser. Drumwright and Murphy (2009) proposed that the advertising industry and the organizations that comprise the industry are in the midst of radical transformation to organizational, geographical, and technological aspects. For example, advertisers expect advertising agencies to keep pace with product innovations and technological advancements. And agencies expect new members to keep pace with innovations by acknowledging that graduates of advertising programs without digital knowledge are "deal breakers" as potential employees (Book et al., 2012). Advertising agencies are merging, moving headquarters overseas, and being bought out by large conglomerates (Thorson & Duffy, 2011). Some agencies collaborate with one another as opposed to compete for business (Keeley, 2011), while other agencies compete with clients by developing and marketing their own products (Boon, 2011). As the industry evolves and advertising services change, it will be important to acknowledge how the superordinate goal changes as well.

Organizational culture also tells us who is involved in the purposeful and ordered actions of the preparation of paid announcements. These people are internal and external to the advertising agency and make up the advertising industry by working for advertisers, advertising agencies, media companies, suppliers and vendors, and even universities. Those internal to an advertising agency provide creative services, including copywriting, graphic design, layout, and art direction; strategic services, including strategic planning and research; media services, including media planning and media buying; and account management services (Shimp, 2010). Advertisers, or the clients of the advertising industry, are businesses and organizations with a product or service to sell and/or information to share. Media companies include newspapers, televisions stations, radio stations, outdoor/billboard companies, and Internet companies, which sell the space and the time for advertisements to run. And suppliers and vendors include printers, paper suppliers, and photographers, to name a few, who assist advertising agencies, advertisers, and media companies with specialized products and services. Universities are included within the advertising industry because of their involvement in recruiting and training the practitioners of tomorrow. Once accepted and enrolled into the program, students of journalism, advertising, public relations, mass communications, strategic communications, business, marketing, etc. become the new advertisers, agency account executives, and media producers of tomorrow. It is important to note that Keyton (2005) acknowledges the influence external members have on acts of organizing. Organizations, interrelated within any industry, draw on one another for resources to accomplish goals (Putnam & Nicotera, 2009). Advertising agencies work with advertisers, who serve as both clients and partners, and with media companies and other service providers to plan for, develop, and place paid announcements. And while external to an advertising agency, these members help with the development of paid advertisements and, therefore, have an influence on the purposeful and ordered actions of an organization.

The members of an organization are those that share a cultural perspective. Schein (1990) defines culture as the shared basic assumptions that a group of people has learned as a result of solving their problems, which is influenced by external and internal pressures. These assumptions have worked well enough and, therefore, are considered valid and taught to new members of the group as the correct way to think and feel in relation to solving those problems. Therefore, organizational culture, which describes social action, depends upon the meaning it has for those involved (Alvesson, 2002). Culture gives organizational members a frame of reference through shared beliefs, values, and expressive symbols (Alvesson, 2002). Organizational culture allows members to make sense of their environment and experiences and to share their experiences, feelings, and thoughts with one another (Gabriel, 2000).

Socialization is the process for teaching new members of a group and is what Gabriel (1999) describes as the connection between the individual and an organization. New members of an advertising agency, for example, are taught a philosophy of advertising and, as a result, the correct way to solve clients' advertising problems. This process begins with the leaders of an agency.

Culture is passed down from leadership (Schein, 1990, 2010). The founder of an advertising agency is the first member of the organization and, therefore, the first person challenged with solving the organization's problems as well as the first person to teach new members how to solve problems. If a copywriter is taught by his/her creative director that advertising is meant to be two-way, interactive communication, then the copywriter begins to learn that consumer research is an approach step in the advertising process. In another agency where the copywriter is taught that creativity is king, s/he may develop ads without the consumer in mind.

Acknowledging the shared perceptions of how advertising work is done and how problems are solved does not also assume consensus among organizational members. Keyton (2005) argues that there are both consensual and divided views that constitute organizational culture. Keyton (2005) further acknowledges that organizations are dynamic, and culture is both process and product. Acknowledging culture as dynamic and a process acknowledges the opportunity for divergence and change. Change may include significant departures from existing practices or subtle variations and changes in new ways of doing things. So, while the leader of an advertising agency held religious values that influenced his agency's philosophy of advertising toward creating socially responsible messages, not all employees agreed with this philosophy (Krueger, 1999). Within this agency, there was a divided view on using advertising as a forum to create a society that embodies human values versus a means to sell products on behalf of a client. While leadership may be the first creators of culture, employees socialized into this culture are active participants capable of influencing change (Kunda, 1992).

An organizational environment has a dialectical relationship with its members. Structuration theory provides a perspective for understanding this dynamic relationship, which states that, as organizational members, we create our environment, and our environment recreates us (Giddens, 1984). Processes, including ways of acting and talking, are part of our organizational environment. Therefore, we could extend the theory of structuration to assume that the processes of ethical decision-making are influenced by and influence the organizational environment. Hackley (1999) argues that ethical discourse has performance character, meaning that what people say within a social group reinforces the norms of that group, which might include relations of power, ideology, and selfhood. In Giddens' terms (1984), organizational actors, with agency to act, are both enabled and constrained by their environment and, through action, create and recreate their environment.

Extending this idea into advertising ethics, an organizational environment would have enabling and constraining features on ethical awareness and decision-making, and through acts of decision-making, ethics would create and recreate the organizational environment. This proposition lends itself to research questions for extending advertising ethics. From this proposition, we would want to know the following:

1. What is the organizational culture of an advertising agency?
2. If the organizational environment both enables and constrains ethical awareness, what are the enabling features of the organizational culture that allow members to perceive a problem for its ethical dimensions?

3. What are the constraining features of the organizational culture?
4. How does the ethical decision-making process recreate the organizational environment, if at all?

Organizational Communication

Articulation is an important step in the advertising ethics process as well as for understanding organizational culture. Keyton (2005) suggested that members of an organization are more likely to behave in accordance with organizational values when those values are known. Similarly, Drumwright and Murphy (2004) found that individuals who discussed ethical issues were part of an agency culture that encouraged "moral seeing and talking" (p. 15). This culture was expressed through widely held norms on ethical behavior and the clear articulation of these norms among agency members. Articulation is a social process. As noted earlier, Habermas's (1984) theory of communicative action presents the idea that an ethic should maximize the participation of all competing voices into a dialogue. Furthermore, all utterances of speech contain claims of truth, rightness, and sincerity, which, as part of a social process, are then judged by recipients for these elements. Advertising practitioners judge not only their own ethical standards but those of their colleagues and clients. When comparing these perceptions among advertising executives, Krugman and Ferrell (1981) found that participants regarded their ethical standards as higher than those of their peers.

Individuals act and speak with intention when they come together into dialogue. Communication, situated within a cultural context, shapes our understanding or meaning of the world (Habermas, 1984). In advertising, how we talk about the problems that are faced shapes our understanding of these problems. Therefore, understanding communication situated within this environment is important to understanding the process of advertising ethics.

Rhetoric is the theory that elements of language are purposeful and symbols shared in an attempt to generate a desired response from another or many others (Foss, 1996). Sharing values and assumptions of how an advertising agency works, how an agency should work, and the role of ethics therein are intentional communicative acts. Communication among members of an organization is a process that, overtime and through patterning, constitutes the structure of the organization (Boden, 1994). Recognizing that communication creates structure, Taylor (1993) argued that it is important to study organizations from a communications perspective. Rhetorical theory provides this perspective.

The theory of rhetoric suggests that language can be both action and object. As action, rhetoric is the creation and application of symbols to communicate with one another and to generate an intended response from another (Foss, 1996). Rosen (1985) observed the communication and symbols advertising practitioners used at an annual breakfast to convey culture and how these actions were used as mechanisms for control. Symbols at the event included food served, attire worn, speeches given, and awards presented, and were used for the manipulation and reproduction of bureaucratic forms (Rosen, 1985). Similarly, Brock, Scott, and Chesebro defined rhetoric as "the human effort to induce cooperation through the use of symbols" (1990, p. 14). Rhetoric works to create and shape perspectives that are shared for both cooperation and competition as well as to inform and enact choices (Heath, 2009). Furthermore, "the role of rhetoric enters where there is difference of opinion, doubt, uncertainty, and even firmly held opinions which may be wrong" (Heath, 2009, p. 22). If there were no differences in opinion and no need for negotiating meaning, there would be no need for rhetoric (Heath, 2009).

Rhetoric is considered instrumental and serves a purpose (Brock, Scott, & Chesebro, 1990), which influences social meaning. A rhetorical object that is produced serves a function in facilitating knowledge development, whether intended or unintended. A rhetorical object cannot exist, however, without an agent performing and receiving action. The function of rhetoric cannot exist without agency on both ends, because "all outcomes must be interpreted as they are produced" (Durham, 2005, p. 32).

Extending rhetoric into the advertising ethics process acknowledges that symbols are used to create a perception for ethical awareness, symbols that are both performed and interpreted. The theory of rhetoric is an important contribution to a new agenda for advertising ethics and complements the theory of structuration, which acknowledges an agent's agency to act. To explore rhetoric in advertising ethics and the agent's use of symbols, we would ask the following research questions:

1. What is the meaning of advertising ethics to organizational members?
2. To better understand the process of articulation, what symbols are used to express the meaning of ethics?
3. How do these symbols create a shared meaning versus divided views?
4. What are the consequences of using these symbols as part of the advertising ethics process?

An Organizational Approach to Research

The culture of one organization, and specifically of an advertising agency, is unique from any other. Comprised by its members, an agency's culture defines the values, ethical principles, and norms of behavior (both stated and unstated) that are expected of its employees (Jones, 1999). It should be acknowledged that the findings of a context-dependent study are not generalizable. However, with research findings accumulated over time and across organizations, patterns should begin to emerge. One of these patterns may be the process of ethical decision-making and the relationship this process has with its organizational context.

Previous research on advertising ethics has asked what are the biggest problems faced in advertising or the problems faced most often. A new approach to advertising ethics mandates a new approach for research conducted in context. An organizational approach to studying advertising ethics seeks to understand these problems as situated within an organizational environment influenced by culture and communication.

An organizational approach to advertising ethics research is less concerned with problems (at least in isolation) and more concerned with the context in which the problems arise and the relationship between the two. Research questions, as noted earlier, shift the focus onto the organization, organizational members, organizational culture, and organizational communication. The researcher becomes concerned with the environment or context where advertising work is done by asking questions such as: 1) What is it like to work for the advertising agency? 2) What are the shared values and assumptions of how work is done? 3) What is the consensus view, and what are the divided views on values and assumptions of how work is done and how problems are solved? and 4) How do shared values and assumptions pervade and pattern the work that is done?

If organizational culture depends upon the meaning it has for those involved (Alvesson, 2002), then the researcher must become involved in this action. The methodology of participant observation, or organizational ethnography, is the foundation for such an approach by placing the researcher in an organizational environment to experience, first hand, the purposeful and ordered actions of preparing paid announcements. Organizational ethnography is an involved and time-consuming method, making it a rigorous method and one appropriate for an in-depth study of culture.

Method of Participant Observation

There are five implications for participant observation as indicated by Bruyn (1963), making it an ideal organizational approach to studying the process of advertising ethics. First, the participant observer shares in activities and sentiments of advertising practitioners. Second, the participant observer is both involved in and detached from these experiences to garner an insider's and outsider's perspective. Third, the researcher's role in the setting is determined by the requirements of research and fit with the culture. Fourth, the researcher's methods and theoretical perspectives are interdependent with the culture. And fifth, the social role of the researcher is a natural part of the culture of the observed because a researcher is human first and researcher second.

Acknowledging the social role of participant observation is referred to as reflexivity in ethnographic fieldwork. Reflexivity recognizes the researcher as part of the social events and processes that are not only those observed but those narrated by the researcher through his or her involvement (Atkinson & Coffey, 2002). Reflexivity balances the insider's and outsider's perspective of participant observation (Bruyn, 1966). A participant observer is both participant (insider) and observer (outsider), who is influenced by and influences his/her social environment. To overemphasize one's position as researcher to change things swells one's importance, while to deny one's being there construes the properties of the method (Atkinson & Coffey, 2002). It is, therefore, important to acknowledge reflexivity as the balance of involvement and influence with detachment and observation. Within this balance, the researcher should acknowledge and record his/her own personal thoughts, reactions, and feelings while conducting fieldwork.

There are four elements contributing to the written ethnography (i.e., the outcome of fieldwork, participation, and observation), which include:

> 1) the assumed relationship between culture and behavior (the observed), 2) the experiences of the fieldworker (the observer), 3) the representational style selected to join the observer and the observed (the tale), and 4) the role of the reader engaged in the active reconstruction of the tale (the audience).
>
> (Van Maanen, 1988, p. xi)

The task of the researcher is to describe and analyze the world from the perspective of those involved in the organization's goal-oriented activities (Rosen, 1991). Therefore, the outcome of ethnography is a representation of the social reality of others in an ethnographic tale (Van Maanen, 1988). Van Maanen (1988), Emerson, Fretz, and Shaw (1995), Goodall (2000), and Yanow (2009) acknowledge the active role of writing in this social construction of reality. Writing is considered active because, as the researcher writes, within and upon leaving the field, s/he is still analyzing, interpreting, and developing findings (Emerson et al., 1995). Therefore, active writing should not be separated from the involvement or participation and time spent in the field (Yanow, 2009).

Implications for Education

Ethnographic tales written on advertising ethics, which develop knowledge beyond the micro-level of problems, will advance advertising education. Proposed here are three ways in which an organizational approach will advance advertising education. First, an organizational approach brings real-word, industry examples into the classroom. Second, these examples produced from time spent in the field can emphasize the positive. And third, an organizational approach paints a broader picture of advertising as one element in a larger society.

Providing up-to-date insights on what goes on in advertising, on the operations of an agency, and on who works there are essential to informing advertising students who may not have opportunities to work in the industry before graduation day. Stuhlfaut and Farrell (2009) argued that the main courses of advertising education are about the management, creation, and implementation of strategic communication, while legal, ethical, and societal topics are viewed as supplementary. A new approach to studying advertising ethics and the knowledge gained from this approach will integrate ethical issues into advertising educational content, thus elevating the importance of ethics. An organizational approach places advertising ethical issues into the curriculum of management, planning, creation, and implementation of advertising.

This new organizational approach, due to the depth of study, provides case studies. Oftentimes, case studies in media ethics showcase real-life or propose hypothetical dilemmas that reflect the negative outcomes of decision-making, including acts of dishonesty, abuse of consumer privacy, or the use of stereotypes, to name a few examples. Case studies in advertising ethics should include scenarios of decision-making, resulting in positive outcomes. Case studies are organizational stories that can pass along organizational culture, act as repositories of ideas, and generate emotion (Gabriel, 2000). Therefore, through story-telling, positive stories can be shared, thus setting examples and expectations for morally aware practices in advertising. While Gabriel (2000) argued that many stories focus on the positive, in advertising ethics literature, specifically, positive examples showcasing the morality of a decision are often lacking. An organizational approach can build a repository of positive stories to share.

Advertising students of today are the practitioners of tomorrow. Therefore, awareness of ethical problems, as the first step in the advertising ethics process, and of the environment in which these problems arise starts in the classroom. The new approach to studying advertising ethics informs students, then, not only of what the ethical problems are but also of what the contextual factors for facing these problems may be. Students should begin to understand their role as an individual member contributing to and being affected by an organizational context in which they soon will be employed. Students should understand that an advertising executive is an individual with a personal set of values and beliefs as well as an organizational member operating within an organization characterized by a unique set of values and beliefs, which might be oppositional to his/her personal beliefs. Understanding this individual role situated within a larger context can prepare students for the organizational and ethical challenges that they will face, as well as provide them with an understanding of the enabling and constraining features of that environment. Through this awareness, advertising students may begin to see the bigger picture of advertising and of their role in the planning and creation of advertising, something that often comes only after many years of working experience.

Challenges of an Organizational Approach

A new approach to advertising ethics, and the required research methods, does not come without challenges. For example, challenges of participant observation include those related to reflexivity, as well as to granting confidentiality, narrowing the research focus, and capturing events and behaviors. Challenges will also arise due to issues of accessibility into an organizational environment and issues of accessibility into the processes of advertising within that environment.

A challenge true to all participant observation is the ability to capture events and conversations happening within a new environment, such as an advertising agency, as well as capturing the role and influence of the researcher within that environment. Reflexivity, as presented by Atkinson and Coffey (2002), is the means to acknowledge the methods and role of the researcher within a new social environment as influential, without overstating or minimizing that role.[1] Instead of trying to eliminate the effects of the researcher (his contamination, if you will), the researcher should try to understand this influence (Hammersley & Atkinson, 1983). Copious fieldnotes combat this challenge. Field notes should capture what is observed, e.g., events such as meetings, the people involved, behavior, attire, body language, what is said, dialogue, and reactions between the people involved; what is personally felt, e.g., the researcher's reaction to, thoughts, feelings, and comments during these events; and the perceived relationship between what is observed and what is felt.

Challenges of accessibility begin prior to fieldwork. Entering into an agency will prove challenging due to the nature of the business. An advertising agency is a multifaceted and complicated organization. An advertising agency employs many practitioners and works with a multitude of clients and service providers. The nature of the business, as a service provider to other businesses, makes the organization and the work quite sensitive. It is, therefore, important not only to promise confidentiality, but also to stress the topics, events, people, and other personally identifiable information that will be protected. A researcher may be asked and should be willing to sign the agency's non-disclosure agreement (NDA). An NDA is a standard agency document that a new employee signs but that also applies to the researcher. Terms may include what cannot be disclosed, such as trade secrets and confidential information, and non-compete clauses, which means that the employee/researcher will not recruit from the agency any business, clients, or employees of the agency. In addition, the researcher should inform the agency of the possible published materials, such as journal articles, book chapters, dissertations, etc.; promise confidentiality therein for the agency, agency employees, clients, and service partners; and promise confidentiality for any other potentially sensitive information, such as financial data, number of employees, geographic location, etc.

In return for the time spent within an advertising agency, the researcher may want to offer an incentive, which will help alleviate the challenge of accessibility. Options include consultation. Perhaps the agency is experiencing an organizational challenge that the researcher can diagnose and for which they can offer recommendations. Another option may be providing research services to the agency and their respective clients. While some agencies have their own researchers and account planners, and some of their clients have the same, other smaller agencies may not. It should be noted that offering to work for the agency while conducting research places the researcher in a position of participant first, observer second. This option comes with its own set of challenges and opportunities. And finally, the researcher may offer to produce a report, personalized for the agency, on organizational culture.

Upon entering the field, determining what to observe and gaining access to these events will present a new set of challenges. Determining what to observe will be guided, in part, by research questions and the theoretical perspective of the investigator. However, what an ethnographer sets out to study is oftentimes challenged by and, as a result, changed due to time spent in the field. Therefore, a researcher may indeed benefit from developing a focus during the proposal and early stages of participant observation. Also, gaining access into specific events, meetings, conversations, etc. may not be granted. This should not be seen as a limitation, but as another data point. According to Hammersley and Atkinson (1983), access problems can turn into data. Furthermore, access is not merely physical or geographic, but it also involves access into a person's beliefs, thoughts, etc. Whether the research focus changes over time or issues of access arise, the researcher should be open to the dynamic nature of the field and willing to learn from the opportunities and challenges that arise.

Conclusion

A new approach to advertising ethics is proposed. The new approach takes an organizational perspective by acknowledging the context where problems arise. Organizational culture provides a deeper understanding of the advertising agency, comprised by shared values, beliefs, and assumptions. This culture is determined, in part, by the problems that are faced and resulting solutions to those problems. Therefore, it is important to acknowledge the dynamic relationship that advertising ethics, as a process of awareness and decision-making, has in shaping organizational values and, reciprocally, the influence that organizational culture has on advertising ethics.

Note

1 As I sit in the field as a participant observer for a current study and while typing this very sentence, two agency employees walk past sharing a joke. At first, I hear the conversation going on in the background. One took the other's pen, and the first employee, upon returning the pen, stated, "Here's your f'n pen back. You get an f-bomb." The reply from the second employee was, "F-bombs are part of our culture." "No, they're not," the first employee replied, while pointing at me indicating that that comment does not go in my study as an accurate representation of their culture. This is just one of many examples that my presence, as a participant observer, is acknowledged by agency members and that awareness for why I am here at the agency (i.e., to study culture) is articulated.

References

Alvesson, M. (2002). Understanding Organizational Culture. *Thousand Oaks Sage*.

Applegate, E. (2008). The development of advertising, 1700–1900. In W. D. Sloan (Ed.), *The Media in America: A History* (7th ed., pp. 267–286). Northport, AL: Vision Press.

Aristotle. (1998). *Nicomachean Ethics* (D. P. Chase, Trans. Dover Thrifted.). Toronto: General Publishing Company.

Atkinson, P., & Coffey, A. (2002). Revisiting the relationship between participant observation and interviewing. In J. F. Gubrium & J. A. Holstein (Eds.), *Handbook of Interview Research*. Thousand Oaks: Sage.

Baker, S. (2008). The model of the principled advocate and the pathological partisan: A virtue ethics construct of opposing archetypes of public relations and advertising practitioners. *Journal of Mass Media Ethics*, 23, 235–253.

Baker, S., & Martinson, D. (2001). The TARES test: Five principles of ethical persuasion. *Journal of Mass Media Ethics*, 16 (2&3), 148–175.

Boden, D. (1994). *The Business of Talk: Organizations in Action*. Cambridge, U.K.: Polity Press.

Bok, S. (1983). *Secrets: On the Ethics of Concealment and Revelation*. New York: Vintage.

Book, B., Dycus, P., Kell, J., Kilcullen, C., Leahy, J., & Stevens, J. (2012, February 14). [Creative Panel Discussion, Ad Club St. Louis].

Boon, W. (2011). Amsterdam agencies become their own clients by bringing products to market. June 12. Retrieved from www.advertisingage.com

Brock, B. L., Scott, R. L., & Chesebro, J. W. (1990). *Methods of Rhetorical Criticism: A Twentieth-Century Perspective* (3rd ed.): Wayne State University Press.

Bruyn, S. T. (1963). The methodology of participant observation. *Human Organization*, 22 224–235.

Bruyn, S. T. (1966). *The Human Perspective in Sociology: The Methodology of Participant Observation*. Englewood Cliffs, New Jersey: Prentice-Hall, Inc.

Burnett, L. (2012) Retrieved 2/7/2012 from http://www.brainyquote.com/quotes/authors/l/leo_burnett.html

Burt, F. A. (1940). *American Advertising Agencies, an Inquiry into their Origin, Growth, Functions and Future*. New York: Harper & Brothers.

Bush, V., Harris, S., & Bush, A. (1997). Establishing ethical boundaries for service providers: A narrative approach. *The Journal of Services Marketing*, 11 (4 SRC—GoogleScholar), 265–277.

Carlson, D., Perrewe, S., & Pamela, L. (1995). Institutionalization of organizational ethics through transformational leadership. *Journal of Business Ethics*, 14 (10), 829–838.

Carroll, A. B. (1987). In search of a moral manager. *Business Horizons*, 7–25.

Christians, C. G., & Cooper, T. W. (2009). The search for universals. In L. Wilkins & C. G. Christians (Eds.), *The Handbook of Mass Media Ethics*. New York: Routledge.

Christians, C. G., Rotzoll, K. B., & Fackler, M. (1991). Media ethics: Cases and moral reasoning (3rd ed., New York: Longman, Chapter 7, Advertising (Vol. 8 SRC—GoogleScholar, pp. 199–242).

Cunningham, P. H. (1999). Ethics of advertising: Oxymoron or good business practice? In J. P. Jones (Ed.), *The Advertising Business*. Thousand Oaks, CA: Sage.

Davis, J. J. (1994). Ethics in advertising decision making: Implications for reducing incidence of deceptive advertising. *Journal of Consumer Affairs* 28 (2 SRC—GoogleScholar), 380–403.

Drumwright, M. E. (2007). Advertising ethics: A multi-level theory approach. In G. J. Tellis & T. Ambler (Eds.), *The Sage Handbook of Advertising*. London: Sage.

Drumwright, M. E., & Murphy, P. E. (2004). How advertising practitioners view ethics: Moral muteness, moral myopia, and moral imagination. *Journal of Advertising*, 33 (2), 7–24.

Drumwright, M. E., & Murphy, P. E. (2009). The current state of advertising ethics: Industry and academic perspectives. *Journal of Advertising*, 38 (1 SRC—GoogleScholar), 83–107.

Durham, F. (2005). Public relations as structuration: A prescriptive critique of the StarLink Global food contamination case. *Journal of Public Relations Research* 17 (1 SRC—GoogleScholar), 29–47.

Emerson, R. M., Fretz, R. I., & Shaw, L. L. (1995). *Writing Ethnographic Fieldnotes*. Chicago, IL: The University of Chicago Press.

Foss, S. K. (1996). *Rhetorical Criticism: Exploration & Practice* (2nd ed.). Prospect Heights, IL: Waveland Press, Inc.

Gabriel, Y. (1999). Organizations in Depth: The Psychoanalysis of Culture (pp. 191–210). London: Sage.

Gabriel, Y. (2000). *Storytelling in Organizations: Facts, Fictions, and Fantasies.* Oxford; New York: Oxford University Press.

Giddens, A. (1984). *The Constitution of Society: Outline of the Theory of Structuration.* Berkeley, CA: University of California Press.

Goodall, H. L. (2000). *Writing the New Ethnography.* Lanham, Maryland: Rowman & Littlefield Publishers, Inc.

Habermas, J. (1984). *The Theory of Communicative Action* (Vol. 1: Reason and the rationalization of society (T. McCarthy, Trans.)). Boston: Beacon Press.

Hackley, C. E. (1999). The meanings of ethics in and of advertising. *Business Ethics: A European Review*, 8 (1), 37–42.

Hammersley, M., & Atkinson, P. (1983). *Ethnography, Principles in Practice.* London: Tavistock.

Heath, R. L. (2009). The rhetorical tradition: Wrangle in the marketplace. In R. L. Heath, E. L. Toth & D. Waymer (Eds.), *Rhetorical and Critical Approaches to Public Relations II*. New York Routledge.

Hill, T. E. (2006). Kantian normative ethics. In D. Copp (Ed.), *The Oxford Handbook of Ethical Theory*. New York: Oxford University Press.

Holland, D. R. (1976). Volney B. Palmer (1799–1864): The nation's first advertising agency man. *Journalism Monographs*, 44, 1–40.

Hunt, S. D., & Chonko, L. B. (1987). Ethical problems of advertising agency executives. *Journal of Advertising*, 16 (4 SRC—GoogleScholar), 16–24.

Jones, J. P. (1999). The culture of an advertising agency. In J. P. Jones (Ed.), *The Advertising Business*. Thousand Oaks, CA: Sage.

Keeley, E. (2011). How to ensure you're getting the most out of collaboration. *Advertising Age*, 82 (20), 28.

Keyton, J. (2005). *Communication & Organizational Culture: A to Understanding Work Experiences.* Thousand Oaks, C.A.: Sage.

Kirkpatrick, J. (1994). *In Defense of Advertising: Arguments from Reason, Ethical Egoism, and Laissez-faire Capitalism.* Westport, CT: Quorum Books.

Krueger, D. (1999). Ethics and values in advertising: Two case studies. *Business and Society Review*, 99 (SRC—GoogleScholar), 53–65.

Krugman, D. M., & Ferrell, O. C. (1981). The organizational ethics of advertising: Corporate and agency views. *Journal of Advertising*, 10, 21.

Kunda, G. (1992). *Engineering Culture: Control and Commitment in a High-Tech Corporation.* Philadelphia: Temple University Press.

McDonald, & Scott. (2007). A history of advertising. In G. J. Tellis & T. Ambler (Eds.), *The Sage Handbook of Advertising*. London: Sage.

Murphy, P. E. (2005). Developing, communicating and promoting corporate ethics statements: A longitudinal analysis. *Journal of Business Ethics*, 62 (2), 183–189.

Nwachukwu, S. L. S., & Vitell, S. J. J. (1997). The influence of corporate culture on managerial ethical judgments. *Journal of Business Ethics*, 16, 757–776.

O'Barr, W. M. (2005). The advertising profession in the public's eye. *Advertising & Society Review*. Retrieved from

O'Guinn, T., Allen, C., & Semenik, R. (1998). *Advertising.*Cincinnati, Ohio: South-Western College Publishing.

O'Guinn, T., Allen, C., & Semenik, R. (2009). *Advertising and Integrated Brand Promotion* (5th ed.). Mason, Ohio: South-Western Cengage Learning.

O'Toole, J. (1980). *The Trouble with Advertising: A View from the Inside* (2nd ed.). New York: Times Books.

Patterson, P., & Wilkins, L. (2008). *Media Ethics: Issues and Cases* (6th ed.). Boston: McGraw Hill.

Preston, I. L. (2010). Interaction of law and ethics in matters of advertiser' responsibility for protecting consumers. *The Journal of Consumer Affairs*, 44 (1), 259–264.

Putnam, L. L., & Nicotera, A. M. (2009). *Building Theories of Organization: The Constitutive Role of Communication*. New York Routledge.

Rosen, M. (1985). Breakfast at Spiro's: Dramaturgy and dominance. *Journal of Management*, 11 (2 SRC—GoogleScholar), 31–48.

Rosen, M. (1991). Coming to terms with the field: Understanding and doing organizational ethnography. *Journal of Management Studies*, 28 (10), 1–24.

Schein, E. H. (1990). Organizational culture. *American Psychologist* 45 (2 SRC—GoogleScholar), 109–119.

Schein, E. H. (2010). *Organizational Culture and Leadership* (4th ed.). San Francisco, CA: Jossey-Bass.

Shafer-Landau, R. (2010). *The Fundamentals of Ethics*. New York: Oxford University Press.

Shaw, W., & Barry, V. (1995). *Moral Issues of Business* (6 ed.). Belmond, CA: Wadsworth, Inc.

Shimp, T. A. (2010). *Advertising, Promotion, and Other Aspects of Integrated Marketing Communications*. Mason, OH: South-Western Cengage Learning.

Singhapakdi, A., & Vitell, S. J. (1990). Marketing ethics: Factors influencing perceptions of ethical problems and alternatives. *Journal of Macromarketing*, 12, 4–18.

Standards of Practice of the 4A's. (1924, June 7, 2011) Retrieved July 24, 2012, from http://www.aaaa.org/about/association/Documents/AA110.pdf

Steel, J. (1998). *Truth, Lies & Advertising: The Art of Account Planning*. New York: John Wiley & Sons, Inc.

Stuhlfaut, M. W., & Farrell, M. (2009). Pedagogic cacophony: The teaching of ethical, legal, and societal issues in advertising education. *Journalism & Mass Communication Educator*, 64 (2), 173–190.

Taylor, J. R. (1993). *Rethinking the Theory of Organizational Communication: How to Read an Organization*. Norwood, NY: Ablex.

Thorson, E., & Duffy, M. (2011). *Advertising Age: The Principles of Marketing Communication at Work*. Mason, OH: South-Western Cengage.

Van Maanen, J. (1988). *Tales of the Field: On Writing Ethnography*. Chicago: The University of Chicago Press.

Vos, T. P. (2010). *Explaining the Origins of the Advertising Agency*. Paper presented at the Association for Education in Journalism and Mass Communication (AEJMC), History Division, Denver, CO.

Wilcox, D. L., Cameron, G. T., Reber, B. H., & Shin, J. (2011). *Think Public Relations*. Boston: Allyn & Bacon.

Yanow, D. (2009). Organizational ethnography and methodological angst: Myths and challenges in the field. *Qualitative Research in Organizations and Management An International Journal*, 4 (2), 186–199.

Chapter 8

Clarifying, Confusing, or Crooked?

How Ethically Minded Consumers Interpret Green Advertising Claims

Lucy Atkinson

For today's ethically minded consumer, everyday consumption choices can be fraught with anxieties and misgivings. Take the morning cup of coffee, for example. Is it made with beans that are shade grown? Is the sugar fair trade? Is the cream organic? Is the travel mug BPA-free? Contemporary consumer culture is increasingly inflected with ethical concerns, and for the average consumer, it can be a complicated path to navigate.

On the one hand, consumers face a growing number of ethical purchase options. Between 2009 and 2010, the number of "greener" products, or products claiming to be environmentally friendly, increased by 73% (TerraChoice, 2011). The global market for organic food has more than doubled since 2002 to $27 billion in 2010, with the U.S. market accounting for almost half that total (Bouckley, 2012; Hunt & Dorfman, 2009). On the other hand, not all of these ethical products are created equal. Store shelves are stocked with products that claim to be ethical—be they "all natural" or "green"—but are actually not much different from conventional products. Sometimes this misinformation is willful, as in greenwashing or deceptive advertising that paints a conventional product as environmentally friendly when in reality it falls short of established guidelines. Other times, this misinformation can be accidental, as was the case with Whole Foods Market, which felt the wrath of dissatisfied consumers when news reports revealed that food grown in China and labeled organic might not have met the standards for certification (Neuman & Barboza, 2010). Consumer backlash quickly prompted the self-billed "natural and organic" grocery store to alter its sourcing policies and reduce the number of products it carries from China.

Whether intentional or inadvertent, this marketing misinformation combined with a staggering number of ethical product options helps partly explain why many would-be ethical consumers are unwilling or unable to act. Indeed, one of the biggest issues in the area of ethical consumption is the sizable gap that exists between consumer intentions and consumer behaviors. Called the attitude–behavior gap or word–deed gap, this disconnect describes the all-too-common situation in which self-described conscientious or ethical consumers claim they are willing to choose and pay more for ethical products over conventional ones, but fail to follow through with these intentions at the cash register (Bonini, Hintz, & Mendonca, 2008; Kalafatis & Pollard, 1999; Peattie, 2010).

This chapter offers a partial explanation for this gap. In contrast to most research exploring the attitude–behavior gap, I focus on the way consumers interpret and derive meaning from green advertising claims. This is in contrast to the majority of scholarly work looking into this attitude–behavior gap, which focuses on identifying the typical ethical consumer and those antecedent attitudes, values, and behaviors that will best predict ethical product purchase (for example: Anderson & Cunningham, 1972; Prothero, 1990; Schlegelmilch, Bohlen, & Diamantopoulos, 1996; Shrum, McCarty, & Lowrey, 1995). Instead, I focus on the ethical frameworks consumers use as they contemplate their morally infused consumption choices and the complicated and multifaceted ways in which they read and understand green advertising messages. This contributes to much-needed research in the ways advertising influences ethical consumption (Iyer & Banerjee, 1993; Kilbourne, 1995; Manrai, Manrai, Lascu, & Ryans, 1997; Obermiller, 1995).

Specifically, this chapter explores how ethically minded consumers understand and interpret green advertising claims. Based on focus group interviews with 21 self-identified, ethical consumers, the data suggest consumers draw complex interpretations of green advertising claims, including those that could be classified as misleading or "greenwashing." Rather than viewing green claims as deceptive or self-serving, consumers frame them in much more nuanced ways, balancing the realities of a disengaged mass consumer culture with the idealistic and lofty goals of environmentally friendly consumption. This ambivalence helps explain the well-documented attitude–behavior gap among ethically minded consumers who claim to be motivated by pro-social concerns, such as the environment, but fail to follow through with these concerns in their actual purchases.

This chapter is organized as follows. It begins with a discussion of ethical consumption and ethical consumers. This first section outlines what constitutes ethical consumption, how ethical consumers are defined, and the different ethical approaches that have been used to explain ethical consumption. The second section considers the marketing side of ethical consumption. It explores how consumers understand corporate ethics, especially as it relates to advertising. Special attention is given to the problem of green advertising or potentially deceptive advertising about ethical products. The third section offers a case study of a particular green advertisement that could easily be classified as greenwashing or misleading. It first describes how consumers make sense of green advertising in general, then, drawing on focus group data, it details how consumers interpret a particular problematic advertisement for bottled water. The chapter ends with a discussion of managerial implications and directions for future research.

Ethical Consumption and Ethical Consumers

After more than three decades of research, ethical consumption and green advertising represent a well-established field of inquiry (for example: Henion & Wilson, 1976; Kilbourne, 1998; Kilbourne & Beckmann, 1998; Kinnear, Taylor, & Ahmed, 1974; Obermiller, 1995; Peattie, 2010; Schuhwerk & Lefkoff-Hagius, 1995; Shrum et al., 1995; Tanner & Kast, 2003), yet there remain a number of undertheorized issues (Crane, 2000; McEachern, 2008). In particular, not enough is known about how consumers interpret and process green advertising (Iyer & Banerjee, 1993) and how consumers perceive the ethical behavior of corporations (Brunk, 2010).

As a category, the term ethical consumer[1] denotes a broad collection of consumption orientations, assumes multiple forms, and encompasses a variety of consumer practices, including fair-trade purchasing, community-supported agriculture, and ethical investing. It can be informed by a number of motivations, simultaneously individual and private as well as community-oriented and public. It goes by a number of names, including responsible consumption (Fisk, 1973), ecologically concerned consumption (Henion, 1976; Kinnear et al., 1974), socially responsible consumption (Antil, 1984; Antil & Bennett, 1979), socially conscious consumption (Webster, 1975), and political consumption (Micheletti, 2003; Micheletti & Stolle, 2008; Stolle, Hooghe, & Micheletti, 2005). Despite the variety in terminology, each one is concerned with the same larger construct, albeit in differing degrees (Antil & Bennett, 1979).

Consistent across all these semantic variations, the concept of ethical consumption incorporates matters of conscience and can include issues of animal welfare, workers' rights, localist concerns, health-related matters, and environmental issues (Auger & Devinney, 2007; Carrigan, Szmigin, & Wright, 2004; Crane, 2001). It involves "the conscious and deliberate choice to make certain consumption choices due to personal and moral beliefs"(Crane &Matten, 2004). As a practical matter, it tends to include either positive ethical consumerism in the form of buycotting, or deliberately buying products and services that are minimally harmful to people, animals, and the environment, and negative ethical consumerism in the form of boycotting, or deliberately avoiding products and services that do not take into account the impact on people, animals, and the environment (Smith & Williams, 2011). At its heart, ethical consumption "seeks to embed altruistic, humanitarian, solidaristic and environmental commitments into the rhythms and routines of everyday life—from drinking coffee, to buying clothes, to making the kids' packed lunch" (Clarke, Barnett, Cloke, & Malpass, 2007, p. 233).

Scholarship into ethical consumer behavior has its roots in studies of socially responsible behavior (Berkowitz & Lutterman, 1968), which revealed that individuals who score high on the social responsibility scale were more likely to be involved in their communities, not just in conventionally viewed civic ways, such as membership in PTAs, but also in more consumer-oriented ways, such as donating money to charity. This work was extended by Anderson and Cunningham (1972), who identified the typical socially responsible consumer as young, well-educated, and of relatively high occupational attainment and socioeconomic status; these consumers are also more cosmopolitan, less conservative, and less status conscious. Based on early studies, the overall picture of the ethical consumer is of a person who feels efficacious, confident, and socially integrated. Webster (1975), for example, noted that the socially conscious consumer is well-adjusted to community norms, although not a conformist, and feels capable of influencing the community and wider world. Brooker (1976) showed that socially conscious consumers are more likely to be self-actualizing individuals, concerned with actions that "will satisfy the needs of others at the same time that individual's own needs are satisfied" (p. 107).

The majority of contemporary research has been concerned with developing a typology of ethical consumers and identifying what attitudes, values, and behaviors define this group (Crane, 2001; Kilbourne, 1998). Past research suggests that ethical consumers are wealthier and better educated, and hold white-collar jobs (Iyer & Banerjee, 1993); however, demographics are rarely found to be consistent, strong predictors of ethical consumer behavior (Belk, Devinney, & Eckhardt, 2005; Shrum et al., 1995). Instead, attitudes and past behaviors have been found to be more useful. For example, individuals who demonstrate greater perceived consumer efficacy, environmental concern, brand loyalty, information seeking, and collective orientation are more likely to shop in ethical ways (Ellen, Wiener, & Cobb-Walgren, 1991; Follows & Jobber, 2000; Kilbourne & Beckmann, 1998; Shrum et al., 1995).

Still, there remains a lack of powerful factors that can consistently and reliably predict ethical consumption and explain under what conditions ethically minded consumers are likely to put their wallets where their attitudes are. That is to say, the well-documented attitude–behavior gap among would-be ethical consumers remains insufficiently explained (Carrigan & Attalla, 2001; Carrington, Neville, & Whitwell, 2010; Kalafatis & Pollard, 1999).

Part of the problem is that models of ethical consumer behavior assume that intention naturally translates into behavior, when in reality any number of events can transpire to inhibit consumer intention moving on to consumer behavior (Carrington et al., 2010). In the actual consumption moment, ethically minded consumers may be more influenced by price or product attributes, rather than ethical characteristics (Belk, 1975; Belk et al., 2005; Boulstridge & Carrigan, 2000; Carrigan & Attalla, 2001). More generally, consumers may feel a lack of efficacy or belief that their ethical actions could have an impact (Carrigan & Attalla, 2001; Kalafatis & Pollard, 1999). For others, the desire to make ethical purchases is forestalled by what many perceive to be a lack of credibility and honesty in advertising in general and in environmental claims in particular (Crane, 2000; Hulm, 2010; Leire & Thidell, 2005).

Persuasive and informative mass media exert a strong influence, both positive and negative, on consumers' likelihood of adopting ethically minded consumption attitudes and of engaging in ethical consumption. This influence can be enduring or momentary. General, on-going media exposure can influence certain attitudes and beliefs that are conducive to ethical consumption. For example, viewing public affairs and nature documentaries positively predicts environmentally friendly behaviors (Holbert, Kwak, & Shah, 2003), and news consumption has been shown to predict ethical consumption, while entertainment content has not (Cho & Krasser, 2011; Shah, McLeod et al., 2007).

Marketing's influence is more complicated. Ethical consumers tend to be information seekers but view advertising with a fair degree of skepticism (Shrum et al., 1995). Interviews with typical consumers suggest marketing information would be viewed positively, especially among those who are less informed, but that they would be more likely to respond to negative information, i.e., information about unethical corporate behavior, than positive information (Carrigan & Attalla, 2001). Advertising, particularly green advertising, is perceived as unreliable and not credible (Johnston, 2008; Kalafatis & Pollard, 1999; Manrai et al., 1997). Fears of greenwashing, or advertising that includes environmental claims that are trivial, misleading, or deceptive, are a concern (Kangun, Carlson, & Grove, 1991). Consumer doubt regarding advertising claims is especially salient with respect to issues of environmental consumption since so many of these claims fall under the category of credence attributes, i.e., benefits or attributes that cannot be verified through information or personal experience (Darby & Karni, 1973; Nelson, 1970, 1974). When a consumer buys an organic apple, she must trust that the organic label is truthful and that the apple is indeed organic.

Given the equivocal influence of demographics, attitudes, and mass media on ethical consumption, scholars are increasingly turning to consumers' ethical orientations as a way to explain the attitude–behavior gap (Carrington et al., 2010). For example, personal values and ethics have been shown to positively influence ethical consumption in the context of fair trade and of organic and sustainable food (Arvola et al., 2008; Shaw & Clarke, 1999; Shaw & Shui, 2002; Vermeir & Verbeke, 2008).

As a lens through which to analyze consumption, ethical orientations offer considerable leverage. Consumption, according to Hall (2011), is an inherently ethical or moral matter. Consumption raises questions of fairness, of weighing individual needs against group interests, of balancing immediate versus delayed gratification.

> In this sense, the very negotiations upon which consumption is based—moral concepts such as justice and power, and basic ethical principles of right vs. wrong and good vs. bad—render consumer behavior as an outlet for the expression of personal ethics.
>
> (Hall, 2011, p. 627)

Early research into the socially conscious consumer reflected this moral component of consumption choices, with those scoring high on the social responsibility scale (used as a proxy for socially conscious consumer orientations) also showing a deep concern for broader ethical and moral issues as well as a strong sense of justice (Anderson & Cunningham, 1972; Berkowitz & Lutterman, 1968).

Yet the influence of personal ethics on consumer choices is complicated (Auger, Burke, Devinney, & Louviere, 2003), as illustrated by the case of child labor. While very few consumers would explicitly condone using child labor in the manufacture of clothing or electronics, for example, the alternative is not necessarily an improvement, and sanctions against child labor do not automatically mean children are better off. "I don't believe that the people who buy Gap and Nike want these girls to work in brothels because they lost their jobs at the garment factory" (Chon, 2000).

As well, ethical consumption choices can have an impact on a consumer's subsequent ethical beliefs. Mazar and Zhong (2010) have shown that, although green consumers are perceived as more altruistic, ethical, and cooperative than their non-green counterparts, individuals who purchase green products are more likely to engage in unethical behaviors, such as lying and stealing, than those who do not buy green products. They suggest that the halo effect of green consumerism needs to be taken with reservations. Green consumption choices seem to give these consumers free license to engage in indulgent and unethical behaviors.

In reality, ethical choices are often a result of trade-offs and compromises. Consumers balance their interests against others' interests, taking into account the information they have at hand. As a result, consumers might have multiple, frequently contradictory opinions about what is the ethically right decision to make (Szmigin, Carrigan, & McEachern, 2009).

Indeed, scholars have identified a number of different ethical frameworks to describe the ways consumers think about and understand their ethical consumption choices. Deontological approaches rely on rules. Consumers evaluate their consumption choices as right or wrong in reference to some higher morals, norms, or laws. Within deontological ethics, individuals act ethically because it is the right thing to do, regardless of the outcome. A teleological or consequentialist approach focuses on the outcomes of particular actions, taking into account the probability, desirability, and severity of positive or negative impacts (Brunk, 2010). Using the example of sweatshop labor, an ethical consumer motivated by deontological reasoning would view sweatshop labor as universally abhorrent since it goes against deeply held beliefs about how people should be treated. From the consequentialist perspective, however, sweatshop labor might be viewed as the more desirable outcome if the alternative means workers would have to seek other, more dangerous work, such as prostitution.

Virtue ethics offers a third explanation for why consumers might make ethical purchase choices. Whereas the deontological and consequentialist perspectives both consider self-interest to be an obstacle to altruism and ethical behavior, virtue ethics acknowledges an "enlightened self-interest in caring for others" (Barnett, Cafaro, & Newholm, 2005, p. 17). While consequentialist and deontological approaches focus on duties and responsibilities, virtue ethics is concerned with the good life and how to achieve it (Atkinson, 2012). The good life here is one that leads to well-being, maximizes moral self-realization, and fosters harmonious social relations and intellectual development (Cafaro, 2001). Ethical consumption fits neatly into this view and recognizes that these kinds of consumer choices are "not simply a matter of wholly selfless beneficence" but are a combination of "other-regarding and self-regarding virtues" (Barnett et al., 2005, p. 14).

Lastly, the social connection model (Young, 2004, 2006) argues that, as consumers in a global, interconnected marketplace, we are implicated in the various injustices carried out in the name of production and consumption, such as child labor, environmental degradation, and workers' rights. As consumers, we are socially connected to other actors in ways that supersede nation-state borders and local in-group affiliations. As such, consumers share a responsibility in not only rectifying these marketplace injustices but also challenging the underlying structures that make these injustices possible.

Consumers bring their particular ethical perspectives to bear while navigating the marketplace and making decisions about what to buy. Ethically minded consumers who adopt a consequentialist viewpoint, for example, will consider how the un/ethical behaviors of corporations impact various domains, such as workers, the environment, or the local community (Brunk, 2010). However, scholars have found that when consumers bring their ethics to bear on marketplace decisions, they do so inconsistently. For example, consumer attitudes are more likely to be affected by unethical corporate behavior than ethical corporate behavior (Folkes & Kamins, 1999), and consumers are more likely to punish corporations that are being unethical rather than reward those companies that are acting ethically (Elliott & Freeman, 2001).

Consumer ethics can also be affected by mass media, particularly persuasive content. Auger et al. (2003) demonstrated experimentally that consumer perceptions of what is ethically salient can be altered. When subjects were presented with different combinations of functional and ethical product attributes, certain combinations of ethical product attributes, such as animal testing, were more likely to lead to purchase than other combinations, such as biodegradability. It suggests that consumers could be convinced to change their purchase patterns depending on what kind of relevant ethical information is presented (Auger et al., 2003).

The specifics of this influence, however, are insufficiently understood, and the way in which marketing activity might affect ethical consumer behavior needs greater attention (Carrigan & Attalla, 2001). The following section takes up this point.

Green Advertising

In their determination of what constitutes an ethical product or service, consumers are also keenly aware of what kinds of corporate actions are ethical; however, scholars have only begun to explicate how consumers perceive the ethical qualities of corporations (Brunk, 2010). Studies have shown that ethical branding by companies like Ben & Jerry's and The Body Shop can be received favorably by ethically minded consumers and can translate into commercial success, whereas ethical breaches like that of Shell, for its poor environmental track record, or Nike, for its use of sweatshop labor, can damage brand names and hurt sales (Crane, 2001).

Oftentimes, though, what consumers consider ethical is at odds with what corporations consider ethical. One area where this disconnect is prominent is in the realm of advertising. Corporations, for example, tend to view advertising as one of the least important elements of corporate social responsibility (Perrini, Pogutz, & Tencati, 2006). Consumers are inclined to think the opposite. Relying on in-depth interviews with consumers, Brunk (2010) demonstrated that questionable advertising practices were a core concern. Brunk's informants believed that advertisers target and take advantage of weak and vulnerable consumers, such as young children and the elderly, and promote misleading, deceptive, even false product information. An often-cited example is that of Nestlé. Beginning in the late 1970s, Nestlé faced severe backlash from consumers when it advertised infant formula in less economically developed countries in

Africa and Asia. As a result, Nestlé has been the target of a three-decades-plus boycott. It is important to note that Nestlé was not criticized for the product it was selling, which in more developed countries is not as dangerous for infants, so much as for the aggressive marketing tactics it employed (Crane, 2001). Although generally considered a safe product in more developed countries, baby formula represents a much riskier option in areas where there is limited availability of clean drinking water to mix with the powdered formula and reduced access to the means to sanitize bottles. As a result, formula-fed infants in developing countries are at greater risk of death than are breastfed infants (UNICEF, 2005). Nestlé has been criticized for misrepresenting formula as superior to breast milk and for knowingly targeting illiterate and uneducated mothers who are unsure about how to use the product correctly and how to clean the bottles and nipples effectively (Time, 1976).

While extreme cases like that of Nestlé are more easily interpreted as aggressive and unethical, much less is known about how consumers interpret more mainstream, ethically minded advertising (Mohr, Webb, & Harris, 2001). The case study in the next section of this chapter offers insight into this domain. First, the remainder of this section offers a discussion of the kinds of persuasive communication available to ethically minded consumers, focusing on green advertising and the risk of greenwashing.

When it comes to marketing ethical product attributes, manufacturers have a number of options, including advertising, in-store promotions, and packaging. Some ethical attributes may also be marketed by way of eco-labels (or certification seals) that indicate the product has met certain guidelines.[2] Regardless of the kind of marketing, consumers tend to be at a disadvantage in that many of these ethical product claims, referred to as credence claims, cannot be verified by the individual consumer. Instead, they must trust that the claims are truthful. Whereas many product attributes can be verified through personal experience or information search, credence claims must be accepted at face value as truthful (Darby & Karni, 1973; Nelson, 1970, 1974). For example, a consumer buying coffee is able to confirm attributes like taste and price by drinking it (experience) and comparing price (information), but if a particular brand claims to be cultivated using organic farming principles, the consumer has no practical way of verifying such a claim.

Given the near impossibility of consumers to verify credence claims, marketing regarding these kinds of attributes is often viewed more skeptically than are claims about search and experience attributes. Marketing messages for these kinds of claims, then, must be perceived as highly credible and trustworthy to be effective (Ford, Smith, & Swasy, 1990; Grunert, Bech-Larsen, & Bredahl, 2000; Hansen & Kull, 1994; Thøgersen, 2000, 2002). Cultivating trust is important. Consumer trust has been shown to have a powerful impact on marketplace attitudes and behaviors, with a long tradition of scholarly work demonstrating that persuasion depends on trust (Boush, Chung-Hyun, Kahle, & Batra, 1993; Hovland & Janis, 1959; McGuire, 1968). Consumer trust leads to greater attention to persuasive messages, more favorable brand attitudes, and stronger brand loyalty, whereas lack of trust can negatively impact brand affect and beliefs (Chaudhuri & Holbrook, 2001; Du, Bhattacharya, & Sen, 2007; Harris & Goode, 2004; Mizerski, Pucely, & Patti, 1986).

In these moments of consumer uncertainty, trust acts as a lubricant and works as a simplifying strategy for consumers. If consumers trust the brand or the manufacturer, they are more likely to accept the organic claim as credible and honest. When consumers do not trust the content of the marketing claims or suspect an advertising message of deception or greenwashing, they are much less likely to purchase the product or adopt a favorable attitude toward it (Kangun et al., 1991; Thøgersen, 2002).

Misjudging how consumers interpret green advertising or understating the importance of consumer trust can be fatal. For example, early green advertising in the 1990s faced a backlash from consumers when green marketing failed to live up to its environmental claims or was used to hawk inferior products (Crane, 2000; Prothero, 1990). As a result, consumers in the 1990s viewed advertising as the least credible source of environmental information (Iyer & Banerjee, 1993), and a content analysis of advertising in the same time period showed 58% of environmental advertising contained at least one misleading or deceptive claim (Kangun et al., 1991).

Despite the importance of understanding the advertising side of the ethical consumption equation, the majority of attention remains focused on the consumer side and identifying typical ethical consumers (Iyer & Banerjee, 1993; Kilbourne, 1995). A handful of studies have analyzed green advertising messages, taking either a content analysis approach to document what different kinds of green advertising exist or an experimental approach to test which advertising frames resonate with consumers. In their content analysis of green print advertising, Iyer and Banerjee (1993) showed that most green appeals focused on promoting an environmentally friendly corporate image and on describing the environmentally friendly steps being taken in the production phase (i.e., careful use of natural resources) rather than the consumption or disposal phases. Experimental studies have explored which kinds of green appeals work best. In tests of environmental claim strength, results show moderate claims regarding pollution reduction are more convincing than weak or strong claims about pollution reduction (Manrai et al., 1997). Taking into account issue salience, Obermiller (1995) demonstrated experimentally that "sick baby" appeals (negative appeals that focus on the problem and its severity) are more effective than "well baby" appeals (positive appeals that reaffirm the individual's ability to effect change) for low-salience green issues, whereas the opposite is true for high-salience green issues.

From a regulatory perspective, government and consumer groups provide guidelines on what constitutes appropriate green advertising and what could be construed as deceptive or misleading. The Federal Trade Commission released its first Green Guide in 1992 and then revised it in 1996 and 1998 (FTC, 1998). It is currently undergoing additional revisions to address emerging green claims, such as carbon-offsets, and new technology (FTC, 2010). These guides advise manufacturers on a variety of aspects about green advertising, such as staying away from overstating environmental attributes or including environmental claims that cannot be substantiated.[3] Consumer and media groups, like SourceWatch and Greenpeace, offer guides to consumers to help identify greenwashing. TerraChoice, an environmental marketing firm, lists the seven Sins of Greenwashing (TerraChoice, 2011) that are to be avoided, including the sin of no proof, the sin of vagueness, and the sin of lesser of two evils.

What remains largely absent from the academic literature, however, is an understanding of how consumers understand green advertising in a non-experimental setting, and how green advertising, including so-called greenwashing, is received by audiences. Content analyses can tell us what kinds of green advertising exist. Experiments can show us how artificially manipulated factors can influence consumer responses. But neither provides robust insight into how consumers understand real-world green advertisements, how these advertisements are understood as truthful or deceptive, and how consumers weigh the various competing interests (i.e., price, availability, performance) in their determination of what makes a suitable green product.

The next section addresses these gaps through a case study analysis of a green advertisement for bottled water.

Case Study: Ozarka Natural Spring Water

This section synthesizes the discussion of the previous two sections by exploring how real consumers understand a real advertisement. The advertisement is a magazine advertisement for Ozarka bottled water that relies very heavily on environmental appeals.

Food is a suitable product to use for a case study about ethical advertising, as food is central to the issue of ethical and sustainable consumption (Johnston, 2008). Food cannot be separated from the issue of morals, and "moral concern with food intake is as old as morality itself" (Zwart, 2000, p. 113, cited in Buller, 2010). For example, in western society, it is considered immoral to eat dogs; in the Hebrew faith, there are numerous divine laws regarding what food is admissible and what is not; in the

Hindu religion, the cow is a sacred animal. In western consumer culture, food remains a morally charged category. "We now define ourselves not by what we eat—and perhaps less by what we choose not to eat—but by how we eat" (Buller, 2010, p. 1877). As a consumer commodity, food touches on all potential dimensions of ethical consumption, including issues of localism, organic food production, and fair trade, etc. (Johnston, 2008). It also represents a means for individuals to pass moral judgments on others. In the 1950s, for example, women who used instant coffee were characterized as lazy, spendthrift, inferior housewives (Antil, 1987). Given the well-established connection between food and ethics, it was deemed an appropriate commodity for an advertising case analysis.

The Ozarka Natural Spring Water advertisement ran in women's lifestyle magazines, like *Better Homes and Gardens* and *O, The Oprah Magazine*, in 2008. Ozarka, which was acquired by Nestlé in 1987, bills itself as 100% natural, locally sourced spring water.[4] The advertisement discussed here is part of Ozarka's campaign promoting its new environmentally friendly bottle design. The advertisement features an Ozarka bottle in the center foreground, situated against a pristine nature backdrop featuring a bright blue sky, rolling hills, a wide, slow-moving stream, green grass, wildflowers, and a setting sun low on the horizon behind some low hanging clouds. The headline reads: "When it comes to the environment, we're doing less." Underneath the bottle, the body copy reads: "100% natural spring water deserves an Eco-Shape bottle that has less impact on the earth. Ozarka Natural Spring Water. A little natural does a lot of good." The reader's attention is then directed to three aspects of the bottle. The first tag points to the cap and the descriptor "dye-free cap," the second points to the label and the descriptor "less paper," while the third points to the body of the bottle and the descriptor "30% less plastic." The claim of "less paper" refers to the fact that Ozarka's Eco-Shape label is a third of the size. The claim of "30% less plastic" is in comparison to other half-liter bottles on the market, including those for carbonated beverages, which are heavier to retain the carbonation (Bialik, 2007). The evidence supporting these two claims is found in a footnote at the bottom of the advertisement and is presented in very small font.

TerraChoice's Sins of Greenwashing (2011) offers a guide to assess the Ozarka ad. The environmental marketing firm lists seven green claims that advertisers should avoid or run the risk of being seen as misleading, deceptive, or deceitful. These "sins of greenwashing" list the kinds of claims that marketers might be tempted to make in an effort to present their product or service as more environmentally friendly, but TerraChoice cautions that misappropriating these green claims can backfire on a brand. A close reading of the Ozarka ad suggests the company has committed four of the seven sins of greenwashing:

- The *Sin of the Hidden Trade Off* is "committed by suggesting a product is 'green' based on an unreasonably narrow set of attributes without attention to other important environmental issues" (TerraChoice, 2011, p. 9). Here, Ozarka suggests its bottled water is green because of the Eco-Shape bottle, without taking into account the other elements of production (energy use, greenhouse gases, air pollution) that are environmental issues.
- The *Sin of No Proof* is "committed by an environmental claim that cannot be substantiated by easily accessible supporting information or by a reliable third-party certification" (TerraChoice, 2011, p. 9). Although Ozarka provides evidence for its claims about less plastic and less paper, these claims are relegated to very hard to read fine print in a footnote. As well, claims about using 30% less plastic are not in reference to Ozarka's own bottles, or even to other water bottles, but to national averages that include heavier, carbonated beverage bottles.
- The *Sin of Vagueness* is "committed by every claim that is so poorly defined or broad that its real meaning is likely to be misunderstood by the consumer" (TerraChoice, 2011, p. 9). The Ozarka ad includes the three-arrowed recycling logo at the bottom right and asks consumers to please recycle. However, it does not mention that, in most municipalities, recycling facilities will not accept bottle caps because they are made of a different plastic material than the bottle (Earth-Talk, 2008).
- The *Sin of Lesser of Two Evils* is "committed by claims that may be true within the product category, but that risk distracting the consumer from the greater environmental impacts of the category as a whole" (TerraChoice, 2011, p. 9). Like organic cigarettes or fuel-efficient SUVs, water in a plastic bottle, even if the bottle uses 30% less plastic, is more environmentally problematic than tap water.

Based on TerraChoice's criteria, the Ozarka ad hits four of seven sins and clearly comes down on the side of greenwashing.

But is it really?

I presented this ad to members of three focus groups, and the real-world consumer interpretations were both complicated and nuanced.[5] In examining consumer responses to green advertising, this research fills a gap in scholarly work about ethical consumption. With just a few exceptions (Ellen et al., 1991; Obermiller, 1995; Schuhwerk & Lefkoff-Hagius, 1995), academics have paid only passing attention to how green advertising's design and copy affect consumer message processing (Manrai et al., 1997).

As well, by relying on qualitative techniques, I am able "to explore complex behavior and to experience the consumer's 'eye view' of the world," an approach that is well suited for preliminary data collection in under-researched areas and topics like this one (Carrigan & Attalla, 2001, p. 567). Unlike survey questions, which can introduce elements of social desirability when discussing ethical behavior (Carrington et al., 2010), and experiments, which place consumers in highly controlled, artificial situations, focus groups yield rich insight into consumer understandings of ethical consumption and green advertising. Although lacking in generalizability to the broader population, focus groups make up for this with the depth of data they reveal. Compared to in-depth interviews, the focus group allows respondents to interact, which can lead to deeper discussions than might be had during individual contributions (Carrigan & Attalla, 2001).

The focus groups in this project consisted of three groups of seven women each. Consumers were between the ages of 30 and 62 (average age was 42.9), were the primary shoppers in their households, and regularly watched or read lifestyle programming, like Oprah Winfrey or Martha Stewart. Participants need not have been ethical consumers, although the vast majority identified themselves as such when asked. Like most consumers, these participants were skeptical of advertising and business (Bonini, McKillop, & Mendonca, 2007). Similar to other findings (Webb & Mohr, 1998), these consumers were skeptical and expressed concern that they, as consumers, were being taken advantage of and that advertising about ethical or prosocial product attributes was a gimmick. At best, advertising is viewed by these women as inherently biased and self-serving; at worst, patently misleading and deceptive:

> Advertising is out there so that you will choose their product as opposed to someone else's product. If you really don't have all of the information, it's like anything else, people are going to put out so much to make their product more appealing, and who knows the more important information that they could be holding that will maybe help make a determining factor. They put out stuff that's to their advantage with regards to a lot of what they're trying to sell.
>
> (Participant #3, Focus Group #1)

> One of my main concerns with green products is greenwashing. I just want it to be very upfront you know, as far as what it is. And sometimes I feel like I have to go out of my way to do additional research because it's not always exactly what it may claim to be, and the way that it's packaged may not always exactly be that.
>
> (P5, FG1)

> And I'm just going to throw out that all of that seems really deceptive to me. I mean, anybody can do that. There aren't a lot of standards

around it yet. So that's why I rely more on a website like Grist,[6] because it gives me more information on the carbon footprint of the companies that are producing things, because looking at the packaging just doesn't give me enough information.

(P7, FG2)

These consumers were also aware that some green claims, like being organic or "natural," were nothing more than marketing gimmicks. For many of them, a primary concern with green advertising was greenwashing.

It was like ok this is a gimmick. Everybody's doing this, and just putting it on there. So yeah, you could end up being like that, like all right you're green now, too. Are you really or are you just trying to sell?

(P7, FG2)

Yeah, it's vogue right now. Being green is vogue right now. So every company is going to try to have their ... you know, even if they've been doing the same thing for 40 years, they're going to try to find a way to let you know that it's green.

(P6, FG3)

These participants, then, displayed a distrust of advertising broadly and skepticism about green advertising in particular that mirrors consumers in general (Kanter, 2009). It was surprising, then, to hear their interpretation of the Ozarka ad.

Initial reactions to the water bottle ad were as expected. Participants were skeptical and critical about the product and the green framing of the message. Participants echoed the sentiment of TerraChoice's *Sin of Lesser of Two Evils* (2011) and wished consumers would opt for reusable bottles that could be refilled with tap water rather than disposable, one-shot plastic bottles. One informant said, "It's kind of a joke to me ... 30% less plastic, but it's still plastic and it's still ... where are you going to put all these bottles?" (P3, FG2).

But in all three focus groups, the discussion became more complicated and, unprompted by the moderator, participants began weighing the various factors at play in a consumer's mind and started talking about the positive aspects of the ad. This turn in the conversation, which happened in all three focus groups, reveals two main themes that help rationalize and justify why consumers, despite their best ethical intentions, choose not to buy ethical products in the marketplace.

The first theme argued for the idea that consumers have to make personal trade-offs. Purchase decisions must reflect not only the individual consumer's wishes, but also the realities of the consumption situation and the demands of other family members. One participant mentioned that the tap water in her rental house tasted horrible. If she owned the house, she would buy a water filter, but as a renter, she felt her only option was to buy bottled water.

Two other informants mentioned that, for households with children, having bottled water at hand was much healthier than soda or juice. Another participant said that, because Ozarka is locally sourced, it represents a positive ethical attribute that should be kept in mind. Being local means being healthier and less processed.

> It just looks refreshing, just coming from the spring, and it's an actual natural spring in Texas and really good water. You don't have to process it a lot, so...and coming from an environmental background, I know there's a ton of processes going on.
>
> (P7, FG1)

The second rationalization offered by participants was the idea that, while bottled water may not be ideal, at least this Ozarka brand is a step in the right direction with its Eco-Shape bottle. Buying bottled water can be rationalized as the right choice because consumers are supporting a company that is making an effort at reducing plastic waste.

> People do buy it, so if people are going to continue to buy it, they're going to continue to make it. So if they're going to make it more environmentally friendly, then that's good.
>
> (P2, FG1)

> I mean, for me, I look at it and think, well, a lot of people drink bottled water. They say reuse, recycle, but sometimes people just don't. And if you can at least make it a little bit better so that people can do it, then great. I mean, standing ovation for that.
>
> (P7, FG1)

> It will make them feel better about it. It's better than the alternative.
>
> (P4, FG3)

Ultimately, participants presented a conflicted story in response to the Ozarka ad. It was recognized as greenwashing and as an ethical product of dubious character. But it was also justified as an appropriate purchase, given the trade-offs consumer are forced to make. It may not be ideal, but participants can rationalize it as making the best of a bad situation.

The reality of it is we can't always...we have really busy lives, and we can try as hard as we can to do everything as natural as possible, but the reality of it is, we don't all live on farms and we don't ... I mean, we're living in a metropolitan city, most of the people have one or both parents working, and it's just a reality of the situation and at some point you have to say, look, I've done the best I can, so I do think this is better than the other alternatives.

(P6, FG3)

The results suggest consumers are complicated and oftentimes contradictory in their assessment of green advertising and ethical products. It underscores work done by Crane (2001), who has argued that the idea of an ethical product is a fallacy. Rather than classifying individual products as ethical or unethical, it is better to think of them as bundles of ethical attributes that relate to any number of ethical issues. Following this logic, there can be no such thing as an ethical product, only ethical attributes. Even these ethical attributes represent just one aspect of the product. Consumers are still motivated by other factors, such as price and performance, and will often find themselves in the situation of having to choose one attribute over another. For the focus group participants, then, the Ozarka water bottle occupied a middle ground between ethical and unethical. It offered some ethical attributes (less plastic, a dye-free cap) that helped justify purchasing it over competing but less ethical brands.

Similarly, the work by Kilbourne (1995) helps explain why participants were not uniformly put off by the Ozarka ad as an example of greenwashing. Kilbourne has argued that green advertising can be situated on a continuum from ecological to environmental. On the ecological end, advertising could be described as Green (with a big "G"), whereas on the environmental end, advertising could be described as green advertising (with a little "g"). On the one hand, Green/ecological advertising is more robust and represents a challenge to the dominant social paradigm. It advocates a reformist or radical approach, including an eco-centric (rather than anthropocentric) perspective. On the other hand, green/environmental advertising is concerned with promoting the status quo. Environmental solutions are seen to rest with consumption, science, and technology. In this view, nature is a resource to be managed by humans. Following this logic, we might fairly position the Ozarka ad at the green/environmental end of the continuum. It addresses an environmental issue, but it does so in a way that seeks to maintain the status quo: Resolving the environmental crisis requires consuming, albeit consuming differently. Participants seemed to recognize this advertising appeal as a form of acceptable, although weak, green advertising.

Implications and Future Research

The insights from these focus groups suggest consumers are very nuanced in their assessments of green advertising. While an ad may be read objectively and in isolation as greenwashing, consumers interpret the message with a rich and changing mental calculus. This complex dynamic helps explain why individuals may claim to hold environmental values and to be green consumers, but their actual marketplace choices are not always in keeping with those attitudes. In actuality, the distance between a consumer's green attitudes and their green purchases is fraught with the pressures of day-to-day reality such that, as past research into the green attitude–behavior gap suggests, consumers may talk the green talk, but frequently fail to walk the green walk.

The data in this study suggest there is a complicated process of rationalization and justification happening to prevent green intentions from manifesting as green behaviors. While research has focused on identifying the presence of this gap, very little research has sought to chart the dimensions of the gap itself. That is to say, the failure of green attitudes to result in green purchases has been well-documented, but what is missing from the literature is an empirical focus on the various consumer orientations that, in the moment, prevent otherwise green individuals from enacting their green values in the marketplace. I propose a model of ethical consumption that outlines this process and suggests avenues of future research that would help delineate the contours of this gap.

Drawing on the O-S-O-R model of social psychology (Markus & Zajonc, 1985) and political communication (McLeod, Kosicki, & McLeod, 2002), I suggest that ethical consumer behavior can better be understood by examining individual consumer orientations *in combination* with messages about green consumption, particularly green advertising. Most research looking at the attitude–behavior gap assumes a stimulus–response process and adopts one of two guiding perspectives. One approach examines the stimulus (which can be anything from green marketing appeals and word of mouth, to in-store product availability) to understand what kinds of green appeals work best (Hansen & Kull, 1994; Iyer & Banerjee, 1993; Kilbourne, 1995; Manrai et al., 1997; Obermiller, 1995; Schuhwerk & Lefkoff-Hagius, 1995). A second approach looks to the various pre-existing consumer orientations that can inhibit or encourage green consumption, such as perceived consumer efficacy, trust, need for information, and environmental concern (Ellen et al., 1991; Gupta & Ogden, 2009; Kalafatis & Pollard, 1999; Peattie, 2010; Schlegelmilch et al., 1996; Shrum et al., 1995).

Rarely are these two influences studied in tandem to understand how they interact to engender subsequent consumer orientations, which in turn influence green purchase decisions. The O-S-O-R model from social psychology offers a framework to understand this process and suggests that the effects of media messages, like green advertising, are likely to be conditional rather than powerful and direct. The first "O" in the model stands for pre-existing consumer orientations, "the set of structural, cultural, cognitive and motivational characteristics" of the audience members who are presented with a mediated message (McLeod et al., 2002, p. 238). These predispositions are essentially individual differences and vary from consumer to consumer. The communication message or stimulus, represented by the "S," encompasses those messages that inform consumers about green consumption choices and could range from persuasive or informative mass-mediated content, to interpersonal or electronic word of mouth. Individuals may respond to the message in various ways, and these subsequent orientations, represented by the second "O," influence how consumers are likely to react or respond, signified by the "R."

Essentially, the model argues that communication, such as a green advertising message, has conditional effects on individuals, effects that are mediated by the individual's pre-existing orientations. It recognizes that individuals bring their unique set of cognitive, affective, and motivational characteristics to the processing of any media message. This basic model and its extensions have been applied successfully to gauge the influence of political media content, such as news or advertising, on civic and political participation (Cho et al., 2009; Rojas & Puig-i-Abril, 2009; Shah, Cho et al., 2007; Sotirovic & McLeod, 2001). Although most work has been done in the area of political communication, the model has been extended in very limited ways to other areas, including environmental concern and political consumption (Shah, McLeod et al., 2007; Zhao, 2012).

As outlined in Figure 8.1, the O-S-O-R model can be fruitfully applied to the area of ethical consumption where it could offer useful, more robust insight into the attitude–behavior gap. Although by no means

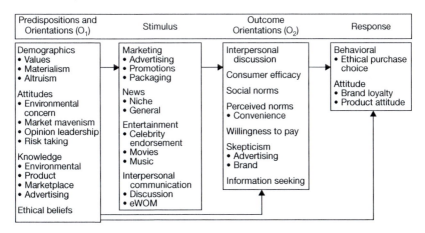

Figure 8.1 O-S-O-R Model

exhaustive, the model identifies some possible predispositions, communication sources, and outcome orientations that could be useful to explore. Specifically, the second O in the model represents the various outcome orientations that might pre-empt consumers' green concerns from manifesting as green purchases. For example, consumer predispositions, such as ethical beliefs or environmental concern, could moderate the influence of interpersonal communication about a particular green brand on a consumer's feeling of efficacy, which in turn influences her decision to purchase the green brand.

To put it in anecdotal terms, imagine a new mother who is deciding what brand of diapers to use with her newborn. She is concerned about the environmental impact of using disposable diapers and believes it is her ethical obligation to be a good steward of the environment. She might log on to an online social group and support network for new mothers in her city, where she comes across comments about cloth diapering. The majority of mothers on the discussion board advocates using cloth diapers and describes how simple and straightforward they are to use, in addition to being vastly superior to disposable diapers in terms of their impact on the environment. Our hypothetical new mother may follow these comments closely and notice that most mothers choose cloth diapers. She may interpret these comments to indicate that social norms within her group behoove her to make the same choice.

As suggested in Figure 8.1, there are numerous ways consumer orientations and communication stimuli can interact to influence subsequent consumer orientations. A number of these secondary orientations are explicated below and represent fertile avenues of future research. Although by no means exhaustive, these examples highlight the usefulness of understanding how predispositions and media messages combine to influence orientations and responses and shed light on the attitude–behavior gap that besets ethical consumption.

Interpersonal Discussion

Work in political communication has indicated that mass media effects do not operate directly on civic and political participation, but rather indirectly through political talk (Shah, McLeod et al., 2007). News media, for example, can prompt political discussion among individuals, which in turn can influence likelihood of voting in an election. This two-step flow of information (Katz & Lazarsfeld, 1955) has been extended to persuasive commuication in the realm of health promotion messages. For example, talking about health campaigns can moderate media effects, thereby increasing memory, persuasive influence, and self-efficacy (Dunlop, Kashima, & Wakefield, 2010; Southwell & Yzer, 2007). The same patterns could be expected in the case of ethical consumption. The willingness of consumers who are presented with green advertising claims to act on these persuasive messages by buying green products is likely to be mediated by interpersonal talk about the products being advertised and the way they are being promoted.

Consumer Efficacy

Perceived consumer effectiveness (PCE) has been identified as an important precursor to ethical consumption (Ellen et al., 1991). For individuals to opt for ethical products, they must feel like their ethical purchases will make a difference. While past research has demonstrated that those high in PCE are more likely than those low in PCE to buy environmentally friendly products (Kinnear et al., 1974; Roberts, 1996), rarely is the construct explored as a function of both pre-existing orientations and media messages. For example, not enough is known about the antecedents of PCE and how different message frames might help counteract low feelings of PCE (Roberts, 1996). The O-S-O-R model of ethical consumption proposed here represents a useful means of parsing out a more nuanced understanding of PCE.

Information Seeking

Claims regarding ethical products and services occupy a special category, known as credence claims, and must generally be accepted by consumers at face value. For example, when a brand of detergent claims to be environmentally friendly or when a brand of coffee claims to be shade grown, consumers have limited means to verify these ethical claims personally. One option they do have is to seek out additional information that confirms or contradicts the ethical claims. Indeed, past research has shown that green consumers are information seekers (Shrum et al., 1995). Information seeking is dependent on a number of individual predispositions, including demographics like education and income, but also certain values and orientations, such as interest in the message content, opinion leadership, and uncertainty reduction motives (Atkin, 1972; Boyle et al., 2004; Lazarsfeld, Berelson, & Gaudet, 1948). Given these moderating influences on information seeking, the O-S-O-R model could be productively used to understand its role in ethical consumption.

In qualitative terms, the focus group data described previously underscore the interactive effects of predispositions and communication content on outcome orientations, which in turn affect ethical consumption. Informants framed their own day-to-day consumption choices in ethical terms and described themselves as ethical consumers. When interpreting a particular example of green advertising, the majority saw it as greenwashing, as gimmicky, and as a hypocritical marketing appeal that was out to dupe consumers. Yet these same individuals also reacted to these ads by rationalizing the environmentally unfriendly act of buying bottled water. Their outcome orientations (O_2), as an interaction of ethical beliefs and marketing content, influenced their perceived efficacy. They rationalized the decision to buy bottled water as a lesser-of-two evils decision. While the task of being an ethical consumer in all decisions is untenable, they can still feel effective as quasi-ethical consumers by making these compromise purchases, i.e., by buying bottled water that comes in more environmentally friendly packaging.

The O-S-O-R model in Figure 8.1 outlines this process of influence, highlighting how predispositions and messages can interact to precipitate additional orientations, which in turn influence behavior choices. This model offers leverage in the study of green consumption by offering explanations for how green intentions are (or are not) translated into green behaviors, with the second O, in particular, shedding light on the missteps that can happen in the gap between attitude and behavior.

Notes

1 Ethical consumption is not aligned with the voluntary simplicity and downshifting movements. Ethical consumption addresses questions of *how* to consume; whereas voluntary simplicity and downshifting address the question of *whether* to consume, and "reject the persona of the consumer" (Clarke et al., 2007).
2 EnergyStar is perhaps the best-known eco-label in the United States and is used to indicate the energy efficiency of various appliances, like fridges and washing machines. These labels are frequently incorporated into advertising and packaging. Unlike other industrialized countries, the United States does not have a single, government-endorsed, multi-attribute eco-label similar to the Blue Angel in Germany or the Nordic Swan in Scandinavia (Case, 2004).
3 The full Green Guide can be found at www.ftc.gov/bcp/grnrule/guides980427.htm.
4 See: www.ozarkawater.com/#/about/about_us.
5 These focus groups were part of a larger project looking at green advertising in cross-platform lifestyle programming (i.e., the website, magazine, and television shows of Oprah, Rachael Ray, Martha Stewart, and Better Homes and Gardens) and how these ads were interpreted by real consumers. Focus group members were presented with five advertisements using green appeals. This chapter is limited to a discussion of consumer interpretations of just the Ozarka ad.
6 Grist.org is a website of environmental news and commentary.

References

Anderson, W. T., & Cunningham, W. H. (1972). The socially conscious consumer. *Journal of Marketing*, 36 (July), 23–31.
Antil, J. H. (1984). Socially responsible consumers: Profile and implications for public policy. *Journal of Macromarketing*, 4(2), 18–39.

Antil, J. H. (1987). Consumer perceptions of convenience food users. *Advances in Consumer Research*, *14*, 558–561.

Antil, J. H., & Bennett, P. D. (1979). Construction and validation of a scale to measure socially responsible consumption behavior. In K. E. Henion & T. C. Kinnear (Eds.), *The Conserver Society* (pp. 51–68). Chicago: American Marketing Association.

Arvola, A., Vassallo, M., Dean, M., Lampila, P., Saba, A., Lähteenmäki, L., & Shepherd, R. (2008). Predicting intentions to purchase organic food: The role of affective and moral attitudes in the theory of planned behaviour. *Appetite*, *50*, 443–454.

Atkin, C. K. (1972). Anticipated communication and mass media information-seeking. *The Public Opinion Quarterly*, *36*(2), 188–199.

Atkinson, L. (2012). Buying in to social change: How private consumption choices engender concern for the collective. *The ANNALS of the American Academy of Political and Social Science*, *644*(1), 191–206.

Auger, P., & Devinney, T. M. (2007). Do what consumers say matter? The misalignment of preferences with unconstrained ethical intentions. *Journal of Business Ethics*, *76*(4), 361–383.

Auger, P., Burke, P., Devinney, T. M., & Louviere, J. J. (2003). What will consumers pay for social product features? *Journal of Business Ethics*, *42*(3), 281–304.

Barnett, C., Cafaro, P., & Newholm, T. (2005). Philosophy and ethical consumption. In R. Harrison, T. Newholm, & D. Shaw (Eds.), *The Ethical Consumer* (pp. 11–24). London: Sage.

Belk, R. W. (1975). Situational variables and consumer behavior. *Journal of Consumer Research*, *2*, 157–164.

Belk, R. W., Devinney, T., & Eckhardt, G. (2005). Consumer ethics across cultures. *Consumption, Markets & Culture*, *8*(3), 275–289.

Berkowitz, L., & Lutterman, K. G. (1968). The traditional socially responsible personality. *Public Opinion Quarterly*, *32* (Summer), 169–185.

Bialik, C. (2007, December 14). The numbers guy: Water bottles slim down. *The Wall Street Journal*. Retrieved from http://blogs.wsj.com/numbersguy/water-bottles-slim-down-238/.

Bonini, S. M. J., Hintz, G., & Mendonca, L. T. (2008, March). Addressing consumer concerns about climate change. *McKinseyQuarterly.com*. Retrieved from www.mckinseyquarterly.com/Addressing_consumer_ concerns_about_ climate_change_2115.

Bonini, S. M. J., McKillop, K., & Mendonca, L. T. (2007, May). The trust gap between consumers and corporations. *McKinseyQuarterly.com*. Retrievedfromwww.mckinseyquarterly.com/The_trust_gap_between_consumers_ and_corporations_1985.

Bouckley, B. (2012, January 25). World organic food sales shine, but dairy in doldrums. *Dairyreporter.com*. Retrieved from www.dairyreporter. com/Markets/World-organic-food-sales-shine-but-dairy-in-doldrums.

Boulstridge, E., & Carrigan, M. (2000). Do consumers really care about corporate responsibility? Highlighting the attitude–behaviour gap. *Journal of Communication Management*, *4*(4), 355–368.

Boush, D. M., Chung-Hyun, K., Kahle, L. R., & Batra, R. (1993). Cynicism and conformity as correlates of trust in product information sources. *Journal of Current Issues & Research in Advertising, 15*(2), 71–79.

Boyle, M. P., Schmierbach, M., Armstrong, C. L., McLeod, D. M., Shah, D. V., & Zhongdang, P. (2004). Information seeking and emotional reactions to the September 11 terrorist attacks. *Journalism & Mass Communication Quarterly, 81*(1), 155–167.

Brooker, G. (1976). The self-actualizing socially conscious consumer. *The Journal of Consumer Research, 3*(2), 107–112.

Brunk, K. H. (2010). Exploring origins of ethical company/brand perceptions: A consumer perspective of corporate ethics. *Journal of Business Research, 63*(3), 255–262.

Buller, H. (2010). Palatable ethics. *Environment and Planning A, 42*(8), 1875–1880.

Cafaro, P. (2001). Economic consumption, pleasure, and the good life. *Journal of Social Philosophy, 32*(4), 471–486.

Carrigan, M., & Attalla, A. (2001). The myth of the ethical consumer—do ethics matter in purchase behaviour? *The Journal of Consumer Marketing, 18*(7), 560–578.

Carrigan, M., Szmigin, I., & Wright, J. (2004). Shopping for a better world? An interpretive study of the potential for ethical consumption within the older market. *The Journal of Consumer Marketing, 21*(6), 401–417.

Carrington, M. J., Neville, B. A., & Whitwell, G. J. (2010). Why ethical consumers don't walk their talk: Towards a framework for understanding the gap between the ethical purchase intentions and actual buying behaviour of ethically minded consumers. *Journal of Business Ethics, 97*(1), 139–158.

Case, S. (2004, June 23). Eco-labels: Making environmental purchases easier? Government Procurement. *American City & Country*. Retrieved from http://americancityandcounty.com/green/eco-labels-making-environmental-purchasing-easier.

Chaudhuri, A., & Holbrook, M. B. (2001). The chain of effects from brand trust and brand affect to brand performance: The role of brand loyalty. *Journal of Marketing, 65*(2), 81–93.

Cho, J., Shah, D. V., McLeod, J. M., McLeod, D. M., Scholl, R. M., & Gotlieb, M. R. (2009). Campaigns, reflection, and deliberation: Advancing an O-S-R-O-R model of communication effects. *Communication Theory, 19* (February), 66–88.

Cho, S., & Krasser, A. H. (2011). What makes us care? The impact of cultural values, individual factors, and attention to media content on motivation for ethical consumerism. *International Social Science Review, 86*(1/2), 3–23.

Chon, G. (2000, December 22). Dropped stitches. *Asiaweek, 26*(50). Retrieved from http://marriottschool.net/teacher/EMBA687/Nike%20&%20Shoe%20Industry/Asiaweek_com__Dropped_Stitches__12-22-2000.htm#more.

Clarke, N., Barnett, C., Cloke, P., & Malpass, A. (2007). Globalising the consumer: Doing politics in an ethical register. *Political Geography, 26*(3), 231–249.

Crane, A. (2000). Facing the backlash: Green marketing and strategic reorientation in the 1990s. *Journal of Strategic Marketing, 8*(3), 277–296.

Crane, A. (2001). Unpacking the ethical product. *Journal of Business Ethics, 30*(4), 361–373.

Crane, A., & Matten, D. (2004). *Business Ethics: A European Perspective: Managing Corporate Citizenship and Sustainability in the Age of Globalization.* Oxford: Oxford University Press.

Darby, M. R., & Karni, E. (1973). Free competition and the optimal amount of fraud. *Journal of Law and Economics*, 16, 67–88.

Du, S., Bhattacharya, C. B., & Sen, S. (2007). Convergence of interests-cultivating consumer trust through corporate social initiatives. *Advances in Consumer Research – North American Conference Proceedings*, 34, 687–687.

Dunlop, S. M., Kashima, Y., & Wakefield, M. (2010). Predictors and consequences of conversations about health promoting media messages. *Communication Monographs*, 77(4), 518–539.

EarthTalk. (2008, April 28). Tops off? Why some towns won't recycle bottle caps. *Scientific American.*

Ellen, P. S., Wiener, J. L., & Cobb-Walgren, C. (1991). The role of perceived consumer effectiveness in motivating environmentally conscious behaviors. *Journal of Public Policy & Marketing*, 10(2), 102–117.

Elliott, K. A., & Freeman, R. B. (2001). *White Hats or Don Quixotes? Human Rights Vigilantes in the Global Economy.* Cambridge, MA: National Bureau of Economic Research, Working Paper No. 8102.

Fisk, G. (1973). Criteria for a theory of responsible consumption. *The Journal of Marketing*, 37(2), 24–31.

Folkes, V. S., & Kamins, M. A. (1999). Effects of information about firms' ethical and unethical actions on consumers' attitudes. *Journal of Consumer Psychology*, 8(3), 243–259.

Follows, S., B., & Jobber, D. (2000). Environmentally responsible purchase behaviour: A test of a consumer model. *European Journal of Marketing*, 34(5/6), 723–746.

Ford, G. T., Smith, D. B., & Swasy, J. L. (1990). Consumer skepticism of advertising claims: Testing hypotheses from economics of information. *Journal of Consumer Research*, 16(4), 433–441.

FTC. (1998). *Guides for the Use of Environmental Marketing Claims.* Washington, DC: Federal Trade Commission,

FTC. (2010, October 6). Federal Trade Commission proposes revised "Green Guides": Seeks public comment on changes that would update guides and make them easier to use. *FTC.gov*. Retrieved from www.ftc.gov/opa/2010/10/greenguide.shtm.

Grunert, K. G., Bech-Larsen, T., & Bredahl, L. (2000). Three issues in consumer quality perception and acceptance of dairy products. *International Dairy Journal*, 10(8), 575–584.

Gupta, S., & Ogden, D. (2009). To buy or not to buy? A social dilemma perspective on green buying. *Journal of Consumer Marketing*, 26, 376–391.

Hall, S. M. (2011). Exploring the "ethical everyday": An ethnography of the ethics of family consumption. *Geoforum*, 42(6), 627–637.

Hansen, U., & Kull, S. (1994). Öko-label als umweltbezogenes informationsinstrument: Begründungszusammenhänge und interessen (Eco-labels as environmental information tool: Reasoning and interest). *Journal of Marketing*, 4(4. kvartal), 265–273.

Harris, L. C., & Goode, M. M. H. (2004). The four levels of loyalty and the pivotal role of trust: A study of online service dynamics. *Journal of Retailing*, *80*(2), 139–158.

Henion, K. E. (1976). *Ecological Marketing*. Columbus, OH: Grid Inc.

Henion, K. E., & Wilson, W. H. (1976). The ecologically concerned consumer and locus of control. In K. E. Henion & T. C. Kinnear (Eds.), *Ecological Marketing* (pp. 131–144). Chicago: American Marketing Association.

Holbert, R. L., Kwak, N., & Shah, D. V. (2003). Environmental concerns, patterns of television viewing, and pro-environmental behaviors: Integrating models of media consumption and effects. *Journal of Broadcasting and Electronic Media*, *47*, 177–196.

Hovland, C., & Janis, I. L. (1959). *Personality and Persuasibility*. New Haven, CT: Yale University Press.

Hulm, M. (2010). *Your Brand: At Risk or Ready for Growth?* Bristol, UK and Chicago: Alterian.

Hunt, N., & Dorfman, B. (2009, January 28). How green is my wallet? Organic food growth slows. *Reuters*. Retrieved from www.reuters.com/article/2009/01/28/us-financial-food-organic-idUSTRE50R01C20090128.

Iyer, E., & Banerjee, B. (1993). Anatomy of green advertising. *Advances in Consumer Research*, *20*(1), 494–501.

Johnston, J. (2008). The citizen–consumer hybrid: Ideological tensions and the case of Whole Foods Market. *Theory and Society*, *37*(3), 229–270.

Kalafatis, S. P., & Pollard, M. (1999). Green marketing and Ajzen's Theory of Planned Behaviour: A cross-market examination. *Journal of Consumer Marketing*, *16*(4/5), 441–460.

Kangun, N., Carlson, L., & Grove, S. J. (1991). Environmental advertising claims: A preliminary investigation. *Journal of Public Policy & Marketing*, *10*(2), 47–58.

Kanter, J. (2009, April 30). Study: For consumers, green is greenwash. *New York Times*.

Katz, E. & Lazarsfeld, P. F. (1955). *Personal Influence: The Part Played by People in the Flow of Mass Communication*. Glencoe, IL: Free Press.

Kilbourne, W. E. (1995). Green advertising: Salvation or oxymoron? *Journal of Advertising*, *24*(2), 7–19.

Kilbourne, W. E. (1998). Green marketing: A theoretical perspective. *Journal of Marketing Management*, *14*(6), 641–655.

Kilbourne, W. E., & Beckmann, S. (1998). Review and critical assessment of research on marketing and the environment, *Journal of Marketing Management*, *14*(6), 513–532.

Kinnear, T. C., Taylor, J. R., & Ahmed, S. A. (1974). Ecologically concerned consumers: Who are they? *Journal of Marketing*, *38* (April), 20–24.

Lazarsfeld, P., Berelson, B., & Gaudet, H. (1948). *The People's Choice*. New York: Columbia University Press.

Leire, C., & Thidell, A. (2005). Product-related environmental information to guide consumer purchases—a review and analysis of research on perceptions, understanding and use among Nordic consumers. *Journal of Cleaner Production*, *13*(10/11), 1061–1070.

Manrai, L. A., Manrai, A. K., Lascu, D.-N., & Ryans, J. K. (1997). How green-claim strength and country disposition affect product evaluation and company image. *Psychology & Marketing*, *14*(5), 511–537.

Markus, H., & Zajonc, R. (1985). The cognitive perspective in social psychology. In G. Lindzey & E. Aronson (Eds.), *Handbook of Social Psychology* (3rd ed., pp. 137–229). New York: Random House.

Mazar, N., & Zhong, C. B. (2010). Do green products make us better people? *Psychological Science, 21*(4), 494–498.

McEachern, M. G. (2008). Guest editorial: The consumer and values-based labels. *International Journal of Consumer Studies, 32*(5), 405–406.

McGuire, W. J. (1968). Personality and susceptibility to social influence. In E. F. Borgatta & W. W. Lambert (Eds.), *Handbook of Personality Theory and Research* (pp. 1130–1187). Chicago: Rand McNally.

McLeod, D. M., Kosicki, G. M., & McLeod, J. M. (2002). Resurveying the boundaries of political communication effects. In J. Bryant & D. Zillmann (Eds.), *Media Effects: Advances in Theory and Research* (2nd ed., pp. 215–267). Mahwah, NJ: Lawrence Erlbaum Associates.

Micheletti, M. (2003). *Political Virtue and Shopping: Individuals, Consumerism, and Collective Action.* New York: Palgrave Macmillan.

Micheletti, M., & Stolle, D. (2008). Fashioning social justice through political consumerism, capitalism and the internet. *Cultural Studies, 22*(5), 749–769.

Mizerski, R., Pucely, M. J., & Patti, C. (1986). *The Influence of Consumer Confidence in the Truthfulness and Accuracy of Advertising on their Subsequent Processing of Ad Messages.* Paper presented at the American Marketing Association, Chicago.

Mohr, L. A., Webb, D. J., & Harris, K. E. (2001). Do consumers expect companies to be socially responsible? The impact of corporate social responsibility on buying behavior. *Journal of Consumer Affairs, 35*(1), 45–72.

Nelson, P. (1970). Information and consumer behavior. *Journal of Political Economy, 78*(2), 311–329.

Nelson, P. (1974). Advertising as information. *Journal of Political Economy, 82*(4), 729–754.

Neuman, W., & Barboza, D. (2010, June 13). U.S. drops inspector of food in China. *New York Times.* Retrieved from www.nytimes.com/2010/06/14/business/global/14organic.html?pagewanted=all.

Obermiller, C. (1995). The baby is sick/the baby is well—a test of environmental communication appeals. *Journal of Advertising, 24*(2), 55–70.

Peattie, K. (2010). Green consumption: Behavior and norms. *Annual Review of Environment and Resources, 35*(1), 195–228.

Perrini, F., Pogutz, S., & Tencati, A. (2006). Corporate social responsibility in Italy: State of the art. *Journal of Business Strategies, 23*(1), 65–91.

Prothero, A. (1990). Green consumerism and the societal marketing concept: Marketing strategies for the 1990s. *Journal of Marketing Management, 6*(2), 87–103.

Roberts, J. A. (1996). Green consumers in the 1990s: Profile and implications for advertising. *Journal of Business Research, 36,* 217–231.

Rojas, H., & Puig-i-Abril, E. (2009). Mobilizers mobilized: Information, expression, mobilization and participation in the digital age. *Journal of Computer-Mediated Communication, 14,* 902–927.

Schlegelmilch, B. B., Bohlen, G., & Diamantopoulos, A. (1996). The link between green purchasing decisions and measures of environmental consciousness. *European Journal of Marketing, 30*(5), 35–55.

Schuhwerk, M., & Lefkoff-Hagius, S. (1995). Green or non-green? Does type of appeal matter when advertising a green product. *Journal of Advertising, 24,* 45–54.

Shah, D. V., Cho, J., Nah, S., Gotlieb, M. R., Hwang, H., Lee, N., McLeod, D. M. (2007). Campaign ads, online messaging, and participation: Extending the communication mediation model. *Journal of Communication, 57* (December), 676–703.

Shah, D. V., McLeod, D. M., Kim, E., Sun Young, L., Gotlieb, M. R., Ho, S. S., & Breivik, H. (2007). Political consumerism: How communication and consumption orientations drive "lifestyle politics." *The ANNALS of the American Academy of Political and Social Science, 611*(1), 217–235.

Shaw, D., & Clarke, I. (1999). Belief formation in ethical consumer groups: An exploratory study. *Marketing Intelligence and Planning, 17*(2), 109–119.

Shaw, D., & Shui, E. (2002). An assessment of ethical obligation and self-identity in ethical consumer decision-making: A structural equation modelling approach. *International Journal of Consumer Studies, 26*(4), 286–293.

Shrum, L., McCarty, J., & Lowrey, T. (1995). Buyer characteristics of the green consumer and their implications for advertising strategy. *Journal of Advertising, 24,* 71–82.

Smith, N. C., & Williams, E. (2011). Responsible consumers and stakeholder marketing: Building a virtuous circle of social responsibility. *Universia Business Review, 30,* 68–78.

Sotirovic, M., & McLeod, J. M. (2001). Values, communication behavior, and political participation. *Political Communication, 18,* 273–300.

Southwell, B. G. & Yzer, M. C. (2007). The roles of interpersonal communication in mass media campaigns. *Communication Yearbook, 3,* 419–462.

Stolle, D., Hooghe, M., & Micheletti, M. (2005). Politics in the supermarket: Political consumerism as a form of political participation. *International Political Science Review/Revue internationale de science pol, 26*(3), 245–269.

Szmigin, I., Carrigan, M., & McEachern, M. G. (2009). The conscious consumer: Taking a flexible approach to ethical behaviour. *International Journal of Consumer Studies, 33*(2), 224–231.

Tanner, C., & Kast, S. W. (2003). Promoting sustainable consumption: Determinants of green purchases by Swiss consumers. *Psychology & Marketing, 20*(10), 883–902.

TerraChoice. (2011). *The Sins of Greenwashing Home and Family Edition, 2010: A Report on Environmental Claims Made in the North American Consumer Market.* Underwriters Laboratories and TerraChoice.

Thøgersen, J. (2000). Psychological determinants of paying attention to eco-labels in purchase decisions: Model development and multinational validation. *Journal of Consumer Policy, 23,* 285–313.

Thøgersen, J. (2002). Promoting green consumer behavior with eco-labels. In T. Dietz & P. C. Stern (Eds.), *New Tools for Environmental Protection: Education Information and Voluntary Measures* (pp. 83–104). Washington, DC: National Academy Press.

Time. (1976, February 16). The Formula Flap, *Time,* 81.

UNICEF. (2005). *Infant and Young Child Feeding.* Retrieved from www.unicef.org/nutrition/index_breastfeeding.html.

Vermeir, I., & Verbeke, W. (2008). Sustainable food consumption among young adults in Belgium: Theory of planned behaviour and the role of confidence and values. *Ecological Economics*, 64, 542–553.

Webb, D. J., & Mohr, L. A. (1998). A typology of consumer responses to cause-related marketing: From skeptics to socially concerned. *Journal of Public Policy & Marketing*, 17(2), 226–238.

Webster, F. E., Jr. (1975). Determining the characteristics of the socially conscious consumer. *The Journal of Consumer Research*, 2(3), 188–196.

Young, I. M. (2004). Responsibility and global labor justice. *Journal of Political Philosophy*, 12(4), 365–388.

Young, I. M. (2006). Responsibility and global justice: A social connection model. *Social Philosophy and Policy*, 23(1), 102–130.

Zhao, X. (2012). Personal values and environmental concern in China and the US: The mediating role of informational media use. *Communication Monographs*, 79(2), 137–159.

Zwart, H. (2000). A short history of food ethics. *Journal of Agricultural & Environmental Ethics*, 12, 113–126.

Crowdsourcing and Co-Creation

Ethical and Procedural Implications for Advertising Creativity

W. Glenn Griffin

Each year, two NFL teams run the gauntlet for a spot in what is arguably the biggest sporting event in the world, the Super Bowl. The game is one of the most watched on television worldwide, and advertisers pay millions of dollars to spend just 30 seconds with that audience. So in 2006, when Doritos announced a contest that invited consumers to create their own Super Bowl spot for the brand, it became one of the hottest plays in ad industry history. It sounded risky (maybe crazy), handing over branding work to novices—particularly in such a high-profile context. Would the contest work? Would the ads be any good? As it turned out, Doritos' "Crash the Super Bowl" concept was a winner. Thousands entered, and five finalists each received $10,000 and a trip to Miami for a private Super Bowl party. The ads they created were highly popular with viewers, ranking among *USA Today's* Ad Meter Top 5 (Brabham, 2009). This user-generated content (UGC) strategy helped stake out a new marketing frontier, and in 2012, "Crash the Super Bowl" marked its sixth anniversary with five spots aired during Super Bowl XLVI. Over the years, as Doritos' contest has grown and other brands have launched similar initiatives, advertising agency professionals and their clients watch and continue to debate the value and wisdom of UGC and other "crowdsourced" strategies. Does this represent the beginning of the end of advertising as we know it? Is the longstanding, negotiated relationship between advertisers and consumers (in which agency minds set the agenda) being turned on its head? Perhaps most importantly, agencies and clients are worried about how all of this will impact their bottom line. But as we enter an era in which advertising is no longer simply targeted at consumers but also *made by them*, perhaps there are other questions that should be asked—questions involving the possible exploitation of creative talent in "the crowd," about the quality and long-term viability of crowdsourced work, and whether or not agencies and their clients have fully considered the impact that crowdsourcing will have on the way they both do business.

Crowdsourcing, User-Generated Content, and Co-Creation

As we prepare to discuss crowdsourcing and its implications for advertising creativity, it is important to remember that the concept is still relatively new, and its definition continues to evolve as professional commentary and scholarship build. Although some of the existing literature asserts that creative *inspiration* is increasingly crowdsourced via online portals such as Pinterest, Tumblr, and other content aggregators, this chapter will limit its view to the practice by advertising agencies of soliciting creative work from consumers (amateur sources of creative ideas/content) or those with specific training and expertise in various creative disciplines, both groups now collectively identified as part of "the crowd."

Defining the Terms

The term "crowdsourcing" was coined by Jeff Howe, a contributing editor at *Wired* magazine, in 2006 (Howe, 2006). The practice is defined as "the act of a company or institution taking a function once performed by employees and outsourcing it to an undefined (and generally large) network of people in the form of an open call" (Brabham, 2008, p. 78). The real genius behind the practice, Howe argues, is "the large network of potential laborers" it can tap into online (Brabham, 2008, p. 78). But the definition does not apply until an advertiser actually chooses from among "the crowd's" ideas and implements one. Crowdsourcing includes user-generated content (UGC), which is created "outside professional routines and practices" (Christodoulides, Jevons,& Blackshaw, 2011, p. 101). While Doritos' "Crash the Super Bowl" sources from an estimated 100 million plus amateur creators in the U.S., many crowdsourcing strategies focus on a smaller pool of creative professionals: freelancers, un- or under-employed creatives looking for projects, or students seeking a foothold in the business (Christodoulides et al., 2011).

"Co-creation" is also a buzzword related to crowdsourcing, referring to the solicitation of ideas from customers (but stopping short of asking them to develop content) by companies seeking to leverage their collective wisdom (Jack, 2009). However, as the term implies, co-creation is a collaborative effort between the two parties. Consider Starbucks Coffee's website, mystarbucksidea.com, which collected more than 17,000 suggestions from patrons in just 14 months, some of which have subsequently been developed and implemented by the company (Winsor, 2009).

When one considers that the terms "crowdsourcing," "user-generated content," and "co-creation" all entered the industry vernacular less than a decade ago, both their staggering growth in popularity and their penchant for generating controversy are underscored. Some say that we are witnessing a shift in power and influence—away from marketers and in favor of the consumer (Christodoulides et al., 2011). Unquestionably, and in a relatively short period of time, these strategies for making "the crowd" part of the process have yielded some remarkable success stories.

Success Stories from "the Crowd"

Make no mistake: Crowdsourcing and co-creation are more than just advertising strategies. For some companies, they are at the heart of the business model. Even a cursory scan of the industry commentary on crowdsourcing reveals some of the big winners that have successfully leveraged the concept. Here, we provide an overview of some of the most prominent case studies.

Getty Images/iStockphoto

The online stock photography site iStockphoto.com crowdsources the work of more than 23,000 amateur and professional photographers (most on a royalty-free basis) for use by art directors and designers (Hempel, 2006). Photographers who submit their work to iStockphoto's collection receive a 20% commission on the sale of their images; some can earn up to 40% if they sign an exclusivity contract (Brabham, 2008). In 2006, stock photography giant Getty Images purchased iStockphoto for a reported $50 million, affording Getty an even greater share of the highly competitive royalty-free and rights-managed photo business (Hempel, 2006).

Threadless.com

Founded in Chicago in 2000, Threadless.com sells t-shirts that are designed by a crowdsourced community of artists and critiqued by users in an ongoing competition (Brabham, 2008). By 2006, the company was selling 60,000 t-shirts a month at a 35% profit margin, and latest company earnings are estimated at $30 million (Brabham, 2008; Burkitt, 2010). Winning designers on the site are awarded $2,000 in cash, a $500 gift certificate, and a $500 bonus each time a design is reprinted (http://threadless.com). Threadless t-shirts, printed by the company using designs from its crowdsourced community, are the lucrative products of a co-creation model.

Peperami

The popular U.K. sausage snack Peperami (a Unilever product) was among the first consumer brands to shock the ad industry by firing its agency of record and launching a crowdsourcing initiative in which "anyone and everyone" could produce and submit Peperami television commercials (Campaign, 2010, p. 12). A $10,000 prize was offered to the winner (a sum representing a mere fraction of what a professionally produced ad would cost), and 1,185 entries were collected. In the end, an ex-creative director from Munich and a copywriter from London (both industry veterans) won the pitch, and Unilever claims the strategy accounted for up to a 70% savings in agency fees (Campaign, 2010).

What's Driving the Growth of Crowdsourcing and Co-Creation?

As the previous case studies demonstrate, companies and brands are building business and deriving significant economic rewards from crowdsourcing and co-creation platforms. But what are the leading rationales that continue to fuel the dramatic growth of these strategies? Why is the sourcing of creative ideas and/or content from "the crowd" so irresistible to so many?

"Millions of Heads Are Better Than One"

Advocates of crowdsourcing and co-creation lead with perhaps the most obvious rationale of all: "millions of heads are better than one" (Brabham, 2009). In a global-minded and hyper-connected business environment, intellectual power and creative talent are widely distributed and represent an untapped resource, they say. Companies that employ full-time creative staff may be limiting their options by drawing upon the talent of a few in an increasingly competitive idea sweepstakes. Why should an advertising agency hire 10 full-time art directors and copywriters to service clients' accounts when it is now possible to distribute a brief among tens of thousands? How does the productivity of an on-site research and development team compare to the possibility inherent in thousands of consumer ideas submitted online? The expertise required to solve problems, develop new ideas, and communicate messages does not necessarily need to live in-house anymore. For advertising industry watchers, this new reality constitutes "a profound paradigm shift" and stands to change the way agencies look and operate (Brabham, 2008, p. 79).

Direct Interaction with Consumers

The sourcing of creative content directly from consumers is also purported to solve another problem for marketers—how to narrow the gap between brand and buyer. For example, competitions like Doritos' "Crash the Super Bowl" can certainly generate excitement and buzz for a brand—effects that traditional ad campaigns may find difficult to deliver (Merritt, 2012). As Wil Merritt, CEO of Zooppa (an online social network for sourcing creative talent), suggests, "brands can motivate groups to build groundswell among a brand's fans, extending the value of traditional ads" (Merritt, 2012). In this digital age, ads and brands are a frequent topic of conversation on Facebook, Twitter, and blogs. Ad content is often shared or forwarded from person to person, and consumers even seek out their favorite brands' fan pages or Twitter IDs as a sign of their allegiance. Perhaps most fascinating, however, is the emergence of a so-called "curator class" among consumers—those who actively promote ad content that they like and demote what they do not (Knutson, 2012). This phenomenon can serve as an important form of feedback for brands that garner positive or negative reactions to their messages, and brand managers are paying attention. Marketers' new appreciation for consumers as true connoisseurs of brand messages likely contributes to the notion that they are also a prime source of creative content. According to one industry observer, this amounts to a relatively simple calculation:

> To draw persuasive messages from the very audience one is trying to persuade is an ultimate form of marketing research. In theory, customers know what they want, and in practice, the goal with crowdsourced advertising is to get customers to produce it in the first place.
>
> (Brabham, 2009)

Essentially, crowdsourcing or co-creating content with the consumer holds the potential to "eliminate the middle man," which is typically the advertising agency. As previously noted, this mindset translates into an unprecedented level of consumer empowerment. More and more companies are looking to their own customers as experts on how to build their brands.

The Inevitability Factor

In 2010, *Fast Company* senior writer Danielle Sacks described an advertising industry at a crossroads, a business that would never be the same again: "Over the past few years, because of a combination of Internet disintermediation, recession and corporate blindness, the assembly line has been obliterated—economically, organizationally and culturally" (Sacks, 2010, p. 111). Clients have become increasingly demanding of their agencies of record (AOR)—particularly in a tough economic climate—and are now more likely to question traditional agency tactics and their potential to deliver maximum return on investment. Some brand managers look at the success of crowdsourcing for big names like Doritos and Unilever and wonder why their AOR is not leveraging it. But many agencies are resistant to change and slow in adopting a more "outsourced" approach (Winsor, 2010). According to John Winsor, CEO of ad agency Victors & Spoils in Boulder, Colorado, "Somewhere along the way, the big-agency business became a lifestyle" (Winsor, 2010). The trust inherent in a longstanding, mutually beneficial client/agency relationship erodes as both parties present competing agendas. Crowdsourcing and co-creation teaches clients that ideas can come from anywhere, while it forces agencies to reexamine everything about the way they are structured. As Winsor observes, "the old system of agencies employing a few creative teams to come up with agenda-setting ideas simply doesn't make sense in a digital era where ideas can and should come from anywhere" (Winsor, 2010). In response, agencies are hiring more digital creatives than any other kind and building more consumer participation and involvement into every new pitch. Increasingly, clients want to see more ideas that draw upon the power of "the crowd" and expect agencies to deliver them. If agencies do not, it is clear that clients have the option to cut them out of the process altogether (think Peperami). The inevitability of crowdsourcing and co-creation, it seems, is rooted in the new gospel that consumers and all that can be learned from them are everything to a brand.

Vital Questions about Crowdsourcing and Co-Creation

As discussed so far in this chapter, crowdsourcing and co-creation are changing the way advertising is made and how both clients and agencies navigate the business of branding. Numerous success stories seem to validate these strategies. Sourcing creativity from "the crowd" is based on the simple idea that many ideas are better than a few; it offers the promise of more direct engagement and interaction with the consumer, and seems destined to change the face of the advertising industry and how it negotiates client relationships. But does this new paradigm also present ethical and procedural challenges for clients, agencies, and "the crowd" itself? Four questions are posed here with intent to examine crowdsourcing through a more critical lens.

Does Crowdsourcing Exploit Creative Talent Intellectually and/or Economically?

If, as some insist, millions of heads really are better than one, then crowdsourcing and co-creation leverages that idea perfectly. As Lévy (1997 [1995]) proposes, intelligence is universally distributed and can be networked to yield a *collective intelligence*, as demonstrated in the online solicitation of ideas and/or content from "the crowd" by various brands.

Advertising Age columnist Bob Garfield agrees and suggests that "the universe of everybody—when properly cultivated—will yield more and better stuff than the universe of the few" (Garfield, 2010, p. 15).

But are members of "the crowd" who submit their work being taken advantage of in the process? To the contrary, crowdsourcing advocates claim. Instead, open calls for creative work represent enormous opportunity. As Victors & Spoils CEO John Winsor sees it, "the current global economic conditions have forced us all to do more with less," and "unemployed [creative professionals] now look for new ways to participate" (Winsor, 2009). Where some see exploitation, others believe that crowdsourcing actually empowers creative people to pick and choose projects like freelancers, with "more agency than Marxist critiques would allow" (Brabham, 2008, p. 86). Winsor (2009) also believes that active members within "the crowd" are afforded the opportunity to "sharpen their creative skills, stay involved with the things they love to do and—most important—get noticed."

A prime motivation for many creative people who respond to calls for their ideas is, in fact, the hope that someone might hire them full time or offer them "a foot in the door" that will lead to more long-term employment, and these hopefuls include students (Krebs, 2011). Whereas in the past a typical college student might never have the opportunity to interview or show a portfolio at a top agency, the crowdsourcing model does afford aspiring creative pros the chance to put their work in front of a creative director or brand manager. More experienced professionals may use the opportunity to establish themselves as entrepreneurs or use assignments to beef up their portfolios in pursuit of a better job (Brabham, 2008). And for a select few, as one of the Doritos' "Crash the Super Bowl" competitors admits, being part of "the crowd" is "doing whatever it takes to get some recognition" (Brabham, 2009). Indeed, crowdsourcing's rewards "are splintering beyond money to include fame and community" (Winsor, 2009). We are, after all, living in the age of the overnight YouTube celebrity.

Despite its rewards, how does crowdsourcing typically treat intellectual property as a commodity? As seen in the case study examples presented earlier in this chapter (iStockphoto, Threadless, Peperami), creative work selected via crowdsourcing or co-creation strategies can be acquired relatively cheaply in comparison to its ultimate retail or marketing value to a company. As previously explained by the definition of the term "the crowd," people who submit ideas or work may be consumers (amateur sources of creative ideas/content) or those with specific training and expertise in various creative disciplines. Some consider "sourcing" from among the ranks of creative professionals as a separate issue from "sourcing" among amateurs and characterize the former as unethical. The American Institute of Graphic Arts (AIGA), an organization representing the interests of graphic artists and designers, is firmly against the crowd-sourcing of creative work from professionals in those fields, based on the idea that professionals should not do unpaid work or submit "spec" (speculative) work to open calls (Schmitt, 2009). Regardless of one's status as either an amateur or a pro, should not anyone whose creative work is chosen via a crowdsourcing or co-creation platform be paid fairly or at least in careful consideration of the work's anticipated value? Unfortunately, this is too often not the case. As Brabham (2008) suggests, "the amount of money paid to the crowd for high quality labor relative to the amount that labor is worth in the market represents a slave economy" (p. 83). Is it fair to pay someone $500 for a piece of artwork that will be used on merchandise sold for tens of thousands of dollars in profit in a single year? What if an ad produced by an amateur airs on the Super Bowl and generates millions in sales in exchange for $10,000 in prize money? Even some proponents of crowdsourcing worry that content acquired at bargain prices from "the crowd" creates a cumulative, downward pressure on the valuation for creative work in the marketplace (Winsor, 2009; Garfield, 2010). Clearly, those from "the crowd" who choose to submit creative work do so with a variety of motivations and of their own free will. However, one hopes that they also possess a thorough understanding of the pros and cons of their participation in these projects as well.

Are the Creative Outcomes of Crowdsourcing Commensurate with its Perceived Advantages?

Given the significant momentum of crowdsourcing and co-creation as high-profile marketing tools, expectations for the quality of creative work derived from "the crowd" are also rather lofty. While few were surprised by the polish and professionalism of Peperami's crowdsourced ad in 2010 (given the fact that a couple of ad pros won the pitch), it can be difficult to predict what amateurs in "the crowd" will contribute in terms of originality. As Christian Barnett, planning director at Coley Porter Bell (U.K.), reminds us, "Consumers may not be using the same criteria to judge creative work" as agencies or clients do (Barnett, 2010, p. 18). When people *outside* the industry create work *for* the industry, they "generally like things they are already familiar with" and imitate existing work (Barnett, 2010, p. 18). Therefore, any collection of content that is "sourced" from amateurs may feel derivative and retread "racial stereotypes, talking babies, and slapstick humor of traditional advertising" (Brabham, 2009).

Also of potential concern when considering the quality of "sourced" creative content is an apparent lack of diversity in "the crowd," which can result in perpetuation of the "aesthetic and values of white, straight, middle-class men" (Brabham, 2008, p. 86). Since most solicitations for creative work are made via online channels, the fact that typical web users are a rather homogenous group could inhibit the quality of work for certain kinds of products. Most members of "the crowd" are also under 30 years of age (Brabham, 2008). Could this mean, for example, that crowdsourcing might be a less viable option for marketers of products made for women or older people?

According to *MediaWeek* writer Eleftheria Parpis, crowdsourced work has its share of detractors in the industry. They call it "gimmicky, say it encourages low quality creative, and eschews strategic thinking and relationship management" (Parpis, 2009). Of course, industry pros are most critical of UGC (amateur work), which is often "shabbily produced, usually pointless and typically self-referential" in that it imitates advertising rather than innovates within the medium (Winsor, 2009). Given this perceived deficit in quality, some suggest that crowdsourcing and co-creation strategies are more valuable as consumer engagement experiences rather than sources of powerful content. In most cases, the best approach, according to *Advertising Age* columnist Bob Garfield, is to "embrace [crowdsourcing] not so much for the ads it may yield, but for experience" (Garfield, 2009, p. 4).

What Are Clients' Motives for Pursuing a Crowdsourcing Approach?

Clients, of course, are well aware that engagement with "the crowd" is about more than just outsourcing creative ideas or content. "Create an ad" competitions and other tactics are also designed to strengthen ties with consumers, generate buzz, and attract attention to their brands. But "sourced" content is also highly prized, particularly in terms of volume. John Ratcliffe, marketing director for the crowdsourcing firm Idea Bounty, reminds brand managers that they could "give a brief to a creative agency and get one idea from a team of two who would spend their time trying to crack the problem, or [they] could get over 100 fresh ideas" (Clark, 2010, p. 13). So, are lots of ideas always better than one? Sourcing ad ideas from the masses could complicate agency efforts to stay "on message," as consumers are unlikely to appreciate or understand a long-term branding strategy and will instead offer myriad divergent solutions.

Do clients with AOR relationships undermine those bonds anytime they look to "the crowd?" Sidestepping the AOR may damage a long-standing partnership by chipping away at trust and, ultimately, a brand's image itself (Krebs, 2011). Nevertheless, clients may still opt to take this risk due to a feeling of helplessness. In many cases, clients feel no sense of control over the creative process as it unfolds within an agency and "just have to trust that something suitable will rise to the top" (Davies, 2010, p. 10). Therefore, crowdsourcing efforts may sometimes amount to "stockpiling" of ideas to assure that all possibilities for promoting a brand are explored, some of which "could be stored for future ... campaign ideas" (Krebs, 2011). In these cases, a client may subject itself to another form of risk—the possibility that an old idea from "the crowd" might later be used without proper attribution or compensation to whomever originally submitted it, exposing companies to potential legal challenges down the road (Krebs, 2011).

Another, and perhaps more cynical, motive for clients and their brand managers to embrace crowdsourcing and co-creation is that it could serve the purpose of cutting advertising agencies out of the process altogether. Or at the very least, companies might leverage "the crowd" as a means of reducing fees that they typically pay to agencies, "because let's face it, public competitions are free pitches by any other name" (Davies, 2010, p. 10). Is this, then, a purely economic rationale, or do some of the high-profile success stories associated with crowdsourcing also call the value of professional expertise into question? Some brand managers "have used the recession as an opportunity to clamp down on paying for 'show ponies'—creative directors who enjoy substantial fees due to their profile" (Clark, 2010, p. 13). If amateurs can produce Super Bowl spots for Doritos at a fraction of the cost, what good is an advertising agency? The fallacy in this logic is that sometimes, clients will get what they pay for.

Does Crowdsourcing Represent an Abdication of Agency Responsibility to Clients?

As advertising agencies seek to justify their value to clients, crowdsourcing and co-creation is a double-edged sword. Agency principals and creative directors understand that many clients see value in these strategies and that any shop claiming to offer cutting-edge creative solutions must be prepared to implement them on a client's behalf. However, as previously discussed in this chapter, some see crowdsourcing and co-creation as a harbinger of disaster for the way agencies do business, or even their long-term viability (Clark, 2010; Davies, 2010). That sobering vision set aside, the fact remains that the competitive landscape for brands is more complex than ever and consumer insights have become absolutely indispensable to marketers. The mass collaboration afforded by crowdsourcing and co-creation strategies addresses both realities and is therefore a necessary tool for the modern agency (Winsor, 2009). In some cases, agencies that develop crowdsourcing platforms for their clients also see it as a savvy business decision, noting that clients often feel they are getting more for their money based on the often copious amounts of consumer data and creative content the strategies can deliver (Boches, 2009). But for traditional agencies that incorporate crowdsourcing strategies into broader media campaigns, more than 100 small firms and start-ups that specialize in this work now represent a significant and imminent competitive threat (Winsor, 2010). Crowdsourcing firms saw their revenues increase by 75% in 2011 to $376 million, according to industry tracking reports (Loten, 2012). If traditional agencies are to survive, crowdsourcing and co-creation will a big part of their future, whether they are ready for it or not.

Perhaps not surprisingly, a growing number of agency professionals express concern about the impact of crowdsourcing on the industry. While one might expect them to be focused on profitability and survival, some of the most passionate voices take a more philosophical tone. One of the major arguments against sourcing ideas and/or content from "the crowd" is that the benefits of these tactics are largely short-term in nature. Mark Hadfield, head of strategy at Nexus/h (U.K.), believes that investing too much in crowdsourcing is not a sustainable course, adding that "a rich, deep and long-lasting client relationship is worth much more than a scattergun approach to ideas" (Jack, 2009, p. 18). The implication here is that agencies should advise clients with the "big picture" in mind and prevent them from allowing consumers to drive strategic decision-making. Bob Seelert, worldwide chairman of agency giant Saatchi & Saatchi, warns against "outsourcing of everything that the agency does" (NavigateNewMedia, 2009). Seelert and others warn that giving "the crowd" too much influence over a brand's message is not in clients' best interests and part of the agency management function is to deliver that advice (NavigateNewMedia, 2009).

Most advertising campaigns for national brands are the result of months (if not years) of research, planning, and ideation that also consider a brand's complete history and anticipate its future. This level of stewardship is arguably what makes the client/agency relationship so valuable, and Wil Merritt, CEO of crowdsourcing firm Zooppa, agrees:

> It's worth stating that nothing can replace a well-researched and well-executed creative campaign. The level of creativity that top-tier marketing teams and agencies generate simply cannot be commoditized. Any attempt to substitute crowd creativity for the imaginations of creative visionaries is destined to be inadequate.
>
> (Merritt, 2012)

This acknowledgment signals the need for agencies to avoid any overemphasis on a single strategy when promoting a brand and to instead choose crowdsourcing (or any other approach) when it fits a brand's specific needs. Crowdsourcing and co-creation strategies should not be implemented because they are trendy but because they fulfill a special role within a broader campaign context.

Even if agencies make decisions about the use of crowdsourcing and co-creation with appropriate discretion, some creative professionals consider ideas and/or content sourced from "the crowd" as inferior and believe that clients are effectively cheated when amateurs or less experienced/educated people do the work. Benjamin Palmer, co-founder and chief creative officer of The Barbarian Group, believes that agencies deliver "the high end of marketing creativity and production" and that "the crowd" cannot match it (Parpis, 2009). The problem, as he sees it, is "by definition you are asking people [to contribute] who are not at the top of their field" (Parpis, 2009). Gordon Comstock, a copywriter and columnist at *Creative Review* (U.K.), agrees, citing the fact that two advertising veterans won the much-publicized Peperami pitch and adding, "we're still much better at this than the general public" (Comstock, 2010, p. 63).

Is "Crowdsourcing 2.0" an Improvement upon the Concept?

If crowdsourcing, like any other marketing strategy, has its pros and cons, it makes sense that this relatively new approach can be improved over time, with adjustments made to amplify its strengths and correct for its weaknesses. In a digital world, does our hyper-connectivity mean that crowdsourcing and co-creation's impact on branding will only grow in significance? Whatever the future holds, crowdsourcing is a dynamic, "sticky" phenomenon for which best practices continue to evolve (Boches, 2009). Amidst this process, industry watchers now cite "Crowdsourcing 2.0" as a more refined, responsible, and sustainable version of the original concept. Here, we define "Crowdsourcing 2.0" and look at a breakthrough agency using crowdsourcing as its business model. We also evaluate the extent to which this latest incarnation of the strategy continues to present ethical issues that can be explored by further research.

"Crowdsourcing 2.0" Defined

"Crowdsourcing 2.0" is a term primarily used in trade magazine articles and essays that discuss the latest applications of the strategy in advertising and share expert opinion on the topic. The distinguishing characteristics of "Crowdsourcing 2.0" are threefold: (1) "the crowd" is not an open, unfiltered community but instead a vetted, credentialed pool of creative people; (2) much more direction and "shepherding" of the process is managed by agency creative professionals; and (3) the exercise of sourcing content from "the crowd" is done in the context of building and maintaining extended working relationships between the agency, the client, and members of the crowd itself (Alberts, 2011; Boches, 2009; Jack, 2009; Winsor, 2009, 2010).

Redefining "the Crowd"

One of the purported improvements in "Crowdsourcing 2.0" is the vetting of members of "the crowd" by the advertising agency. When a call for creative ideas and/or content is made, only those whose experience and qualifications meet an agency's standards receive it. Typically, "the 2.0 crowd" is populated by designers, illustrators, writers, art directors, creative directors, and others whose expertise may be needed. Certainly, this approach helps mitigate concerns about the quality of content that is sourced from an undifferentiated group of consumers, as previously discussed (Barnett, 2010; Brabham, 2009). However, it is less clear how vetting members of "the crowd" might address the likely homogeneity of members, given that white males are overrepresented in most advertising creative roles. Furthermore, the continued solicitation of spec work from "the 2.0 crowd" will not silence critics who believe that professionals should not submit their work for free (Schmitt, 2009). It is important to note, however, that vetting "the crowd" does represent a reclaiming of considerable creative control by agencies that do so. If the goal is to consistently provide clients with quality work, this process increases that likelihood while still casting a large net to catch good work.

More Creative Direction

When sourcing creative from "the crowd" (that is, crowd 1.0), it is unrealistic to expect that most consumers think about a brand from a "big picture" perspective. As a result, some worry that sourced content has the potential to damage a brand's image or confuse its message (Davies, 2010; Jack, 2009; NavigateNewMedia, 2009). Although "the 2.0 crowd" of vetted professionals is likely to be far more sensitive to this issue, these participants are still "outsiders" who may not understand everything they should about the brand's situation. However, the provision of more deliberate and explicit guidance to "the crowd" when calls for work are made should improve the quality of creative work and help protect brands from suffering harm. More careful "shepherding" of the process on the part of agency personnel also helps ensure that the client's interests are being protected, and will presumably improve trust between the two.

Extended Relationships

Many crowdsourcing or co-creation initiatives are "one shot" experiments that generate some short-term excitement for a brand and are then quickly forgotten. But some notable exceptions, like Doritos' Super Bowl concept, are demonstrating to marketers that such activities can be carried forward and become fully integrated into a brand strategy. Now in its sixth year, the "Crash the Super Bowl" program is fully integrated into Doritos' brand work, which is led by its AOR, San Francisco's Goodby, Silverstein & Partners (Pathak, 2012). Although the Doritos competition remains open to anyone, the agency and client maintain tight control over the process. In this case, Crowdsourcing 2.0 is about integrating some of the strategy's key benefits (narrowing the gap between a brand and consumers, building excitement among them) and using it to fulfill long-term marketing goals.

Victors & Spoils: An Advertising Agency Built on Crowdsourcing 2.0

John Winsor, an agency executive cited extensively in this chapter, is a vocal crowdsourcing advocate—and with good reason. As the CEO of Victors & Spoils in Boulder, Colorado, he leads a firm that calls itself "the world's first creative advertising agency based on crowdsourcing principles" (Jack, 2009, p. 18). Founded in 2009, his shop is perhaps the highest-profile "test kitchen" for the long-term viability of crowdsourcing and on the leading edge of defining the term "Crowdsourcing 2.0" (Wåppling, 2009). Victors & Spoils' (V&S) current client roster includes Harley Davidson, Totino's, Axe Shampoo, and the Nike Foundation (www.victorsandspoils.com/).

When he and his partners founded V&S, Winsor knew that the industry would be skeptical about his agency's unique approach, but he views V&S as "an intermediary between brands and crowds ... aiming to address the main criticism that many have leveled at crowdsourcing—it lacks the sustained relationship a long-term agency provides" (Jack, 2009, p. 18). Sometimes V&S works directly for a client or it takes on a project with a brand's AOR as intermediary, but it is essentially organized like any traditional ad agency, with one major difference: Aside from a few creative directors who are full-time employees, the agency's creative department is a digital database of thousands (the agency's "crowd") who are tapped as needed, depending on the project. Although everything that V&S does utilizes its sourced creative pool, it produces whatever a client needs, which extends far beyond UGC competitions or microsites that solicit customer ideas. In other words, V&S's "crowd" works for V&S, which, in turn, works for its clients. The "curation and creative direction" that V&S uses in the vetting of its "crowd" and the content they generate is the key to the agency's success, according to Winsor (Winsor, 2010). Members of the V&S "crowd," after being properly vetted, receive sign-in credentials to access the agency's secure sections whenever a new creative brief (an assignment) is posted. In some cases, V&S will break a project up into smaller pieces and select sub-groups within the crowd to submit ideas, a process that Winsor calls "expertsourcing" (Winsor, 2010). Winsor and his team "want it to feel the same" for clients to work with V&S as they do with any traditional agency and insist that accounts are so "strategically managed" that the work is "headache free" (Winsor, 2010).

Thus far, V&S enjoys good press and word-of-mouth among most industry watchers, but after less than three years in business, it would be premature to call the shop an unqualified success. However, the agency's very existence speaks to the powerful role crowdsourcing and co-creation are playing as game changers in the industry. In the meantime, watch the horizon for the inevitable "Crowdsourcing 3.0."

Questions for Research Persist in the New 2.0

Is "Crowdsourcing 2.0," in fact, a vast improvement on the original concept that addresses the concerns of critics? Certainly, agencies like Victors & Spoils cite numerous "best practices" for crowdsourcing that they consider protective of both creative talent and the agency/client relationship. However, it can be argued that the new-and-improved "2.0" approach does not go far enough in terms of responding to naysayers.

Is the "Crowdsourcing 2.0" Crowd of "Experts" an Improvement in Terms of Diversity?

Among those agencies that engage in more careful vetting of creative talent and more "expertsourcing" when calls for creative work are made, is the diversity issue still at risk of being overlooked? If the members of a credentialed, creative "crowd" of freelancers look anything like the full-time ranks of the ad industry, white males with more industry experience will likely be overrepresented, potentially stifling agency recruitment of minorities and women looking to gain experience and to assume creative roles at less senior levels. How does crowdsourcing impact agency creative recruitment in terms of diversity, given that there are generally fewer full-time creative positions to fill? Does an agency's "vetting" of talent actually make "the crowd" *less* diverse than ever before? In an effort to address these questions, researchers could more closely examine the demographic characteristics of "vetted" creative professionals who regularly respond to crowdsourcing calls (with the goal of creating a profile of the typical "crowd" participant) and query human resources professionals within agencies (via interviews or surveys) to better understand how crowdsourcing may influence the recruitment and hiring of creatives. Furthermore, soliciting commentary from creative directors who supervise work by members of a "crowd" could offer a better understanding for how the "vetting" process actually works and the extent to which diversity is considered therein.

Does "Crowdsourcing 2.0" Address Concerns about the Nature and Quality of the Creative Content it Yields?

Critics of crowdsourcing argue that creative work sourced from an undifferentiated, largely amateur "crowd" will often be inferior in quality to work produced by advertising professionals. As previously discussed, "Crowdsourcing 2.0" is purported to address this issue by limiting "crowd" membership to more seasoned creative minds. But even if the potential for amateurish or unstudied work getting produced is greatly diminished in the "2.0" model, the diversity question remains. Realistically, can a relatively homogenous (albeit more credentialed and vetted) pool of creative talent consistently offer the most distinctive creative work for a vast array of clients and their consumers, or will it fuel a white cultural hegemony that the industry is regularly accused of supporting? A content analysis of advertising and other promotional work yielded from crowdsourcing—analyzed for minority group representation, how distinctive/original the work is in comparison to other content within a given product category, or according to other similar criteria—could help answer this question.

Does "Crowdsourcing 2.0" Help Narrow the "Trust Gap" between Agencies and Clients?

Among the more visible improvements in the "Crowdsourcing 2.0" concept are the methods adopted by agencies to ensure the quality of crowd-generated creative work, such as the vetting of creative talent, more attentive management of the process by creative directors, and a greater focus on long-term creative strategy. These measures were "built in" with hopes of increasing client confidence and keeping agencies relevant to the trend. However, it can be difficult to find evidence that clients see "Crowdsourcing 2.0" very differently or appreciate efforts by ad agencies to attract their business with it. Given the significant "trust gap" between agencies and clients so often discussed in the trade press, clients may view "crowdsourcing" as just another gimmick being used to reinvigorate the image of some agencies and launch new ones.

For example, despite the claim that an agency's creative directors can meticulously shepherd the crowdsourcing of talent and consequently improve the experience for both their clients and members of "the crowd," freelance creatives are likely to bring a different perspective to a crowdsourced assignment than one would expect from a traditional, full-time creative team. Can freelance art directors or writers hired to work on a per-project basis truly understand a brand's story as well as their full-time agency counterparts? Perhaps more importantly, is there much incentive (monetary or otherwise) for them to even make such an effort?

If this is the case, are agencies billing their clients for the same quality of creative work, or are clients being sold an inferior product that cannot realistically serve them well in the long run? It would be interesting to conduct interviews with creative freelancers who are part of "crowds" and try to determine the extent to which they feel integrated as part of the agency team, how they feel about the compensation structure, and whether they consider themselves just as responsible to the client as they are to the agency.

If, in fact, "Crowdsourcing 2.0" represents a significant change in the nature of the agency creative process, it seems that clients should be entitled to understand it and that agencies should value it accordingly. Should agencies bill clients for crowdsourced work differently than they bill for work produced by full-time employees (most significantly at a different rate)? Do clients who have worked with agencies on a crowdsourced project feel that they knew what was going on? What were the positive and negative aspects of the experience? Did they feel that they were treated fairly? What are clients' assessments of the crowdsourcing model both strategically and financially? These and other questions present an interesting opportunity for interdisciplinary work among advertising and economics or finance scholars, given the interplay of both disciplinary and budgetary issues they incorporate.

At this point, it may be too early to assess the long-term viability of the crowdsourcing concept (or agencies like Victors & Spoils built upon it), but close monitoring of not only the effectiveness but also the ethics of crowdsourced creative work over time may offer more answers and reveal its true impact on the agency/client relationship.

Conclusion

Advertising is an industry that sees many trends come and go, so people who work in this field are accustomed to change and adapting to new ways of doing business. But crowdsourcing and co-creation may be more disruptive to the business than anything it has seen before. The sourcing of creative ideas and/or content from outside the agency is proving transformative for those firms, their relationships with their clients and—perhaps most importantly—consumers, who now interact with brands and advertising on a personal level never seen before. The unique perspective that amateur creative work can bring to a brand holds great fascination for many clients. As a result, the crowdsourcing revolution is demanding the renegotiation of power between the advertiser and the consumer, with agencies now struggling to reclaim their role as expert advisers.

Less than a decade into the crowdsourcing phenomenon, ethical issues involving the potential exploitation of creative talent, the quality of crowdsourced creative work, and the dynamics of the agency/ client relationship are important to recognize, particularly as the industry begins to refine its approach in the form of "Crowdsourcing 2.0." This chapter identifies several important research questions that, if pursued by researchers, can contribute to a more holistic and long-term evaluation of the strategy. Both advertising practitioners and scholars should remain engaged in both the debate and the dialogue on crowdsourcing as we continue to witness the evolution of the advertising profession. Perhaps more importantly, this conversation may serve to protect the value of creative work and the integrity of the creative process.

References

Alberts, D. (2011, March 4). Making a stand for crowdsourcing 2.0. *Campaign*, 15.

Barnett, C. (2010, November 25). It's new, it's exciting, but it's not clever. *Design Week*, 18.

Boches, E. (2009, October 29). A crowdsourcing ad agency: can it work? Message posted to http://edwardboches.com.

Brabham, D. C. (2008). Crowdsourcing as a model for problem solving: An introduction and cases. *Convergence: The International Journal of Research into New Media Technologies*, 75(14), 75–90. doi:10.1177/1354856507084420

Brabham, D. C. (2009). Crowdsourced advertising: How we outperform Madison Avenue. *FlowTV.org*. Retrieved March 9, 2012 from http://flowtv.org.

Burkitt, L. (2010). Need to build a community? Learn from Threadless. *Forbes. com*. Retrieved March 7, 2012 from www.forbes.com/2010/01/06/threadless-t-shirt-community-crowdsourcing-cmo-network-threadless.html.

Campaign (2010, August 20). Does Peperami ad make a case for crowdsourcing? *Campaign*, 12.

Christodoulides, G., Jevons, C., & Blackshaw, P. (2011). The voice of the consumer speaks forcefully in brand identity: User-generated content forces smart marketers to listen. *Journal of Advertising Research*, 51(1), 101–108. doi:10.2501/JAR-51-1-101-111

Clark, N. (2010, July 14). Testing the wisdom of crowds. *Marketing*, 13.

Comstock, G. (2010, October). Oi! Crowdsource my tiny Peperami. And step on it! *Creative Review*, 63.

Davies, J. (2010, February 18). A democratic gesture? *Design Week*, 10.

Garfield, B. (2009). How Etsy made us rethink consumer-generated ads. *Advertising Age*, 80(31), 4–5.

Garfield, B. (2010). Crowdsourcing's democracy loses some appeal when your rate card is in jeopardy. *Advertising Age*, 81(27), 15.

Hempel, J. (2006). Crowdsourcing: Milk the masses for inspiration. *Business Week*, 4002, 38–39.

Howe, J. (2006). The rise of crowdsourcing. *Wired.com*. Retrieved March 5, 2012 from www.wired.com/wired/archive/14.06/crowds_pr.html.

Jack, L. (2009, November 26). The people take over the pitch. *Marketing Week*, 14–18.

Knutson, T. (2012). Is crowdsourcing a threat to ad agencies? *New BusinessIntel.com*. Retrieved from www.newbusinessintel.com/read/is-crowdsourcing-a-threat-to-ad-agencies.

Krebs, N. (2011, November 27). Off the board and to the horde! Is crowdsourcing ethical? Message posted to www.nannakrebs.com.

Lévy, P. (1997 [1995]). *Collective Intelligence: Mankind's Emerging World in Cyberspace*. New York: Plenum.

Loten, A. (2012). Small firms, start-ups drive crowdsourcing growth. *Online. WSJ.com*. Retrieved March 9, 2012 from http://online.wsj.com/article/SB1000 14240529702046536045772512931001111420.html.

Merritt, W. (2012). Crowdsourced advertising: It's not just cheap labor. *Adotas. com*. Retrieved March 5, 2012 from www.adotas.com/2012/02/crowdsourced-advertising-it%E2%80%99s-not-just-cheap-labor/.

NavigateNewMedia (2009, December 14). Bob Seelert: A conversation about the digital revolution. *YouTube*. Retrieved April 28, 2013 from www.youtube.com/watch?v=HURSjlAqHpo.

Parpis, E. (2009, November 2). Crowd control. *MediaWeek*, *19*(39).

Pathak, S. (2012, January 4). Doritos' Crash the Super Bowl: The five finalists. *Creativity-Online.com*. Retrieved March 4, 2012 from http://creativity-online.com/news/doritos-crash-the-super-bowl-the-five-finalists/231880.

Sacks, D. (2010). Mayhem on Madison Avenue. *Fast Company*, *151*, 110–144.

Schmitt, G. (2009). How will crowdsourcing trend shape creativity in the future? *Advertising Age*, *80*(14), 13.

Wåppling, D. (2009, October 29) Press release: Victors & Spoils launches first advertising agency built on crowdsourcing principles. Message posted to www.adland.tv/.

Winsor, J. (2009). Crowdsourcing: What it means for innovation. *BusinessWeek.com*. Retrieved March 9, 2012 from www.businessweek.com/innovate/content/jun2009/id20090615_946326.htm.

Winsor, J. (2010). The future of advertising. *BusinessWeek.com*. Retrieved March 9, 2012 from www.businessweek.com/innovate/content/jul2010/id20100712_542186.htm.

Chapter 10

Ethics, Advertising, and Racial Segmentation

An Integrated Social Identity Perspective

Troy Elias

A pluralistic ideology currently frames the American landscape. Today, differences between publics are intentionally delineated and, in many instances, celebrated as the once notable paradigm of mass communication continues to fissure and crack (Chaffee & Metzger, 2001; Katz, 1996). Contemporary media have contributed much to these developments. Modern media have enhanced the ability of audiences to transmit and retrieve information at relatively no cost, while simultaneously augmenting audiences' control over content creation and selection (Chaffee & Metzger, 2001). As a result, consumers now comprise distinctive groups with common interests and values, but perhaps more importantly, they now also wield the ability to discuss any topic that interests them, through whatever media they prize, whenever they see fit to do so. Accordingly, mass media can no longer be considered the dominant source of information that it once was.

Historically, going back 40 years or so, the majority of people living in America could access without cost, at best, three commercial broadcast stations, one public non-commercial TV station, and possibly one independent commercial station (Turow, 1997). Fast-forward to today, and innovative technologies have spawned a virtually unbounded wave of informational and interactive sources for consumers (Appiah & Elias, 2010; Papacharissi & Rubin, 2000). The number of television channels alone, for instance, has grown from an average of 33 in 1990, to over 100 channels by 2003, and more than 150 by 2009 (Tanner, 2011). The enhanced ability of the media to reach countless individuals with diverse interests has stimulated an "attention economy" that places a premium on attracting audiences' attention (Webster & Zsiazek, 2012).

Media firms and advertisers have proven to be major drivers of this economy. Their conscientious endeavors to carve an organically large and nebulous heterogeneous market into smaller, more manageable, homogeneous slices (Hollerbach, 2009) have yielded meticulously monitored communities where distinctive listening, viewing, and reading practices are cultivated (Turow, 1997). This strategy is known as audience segmentation (Nairn & Berthon, 2003). Altogether, audience segmentation refers to the grouping of members of a heterogeneous audience into blocs of consumers who are alike based on valued, principal characteristics (Hollerbach, 2009; Pires & Stanton, 2005). As the degree to which a consumer identifies with a given homogenous consumer segment increases, so too does the expectation that he or she will respond favorably to a tailored offer based on that identity (Pires & Stanton, 2005). The ultimate objective of audience segmentation is, therefore, targeted marketing or the rigorous marketing of a product to a consumer segment based on their principal, valued, shared characteristics (Cui & Choudhury, 2003).

As an overall marketing strategy, audience segmentation and concomitantly target marketing have become cornerstones of modern marketing (Cui & Choudhury, 2003; Smith & Cooper-Martin, 1997). However, while segmented markets propagate a closely knit, marketable community among people of a similar background, they also embellish differences between social factions, which can have an overall deleterious effect on the American public sphere (Gandy, 2005). Although a segment may be defined based on any number of cues that determine an individual's membership in a group (Gandy, 1998; Nairn & Berthon, 2003), this article centers on segmentation of audiences based on race and ethnicity, focusing specifically on the Black demographic.

To date, a review of the existing literature reveals a tendency to depict the Black audience as victims of the media. Blacks as consumers are often regarded as decentered subjects, historically and culturally embedded within social relations, capable of making meaning only through historical and socio-cultural discourses and influences that frame their otherness and their exploitation (Gandy, 1998, 2005; Kates, 1999). A less frequently observed perspective is that of Black audiences as autonomous actors making conscientious decisions as empowered consumers amidst a fractured media landscape (Gandy, 1998, 2005; Turow, 1997). Integration of these two outlooks is noticeably absent in the literature. These perspectives, however, are by no means mutually exclusive. While there are ethical implications at the macro-level, where media firms and ad agencies mine Black audience segments with the objective of shaping their consumer decision making, there is an equally important need to understand how Black consumers and audiences are likely to respond to mediated messages that arise due to advertisers' attempts to commoditize Black identity.

This chapter, accordingly, seeks to address the schism between studies that view race-based audience segmentation and target marketing as debilitating tools that stereotype and malign the Black community versus those that acknowledge Black consumers as independent entities making conscientious assessments as empowered consumers. Concomitant ethical issues related to the practice of audience segmentation and targeted marketing will be addressed. The chapter will conclude with an agenda for future research. Theoretical frameworks such as media dependency, social identity theory, and psychological distinctiveness are utilized to examine and explain the way Black individuals may be inclined to make choices with regard to media selection and usage, as well as how they may most likely respond to the influence of similar others in mediated contexts today and in the future. In sum, this chapter seeks to explore current and future nuances of both the macro- and micro-level tensions at work in the segmenting of Blacks in America.

Racial and Ethnic Segmentation

Effectively executed audience segmentation on the basis of race and ethnicity is deemed a sensible strategy as it resonates strongly along a dimension that is meaningful to the intended audience (Grier & Brumbaugh, 2004). The process of targeting Blacks in America, however, has not evolved without some missteps. In past decades, and still today, advertisers and marketers can be found who believe that Black consumers can effectively be reached by using White or mainstream characters in general media. As argued by African American advertising guru Tom Burrell (2010), however, Black people are not dark-skinned White people. They have distinct psychosocial needs, desires, aspirations, and fears. They also tend to have different approaches to shopping and purchasing than other ethnic groups (Wolburg & Pokrywczynski, 2001). To wit, studies have demonstrated the salience and importance that the race or ethnicity of a source plays as a communication heuristic for ethnic minorities (Appiah, 2002, 2003, 2007; Deshpandé & Stayman, 1994; Elias, Appiah, & Gong, 2011).

Nevertheless, a major concern of advertisers has been that the use of ethnic minorities in advertising campaigns would lead to a White backlash (Bush, Hair, & Solomon, 1979; Chambers, 2008). Extant literature, however, refutes this argument and offers empirical support that the opposite is, in fact, more likely to occur. Experimental studies indicate that White consumers tend to respond no differently to commercial websites that feature a product endorsement from a Black character than they did toward a White character endorsing the product (Appiah, 2007). White viewers have also been found to display no significant differences in their browsing behavior, recall of product and site content, or evaluation patterns of products and main characters based on the racial target of the site (Appiah, 2003). The findings for ethnic minorities, however, are markedly different.

Black consumers have been found to respond more favorably to testimonial ads that utilize testimonials from Black characters than those from White characters (Elias & Appiah, 2010). Blacks have also indicated greater levels of identification with a character, a greater tendency to believe a website and product were meant for "someone like them," and recalled more information from a site that features Black testimonials as opposed to a site with either White testimonials or no testimonials (Appiah, 2007). Other studies also show Black consumers have better recall of Black occupational characters on television than they do White occupational characters (Appiah, 2002), and that even when Blacks do not evaluate Black targeted websites more favorably than White targeted websites, they still tend to spend more time browsing and have greater recall of information from Black-targeted sites than White-targeted sites (Appiah, 2003). Despite these findings, however, advertisers still display a notable degree of reticence to use Black characters and models in advertisements. Further compounding this issue is the growth of other ethnic markets, particularly the Spanish-speaking market.

As the U.S. undergoes shifts in its ethnic and racial composition, which are projected to make it a "majority-minority" society by 2042 (Lichter, 2012), much of the attention of advertisers has shifted to the Hispanic market. At face value, this is understandable. Hispanics currently represent the largest ethnoracial minority population in the U.S., at 16% of the total population (Lichter, 2012), and they are already a significant segment of the workforce (Cartegena, 2012). They are expected to keep increasing in size faster than other minority groups, and they have migrated not just to traditional locations such as the Southwest, California, Texas, New York, and Miami, but to rural areas as well (Quian & Lichter, 2007; Lichter, 2012). Awareness of these demographic shifts has prompted a lack of urgency with regard to using Blacks in racially authentic and culturally relevant ways in ads (Miller & Kemp, 2006). Advertisers have grown complacent in their pursuit of insights related to the Black demographic. This has been reflected in reduced spending, a notable increase in generic messaging, and inadequate levels of market research into major aspects of the lifestyles of Blacks (Miller & Kemp, 2006). This is especially unfortunate given how much the Black population has to offer.

The Appeal of the Black Demographic

According to the 2010 Census's racial and ethnic data, America is more ethnically diverse today than it has ever been (Mobolade, 2011). Blacks, specifically, continue to grow and make strides in income and education at a rate that exceeds that of the overall population (Nielsen, 2011). Nielsen (2011) reports that Black households in the U.S. earning more than $75,000 per annum grew by 63.9% between 2000 and 2009, while Black households earning $50,000 or less decreased in the same span.

This rate of increase was 11.7% greater than the change of the overall population, representing, according to Nielsen (2011), "a full shift upward in the income of the overall [Black] community" (p. 6). Also increasing over the years has been Black buying power. Hallman (2008) reports increases in U.S. Black buying power from $318 billion in 1990 to $590 billion in 2000, and $1.1 trillion in 2011, a 237% increase in 22 years (Hallman, 2008). Scholars contend that these gains reflect more than mere population growth and inflation and are indicative of sustainable, improved employment opportunities and higher levels of education (Humphreys, 2008). The true value of the Black demographic, however, extends beyond their available wealth as a group and into their potential impact on American culture. Blacks are often considered one of the primary influencers of mainstream culture (Miller & Kemp, 2006).

Pettigrew (2008) contends that, given their disadvantaged status, Blacks have constantly found it necessary to be creative to survive. Hence, from the time of slavery to the present day, Blacks have affected language, music, dance, and style as forms of self-expression. In many instances, when Blacks start wearing a new style of clothing, the country soon follows (Miller & Kemp, 2006; Patterson, 2006). Culturally related music such as rap and hip hop is quickly adopted by members of other ethnicities, including Asians, Latinos, and Whites (Miller & Kemp, 2006; Patterson, 2006). The same can also be said of African American slang, which is often quickly adopted by mainstream culture (Pettigrew, 2008). On the other hand, Blacks are unlikely to look to other cultures for cues about clothing, language, music, or behavior (Miller & Kemp, 2006). All things considered, it seems counterintuitive to not extend every effort to speak in a culturally significant way to a demographic that often dictates to the rest of the planet what cool is. With Black America showing economic progress and population growth, and with its potential for influence, it is advisable for advertisers and those who study advertising to have some understanding of the way that this demographic operates under existing segmentation influences.

Advertising as Adversary

As previously mentioned, a primary driver of audience segmentation is the advertising industry (Nairn & Berthon, 2003; Turow, 1997). Advertising plays an integral role as the major support system of U.S. media (Turow, 1997), but perhaps more importantly, it helps define the borders between those who are to be considered within the group and those who represent members of an out-group (Entman & Rojecki, 2000; Gandy, 1998). As has been the case for several decades, advertising messages in the media implicitly and explicitly tell members of society where they belong, who they are, and how they should act toward others (Coltrane & Messineo,

2000; Entman & Rojecki, 2000; Gandy, 2005). With U.S. ad spending projected at roughly $170 billion for 2012 alone (Hof, 2012), advertising continues to surpass major institutions such as the church, family, and school in its ability to provide cultural guidance about an individual's place in society (Nairn & Berthon, 2003; Turow, 1997). African Americans, however, have long held an adversarial relationship with the advertising industry (Entman & Rojecki, 2000), more so, in fact, than any other racial or ethnic group in the U.S. (Chambers, 2008).

Chambers (2008) posits that Black consumers and image makers have long sought advertising messages that reflect the diversity of the Black experience and which portray overlooked nuances of Blacks' lifestyles, culture, and aspirations. The depictions that have been most prevalent, however, have typically been crafted by White image makers for the larger portion of the twentieth century and have been largely negative and stereotypical. The deleterious effect of these messages on the psyche of Blacks in America, as well as the impact of its shaping of negative perceptions of Blacks held by those who wield power, cannot be overstated. Coltrane and Messineo (2000) argue that, while audiences are not expected to automatically mimic what they see in the media, media images still manage to become incorporated into cognitive schema and are "called up during processes of identity formation, self-evaluation, attribution, and social comparison" (p. 365). They argue that media images sanction restrictive and stereotypical worldviews, promote approval of current social standards, and assure people that the status quo is the way things ought to be. Not surprisingly, given the influence of advertising on shaping identity in the U.S. (see Coltrane & Messineo, 2000 for a full review), a great deal of attention has been and continues to be paid to related ethical issues that arise in advertisers' segmenting and targeting of Blacks in the U.S.

Audience Segmentation—Ethical Implications

Critics of audience segmentation often argue that segmented audiences are much more analogous to victimized publics than they are to endowed individuals acting with power and autonomy (Gandy, 2005). Gandy (1998) contends that advertisers and media firms use audience segmentation to strip consumers of the diversity that makes them unique. For instance, in order for racial and ethnic segmentation to be effective, group members must identify based on traits such as shared ethnicity and cultural experiences. Those that identify are expected to respond in the same way to targeted offers (Pires & Stanton, 2005). The reality for Blacks, however, despite the overtures of advertisers and general media, is that there is no single Black experience (Miller & Kemp, 2006). Variables such as age, education, economics, geography, sexual orientation, skin color, and differences in degrees of family and community support can affect how one Black person's experience in the U.S. might be similar to or different from that of another Black person (Miller & Kemp, 2006). The practice and product of audience segmentation, however, routinely fail to make this distinction (Smith & Cooper-Martin, 1997). As such, a critical fall-out of audience segmentation processes is the reinforcement of stereotypes of the very groups they seek to attract (Gandy, 1998).

Advertisers are often believed to have the most accurate gauge of the sensitivities and inclinations of the audiences that they mine (Gandy, 2005). Entman and Rojecki (2000) contend that there is no group more expert in a society's cultural values and taboos than those who create television advertisements. They argue that ads often provide extremely precise indicators of a culture's racial heartbeat. Historically, however, African Americans have been portrayed as inferior and subservient to Whites in mainstream media (Entman & Rojecki, 2000). Not surprisingly, the reality for most agencies is that they have been and remain underrepresented by ethnic minority employees at virtually every position (Boles, 2006). Chambers (2008) posits that, for the majority of the twentieth century, predominantly White advertisers and ad agency personnel did not believe Black professionals in the field were necessary. African American expertise and insight was not considered a valuable asset. Again, it was believed that a White backlash would result from the use of Blacks in ads. Furthermore, it was presumed that White consumers would view positive images of Blacks as a direct challenge to White authority and societal norms, and that Blacks did not have adequate economic sway to be an important consumer group anyway. As a result, expertise and insight into the Black audience was not sought out, and Black personnel were not recruited except for the most menial of agency positions. Therefore, for most of the twentieth century, advertisements and the ad industry remained bereft of representation within its own ranks from members of the same Black segments whose identity and culture they were supposed to be representing. Nonetheless, a number of notable African American ad agencies, such as Global Hue, Carol H. Williams, and the Burrell Communications group, exist, and they strive to provide more accurate and insightful campaigns, using Black models where needed and employing Black executives in relevant agency positions. Firms like these can hopefully help minimize the occurrence of additional ethical issues related to simplistic understandings of Black markets and problematic portrayals of Black consumers. This may still be a particularly challenging task, however, when it comes to one particular Black issue: the inclusion of non-stereotypical and non-offensive imagery of the Black homosexual in mediated narratives of Black life.

Multiple minorities, specifically those that are sexual minorities as well as Black, experience a unique conflict: homophobia in the Black community and racism in the gay community (Smith, 1999). Homophobia and sexual prejudice can be motivated by multiple factors. These include religious pronouncements (Smith, 1999), disagreeable exchanges with gay/lesbian individuals that become generalized attitudes toward the entire group, heterosexuals' discomfort with their own sexual urges or gender compliance, and perhaps most likely for Blacks, the impact of in-group norms that are at odds with homosexual individuals and their life-style (Herek, 2000). The reality, however, is that not all Black people are straight, and not all gay people are White (Carbado, 2000). Heterosexual Black America, however, tends to view the gay community as White, affluent, highly privileged, and politically formidable (Smith, 1999). Car-bado (2000) argues that the idea that homosexuality is something that White people do and Black people shouldnot do has been circulated and reified in the Black community since the 1960s. To many Blacks, a Black person's ethnic authenticity is linked to his or her sexual identity (Car-bado, 2000). Black gays and lesbians have to decide, therefore, whether they want to be Black or gay. Implicit in this outlook is the idea that Blackness is a static, unchanging identity, while homosexuality is a choice or lifestyle. Furthermore, Smith (1999) contends that, because Black gay and lesbian individuals are rendered invisible in both Black and gay con-texts, it has become easier for the Black community to express homopho-bia and oppose gay rights without taking into consideration that these attacks affect their own members. It is as important today as it has been at any other time for the Black community to embrace all of its mem-bers, regardless of sexual orientation. There are already sufficient outside threats to the existence of Blacks without attacks or marginalization of an already marginalized group by its own in-group members.

A relevant example of an outside threat is the targeting of harmful products solely to the Black consumer. In past decades, there has been a significant push to prevent targeted marketing of harmful products to vulnerable markets (Smith & Cooper-Martin, 1997). Constituents of these markets are thought to include children, the elderly, those prone to addiction or compulsion, or those considered disadvantaged due to their socioeconomic status (Cui & Choudhury, 2003; Smith & Cooper-Martin, 1997). Targeted marketing has generally been considered a boon to both consumers and marketers in that it encourages fewer wasted resources on the management side, while providing, ideally, consum-ers with products they are most likely to be interested in (Calfee, 1991). However, numerous cases exist of consumer interest groups expressing dissatisfaction with the targeting of harmful products to vulnerable con-sumers (Cui & Choudhury, 2003). Two of the more famous instances in past years involve products targeted exclusively to Blacks: Uptown ciga-rettes from R.J. Reynolds Tobacco Co., and high-powered malt liquor, Power Master, from G. Heileman Brewing Co. Uptown provided higher levels of menthol, and Power Master had stronger alcoholic content than similar general-market products in the same product categories. These products were meant to target the Black demographic exclusively. Ultimately, they were both withdrawn from consideration amidst a deluge of criticism from health specialists, community groups, activists, and even clergy (Calfee, 1991; Smith & Cooper-Martin, 1997).

Going forward, however, it is clear that it is important that marketers and advertisers adequately address ethical problems that involve Black consumers and their potential susceptibilities in relation to the types of products being targeted toward them. Naturally, there are implications in how the term "vulnerable" is being operationalized. Cui and Choudhury (2003) argue that consumers' abilities to perceive the harmfulness of a product tend to fall on a continuum that extends from sophisticated to at-risk, then to vulnerable. According to Cui and Choudhury, sophisticated consumers are labeled as such usually due to maturity, higher levels of education, or prior experience. At-risk consumers refer to those prone to addiction but who may still possess basic skills and abilities, while those that are vulnerable are categorized by factors such as age, education, and physical and mental health problems. The Black community, like many other demographic units, is inherently heterogeneous. There are sections within the population that would fit within any one of the three aforementioned categories at any given point in time. Advertisers need to determine in advance what aspect of Black life they are seeking to target, as that may have implications for any conceivable ethical issue. For instance, the argument that Power Master malt liquor was taken off the shelves because it targeted Blacks should really be qualified by the argument that it targeted poor Blacks who were not sufficiently informed about the possible and likely accumulative negative effects of high-powered alcohol consumption on their health. Saying that Power Malt and Uptown were dropped for targeting Blacks is excessively simplistic and mechanistic. The reality is much more complex.

Regardless, advertisers need to ascertain in advance whether their target audience is capable of understanding the benefits and hazards that accompany a product. Customers need a certain level of mental, physical, and economic abilities to fully engage in a marketing exchange (Cui & Choudhury, 2003). Marketers need to ensure that, before that exchange occurs, consumers have adequate levels of each. Advertisers also need to determine whether targeted markets have been provided sufficient information to conclude whether their expectations will be fulfilled after a purchasing decision, and that targeted markets are provided with the option of going elsewhere (Cui & Choudhury, 2003). Although it sounds extreme, the alternative is potential negative public fall-out with an already issue-ridden Black consumer segment and the possibility of expensive litigation. Additionally, while targeting vulnerable populations with harmful products is clearly unethical, choosing not to target ethnic segments or not to provide them with the option of using a product or service is also fraught with controversy and ethical issues (Cui & Choudhury, 2003). Firms may be concerned about making a mistake in ethnic marketing because of the political implications, so they may elect to do nothing or to do what everybody else has done in order to avoid difficulties (Zuckoff, 1992). Targeting Blacks or any other ethnic group using a unique marketing mix for products that provide universal benefits is considered unethical and unfair (Cespedes, 1993) as it reduces opportunities and options for other consumers by excluding them; such actions limit consumer choices.

Another common ethics-based critique of audience segmentation, one that affects Blacks much more indirectly than the preceding issues, is that audience segmentation processes place the overall U.S. public sphere at risk. It has been argued that, in the audience production process, advertisers actively seek rifts in the social fabric and then fortify and expand those rifts for their own economic advancements (Turow, 1997). While segmented markets may develop a closely knit community among people of a similar background, highlighting differences between groups can induce a host of anti-communal effects, such as increased suspicion of others, easily accessible racial and gender stereotypes, perpetuation of subtle forms of racial prejudice, limited opportunities for community building, and the setting of cognitive limits on the potential for social change (Coltrane & Messineo, 2000; Entman & Rojecki, 2000; Turow, 1997). Katz (1996) argues that, except for occasional media events, the nation no longer congregates together through the media. Given the exponential increase in available channels of information, media have largely ceased to function as a shared public space in its traditional sense. According to Katz (1996), the mass democracy of the U.S. landscape is being deprived of a common meeting ground, and, should theories of technological determinism be accurate, the very cohesion of the nation-state itself is in jeopardy. Implicit in this argument lies a major issue with much of the criticism of audience segmentation addressed thus far. The critiques offered take on a technologically deterministic slant and largely fail to recognize the agency of the consumer. Even the staunchest critic of audience segmentation needs to address the socially deterministic attitude inherent in the element of segmentation. As Gandy (2005) argues, "the construction of the audience as a market grants some autonomy to individuals as rational actors who select those goods and services that have the greatest potential for meeting their needs within the limits of their budgets" (p. 3). Accordingly, an important consideration that needs to be examined is the gratifications gained by audiences in using the media. One notable argument provided in extant literature is that, as society becomes more complex, individuals turn to the media to help them understand what is expected of them and to help them find their place in the world.

Media Dependency

Proponents of the dependency model of mass communication effects argue that audiences approach mediated messages with pre-established beliefs, values, and norms that have been established through their valued group associations (Ball-Rokeach & DeFleur, 1976). Messages stemming from the media are perceived and interpreted through the filter of an individual's social reality. Social reality is certainly derived from an individual's direct experiences, which provide meaning and understanding of the world through symbolic interactions with others, but it also is derived through a dependency on the media. Media contribute to social reality by informing, explaining, and providing valuable information about nuances and subtleties of the world in which we live (Gamson, 1995; Johnson-Cartee, 2005).

As society progressively becomes more convoluted, dependency on the media to explain complex issues heightens. Like everyone else living in a complex world, Black individuals are often required to make determinations about issues (i.e., vote for public officials, espouse ideals, or express opinions), which may be outside their normal frame of reference. Resultant feelings of ambiguity, ambivalence, and even anxiety, particularly in situations where the issue is imperative, can drive individuals to the mass media for information and guidance (Gamson, 1995; Johnson-Cartee, 2005). By interpreting media messages as "real," however, and not fully considering the way these messages are produced, Blacks can acquire a sense of reality that is not based on any objective reality (Johnson-Cartee, 2005). The ramifications of this can be especially problematic, considering that knowledge is often constructed through the media (Deutsch & Gerard, 1955). Media narratives, particularly through advertising and to a lesser extent through the news, are often carefully constructed channels of culturally transmitted messages that re-affirm cultural and behavioral mores (Armstrong, Neuendorf, & Brentar, 1992).

Turow (1997) contends that society is, debatably, a construct created through acts of communication. The media communicate to audiences the norms and mores of a society, the types of individuals that make up that society, traits they tend to have, general behavioral orientations of prototypical members, valuable traits they may share, and likewise, actions they perform that are altogether unfavorable. Advertising and media practitioners, therefore, help facilitate the construction of attitudes toward women, men, homosexuals, African Americans, White Americans, Hispanic Americans, the affluent, seniors, democrats, and even children within U.S. society (Turow, 1997). Problems arise, however, when individuals' only contact with members of out-groups lies in mediated messages.

Scholars have long maintained that separation and unfamiliarity with an out-group breed stereotypes and intergroup prejudice, which give rise to negative attitudes and varying degrees of hostility (Allport, 1954; Brewer & Gaertner, 2004). Increased contact with out-group members, particularly under cooperative, interactive conditions, however, can undermine negative attitudes and change attitudes toward and beliefs about a group as a whole (Brewer & Gaertner, 2004). This is supported by studies on heterosexual attitudes toward homosexuality that indicate that the more gays and lesbians a person knows, the less homophobic he or she is likely to be (Finlay & Walther, 2003; Liang & Alimo, 2005), particularly when those individuals are friends or family members. Unfortunately for the majority of us living in the U.S., diversity, for the most part, is restricted to the workplace (Miller & Kemp, 2006).

In fact, outside of places of employment and college campuses, collaborative, interactive, inter-ethnic group contact in the U.S. is a rarity. For example, the majority of Blacks in the U.S. choose to live, worship, and socialize exclusively with each other (Miller & Kemp, 2006). Although they may work with other ethnic groups, they are otherwise reading Black newspapers and magazines, visiting Black websites, listening to Black radio (i.e., hip-hop, rhythm and blues, or jazz), and experiencing culturally targeted messages primarily in the neighborhoods in which they reside (Miller & Kemp, 2006). Blacks are by no means the exception. For instance, even though Blacks are inclined to live and play amongst their own kind, their numeric minority status in the U.S. means that they are more likely to experience interracial contact than Whites (Trawalter & Richeson, 2008). Furthermore, as argued by Fischer (2011), college represents the first time that Whites come into significant contact with members of other ethnic groups, despite the overall changing nature of interracial relations in the U.S. As the U.S. grows exceedingly more diverse (Humphreys, 2008; Mobolade, 2011), however, the frequency of interracial contact for every ethnicity is likely to change. A fragmented media and interpersonal landscape holds numerous implications for ethnic minorities. Social identity theory and the distinctiveness principle are two theoretical frameworks that can help address these implications.

Social Identity Theory of Intergroup Behavior

Social identity theory examines the social psychological processes of intergroup behavior (Tajfel, 1974; Tajfel & Turner, 1986). Social identity can be defined as "that part of an individual's self-concept that is derived from his knowledge of his membership of a social group (or groups) together with the emotional significance attached to that membership" (Tajfel,

1974, p. 69). One of the major assertions of this theory is that posi-tive social identity is based on comparisons made between the in-group and some relevant out-group such that an individual's in-group is viewed more favorably. Generally, when individuals' social identity is considered unsatisfactory, they will either strive to leave their existing group and join some other, more positively distinct group, or they will try to make their existing group more positively distinct (Tajfel & Turner, 1986).

The inherent human motivation for maintaining positive social identity, as argued by social identity theorists (see Hogg, 2004; Tajfel & Turner, 1986), is the enhancement and maintenance of self-esteem. People are assumed to have a fundamental need to achieve and maintain positive social identities for the social groups to which they belong as a means of enhancing their sense of worth. The implications of this are especially rel-evant to ethnic minorities, such as Blacks, given that minority size tends to be highly correlated with disadvantages in power and status (Brewer, 1991). Arguably then, ethnic minorities should be more motivated in general than members of an ethnic majority to improve perceptions of their self-worth. This should lead to higher levels of ethnic identification among ethnic groups as the outcome, and the reputation of each group is indelibly linked to its members' self-worth (Brewer, 1991).

What has been overlooked in much of the literature is the fact that all ethnic minorities, including Blacks, may not necessarily respond the same way or feel the same way about their racial or ethnic member-ship (Elias, Appiah, & Gong, 2011). For many Blacks, race might be an important social identity; however, a great deal of variability in terms of how strongly individuals identify with their ethnic groups has been found over the years. Studies on the identity of minorities have indicated indi-vidual variation in the strength of ethnic identification among minorities (see Phinney, 1992). This variation in the degree to which members of an ethnic group value and identify with their ethnic group is labeled *eth-nic identity*. Phinney (2005) defines ethnic identity as "a self-constructed understanding of oneself in terms of one's cultural and ethnic background and the attitudes and feelings associated with that background" (p. 189). It has since been found that mainly minorities with strong ethnic identity tend to clearly exhibit in-group, same-race favoritism in media responses and social interactions (Appiah, 2004). Another key variable that may potentially affect Blacks' responses to targeted ads is the impact of group size relative to the size of the out-group.

Effects of Group Size

While variation in minority members' ethnic affiliation and identifica-tion has proven helpful in elucidating the ways in which minority groups interact with culturally or racially targeted content, another significant finding in the literature has been the impact of group size on the salience of group membership. Deshpandé and Stayman (1994) found that minority-group consumers (Hispanics) are more likely to spontaneously invoke their ethnic identities when they are in a social context where they make up the numeric minority rather than a numeric majority in their cities. The results of their study demonstrated that Hispanics who reside in a social environment where they are the numeric minority (Austin, Texas) are more likely to believe that a Hispanic spokesperson is trustworthy, and evaluate the brand of a product endorsed by a Hispanic higher than Hispanics who reside in a social environment where they are the numeric majority (San Antonio, Texas). This finding was consistent for Blacks as well. Black consumers who represent a numeric minority in their immediate social environment show significantly more favorability toward targeted online ads than Black consumers who reside in a social environment where they make up the numeric majority (Elias & Appiah, 2010). These findings offer significant implications for distinctiveness.

Distinctiveness Principle and Distinctiveness Theory

The distinctiveness principle refers to a general human motive within individuals' identity to establish and maintain a sense of differentiation from others (Breakwell, 1986; Brewer, 1991; Vignoles, Chryssochoou, & Breakwell, 2000). The distinctiveness principle contends that individuals have a need to see themselves as unique (Snyder & Fromkin, 1980), as well as a need to establish a sense of differentiation from others (Brewer, 1991). At the same time, however, individuals also have a need to belong to some larger social collective (Brewer, 1991). Brewer (1991) argues that individuals that are highly individuated are susceptible to isolation and stigmatization, while individuals that are fully deindividuated lack a basis for comparative appraisal or self-definition.

Fundamentally, the distinctiveness principle asserts that individuals will tend to perceive characteristics that provide them a sense of distinctiveness as central to their identity and will oftentimes display opinions and behaviors that exhibit their distinctiveness from others (Vignoles et al., 2000). Research has indicated that individuals from several cultures and subcultures are particularly motivated to distinguish themselves from others and are likely to do so when their distinctiveness or identity is threatened, challenged, or salient (Jetten, Spears, & Manstead, 1996; Mastro, 2003), which is particularly true for Blacks.

Distinctiveness theory argues that a person's distinctive traits (race and ethnicity, for instance) will be more salient to him or her than the more prevalent traits that are possessed by other people in the environment (Appiah, 2003; Deshpandé & Stayman, 1994). The theory asserts that people tend to define themselves on the basis of traits that are numerically rare in their social environment (Grier & Brumbaugh, 2004; McGuire, 1984; McGuire, McGuire, Child, & Fujioka, 1978). When individuals are required to consider their identity, those identities that will take precedence over others tend to be those that are rare in their "social milieu" (McGuire, 1984). The classic example given for this is that a Black woman is more likely to be aware of her gender when she is in a room filled with Black men, but more aware of her race when she is in a room full of White women (Grier & Brumbaugh, 2004). Therefore, for ethnic minority groups living in the U.S., race and ethnicity should tend to be salient characteristics in their day-to-day communication and interaction behavior in both personal and mediated situations given their numeric minority status. Whites, on the other hand, may for the most part tend to not be as affected given that they represent a numeric majority in the U.S.

Generally, the literature indicates that Whites do not think of themselves as a specific ethnic group (Phinney, 1992) and tend to be guided by more nonracial cues, such as occupation and social class status, than by race (Smedley & Bayton, 1978). As mentioned earlier, Appiah (2007) found that, unlike Blacks, White consumers respond no differently to commercial websites whether the character endorsing a product is Black or White. White viewers have also been found to display no significant differences in their browsing behavior, recall of product and site content, or evaluation patterns of products and main characters based on the racial target of the site (Appiah, 2004). These findings imply that Whites tend not to explicitly use race as their primary cue when identifying with a source or while making similarity judgments (Smedley & Bayton, 1978). Blacks, on the other hand, given that they represent a numeric minority in their social environment, tend to be much more cognizant of their race, thereby leading them to be more sensitive to same-race mediated characters and subsequently leading them to evaluate stimuli associated with same-race characters more favorably.

A Look Ahead

As an overall marketing strategy, audience segmentation and target marketing have become cornerstones of modern marketing (Cui & Choudhury, 2003; Smith & Cooper-Martin, 1997). There is a great likelihood that these strategies will be in use for some time. Given the subtle ways that advertising affects group formulation, it is important to examine the effects of segmentation on the Black community. A yet-to-be addressed issue in this chapter is what role advertising plays in the crystallization or fragmentation of the Black community, if any. Although the Black experience varies based on diverse experiences and countless variables, there are still shared cultural experiences that frequently promote a strong sense of group unity. It can be argued, however, that the once close-knit Black community has also felt the effects of audience segmentation. For instance, while older Blacks are more inclined to believe that being Black is a static entity, changes afforded by segmentation potentially show younger generations being much more open to redefining what it means to belong to a particular ethnic group.

For instance, despite longstanding acceptance of the one drop rule (i.e., one drop of Black blood made a person Black under the eyes of the law in the U.S.) that harkens back to the 1920s (Gandy, 1998), Census data from 2000 indicate that audiences 25 and under are twice as likely as older adults to identify themselves as multiracial (La Ferle, 2003). Furthermore, 44% of Blacks aged 18–29 no longer consider it appropriate to label Black people as comprising a single race (Williams, 2007). Therefore, the challenge of identity formation and classification has been exacerbated in light of the current era of fragmentation, multiculturalism, and the apparent celebration of differences that defines U.S. audiences today. It can be argued that these developments have largely been spawned by an increase in the number of easily accessible media sources, owing in no small part to technological advancements in information and communication technologies, and a market defined by firms with economic interests in creating ever-increasing possibilities for more information to become available (Chaffee & Metzger, 2001). Ostensibly, the implication here is that the Black audience may be increasingly easier to talk to given the omnipresence of media. The reality is that it may be more challenging to develop messages that truly resonate with this demographic given that their interests and views may be more diverse than in years past. Additionally, in the event of ever-increasing information, theories such as media dependency can help illuminate the interactions of Black individuals with the media.

As society grows in complexity and information becomes ubiquitous, dependency on the media to explain complex issues intensifies. Life in a complex world requires the ability to manage information effectively, which may drive individuals to the media for information and guidance (Gamson, 1995; Johnson-Cartee, 2005). Individuals may not necessarily be trying to access information from established media sources but may also be looking to connect with social in-group members. This seems to be especially relevant for Blacks who trust targeted media and who tend to pay much closer attention to communication generated from a source that looks like them. This offers significant implications for social identity theory. Additionally, given that ethnic minorities are also frequently a numeric minority in their social environment, the salience or distinctiveness of their numerically rare trait (i.e., ethnicity) in their social milieu may continue to provide a means of differentiation of positively distinguishing self from other. This is likely to be the case at least until America becomes a lot more balanced in the racial ratio of its populations. There are implications for future studies.

Future Research

Audience segmentation based on race in the U.S. has largely been a response by marketers and media firms to ongoing socioeconomic, technological, and demographic trends. The ramifications of this popular marketing-based strategy are far-reaching and provide numerous opportunities for empirical research. Rigorous academic study is needed to explore variables and contexts that may ultimately mitigate the negative effects of market segmentation while enhancing its positive effects. One related yet seemingly innocuous area that future research can explore is the impact of racially coded marketing buzzwords such as "ethnic," "multicultural," "urban," and "diversity." Miller and Kemp (2006) believe that this language tends to be grossly overused by both marketers and the general public. They argue that the overuse of this type of language helps create messages that commoditize Black culture, identity, and the overall Black community's value. Buzzwords such as "urban" often minimize relevant cultural nuances that are unique to the Black experience and can severely limit positive distinctions that should be associated with "urban's" source—the Black experience (Miller & Kemp, 2006). Additional research should also extend into the realm of political discourse.

Recent political rhetoric has engaged discourse or terminology with far greater latent derogatory connotations. Kilgore (2012) quotes Fox News media personality Juan Williams as taking issue with the language of GOP ("Grand Old Party"/Republican Party)racial politics. According to Williams, the use of polarizing and racially coded euphemisms such as "entitlement society," as used by Mitt Romney, and "poor work ethic" and "food stamp president," as used by former House Speaker Newt Gingrich, allows for race-baiting a group that may already generate rubber-stamped stereotypical impressions as an underprivileged underclass, while also providing deniability of any perceived racial content in the message. Research should examine the impact of such rhetoric on both Black and White audiences as well as on members of competing political ideologies.

Another research topic that ought to be addressed in the future is the dearth of Black gay/lesbian models in ads alongside Black heterosexual models as a means of appealing to both heterosexual and LGBT consumers. Attitudes toward homosexuality in the U.S. are still characterized by racial differences (Glick & Golden, 2010). In contrast to Whites, the proportion of Blacks that believe homosexuality to "always be wrong" has decreased relatively little between the early 1970s and the late 2000s (Glick & Golden, 2010). Beliefs about homosexuality and support for gay rights also vary substantially by religion (Clay, Jill, & Edward, 2009; Lewis, 2003), such that condemnation is highest among those who attend religious services frequently, who pray frequently, and who state that religion is very important in their lives (Lewis, 2003). Attribution of causality also plays a major role, such that, when the cause of homosexuality is perceived as being a genetic disposition as opposed to an individual choice, positive affect toward homosexuals and increased support for policies results (Haider-Markel & Joslyn, 2008). Hypermasculinity, an exaggeration of traditionally masculine traits, is another major force within Black communities that affects attitudes toward homosexuality.

This social construct is often enacted through hardcore gangsta rap and "cool pose" of Black males, which typically reflects a complex ritualized form of masculinity that emphasizes strength, toughness, emotionlessness, and the quest for sexual gratification (Ward, 2005). Ward (2005) contends that Black people and churches have also been influenced by the homophobia prevalent in the larger U.S. society, and by related U.S. notions of masculinity. An argument could be made that this construction of masculinity has been heavily influenced by images in the media. Blacks' overtly adverse response to homosexuality especially within its ethnic ranks suggests a tremendous value placed on traditional heterosexual male gender roles. Ward (2005) argues that, to many Blacks, Whiteness and homosexuality connote weakness and femininity, while Black masculinity has been constructed in hypermasculine terms. The construction and deconstruction of Black homosexuality in the media should be further examined. Specifically, future studies can address ways in which Black gay/lesbian models can be used in non-stereotypically depicting ways to mitigate prejudice and discrimination in the Black community, as well as in larger society. Few, if any, Black, gay models from any walk of life come to mind in the context of advertising. This might suggest a fear of ostracism and public rejection shared by fringe members of an already marginalized group. In the future, it may prove beneficial to examine the attitudes of Black heterosexual and homosexual consumers who have been exposed to ads that integrate same-sex partners in either mainstream ads or targeted ads with other models who were clearly heterosexual. As in the case of any other social identity group, it might be discovered that homosexual Black consumers who strongly identify with the uniqueness of their sexual orientation may not respond favorably to efforts to integrate or incorporate homosexuals into mainstream advertising. On the other hand, Black homosexuals that value mainstream assimilation may relish the opportunity to be included in mainstream advertising. This also raises the issue of heteronormativity and the impact of using gays and lesbians in mainstream ads that do not comfortably fit heterosexuals' conceptualization of what a homosexual model should look and act like (e.g., clean cut, attractive, and not overtly homosexual).

In terms of the earlier discussion of targeting Blacks with harmful products, future studies could examine the ethical implications behind the marketing of unhealthy fast-food establishments to the Black community. As previously discussed, many commercial institutions have ignited consumer dissatisfaction due to the marketing of harmful products to vulnerable social groups. McDonald's has been targeting Blacks with the argument that the ethnic consumer tends to set trends. Helm (2010) argues that, as Whites head toward minority status by 2050, McDonald's goal is to shape majority marketing by appealing to ethnic consumers that set trends. Again, while targeting a demographic is not inherently wrong, the question does arise of why it never seems to be companies or products that provide overtly beneficial or healthy products and services that seem to be as enthusiastic to target African Americans.

Finally, changes in the hiring process due, in no small part, to the emergence of online business and social networking services like LinkedIn may hold special implications for Blacks in the professional world in general, and in advertising specifically (VanRysdam, Chun, & Elias, 2012). For instance, as of March 2012, hundreds of thousands of job applications have been submitted using "Apply With LinkedIn." This service encourages participants to include their photograph as part of their online profile. This is a noteworthy deviation from the typical American employee's résumé. In fact, historically, the Equal Employment Opportunity Commission has dissuaded potential employees from sharing their likeness on résumés to limit the likelihood that candidates would be evaluated based on their gender, age, or race and ethnicity. In today's voyeuristic electronic age, however, not revealing one's physical appearance has become something of an aberration. While, in fairness, agencies may not explicitly reject candidates based on race and ethnicity, they may, however, implicitly choose candidates that they believe best fit their organization's culture and style and who they think may best gel with the existing workforce. The issue, of course, being that candidates that do not look like their potential employers or the majority of employees in terms of ethnicity or even age or sexual orientation may end up being overlooked in their job search. Future research could examine what checks and balances are in place to ensure that this does not happen with a high degree of frequency. Future studies can also examine whether or not the use of visual cues play a role based on a particular agency job versus others (i.e., does race matter more for the account executive position than it does for creatives or brand strategists?). As technology continues to proliferate and progress, and as we continue to march to an uncertain economic future, these questions offer a bounty of research material for those interested in the nexus of race, communication, and technology. Arguably, at no point in our nation's history have the answers to these questions been more significant.

References

Allport, G. W. (1954). *The Nature of Prejudice*. Garden City, New York: Doubleday.

Appiah, O. (2002). Black & White viewers' perception & recall of occupational characters on television. *Journal of Communication, 52*(4), 776–793.

Appiah, O. (2003). Americans online: Differences in surfing and evaluating race-targeted web sites by Black and White users. *Journal of Broadcasting and Electronic Media, 47*(4), 534–552.

Appiah, O. (2004). Effects of ethnic identification on web browsers attitudes toward, and navigational patterns on, race-targeted sites. *Communication Research, 31*(3), 312–337.

Appiah, O. (2007). The effectiveness of "typical-user" testimonial ads on Black & White browsers' evaluations of products on commercial web sites: Do they really work? *Journal of Advertising Research, 47*(1), 14–27.

Appiah O., & Elias, T. (2010). Race specific advertising on commercial websites: Effects of computer-generated characters in a digital world. In M. S. Eastin, T. Daugherty, & N. M. Burns (Eds.), *Handbook of Research on Digital Media and Advertising* (Chapter 8). Hershey, New York: Information Science Reference.

Armstrong, B., Neuendorf, K., & Brentar, J. (1992). TV entertainment, news, and racial perceptions of college students. *Journal of Communication, 42*(3), 153–176.

Ball-Rokeach, S. J., & DeFleur, M.L. (1976). A dependency model of mass media effects. *Communication Research, 3*, 3–21.

Boles, M. (2006). The fundamental reason ad agencies lack diversity. *Seldom TYPQL*. Retrieved March 7, 2012 from http://seldomtypql.com/64/the-fundamental-reason-ad-agencies-lack-diversity.

Breakwell, G. M. (1986). *Coping with Threatened Identities*. London: Methuen.

Brewer, M. B. (1991). The social self: On being the same and different at the same time. *Personality and Social Psychology Bulletin, 17*, 475–482.

Brewer, M. B., & Gaertner, S. L. (2004). Toward reduction of prejudice: Intergroup contact and social categorization. In M.B. Brewer & M. Hewstone (Eds.). *Self and Social Identity* (Chapter 22). Malden, MA: Blackwell Publishing.

Burrell, T. (2010). *Brainwashed: Challenging the Myth of Black Inferiority*. New York: Smileybooks.

Bush, R. F., Hair, J. F., &Solomon, P. J. (1979). Consumer's level of prejudice and response to Black models in advertisements. *Journal of Marketing Research, 16*, 341–345.

Calfee, JohnE. (1991, July 22). Targeting the problem: It isn't exploitation, it's efficient marketing, *Advertising Age*, 18.

Carbado, D. W. (2000). Black rights, gay rights, civil rights. *UCLA Law Review, 47*(6), 1467–1519.

Cartegena, C. (2012, April 11). Are you ready to capitalize on the rise of Hispanics as a mega buying force? *Advertising Age*. Retrieved April 26, 2012 from http://adage.com/article/the-big-tent/hispanics-a-mega-buying-force/234056/.

Cespedes, F. V. (1993). Ethical issues in distribution. In N. Craig Smith & John A. Quelch (Eds.), *Ethics in Marketing* (pp. 473–490). Homewood. IL: Richard D. Irwin.

Chaffee, S.H., & Metzger, M.J. (2001). The end of mass communication? *Mass Communication & Society*, 4(4), 365–379.

Chambers, J. (2008). *Madison Avenue and the Color Line*. Philadelphia, PA: University of Pennsylvania Press.

Clay, S.D, Jill, C, &Edward, R.S (2009). The index of attitudes toward homosexuals 30 years later: A psychometric study. *Research on Social Work Practice*, 19(2), 214–220.

Coltrane, S., & Messineo, M. (2000). The perpetuation of subtle prejudice: Race and gender imagery in 1990s television advertising. *Sex Roles*, 42(5/6), 363–389.

Cui, G.,& Choudhury, P. (2003). Consumer interests and the ethical implications of marketing: A contingency framework. *Journal of Consumer Affairs*, 37(2), 364–387.

Deshpandé, R., & Stayman, D. (1994). A tale of two cities: Distinctiveness theory and advertising effectiveness. *Journal of Marketing Research*, 31, 57–64.

Deutsch, M., & Gerard, H. (1955).A study of normative and informational influence upon individual judgment. *Journal of Abnormal and Social Psychology*, 51(November), 629–636.

Elias, T., & Appiah, O. (2010). A tale of two social contexts: Race-specific testimonials on commercial web sites and their effects on numeric majority and numeric minority consumer attitudes. *Journal of Advertising Research*, 50(3), 250–264.

Elias, T., Appiah, O., & Gong, L. (2011). Effects of Black's strength of ethnic identity on consumer attitudes: A multiple-group model approach. *Journal of Interactive Advertising*, 11(2), 13–29.

Entman, R. M., & Rojecki, A. (2000). Advertising Whiteness. In R. M. Entman & A. Rojecki, *The Black Image in the White Mind* (pp. 162–181). Chicago: University of Chicago Press.

Finlay, B., & Walther, C.S. (2003). The relation of religious affiliation, service attendance, and other factors to homophobic attitudes among university students. *Review of Religious Research*, 44(4), 370–393.

Fischer, M. (2011). Interracial contact and changes in the racial attitudes of white college students. *Social Psychology of Education*, 14(4), 547–574.

Gamson, W. (1995). Constructing social protest. In H. Johnston & B. Klandermans (Eds.), *Social Movements and Culture* (pp. 85–106). Minneapolis: University of Minnesota Press.

Gandy, O. (1998). *Communication and Race. A Structural Perspective*. London: Arnold.

Gandy, O. H. (2005). Audience segmentation: Is it racism or just good business? *Media Development*, 2, 3–6.

Glick, Sara Nelson, & Golden, Matthew R. (2010). Persistence of racial differences in attitudes toward homosexuality in the United States. *Journal of Acquired Immune Deficiency Syndromes*, 55(4), 516–523

Grier. S.A., & Brumbaugh, A.M. (2004). Consumer distinctiveness and advertising persuasion. In J.D. Williams, W. Lee, & C.P. Haugtvedt (Eds.), *Diversity in Advertising* (pp. 217–236). Mahwah, NJ: Lawrence Erlbaum Associates.

Haider-Markel, Donald P., & Joslyn, Mark R. (2008). Beliefs about the origins of homosexuality and support for gay rights. *Public Opinion Quarterly*, 72(2), 291–310.

Hallman, C. (2008, January 10). By 2011 Black buying power to hit trillion-dollar mark. *New America Media*. Retrieved January 10, 2011 from http://news.newamericamedia.org/news/view_article.html?article_id=990c03344a0ec68e9edcfcaaa70e7563.

Helm, B. (2010, July 8). Ethnic marketing: McDonald's is lovin' it. The BBW50 chain taps Latino and Black culture for mainstream ads. *Bloomsburg Businessweek*. Retrieved April 27, 2012 from www.businessweek.com/magazine/content/10_29/b4187022876832.htm.

Herek, G. M. (2000). The psychology of sexual prejudice. *Current Directions in Psychological Science, 9*, 19–22.

Hof, R. (2012). Online ad revenues to pass print in 2012. *Forbes*. Retrieved May 5, 2013 from www.forbes.com/sites/roberthof/2012/01/19/ online-ad-revenues-to-pass-print-in-2012/.

Hogg, M.A. (2004). Social categorization, depersonalization, and group behavior. In M.B. Brewer and M. Hewstone (Eds.), *Self and Social Identity* (pp. 203–231). Malden, MA: Blackwell Publishing.

Hollerbach, K.L. (2009). The impact of market segmentation on African American frequency, centrality, and status in television advertising. *Journalism of Broadcasting and Electronic Media, 53*(4), 599–614.

Humphreys, Jeffrey M. (2008). *The Multicultural Economy 2008*. The Selig Center for Economic Growth. Retrieved December 12, 2009 from www.terry.uga.edu/selig/docs/buying_power_2008.pdf.

Jetten, J., Spears, R., & Manstead, A. (1996). Distinctiveness threat and prototypicality: Combined effects on intergroup discrimination and collective self-esteem. *European Journal of Social Psychology, 27*, 635–657.

Johnson-Cartee, K.S. (2005). *News Narratives and News Framing: Constructing Political Reality*. Lanham, MD: Rowman & Littlefield.

Kates, S.M. (1999). Making the ad perfectly queer: Marketing "normality" to the gay men's community? *Journal of Advertising, 28*(1), 25–37.

Katz, E. (1996). And deliver us from segmentation. *Annals of the American Academy of Political and Social Science, 546*, 22–33.

Kilgore, E. (2012, January 30). Will Juan Williams get fired again? *Washington Monthly*. Retrieved March 28, 2012 from www.washingtonmonthly.com/political-animal-a/2012_01/will_juan_williams_get_fired_a035091.php.

La Ferle, R. (2003, December 28). Generation E.A: Ethnically Ambiguous. Retrieved December 28, 2003 from www.nytimes.com/2003/12/28/fashion/28ETHN.html.

Lewis, G. B. (2003). Black–white differences in attitudes toward homosexuality and gay rights. *Public Opinion Quarterly, 67*, 59–78.

Liang, C. T. H., & Alimo, C. (2005). The impact of White heterosexual students' interactions on attitudes toward lesbian, gay and bisexual people: a longitudinal study. *Journal of College Student Development, 46*, 237–250.

Lichter, D. T. (2012). Immigration and the racial diversity in rural America. *Rural Sociology, 77*(1), 3–35.

Mastro, D. E. (2003). A social identity approach to understanding the impact of television messages. *Communication Monographs, 70*(2), 98–113.

McGuire, W. (1984). Search for the self: Going beyond self-esteem and the reactive self. In R.A. Zucker, J. Aronoff, & A. I. Rabin (Eds.), *Personality and the Prediction of Behavior* (pp. 73–120). New York: Academic Press.

McGuire, W., McGuire, V., Child, P., & Fujioka, T. (1978). Salience of ethnicity in the spontaneous self-concept as a function of one's ethnic distinctiveness in the social environment. *Journal of Personality and Social Psychology*, 36, 511–520.

Miller, P., & Kemp, H. (2006). *What's Black About It? Insights to Increase your Share of a Changing African-American Market*. Ithaca, NY: Paramount Market.

Mobolade, O. (2011, March 21). How brands must adapt to the "new majority marketplace." *Ad Age*. Retrieved August 28, 2010 from http://m.adage.com/article?articleSection=cmostrategy&articleSectionName=CMOStrategy&articleid=http%3A%2F%2Fadage.com%2Fcmostrategy%2Farticle%3Farticle_id%3D149507.

Nairn, A., & Berthon, P. (2003). Creating the customer: The influence of advertising on consumer market segments. *Journal of Business Ethics*, 42(1), 83–99.

Nielsen Report. (2011, September The Power of the African-American Consumer. Nielsen. Retrieved November 1, 2011 from http://blog.nielsen.com/nielsenwire/consumer/report-the-power-of-the-african-american-consumer/.

Papacharissi, Z., & Rubin, A.M. (2000). Predictors of Internet use. *Journal of Broadcasting and Electronic Media*, 44(2), 175–196.

Patterson, O. (2006, March 26). A poverty of the mind. *The New York Times*. Retrieved April 26, 2012 from www.nytimes.com/2006/03/26/opinion/26patterson.html?pagewanted=all.

Pettigrew, T. (2008, April 14). Black America is the soul of the urban market. *Ad Age*. Retrieved April 26, 2012 from http://adage.com/article/the-big-tent/black-america-soul-urban-market/126372/.

Phinney, J. S. (1992). The multigroup ethnic identity measure: A new scale for use with diverse groups. *Journal of Adolescent Research*, 7(2), 156–176.

Phinney, J. S. (2005). Ethnic identity in late modern times: A response to Rattansi and Phoenix. *Identity*, 5(2), 187–194.

Pires, G.D., & Stanton, P.J. (2005). *Ethnic Marketing: Accepting the Challenge of Cultural Diversity*. Southbank, Victoria: Thomson Learning Australia.

Pires, G.D., & Stanton, P.J. (2009). *Ethnic Marketing: Accepting the Challenge of Cultural Diversity*. Southbank, Victoria: Thomson Learning Australia.

Quian, Z., & Lichter, D.T. (2007). Social boundaries and marital assimilation: Interpreting trends in racial and ethnic intermarriage. *American Sociological Review*, 72, 68–94.

Smedley, J. W., & Bayton, J. A. (1978). Evaluative race-class stereotypes by race and perceived class of subjects. *Journal of Personality and Social Psychology*, 36(5), 530–535.

Smith, B. (1999). Blacks and gays: Healing the divide. In E. Brandt (Ed.), *Dangerous Liaisons: Blacks, Gays, and the Struggle for Equality* (pp. 15–24). New York: New Press.

Smith, N., & Cooper-Martin, E. (1997). Ethics and target marketing. The role of product harm and consumer vulnerability. *Journal of Marketing*, 61(3), 1–20.

Snyder, C. R., & Fromkin, H. L. (1980). *Uniqueness: The Human Pursuit of Difference*. New York: Plenum.

Tajfel, H. (1974). Social identity and intergroup behaviour. *Social Science Information*, 13(2), 65–93.

Tajfel, H., & Turner, J. C. (1986). The social identity theory of intergroup behavior. In S. Worchel & W. G. Austin (Eds.), *Psychology of Intergroup Relations* (pp. 7–24). Chicago: Nelson-Hall.

Tanner, M. (2011, June 8). How 300+ TV channels affect your brain. *US Television*. Retrieved March 6, 2012 from http://ustelevision.com/2011/06/08/how-300-tv-channels-affects-the-brain/.

Trawalter, S., & Richeson, J.A. (2008). Let's talk about race, baby! When Whites' and Blacks' interracial contact experiences diverge. *Journal of Experimental Social Psychology, 44*, 1214–1217.

Turow, J. (1997). *Breaking up America: Advertisers and the New World*. Chicago: University of Chicago Press.

VanRysdam, M.K., Chun, J., & Elias, T. (2012). Online agency hiring in the age of LinkedIn: The role of visual cues in the hiring of account executives. Unpublished. College of Journalism and Communications, University of Florida.

Vignoles, V., Chryssochoou, X., & Breakwell, G. M. (2000). The distinctiveness principle: Identity, meaning, and bounds of cultural relativity. *Personality and Social Psychology Review, 4*(4), 337–354.

Ward, E. G. (2005). Homophobia, hypermasculinity and the US black church. *Culture, Health and Sexuality, 7*, 493–504.

Webster, J.G., & Zsiazek, T.B. (2012). The dynamics of audience fragmentation: Public attention in an age of digital media. *Journal of Communication, 62*, 39–56.

Williams, J. (2007, November 13). Redefining what it means to be Black in America. *NPR*. Retrieved December 15, 2007 from www.npr.org/templates/story/story.php?storyId=16266326.

Wolburg, J., & Pokrywczynski, J. (2001). A psychographic analysis of Generation Y College students. *Journal of Advertising, 41*(5), 33–53.

Zuckoff, Mitchell (1992, June 28). Reaching out to minority consumers. *Boston Globe, 73*, 77.

Chapter 11

DTC Prescription Drug Advertising

Focusing on Ethics

Michael Mackert and Marie Guadagno

The practice of direct-to-consumer (DTC) prescription drug advertising is unique to the United States and New Zealand. Given the vast spending on DTC advertising in the U.S., it is hardly surprising that researchers have explored the potential benefits (e.g., informing patients about symptoms of health conditions) and problems (e.g., a negative impact on the physician–patient relationship) associated with the advertisements. As researchers have explored a host of issues around DTC advertising, the ethics of DTC advertising in general and of the specific techniques and tactics employed in the ads is often secondary to the formal study goals. In other instances, the ethical issues are more philosophical in nature and not directly related to a specific research question or investigation. As such, there is a need for more structured and formal discussion of the ethics of DTC prescription drug advertising that might benefit all parties involved—a better and more ethical system of DTC drug advertising could benefit consumers, healthcare providers, and pharmaceutical companies. The purpose of this chapter is to highlight ethical issues and questions related to DTC drug advertising that to this point have not been sufficiently addressed in the literature.

This chapter first provides background on DTC drug advertising for context. A review of the potential benefits and concerns of DTC advertising is followed by a broad discussion of ethical questions related to this research. A more focused look at health literacy and patient understanding of DTC drug advertisements leads to a discussion of ethical questions in this narrower and more crucial area. Finally, the chapter concludes with a call to action for increased attention to the ethics of DTC advertising and a proposed research agenda.

Background

Direct-to-consumer (DTC) advertising of prescription drugs in the United States expanded rapidly after a 1997 guidance directive issued by the Food and Drug Administration (FDA) that relaxed the standards for prescription drug advertising. Prior to 1997, DTC advertising of prescription drugs was limited, mostly to print media, due to a requirement that adverse reactions and contraindications of the drug had to be included (Frosch, Grande, Tarn, & Kravitz, 2010). The FDA Final Guidance in 1999 allowed for a specific drug name and use to be mentioned in broadcast ads without the full risk information associated with the drug. Under the new regulations, DTC ads for prescription drugs must make "adequate provision" for attaining risk information by referring consumers to toll-free phone numbers, websites, concurrent print ads, physicians, and/or pharmacists (U.S. Food and Drug Administration, 1999). The guidance states that DTC ads cannot contain false or misleading information and also requires a "fair balance" presentation of the drug risks and benefits through a "major statement" within the advertisement. Currently, prescription drug advertising to consumers is only legal in the United States and New Zealand.

The new FDA guidelines brought a dramatic shift in the way pharmaceutical companies advertised prescription drugs. Advertising budgets, which were once spent primarily on print media, were expanded and refocused to broadcast. The majority of DTC advertising budgets are now spent on television ads, although print channels have slightly regained market share in recent years (Auton, 2004; The Nielsen Company for DTC Perspectives, 2011). To illustrate the dramatic swing in DTC advertising growth, total DTC advertising expenditures went from approximately $47 million in 1990 to more than $4.9 billion in 2007 (Kaphingst, Rudd, DeJong, & Daltroy, 2004; The Nielsen Company, 2009). However, overall spending for DTC advertising began to drop in 2008 due to the economic downturn and the increase in the availability of generic drugs. Recent analysis puts total DTC advertising expenditures at approximately $3.97 billion annually, with the top 20 prescription drug brands comprising more than half of that spending (The Nielsen Company for DTC Perspectives, 2011). Given such enormous promotional expenditures, it is not surprising that the reach of DTC advertising is widespread. In one year, the average consumer will watch 16 hours of DTC drug advertisements on television (Mulligan, 2011). Literature suggests that DTC advertising drives sales of brand name drugs for relief of chronic conditions that have large "market potential"—evidenced by just 20 prescription drug brands accounting for approximately 60% of DTC advertising industry spending (Hollon, 2005; The Nielsen Company for DTC Perspectives, 2011). According to Hollon (2005), physicians identify the three most common conditions for which DTC advertising prompts healthcare as erectile dysfunction, arthritis, and allergies.

The role of DTC advertising in the U.S. healthcare system has sparked serious debate since its rapid expansion in the late 1990s. Due to the inherent risks of promoting a prescription drug to consumers, and noting that prescription drugs differ from other consumer commodities, DTC advertising has led to a substantial body of research attempting to unearth both its potential harms and its benefits to society. The majority of this research has been observational analysis and survey-level data (Hollon, 2005). Research has broadly focused on policy, doctor/patient relationships, and public health. While researchers investigate DTC advertising from a neutral point of view, it is convenient to consider findings in terms of potential benefits and harms of DTC advertising.

Potential Benefits

Given the immense financial expenditures and the fundamental risks associated with prescription drug advertising, academic research has often focused on finding the potential "net benefits" that DTC advertising can offer society. Supporters of DTC advertising cite research that DTC advertising can provide a host of benefits, such as reducing under-treatment of particular conditions, improving the quality of care, increasing patient adherence to prescribed medications, educating consumers, and thereby increasing awareness of one's health status (Auton, 2004; Frosch et al., 2010; Hollon, 2005; Mastin, Andsager, Choi, & Lee, 2007; Murray et al., 2004; Schwartz, Silverman, Hulka, & Appel, 2009). Surveys conducted by the FDA found that the U.S. public had an overall favorable response to DTC advertising (Auton, 2004).

Advocates of DTC advertising affirm that it can conquer the under-treatment of disabling conditions that many Americans suffer from but have not yet been diagnosed with or prescribed suitable medications for. Examples of these conditions include diabetes, arthritis, high blood pressure, high cholesterol, and depression, to name a few. Research estimates that diabetes alone affects the lives of nearly one-third of Americans and contributes to more than $98 billion in healthcare costs and lost productivity each year (Auton, 2004). Similarly, research indicates that burdensome conditions such as clinical depression and osteoporosis are also under-diagnosed and/or under-treated in the United States, while effective and economical treatments are available but unused (Auton, 2004). Supporters credit DTC advertising for informing consumers about common conditions and their treatments, and thus directly motivating them to talk to their doctor about previously undisclosed health conditions (Montoya, Lee-Dukes, & Shah, 2008).

Having consumers take the active step to discuss health concerns with their physicians is also touted as a benefit of DTC advertising. Research found that DTC advertising increases a patient's participation in his or her own medical care and health (Frosch et al., 2010). Consumers reported that DTC advertising prompted them to seek more information about their current and previously undiagnosed medical conditions, and helped them make better decisions regarding their personal health (Weissman et al., 2004). While research concerning the positive or negative effects of DTC advertising on the physician/patient relationship is not conclusive, most doctors and patients agree that prescription drug advertising can trigger necessary conversations regarding health (Frosch et al., 2010). Auton (2004) also argues that consumers are no longer just passive patients who accept a physician's orders. Instead, due to communication technology and better public health, many patients seek out health information from media outlets such as the Internet. DTC advertising can fill a role for those people who need and want information about medical conditions.

In addition to these perceived benefits, proponents of DTC advertising argue that it can play a crucial part in increasing patient adherence to prescribed medication. Not adhering to prescribed medication is estimated to cost more than $100 billion a year in medical expenditures and lost productivity (Johnson & Bootman, 1995). Supporters posit that merely seeing an ad for prescription medicine, even one unrelated to a patient's own health, can remind patients of their medical condition and improve prescribed drug adherence. Although there is some evidence that DTC advertising may increase compliance to a drug regime, there has not been sufficient evidence to clearly conclude such findings (Auton, 2004; Frosch et al., 2010).

Related to the previously discussed potential benefits, one of the most often used justifications for DTC advertising is that it has great educational value. Proponents argue that DTC advertising can educate consumers, and therefore provide a public health benefit. This should not be confused, however, with a marketing campaign that has a pro-social focus, such as a public service announcement, where improving public health is the central goal (Mackert, 2011).

In surveys measuring public perceptions of DTC advertising, approximately 75% of respondents agreed that drug ads improved their comprehension of diseases and their treatments (Murray et al., 2004). While surveys suggest that DTC advertising can serve an educational purpose to consumers, evidence that DTC advertising can educate the public remains open to debate for reasons that will be highlighted in the next section of this chapter.

Potential Harms

The advertising of prescription drugs has been a heated, ongoing controversy—notably after the FDA's 1999 Final Guidance that relaxed the standards for DTC advertising. Opponents of prescription drug advertising argue that pharmaceuticals should not be a "consumer market." They contend that DTC advertising leads to inappropriate over-diagnosis and prescribing, strains the doctor/patient relationship, deceives the public, increases healthcare costs, diverts funds away from true research and development, presents risks associated with new drugs, and medicalizes conditions common to aging—all for the financial benefit of pharmaceutical companies (Auton, 2004; Mulligan, 2011; Royne & Myers, 2008).

A main concern surrounding DTC advertising is that it leads to inappropriate prescribing practices that could be costly and dangerous to patients. Surveys on the subject have found that half of the prescription drug requests that were prompted by an ad viewed by patients were clinically inappropriate (Murray et al., 2004). Although most physicians acknowledge that DTC advertising can educate patients, 80% of surveyed doctors believe that DTC advertising prompts patients to make unwarranted requests for treatments they may not need, and more than half of the time, the doctor prescribed the medication to accommodate the patient's request (Hollon, 2005; Montoya et al., 2008).

Research has found that doctor visits motivated by DTC advertising resulted in 25% of patients receiving a new diagnosis—of that 25%, more than 40% of the conditions were deemed "high priority" (Hollon, 2005). Evidence suggested that DTC advertising increased diagnosis and prescriptions for both appropriate and inappropriate conditions (Frosch et al., 2010).

Related to the concern that DTC advertising increases improper diagnoses is the argument that DTC advertising leads to medicalization, "the process by which nonmedical problems come to be defined as treatable illnesses" (Frosch et al., 2010, p. 27). Essentially this broadens what is defined as an illness to expand the markets for pharmaceuticals. Auton (2004) described these as "lifestyle drugs" that are between the hazy area of true medical conditions and social health conditions. Examples of these include plights related to aging, such as baldness, weight gain, and wrinkles of the skin (Auton, 2004).

Although many physicians feel that DTC advertising can prompt important conversations of true medical conditions, even about those that are deemed "embarrassing," like erectile-dysfunction, there is a concern that DTC advertising can negatively impact the doctor/patient relationship. If a patient requests a certain medication, and that request is denied by his or her physician, fallout in the relationship could take place (Auton, 2004). This could lead to the patient leaving the current physician and seeking one who will prescribe the medication, whether that drug is appropriate or not (Auton, 2004; Murray et al., 2004).

Critics of DTC advertising also cite that it increases overall pharmaceutical costs and redirects important funds away from true research and development to promotional activities (Auton, 2004). A majority of surveyed consumers perceived that DTC advertising does increase the cost of prescription drugs (Murray et al., 2004). U.S. spending on prescription drugs has increased nearly six times over since the early 1990s—from $40.3 billion in 1990 to an estimated $234 billion in 2008 (Kaiser Family Foundation, 2010). While prescription drug expenditures are not the largest sector of healthcare in the U.S., it is the fastest growing sector (Auton, 2004). Although there is not a direct correlation between the rise in drug costs and DTC advertising, research has indicated that DTC advertising does have an influence on the price of drugs (Kaiser Family Foundation, 2010). The top 50 most advertised medications accounted for nearly 50% of the increase in drug spending between 1999 and 2000 (Auton, 2004). Research also found that pharmaceutical companies have shifted large portions of their budgets to promotional activities (such as DTC advertising) instead of focusing them on research and development (Auton, 2004).

Perhaps the most damning critique of DTC advertising is that it uses tactics that mislead the public (Auton, 2004; Hollon, 2005). Opponents of DTC advertising claim that a pharmaceutical company's goal is to drive sales and market share and that promotional activity utilizes ploys that are contradictory to improving public health (Auton, 2004). Research has indicated that prescription drug ads exaggerate the benefits of the medication by using qualitative and vague terms while downplaying the drug's risks (Frosch et al., 2010). This can lead to inaccurate comprehension of both benefits and risks associated with the drug (Kaphingst, Rudd, Dejong, & Daltroy, 2005). Many consumers also assume that DTC ads are subject to government approval (Bell, Wilkes, & Kravits, 2000). Research consistently has found that DTC advertisement content is written at a higher reading level than recommended for general consumer audiences (Kaphingst, Rudd et al., 2004). This is often cited as problematic because the majority of DTC advertisements may be difficult for the average consumer to understand (Kaphingst & DeJong, 2004; Mackert & Love, 2011a), a concern which will be explored in more depth later in this chapter.

Balancing Benefits and Harms: Ethical Issues

As scholars, advocates, and critics discuss potential benefits and harms of DTC prescription drug advertising, a number of ethical issues emerge as worthy of further investigation and consideration in the broad DTC debate.

As a first example of these broader questions, advocates and critics both acknowledge the ads can stimulate conversation between patients and healthcare providers. Advocates point to conversations that may never have happened without the ads, while critics worry about a negative impact on provider–patient communication. In the extreme, patients can demand drugs that are not appropriate and put significant pressure on healthcare providers, at times resulting in providers inappropriately prescribing the demanded medications or losing patients when patients decide to find a more agreeable healthcare provider. The ethical issue here has two levels. First, what responsibility do drug advertisements bear for driving patients to healthcare providers and demanding medications? And second, what responsibility do advertisers bear when patients are prescribed a medication that is not appropriate? It is certainly reasonable to argue that advertisements contribute to patients demanding a particular medication they see an advertisement for, but ads typically encourage consumers to "talk to" their physician—they certainly do not advocate demanding a medication. If healthcare providers decide to prescribe an inappropriate medication—rather than anger or lose a patient demanding a drug she saw advertised—it would seem that is more an ethical issue for the provider than the advertisement that initiated the conversation.

As noted, prescription drug advertising has been criticized for medicalizing the process of aging. Auton (2004) provides examples such as baldness and weight gain. Categorizing weight gain as a lifestyle issue would seem to trivialize a health issue with recognized and serious outcomes for patients. Even ignoring weight gain, issues such as baldness or erectile dysfunction—which could be considered lifestyle issues and the process of aging—could also be considered quality of life issues. Critics who frame the issue as medicalization, and advocates who might frame it as a quality of life concern, are to a large degree arguing past each other. It would seem that getting at the basic ethical questions regarding the role of prescription drugs in addressing lifestyle health issues and how the ethics of advertising of these drugs might be different (or not) from non-lifestyle health issues will require moving past simply framing the issue in a way that serves the preconceptions of advocates and critics.

When it comes to serious health issues, DTC advocates suggest that advertisements can help raise awareness of symptoms, educate consumers, and bring patients into healthcare providers' offices to be diagnosed. While this is certainly a positive outcome, it should be noted that many health conditions exhibit disparities—the burden of illness might disproportionately impact ethnic and racial minorities, individuals living in rural areas, or those of lower socioeconomic status. Heart disease is the number one cause of death among African Americans, for example, but ads for medications related to heart disease are lacking in African American publications (Mastin et al., 2007). This suggests the ethics surrounding the argument that DTC ads raise awareness of health conditions is more complicated, of course. Should drug companies and their advertising agencies be expected to design their campaigns to address these kinds of health disparities? Where is the line between what a corporation can be expected to do in serving public health and what it actually needs to do in advertising its products in the most efficient and profitable manner possible?

Also related to education, advertising professionals have pointed to the Gardasil "One Less" campaign as a positive example of a DTC campaign that educated consumers about a health issue (Mackert, 2011). Criticism and investigation of how Gardasil helped transform cervical cancer and how the public perceived it from an "obscure killer confined mostly to poor nations to the West's disease of the moment" have been present in the mainstream media (Rosenthal, 2008); however, this suggests even successful examples of consumer education are not necessarily that clear. If this campaign means some women are saved from cervical cancer, then that is obviously a positive outcome. But the pharmaceutical companies certainly profit from selling prescription drugs designed to prevent cervical cancer, and DTC advertising campaigns shape public perception about the severity and prevalence of the problem. What are the ethics of exaggerating a health concern when the end result is both improved health for women and increased sales and profits for pharmaceutical companies?

Health Literacy, Patient Understanding, and Advertising Ethics

Much of the research and the issues to this point have assumed that consumers can actually understand and make use of the information in DTC drug advertisements. This is not the case, however, due to the fact that many who see DTC advertisements do not have the health literacy to understand and appropriately take action on the information included in the advertisements.

Health Literacy

Health literacy is broadly defined as an individual's ability to obtain, process, and act appropriately on health information (Ad Hoc Committee on Health Literacy, 1999). Zarcadoolas, Pleasant, and Greer (2006) further conceptualized health literacy by applying four dimensions: fundamental literacy (reading, writing, and numbers), scientific literacy (understanding technology and scientific processes), civic literacy (understanding the relationship between personal and public health issues), and cultural literacy (understanding different cultures and customs as they relate to health). A person who has difficulties in these areas is said to have low health literacy.

Low health literacy often leads to poorer health outcomes due to individuals' inability to understand important health information. This can range from not understanding informational brochures to not comprehending prescription medication instructions. Patients who are low health literate may have problems communicating with health providers

(Zarcadoolas, Pleasant, & Greer, 2006). Factors such as age, low socio-economic status, being part of a minority or immigrant population, and not being a native English speaker can often impair health literacy (Ad Hoc Committee on Health Literacy, 1999).

Both the health and financial implications of low health literacy are significant. An estimated $69 billion per year is spent on problems encountered by individuals with low health literacy, and research estimates this number will continue to rise (Nielsen-Bohlman, Panzer, & Kindig, 2004; Vernon, Trujillo, Rosenbaum, & DeBuono, 2007). This includes more visits and revisits to healthcare providers, patient non-adherence to prescribed medication, longer hospital stays, and a general lack of understanding of how to navigate the healthcare system (Aspden, Wolcott, Bootman, & Croenwett, 2006; Cuban, 2006; Weiss & Palmer, 2004).

Health Literacy and DTC Advertising Understanding

As discussed previously, research has found that the majority of DTC television advertisements rely on qualitative and vague appeals and provide minimal health education information. Benefits are often described in vague, qualitative terms, and supporting evidence is not typically included (Hollon, 2005; Kaphingst et al., 2005; Royne & Myers, 2008). Beyond this, ads contain content that exceeds the recommended reading level for the general public. This is of concern due to the fact that nearly 43% of American adults can only perform simple literacy activities (National Center for Education Statistics, 2003). An estimated one-third to one-half of American adults has difficulties understanding health information and is considered to have low health literacy (Nielsen-Bohlman et al., 2004). Research indicates that individuals with low health literacy find it challenging to obtain information from DTC drug advertisements (Kaphingst, Rudd et al., 2004; Kaphingst et al., 2005).

The ways DTC advertisements are structured, displayed, and written prove to be disconcerting. Content analysis of DTC advertisements routinely has found that television ads allow the viewer more time to process the benefits associated with a drug than the risks (Kaphingst, Dejong et al., 2004). The use of narratives often exaggerates the drug's benefits and obscures the drug's effectiveness and/or risks (Frosch et al., 2010). Although guidelines require a "major statement" to present the drug's risks, that information is typically provided in one long, continuous stream (Kaphingst, Dejong et al., 2004) that is often comical.

Likewise, research focused on DTC print advertisements found content that could be confusing to average patients. Examples of this include copy that is higher than the recommended reading level for average audiences and text that is often difficult to read (e.g., too small of font, too blended in with the background) (Kaphingst et al., 2005). Design decisions made to appeal to consumers are often at odds with best practices for designing written materials for low health literate audiences (Mackert & Love, 2011a). Research found that, in the decade between 1992 and 2002, the educational content included in DTC advertisements declined and promotional content expanded (Curry, Jarosch, & Pacholok, 2005). As noted, DTC ads can contain less educational content if they provide a direction for the consumer to access more information (such as websites or toll-free phone numbers). However, prescription drug websites reflect the concerns many opponents have with ads on traditional mediums—that the benefits are easily accessibly (i.e., on the home page), whereas the risks often are buried somewhere on the site and take multiple clicks to access (Frosch et al., 2010).

Although many critics cite these tactics and question the motivation of pharmaceutical companies and DTC advertising campaigns, research also finds that both pharmaceutical marketing and advertising professionals understand the concern and are frustrated by regulations that make "simple" communication difficult (Mackert, 2011). It is also possible that principles criticized for inclusion in DTC advertisements—the use of emotion and stories to engage consumers, for example—could be used to improve the design of public health campaigns (Mackert & Love, 2011b).

Health Literacy and DTC Advertising: Ethical Issues

Shifting from the broader ethics of DTC advertising to issues related to health literacy and patient understanding, the ethical issues become more complicated and nuanced. The fact is that DTC ads often include complex information, as well as formatting and design apt to make it more difficult for lower health literate audiences to understand the content of the ads. Advocates must recognize these concerns; else their argument that DTC ads can educate consumers—particularly those consumers most in need of additional health education—is, at best, disingenuous. It is possible that better design could benefit both lower health literate consumers and pharmaceutical companies, given that more understandable ads would lead to more consumers hearing the intended message, learning about health conditions, and talking to their healthcare provider about relevant health issues and potential treatments; better campaigns could lead to improved health outcomes for patients and better sales and compliance for drug companies. Even assuming implementation of better regulations that might make use of plain language (using the less medically precise "kidney" that more consumers might understand, rather than a more complicated word like "renal"), to what degree should advertisements be expected to compromise their design to follow best practices for communicating with lower health literate audiences (National Cancer Institute, 2003)?

Ethical concerns about health literacy and patient understanding go beyond branded advertisements. Mackert, Love, and Holton (2011) investigated a novel drug advertising campaign that incorporated characters from the children's movie *Happy Feet* and how media covered the campaign. The sponsor of the non-branded disease education website central to this campaign—and the implications of the sponsorship—would likely not have been clear to lower health literate consumers visiting the website; while a narrow majority of articles covering the campaign did report that the pharmaceutical manufacturer operated the non-branded website, none mentioned other antiviral treatment options or nonmedical ways to prevent the flu. The use of non-branded advertising content, primarily focused on disease education, could be considered to serve more of a public health function than branded ads for a specific prescription drug. However, these kinds of disease awareness campaigns only make sense for market leaders (Mackert, 2011), and less media literate consumers are probably least likely to understand the source of the information and implications. As such, there is a serious ethical question about how the public health benefit (disease awareness and education) must be balanced against how lower health literate consumers will understand these messages and their sources.

DTC Advertising and Ethics: A Proposed Research Agenda

The ethical issues discussed to this point—regarding the benefits and concerns about DTC advertising broadly, as well as those specific to health literacy and patient understanding—have highlighted ethical considerations that are often secondary to primary study objectives. Research focused on the use of persuasive appeals, how visuals complement text, the readability of drug advertisements, how advertising impacts healthcare provider–patient interactions, and other major areas of investigation are, of course, valuable. But increased focus on the ethics of DTC advertising, with ethical questions driving the investigation, is needed. This section provides a call to action for research focused specifically on the ethics of DTC drug advertising and issues involved with pursuing that research agenda.

First, there is a pressing need to involve more voices in the conversation surrounding the ethics of DTC advertising. Researchers interested in studying a particular aspect of DTC advertising can easily come to one conclusion about the intent behind an advertisement (e.g., advertisers purposely complicating the text of the fair balance information to make it harder to understand), while actually talking to the people who design the advertisements could reveal a different reason (e.g., regulations and concerns about legal liability lead to more precise and complicated medical terminology). If investigation of the ethics of DTC advertising is to progress and actually improve the practice of DTC advertising in the U.S., it will be imperative to invite more perspectives on the issue. This might mean more focus on ethical questions with stakeholders that have already been represented in DTC advertising research, such as consumers, physicians, and (to a lesser extent) other healthcare providers with prescriptive authority (e.g., nurse practitioners) or clear interests in prescription drug advertising (e.g., pharmacists). It will also mean reaching out to those who have been largely absent from the discussion to this point, particularly government regulators, professional advertisers and marketers working in the field, and other pharmaceutical executives. The ethical issues surrounding DTC advertising cannot be fully understood or addressed without incorporating the perspectives of all stakeholders.

More fully integrating the perspective of marketers and advertisers working in the DTC advertising field will help address a second issue—ethical questions surrounding DTC advertising must remain grounded in the fact that these are marketing messages and not public health campaigns. As an example, prior research has indicated that 91% of DTC television ads use positive or neutral images when information regarding drug risk is being communicated (Kaphingst, Dejong et al., 2004). This could be perceived as drug companies purposely manipulating nonverbal communication and imagery to lessen the impact of negative information about drug risk. Practically speaking, though, what can advertisers realistically be expected to show? Federal regulations could certainly compel advertisers to show negative images, similar to what the FDA is proposing for cigarette packaging (U.S. Food and Drug Administration, 2012). Failing that, though, it seems unrealistic to expect an advertiser to show anything but positive or neutral images in an advertisement designed to sell a product. Scholars considering the ethics of prescription drug advertising will make more progress if they are realistic about the actual practice of producing and using advertisements to promote prescription drugs.

As scholars consider what drug companies and their advertising agency partners can realistically be expected to include in prescription drug advertisements, it is important to consider how the undisputed profit motive might color their perspective on ethical issues (Mackert & Love, 2011b). Critics have expressed concerns about the use of emotional appeals in drug advertisements, rather than educational messages, to engage consumers. The entire field of social marketing, however, is based on this concept of applying the concepts of marketing to promote health behavior change. In the context of public health, emotional appeals largely devoid of educational content have been used to promote preventive health for men, for example (Mackert & Love, 2011b). Scholars must consider whether the profit motive driving DTC advertisements actually changes whether a particular communication tactic is ethical or not, or if that profit motive is simply coloring their perspective on what should be considered ethical. Related to this, investigation of how more strategic corporate social responsibility (CSR) efforts might improve the perception of pharmaceutical companies and DTC advertising is necessary, to build on existing scholarship on the strategic implementation of CSR to create value for firms (Burke & Logsdon, 1999).

In terms of bigger ethical questions that merit additional attention, one obvious issue is how to balance the question of how DTC advertising contributes to getting treatment for undiagnosed people and contributes to overtreatment. If prescription drug advertising contributes to both of these phenomena, there is an issue of balance—at what point does the problem with overtreatment outweigh the benefits of getting treatment for patients who would otherwise go undiagnosed? To further complicate the ethics of this issue, healthcare reform in the U.S. means the costs of the advertised prescription drugs—both for people who would have otherwise gone undiagnosed and those who might not actually need treatment—contribute to rising healthcare costs for the entire country. What are the ethical issues of taxpayers helping to shoulder the costs of those who do not actually need treatment, along with those who do? How do the answers to these questions change the role of DTC advertising and the regulation of these marketing messages?

Another issue deserving more attention is how DTC campaigns reach, or fail to reach, vulnerable populations impacted by health disparities. As noted earlier, ads for heart disease medication are lacking in African American publications, a potential issue when one considers heart disease is the number one cause of death among African Americans (Mastin et al., 2007). There are other, less obvious vulnerable populations that have not been reached by DTC campaigns, however. Ball, Manika, and Stout (2011) point out that college students, for example, are similar to older audiences in terms of many health conditions (e.g., allergies, depression, anxiety), but often lack health coverage and may not be seen as ripe targets for DTC advertising. The ethics of DTC advertising campaigns and vulnerable populations is particularly relevant given the potential implications of healthcare reform, as more insured patients would seem to create more opportunities for aligning marketing objectives with public health benefits and addressing disparities impacting vulnerable populations.

Finally, there is a potentially rich field of research into how discussion of the ethics of DTC advertising—among scholars, consumers, and healthcare providers—is shaped by the fact that the topic at hand is advertising. Many of the criticisms of DTC advertising—that they medicalize issues of aging, drive patients to demand inappropriate treatments from healthcare providers, and include information that is too complicated—could also be leveled against journalists writing about health issues, websites dedicated to health information, and online support groups. If the discussion surrounding the ethics of DTC prescription drug advertising is to be fruitful and honest, how the fact that the discussion is focusing on ethics of *advertising* shapes the conversation must be understood and recognized.

Conclusion

The purpose of this chapter was to consider the ethics of DTC advertising, first of DTC advertising broadly and then focused particularly on issues related to health literacy and patient understanding. While issues related to ethics are prevalent in research on prescription drug advertising, the discussion of ethics is often secondary to specific research questions and the primary purpose of academic investigation of the practice of DTC advertising. All stakeholders—scholars, practitioners, and policy-makers—need to address these ethical questions more directly moving forward.

Additional exploration of the ethical issues surrounding DTC prescription drug advertising is particularly crucial given rapid advances in medical treatments, including surgically implanted devices. Ethical issues in the advertising of prescription drugs will become even more salient when marketers are reaching consumers with direct messages about surgically implanted medical devices—the implications of having a medical device implanted can be more complicated and permanent than starting a prescription drug (Mackert & Harrison, 2009). The same holds for the direct marketing of genetic testing services, which has been shown to increase interest in these services (Mouchawar et al., 2005) but—like prescription drug advertisements—has been criticized for containing inaccurate information (United States Government Accountability Office, 2010). Lastly, given the increasing globalization of healthcare, ethics and regulations surrounding the promotion of medical tourism—where a patient travels to another country primarily seeking health or medical services—will become pertinent. Hundreds of thousands of patients already partake in medical tourism, and that number is expected to rise (Cohen, 2010).

Consumer-oriented advertising for prescription drugs is far more prevalent than these newer advances and, as such, provides a useful laboratory for discussing the ethical marketing of treatments that can provide a useful starting point for surgically implanted medical devices, genetic testing services, medical tourism, and whatever else is to come.

More attention to the ethics of DTC advertising, how this field could and should operate, will result in an improved model for advertising prescription drugs to the public. A better system could benefit consumers, pharmaceutical companies, healthcare providers, and the overall healthcare system. Continued and direct discussion of the ethics of DTC prescription drug advertising will help ensure all involved benefit as much as possible from the continued practice of drug advertising as it evolves over time.

References

Ad Hoc Committee on Health Literacy. (1999). Health literacy: Report of the Council on Scientific Affairs. *Journal of the American Medical Association, 281,* 552–557.

Aspden, P., Wolcott, J. A., Bootman, J. L., & Croenwett, L. R. (Eds.). (2006). *Preventing Medication Errors (Quality Chasm).* Washington, DC: National Academy Press.

Auton, F. (2004). The advertising of pharmaceuticals direct to consumers: A critical review of the literature and debate. *International Journal of Advertising, 23*(1), 5–52.

Ball, J. G., Manika, D., & Stout, P. (2011). Consumers young and old: Segmenting the target markets for direct-to-consumer prescription drug advertising. *Health Marketing Quarterly, 28*(4), 337–353.

Bell, R. A., Wilkes, M. S., & Kravits, R. L. (2000). The educational value of consumer-targeted prescription drug print advertising. *Journal of Family Practice, 49*(12), 1092–1098.

Burke, L., & Logsdon, J. M. (1999). How corporate social responsibility pays off. *Long Range Planning, 29*(4), 495–502.

Cohen, G. (2010). Medical tourism: the view from ten thousand feet. *Hastings Center Report, 40*(2), 11–12.

Cuban, S. (2006). Following the physician's recommendations faithfully and accurately: Functional health literacy, compliance, and the knowledge-based economy. *Journal for Critical Education Policy Studies, 4*(2), 220–243. Retrieved from www.jceps.com/?pageID=article&articleID=74.

Curry, T. J., Jarosch, J., & Pacholok, S. (2005). Are direct to consumer advertisements of prescription drugs educational? Comparing 1992 to 2002. *Journal of Drug Education, 35*(3), 217–232. doi: 10.2190/1vak-bcng-ehcc-bvld

Frosch, D. L., Grande, D., Tarn, D. M., & Kravitz, R. L. (2010). A decade of controversy: Balancing policy with evidence in the regulation of prescription drug advertising. *American Journal of Public Health, 100*(1), 24–32.

Hollon, M. F. (2005). Direct-to-consumer advertising. *JAMA: The Journal of the American Medical Association, 293*(16), 2030–2033. doi: 10.1001/jama.293.16.2030

Johnson, J. A., & Bootman, J. L. (1995). Drug-related morbidity and mortality: A cost-of-illness model. *Archives of Internal Medicine, 155*(18), 1949–1956. doi: 10.1001/archinte.1995.00430180043006

Kaiser Family Foundation. (2010). *Prescription Drug Trends.* Publication #3057-08. Retrieved from www.kff.org/rxdrugs/upload/3057-08.pdf.

Kaphingst, K. A., & DeJong, W. (2004). The educational potential of direct-to-consumer prescription drug advertising. *Health Affairs, 23*(4), 143–150.

Kaphingst, K. A., Dejong, W., Rudd, R. E., & Daltroy, L. H. (2004). A content analysis of direct-to-consumer television prescription drug advertisements. *Journal of Health Communication, 9,* 515–528.

Kaphingst, K. A., Rudd, R. E., DeJong, W., & Daltroy, L. H. (2004). Literacy demands of product information intended to supplement television direct-to-consumer prescription drug advertisements. *Patient Education and Counseling, 55,* 293–300.

Kaphingst, K. A., Rudd, R. E., Dejong, W., & Daltroy, L. H. (2005). Comprehension of information in three direct-to-consumer television prescription drug advertisements among adults with limited literacy. *Journal of Health Communication*, *10*, 609–619. doi: 10.1080/10810730500267647

Mackert, M. (2011). Health literacy knowledge among direct-to-consumer pharmaceutical advertising professionals. *Health Communication*, *26*(6), 525–533. doi: 10.1080/10410236.2011.556084

Mackert, M., & Harrison, T. (2009). Marketing medical implants: New challenges and concerns. *Journal of Consumer Marketing*, *26*(1), 4–5.

Mackert, M., & Love, B. (2011a). Educational content and health literacy issues in direct to consumer pharmaceutical advertising. *Health Marketing Quarterly*, *28*(3), 205–218. doi: 10.1080/07359683.2011.595639

Mackert, M., & Love, B. (2011b). Profits and perspectives: Advertising, social marketing, and public health. *Journal of Social Marketing*, *1*(3), 240–246.

Mackert, M., Love, B., & Holton, A. (2011). Journalism as health education: Media coverage of a non-branded pharma website. *Telemedicine and e-Health*, *17*(2), 88–94.

Mastin, T., Andsager, J. L., Choi, J., & Lee, K. (2007). Health disparities and direct-to-consumer prescription drug advertising: A content analysis of targeted magazine genres, 1992–2002. *Health Communication*, *22*(1), 49–58. doi: 10.1080/10410230701310299

Montoya, I. D., Lee-Dukes, G., & Shah, D. (2008). Direct-to-consumer advertising: Its effects on stakeholders. *Journal of Allied Health*, *37*(2), 116–120(115).

Mouchawar, J., Hensley-Alford, S., Laurion, S., Ellis, J., Kulchak-Rahm, A., Finucane, M. L., Ritzwoller, D. (2005). Impact of direct-to-consumer advertising for hereditary breast cancer testing on genetic services at a managed care organization: A naturally-occurring experiment. *Genetics in Medicine*, *7*(3), 191–197.

Mulligan, L. (2011). You can't say that on television: Constitutional analysis of a direct-to-consumer pharmaceutical advertising ban. *American Journal of Law & Medicine*, *37*(2/3), 444–467.

Murray, E., Lo, B., Pollack, L., Donelan, K., & Lee, K. (2004). Direct-to-consumer advertising: Public perceptions of its effects on health behaviors, health care, and the doctor–patient relationship. *The Journal of the American Board of Family Practice*, *17*, 6–18.

National Cancer Institute. (2003). *Clear &Simple: Developing Effective Print Materials For Low-Literate Readers*. Retrieved from www.cancer.gov/cancertopics/cancerlibrary/clear-and-simple/AllPages.

National Center for Education Statistics. (2003). *National Assessment of Adult Literacy*. Retrieved from http://nces.ed.gov/naal/kf_demographics.asp.

Nielsen-Bohlman, L., Panzer, A., & Kindig, D. (Eds.). (2004). *Health Literacy: A Prescription to End Confusion*. Washington, DC: National Academy of Sciences.

Rosenthal, E. (2008, August 19). Drug makers' push leads to cancer vaccines' rise. *The New York Times*. Retrieved June 9, 2010 from www.nytimes.com/2008/08/20/health/policy/20vaccine.html?_r=1&pagewanted=all.

Royne, M. B., & Myers, S. D. (2008). Recognizing consumer issues in DTC pharmaceutical advertising. *Journal of Consumer Affairs*, *42*(1), 60–80.

Schwartz, V. E., Silverman, C., Hulka, M. J., & Appel, C. E. (2009). Marketing pharmaceutical products in the twenty-first century: An analysis of the continued viability of traditional principles of law in the age of direct-to-consumer advertising. *Harvard Journal of Law & Public Policy*, 32(1), 333–388.

The Nielsen Company. (2009, March 13). *U.S. Ad Spending Fell 2.6% in 2008.* Retrieved from www.nielsen.com/us/en/press-room/2009/u_s__ad_spending_fell.html.

The Nielsen Company for DTC Perspectives. (2011). *DTC Perspectives, 10* (2). Retrieved from www.dtcperspectives.com/wp-content/uploads/2011/02/DTCP_0611_web.pdf.

United States Government Accountability Office. (2010). *Direct-to-Consumer Genetic Tests: Misleading Test Results Are Further Complicated by Deceptive Marketing and Other Questionable Practices.* Washington, DC: United States Government Accountability Office. Retrieved from www.gao.gov/new.items/d10847t.pdf.

U.S. Food and Drug Administration. (1999). *Guidance for Industry, Consumer-directed Broadcast Advertisements.* Retrieved from www.fda.gov/cder/guidance.

U.S. Food and Drug Administration. (2012). *Cigarette Health Warnings.* Retrieved March 3, 2012 from www.fda.gov/TobaccoProducts/Labeling/Labeling/CigaretteWarningLabels.

Vernon, J. A., Trujillo, A., Rosenbaum, S., & DeBuono, B. (2007). *Low Health Literacy: Implications for National Health Care Policy.* Washington, DC: George Washington University School of Public Health and Health Services.

Weiss, B. D., & Palmer, R. (2004). Relationship between health care costs and very low literacy skills in a medically needy and indigent medicaid population. *The Journal of the American Board of Family Practice*, 17(1), 44–47. doi: 10.3122/jabfm.17.1.44

Weissman, J. S., Blumenthal, D., Silk, A. J., Newman, M., Zapert, K., Leitman, R., & Feibelmann, S. (2004). Physicians report on patient encounters involving direct-to-consumer advertising. *Health Affairs*, 23, W4-219–233.

Zarcadoolas, C., Pleasant, A., & Greer, D. (2006). *Advancing Health Literacy: A Framework for Understanding and Action.* San Francisco, CA: Jossey-Bass.

Chapter 12

Ads Are Watching You

Advertising Applications of Facial Recognition Technology and Communication Ethics[1]

Seung-Chul Yoo

Imagine this: A person stops in front of a digital billboard near a bank, and suddenly a message appears advertising an investment product that matches the person's interests. This is enabled by a new advertising tool called facial recognition technology, which reads human faces to determine a person's approximate age, gender, and race and then generates advertising for brands appealing to the person's demographic. For example, teenage boys may be shown an ad for basketball shoes, while an older individual is shown an ad for retirement insurance.

Faces convey a wide range of meaningful information about consumers, including their demographics. For advertisers, the capability to identify facial information is important because they can obtain valuable personal information from consumers. Rather than searching through all the consumer information from web cookies on personal computers, advertisers can use facial recognition technology to learn about consumers. Further, facial recognition technology will make inferences about consumers' likes and dislikes based on their facial expressions. That is, facial recognition technology enables advertisers to acquire and use the identities of consumers in fundamentally new ways.

This chapter focuses on the advertising applications of facial recognition technology, which have received their fair share of controversy recently, and the ethical concerns that they raise. First, applications of facial recognition technology in a wide range of fields will be reviewed, and then its applications in advertising will be described. Next, the ethical issues raised by facial recognition technology will be discussed, and finally, new directions for research will be identified.

Facial Recognition Technology and its Applications

The concept of facial recognition technology (FRT) refers to an automatic system for identifying an individual from computerized graphic images (Milligan, 1999). The system works by analyzing salient facial features from a recorded image and comparing them with a facial database (Voth,

2003). For example, an algorithm analyzes and compares the relative position, size, and shape of the eyes, nose, ears, and jaw (Voth, 2003).

Current facial recognition technology has not fully matured enough to perfectly identify an individual by analyzing his facial information. In addition, the accuracy with which the system recognizes an individual by analyzing his face varies widely, and the technology is potentially hampered by changes in the environment, such as positioning, lighting, and shadows that can affect data collection (S. Z. Li & Jain, 2011). Further, facial recognition performs worse in absence of clean frontal photos (S. Z. Li & Jain, 2011). However, facial recognition technology is likely to revolutionize the practice of advertising. That is, the improving accuracy of the technology will continue to provide better means for consumer identification.

Facial recognition technology is increasingly used in a variety of ways, encompassing noncommercial and commercial applications. First, the technology is used for security purposes by law enforcement agencies (Gates, 2011). For example, governments have taken an interest in the technology as an instrument of terrorist detection (Gates, 2011). Several international airports in the U.S. and Europe, such as Fresno Yosemite International (FYI) airport in California, already have the technology in use to compare a passenger's face to a photograph stored in their database or a passenger's passport (Huang, Xiong, & Zhang, 2011). Further, German police agencies have been using a facial recognition tool since 2005, supported by the German Federal Criminal Police Office's centralized facial database (Busch, 2006). Similarly, the Pennsylvania Justice Network allows criminal justice organizations to search crime scene photos and closed-circuit television videotapes in a face database of previous arrests (Park, 2011). Nowadays, law enforcement agencies in the U.S. have started to use a handheld facial recognition application developed for the iPhone to conduct a criminal record check by taking a photo of the suspect's face (Steel & Angwin, 2011).

Facial recognition technology is also widely used by non-governmental sectors for identity verification. For example, several schools in the United Kingdom have already started using facial recognition systems to monitor students' attendance and for timekeeping tasks (Levy, 2010). Further, the technology has started to be used as a security key to confirm a person's identity at an Automated Teller Machine (ATM). Instead of using a bank card, the ATM recognizes a customer's face and compares it to his/her original facial image stored in the bank database (Peter et al., 2011).

There are also a number of commercial and entertainment applications of facial recognition technology, including social media, photo editing software, retail, and even online dating services. For example, Google's Picasa digital photo organizer has a built-in face recognition system (Shankland, 2008). The system automatically organizes users' photos by associating faces with the persons in each photo (i.e., Face ID 981087A is Mindy). Similarly, Apple's iPhoto has a face recognition system by which people can tag faces on photos (N. Lee, 2009). Facebook and Windows Live Photo Gallery provide similar face recognition functions (Lowensohn, 2009). In addition, a dating service named FindYourFaceMate. com uses a sophisticated facial recognition tool to match potential partners based on the psychological theory that people with similar facial features are attracted to each other (Damiano, 2011).

This evolving facial recognition technology provides significant opportunities for advertising. That is, advertisers now have the technology that can conveniently make estimates about their targeted consumers. The following section describes advertising applications of facial recognition technology.

I Saw Your Face and Know You: Advertising Applications Using Facial Recognition Technology

In today's advertising world, advertisers are data rich. From networked resources such as search engines, blogs, social media, and automatic face recognition tools, advertisers are collecting a huge amount of information about consumers. Although the advertising industry has struggled with the impact of the economic recession, advertising based on consumer databases offers distinct advantages for marketing and generates higher revenue due to the fact that consumers are migrating from traditional media to digital platforms. For example, Google made $36.5 billion in advertising revenue in 2011, mainly through the analysis of consumer behaviors on their search engine and in Gmail (Andrews, 2012). Among database advertising methodologies, facial recognition has the potential to significantly change the ways in which advertisers use valuable consumer data to determine where to place ads.

Nowadays, facial recognition technology is not only being deployed by entities with substantial financial and technical capabilities, such as governmental agencies. As the technology evolves, sophisticated facial recognition applications are becoming common in consumers' mobile devices, such as smart phones and tablets, offering a massive opportunity to advertise to large numbers of consumers. While face recognition technology is useful, with a wide variety of applications, it has serious privacy issues since it collects sensitive information about individuals.

Facial data are everywhere on the web. More than 250 million photos are uploaded to Facebook every day by the more than 845 million active users, and their system analyzes millions of pictures daily (Dougherty, 2012). Facebook's facial database has already outnumbered the facial databases of the U.S. Department of State, with over 75 million photographs (Dickter, 2011). Facebook's facial recognition algorithm scans all photos posted to Facebook and identifies users' faces among those people who do not opt out of the feature when posting photos (A. Lee, 2011). When advertising, marketers use demographic or geographic segmentation by grouping people with similar traits to tailor their ads to target the right consumers. Here, facial data is worth more than demographics. By researching their users by facial features and expressions, companies such as Facebook will be able to automatically estimate demographics as well as collect social and emotional information about their consumers.

Increasingly, smart phones use facial recognition technology for advertising and marketing purposes. For example, a mobile application, Scene-Tap, provides mobile users information about bars in big cities in the United States. In the participating bars, facial recognition cameras automatically estimate the number of people at the bar, the male-to-female ratio, and the average age of customers, and potential patrons can access this information on their smart phones and use it in selecting a bar. This app is a very useful mobile marketing channel for advertisers as well as bar owners who want to reach young consumers (Singer, 2011). In the near future, advertising brands on mobile phones with a face recognition function will be much more common (Bilton, 2012).

One major concern among advertisers has been calculating advertising effectiveness in outdoor media, especially for specific target audiences. Facial recognition is also growing in the digital signage sector by presenting an opportunity to extend the advertising effectiveness of the medium. For example, facial recognition technology enables advertisers to estimate the demographics of consumers passing by their billboards, and it can calculate how long a consumer watches the ad (see Figure 12.1) (S. Li

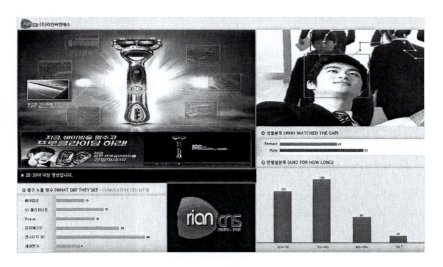

Figure 12.1 Facial Recognition Technology

& Sarno, 2011). Recently, Adidas has started to install large digital signs with Intel's facial recognition technology in their stores (Miller, 2011). UNIQLO also applied in-store digital panels equipped with NEC's face recognition and audience measurement technologies in their large stores in New York, Tokyo, and Seoul (DigitalSignageConnection, 2011).

At this point in time, the advertising applications for facial recognition technology are not comparable in accuracy to those being used by governmental agencies to identify specific individuals (S. Li & Sarno, 2011). Furthermore, advertisers mostly want to know consumers' general demographics, so that they can customize their ad messages. However, more advanced facial recognition can be used to reveal private information related to consumers' identities that is captured by facial recognizers in their publicly available images from blogs, social networks, or personal videos posted on video sharing sites like YouTube (S. Li & Sarno, 2011).

In addition to privacy issues, facial data-based advertising prompts concerns related to stereotypes. Previous studies on the stereotyping effects of race and sex in advertising have shown that representations of certain racial or gender stereotypes influence consumers' attitudes, emotions, and behaviors (e.g., Harris, Henderson, & Williams, 2005). Therefore, creating or at least reinforcing gender and racial stereotypes has been an ongoing concern related to advertising in general (Pollay, 1986). When applying facial recognition, an individual may receive ads on the basis of his skin color. For example, when a Korean American comes close to a digital billboard, it may send him a Chinese food ad even though he is not a huge fan of Chinese food. Further, this practice may result in sexism. That is, a digital billboard may send a message on the basis of a person's gender or age (e.g., skinny jean ads for young females and muscle milk ads for young males). This may strengthen the prejudices based on gender or age. Companies need to remember that the messages they send to targets should reflect healthy and realistic images.

Facial Recognition Technology and Communication Ethics

In the emerging field of digital marketing, the success of brands will greatly depend on the quality of consumer data gathered. Increasingly, advertisers use both online and offline data and integrate them for developing a better marketing strategy. The seamless integration of online and offline data helps advertisers make crucial marketing decisions for creating ads that meet the needs of their target consumers. Facial recognition technology has been integrated in a variety of media services, including online social networks, outdoor billboards, and mobile applications. Here, the data integration that includes facial data raises larger social concerns. For example, a digital sign can detect an anonymous face in the street, deliver an ad, and then share the person's personal information with other digital media, such as mobile phones, for integrated marketing purposes (e.g., a person receives a mobile message after passing by a digital billboard with a facial recognition tool).

The extent to which companies can use facial recognition technology creates controversy and debate. Many consumers are increasingly concerned about their privacy in today's digital media environment. Facial recognition technology will definitely benefit advertisers; however, it poses complex privacy and security concerns. For example, a recent study conducted by Carnegie Mellon researchers demonstrated that facial recognition software can identify not only a person's interests but also his Social Security Number (SSN) using his facial photo in Facebook (Purewal, 2011). Since new media technologies are becoming more and more sophisticated, advertisers will be able to accurately predict more sensitive information about consumers, such as name, interests, SSNs, or credit scores, by taking a picture or analyzing their faces in their blogs or homepages.

Digital privacy, like advertising ethics more generally, can be examined at three main levels: the macro-, the meso-, and the micro-levels (Drumwright, 2007). The macro-, or societal, level is affected by governmental structures, such as the Federal Trade Commission (FTC), the main regulator of interstate commerce and advertising in the U.S. The meso-level involves the dynamics on the level of the organization, such as an advertising agency, an advertiser, or the media. Lastly, the micro-level is the level of the individual (e.g., employee) in the organization.

Despite an increase in the use of face recognition technology, the government has only recently begun to focus on this new privacy risk and consider the possibility of laws and regulations to protect consumers from inappropriate use of facial recognition technologies by the digital advertising industry. For example, the FTC recently held a public workshop, "Face Facts: A Forum on Facial Recognition Technology," on the commercial applications of facial recognition technologies and the related privacy and security issues (Rashid, 2011). At the workshop, government officials, academics, consumer advocates, privacy professionals, advertising industry representatives, and technologists discussed current and future trends of commercial facial recognition technologies, consumer benefits from using it, and the related ethics and privacy concerns. Further, the issues related to targeting vulnerable populations (e.g., children and minorities) were also discussed through the workshop. Based on the findings from the workshop, the FTC is currently working on guidelines related to privacy protections for media using facial recognition technology (Rashid, 2011). Ultimately, baseline privacy legislation must be enacted to protect consumers from advertisers who try to use their information without their permission. For example, the legislation should require companies to securely dispose of the facial data that they collect immediately after finishing the data analysis. It is also important to prevent companies from selling or sharing the data from facial analyses to other commercial entities that may not have appropriate privacy principles. Privacy advocates such as the Electronic Privacy Information Center (EPIC) are also adding pressure on the FTC to suspend the use of facial recognition technology until the federal government can come up with adequate privacy standards to protect citizens (Bilton, 2012). Given the substantial social impact of the technology, legislation should limit the collection of personally identifiable facial data for commercial purposes without the informed consent of the individual consumer.

A company code of ethics is a concise statement of the basic values and norms of an organization. On a meso-level, advertising industry entities such as advertisers, ad agencies, and media companies are putting forth an effort to satisfy both government and consumer demands through self-regulation, such as establishing codes of ethics. Companies' privacy policies are subject to change at any time. In contrast, the organizational code of ethics is a powerful instrument to promote and institutionalize active responsibility of organization members (Stevens, 2008). To foster consumer trust and protect consumer rights, the organizational code of ethics should specify the responsibilities that marketers have when they operate facial recognition technology. Governmental agencies should play a crucial role in developing the industry's self-regulatory privacy codes that cover facial recognition in order to protect consumer rights. For example, the Interactive Advertising Bureau (IAB), the best-known interactive marketing industry organization, should embrace basic ethical guidelines of using facial recognition advertising in their code of conduct, including getting consumers' consent, explicit notifications, avoidance of dishonest or untrue marketing messages, and honest communications with consumers. Further, self-regulatory groups should collaborate with the government in forming their codes. In addition, in designing the codes, the advertising community must consider the opinions of consumers, and the codes must be constantly enforced. Lastly, consumers should be made aware of the extent to which they are monitored by advertisers. Thus, the first step is for governmental authorities, and industry and civic groups to put forth substantial efforts to develop and publish media literacy guidelines specifying the potential privacy risks related to face recognition technology. Further, advertising and marketing associations should put more effort into educating consumers and the advertising community about the ethics of using face recognition technology (Drumwright & Murphy, 2004).

This chapter primarily investigated the current development and use of facial recognition technology in advertising. In particular, the ethical issues raised by facial recognition technology were discussed. This chapter raises a number of important issues for future research in the domain of communication ethics in the digital media era. Future research on this topic might focus on several other things. First, consumers may have ambivalent attitudes toward the use of facial recognition technology for advertising. Therefore, understanding consumers' perceptions of the benefits and risks of facial recognition technology and the way in which they make tradeoffs will be important. According to a study from the American Consumer Institute Center for Citizen Research (Pociask, 2011), nearly two-thirds of consumers do not trust online companies to use their personal information responsibly. In contrast, a study by TNS Global (2009) demonstrated that 53% of respondents would be willing to fill out an anonymous survey to get ads that are relevant to them. From the same study, 84% reported that less than a quarter of the ads they see when using the Internet are relevant to them. That is, consumers are not happy about being tracked, but they still want to get relevant ads that are tailored to their interests (Baek & Morimoto, 2012). For example, consumers are not comfortable with Amazon's marketing activities using their purchase-related history, but they still enjoy Amazon's relevant book recommendations. Here, consumers may perceive Amazon's relevant book recommendations as helpful information rather than ads. The advertising message with high personal relevance (i.e., high involvement) to the recipient has been known to engage consumers more effectively than the message with low relevance (i.e., low involvement) (Petty, Cacioppo, & Schumann, 1983). In this context, facial recognition technology will benefit consumers in some ways by providing highly relevant brand information to the targets. To provide an empirical guide to policy-makers, future studies should attempt to identify consumers' both positive and negative perceptions toward micro targeted advertising using facial recognition technology.

Future research should also consider examining other potential risks of using facial recognition technology, such as stereotyping effects (i.e., racism, sexism, and ageism) due to the selected exposure of ads based on a consumer's facial profile. How is the impact of facial recognition advertising reinforcing the negative stereotypes in our society? How do we avoid or at least minimize the stereotyping of facial recognition advertising? In addition, future researchers could investigate how to protect vulnerable market segments, such as children and teenagers, from highly sophisticated facial recognition advertising. These research questions merit further investigations of advertising ethics in the future. Based on the findings of future research, policy-makers will be able to understand potential harms of using facial recognition advertising before setting up guidelines or regulations.

Facial recognition technology has both positive and negative uses. In the broader view, it is very important that policy-makers, privacy advocates, and industry leaders seek out solutions to protect consumer privacy and rights from the misuse of this powerful technology. If advertisers treat consumers with a high level of respect, their customers will be more loyal to the advertisers' brands. Thus, to be more successful in the long run, advertising agencies and advertising trade associations should adopt comprehensive privacy principles that limit the collection of personal identified consumer data using facial recognition technology without consumers' consent and explicit notifications.

Notes

1 Special thanks to Minette Drumwright in the Department of Advertising and Public Relations at the University of Texas for suggestions on the content of this manuscript.

References

Andrews, L. (2012, February 4). Facebook is using you. *The New York Times*. Retrieved March 1, 2012 from www.nytimes.com/2012/02/05/opinion/sunday/facebook-is-using-you.html?pagewanted=all.

Baek, T., & Morimoto, M. (2012). Stay away from me: Examining the determinants of consumer avoidance of personalized advertising. *Journal of Advertising*, 41, 59–76. doi: 10.2753/JOA0091-3367410105

Bilton, N. (2012, February 22). Behind the Google Goggles, virtual reality. *The New York Times*. Retrieved March 1, 2012 from www.nytimes.com/2012/02/23/technology/google-glasses-will-be-powered-by-android.html.

Busch, C. (2006). Facing the future of biometrics. *EMBO reports*, 7, S23–S25. doi: 10.1038/sj.embor.7400723

Damiano, J. (2011, September 27). New dating strategy helps find a face mate. *Newsday*. Retrieved May 22, 2012 from www.newsday.com/entertainment/pet-rock-1.811972/new-dating-strategy-helps-find-a-face-mate-1.3204283. >

Dickter, A. (2011, December 30). Facial recognition may enhance new apple devices. *Yahoo News*. Retrieved March 12, 2012 from http://news.yahoo.com/facial-recognition-may-enhance-apple-devices-220508333.html.

DigitalSignageConnection. (2011, October 17). NEC provides digital signage for UNIQLO's largest global stores. Retrieved April 2, 2012 from www.digitalsignageconnection.com/nec-provides-digital-signage-uniqlo%E2%80%99s-largest-global-flagship-store.

Dougherty, H. (2012). Ten key statistics about Facebook. *Hitwise*. Retrieved April 25, 2013 from www.experian.com/blogs/marketing-forward/2012/02/07/10-key-statistics-about-facebook/.

Drumwright, M. E. (2007). Advertising ethics: A multi-level theory approach. In G. J. Tellis & T. Ambler (Eds.), *The Handbook of Advertising* (pp. 398–415). London: Sage.

Drumwright, M. E., & Murphy, P. E. (2004). How advertising practitioners view ethics: Moral muteness, moral myopia, and moral imagination. *Journal of Advertising*, 33, 7–24.

Gates, K. (2011). *Our Biometric Future: Facial Recognition Technology and the Culture of Surveillance.* New York: NYU Press

Harris, A. M. G., Henderson, G. R., & Williams, J. D. (2005). Courting customers: Assessing consumer racial profiling and other marketplace discrimination. *Journal of Public Policy & Marketing, 24,* 163–171. doi: 10.1509/jppm.24.1.163.63893

Huang, T., Xiong, Z., & Zhang, Z. (2011). Face recognition applications. In S. Z. Li & A. K. Jain (Eds.), *Handbook of Face Recognition* (pp. 617–638). London: Springer.

Lee, A. (2011, June 8). Facebook rolls out facial recognition for photo tagging. *Huffington Post.* Retrieved March 2, 2012 from www.huffingtonpost.com/2011/06/08/facebook-facial-recognition_n_872983.html.

Lee, N. (2009, January 30). First taste of iLife '09: iPhoto's face recognition. *CNET.* Retrieved March 2, 2012 from http://news.cnet.com/8301-17938_105-10153818-1.html.

Levy, A. (2010, October 4). School installs £9,000 facial recognition cameras to stop students turning up late and teachers could be next target. *Mail Online.* Retrieved April 2, 2012 fromwww.dailymail.co.uk/news/article-1317520/School-installs-9k-facial-recognition-cameras-stop-students-turning-late.html.

Li, S., & Sarno, D. (2011, August 21). Advertisers start using facial recognition to tailor pitches. *Los Angeles Times.* Retrieved March 1, 2012 from http://articles.latimes.com/2011/aug/21/business/la-fi-facial-recognition-20110821.

Li, S. Z., & Jain, A. K. (2011). *Handbook of Face Recognition* (pp. 1–15). London: Springer.

Lowensohn, J. (2009, September 30). Facial recognition face-off: Three tools compared. *CNET.* Retrieved March 2, 2012 from http://news.cnet.com/8301-27076_3-10363727-248.html.

Miller, M. J. (2011, August 25). Facial-recognition technology: Coming to a store near you. *Brandchannel.* Retrieved March 2, 2012 from www.brandchannel.com/home/post/2011/08/25/Facial-Recognition-Technology-Coming-to-a-Store-Near-You.aspx.

Milligan, C. S. (1999). Facial recognition technology, video surveillance, and privacy. *Southern California Interdisciplinary Law Journal, 9,* 295–334.

Park, T. (2011). *Pennsylvania Justice Network 2010–2011 Annual Report.* Harrisburg, PA: Pennsylvania Justice Network. Retrieved March 2, 2012 from www.portal.state.pa.us/portal/server.pt/document/1218064/oa_oit_jnet_annual_report_fy2010-2011.

Peter, K. J., Glory, G., Arguman, S., Nagarajan, G., Devi, V., & Kannan, K. S. (2011). *Improving ATM Security via Face Recognition.* Paper presented at the Electronics Computer Technology (ICECT), 2011 3rd International Conference, Kanyakumari, India.

Petty, R. E., Cacioppo, J. T., & Schumann, D. (1983). Central and peripheral routes to advertising effectiveness: The moderating role of involvement. *Journal of Consumer Research, 10,* 135–146.

Pociask, S. (2011). Online privacy survey results. *The American Consumer Institute Center for Citizen Research.* Retrieved January 10, 2012 from www.theamericanconsumer.org/2011/11/30/online-privacy-survey-results/.

Pollay, R. W. (1986). The distorted mirror: Reflections on the unintended consequences of advertising. *Journal of Marketing, 50*, 18–36. doi: 10.2307/1251597

Purewal, S. J. (2011, August 5). Why Facebook facial recognition is creepy: Redux. *PCWorld*. Retrieved January 2, 2012 from www.pcworld.com/article/237367/why_facebook_facial_recognition_is_creepy_redux.html.

Rashid, F. Y. (2011, December 9). Facial recognition apps carries risk of user privacy violations, FTC warns. *eWeek.com*. Retrieved April 2, 2012 from www.eweek.com/c/a/Security/Facial-Recognition-Apps-Carries-Risk-of-User-Privacy-Violations-FTC-Warns-497289/.

Shankland, S. (2008, September 8). Revamped Google Picasa site identifies photo faces. *CNET*. Retrieved April 1, 2012 from http://news.cnet.com/8301-13580_3-10026577-39.html.

Singer, N. (2011, November 12). Face recognition makes the leap from sci-fi. *The New York Times*. Retrieved January 3, 2012 from www.nytimes.com/2011/11/13/business/face-recognition-moves-from-sci-fi-to-social-media.html.

Steel, E., & Angwin, J. (2011, August 16). Device raises fear of facial profiling. *The Wall Street Journal*. Retrieved January 10, 2012 from http://online.wsj.com/article/SB10001424052702303678704576440253307985070.html.

Stevens, B. (2008). Corporate ethical codes: Effective instruments for influencing behavior. *Journal of Business Ethics, 78*, 601–609. doi: 10.1007/s10551-007-9370-z

TNS Global (2009). *2009 Study: Consumer Attitudes about Behavioral Targeting*. Retrieved April25, 2013 from www.slideshare.net/TRUSTeprivacyseal/trustetns-study-consumer-attitudes-about-behavioral-targeting.

Voth, D. (2003). Face recognition technology. *Intelligent Systems, IEEE, 18*, 4–7.

Chapter 13

Ethical Issues in Marketing Communication in Emerging Markets

The Case of Advertising in the Middle East

Sara Kamal

Prominent marketing scholars such as Prahalad (2004) have long empha-sized the immense potential of developing economies, particularly emerg-ing markets, underscoring that many of these markets provide significant growth opportunities for multinational brands. Indeed, what makes these markets even more critical to bottom line growth for many marketers is the fact that the majority of the world's population hails from coun-tries that can be classified as developing or emerging markets (Mahajan, Banga, & Gunther, 2005). Therefore, as emerging markets continue to become more critical to marketers' success, the role and growth of adver-tising in these markets are of increasing importance.

The Middle East is an emerging market that has witnessed increased economic growth, media expansion, and an uptake of advertising activ-ity, making it an attractive target segment for marketers. Yet relatively lit-tle research attention has been given to advertising practices in the region (Taylor, 2005). Even less attention has been given to advertising ethics.

The primary goal of the current chapter is to examine the issue of adver-tising ethics within the context of an important emerging market region, namely the Middle East. The Middle East region consists of 12 Arab coun-tries, namely Bahrain, Iraq, Jordan, Kuwait, Lebanon, Oman, Palestine (the Gaza Strip and West Bank), Qatar, Kingdom Saudi Arabia (KSA), Syria, United Arab Emirates (UAE), and Yemen. The regional advertising market has been estimated at $13.7 billion in 2010 with a compounded annual growth rate (CAGR) of 12.4% (Pan Arabian Research Center, 2011). The UAE is considered an important market leader because of its enhanced media capabilities and technologies, while KSA remains an important market in the region due to its massive consumer market (Dubai Press Club, 2009). As is characteristic of most emerging markets, nations within the region have a "youth bulge" (Mahajan et al., 2005). That is, over half of the population in the Middle East region is under the age of 30 (Pew Research, 2011), signaling important opportunities for international brands, particularly within the telecommunications, enter-tainment, fashion, education, and services industries. Due to a shared language, religion, and geographic proximity (Beeston, 1974; Cleveland, 1964), researchers have noted that consumers in these markets tend to hold similar cultural norms, values, and beliefs (Karande, Almurshidee, & Al-Olayan, 2006).

This chapter first discusses the role of advertising in emerging economies and provides a brief overview of advertising ethics research in the U.S. It then builds a discussion around the broad themes that have emerged from previous business and marketing communication research in the Middle East related to advertising ethics and the factors that affect it. It then identifies avenues for future research and investigation and discusses their implications for research, policy, and practice.

Advertising in Emerging Economies

The definition of an emerging market has been a topic of some debate among researchers. While some scholars maintain that economic indicators like gross domestic product and economic growth rates are indicative of a country's status, others have noted that such measures are too stringent and do not encompass the full nature of an "emerging" economy. For example, Samli (2004) noted that, based on economic indicators alone, China or India would be classified as "low-income" countries and would not be considered emerging markets. Similarly, countries such as the UAE or Qatar would be considered "high-income" economies, implying economic development and maturity (which may not be the case). Therefore, to address this issue, scholars such as Rahman and Bhattacharyya (2003) underscored the importance of taking into consideration qualitative measures when classifying nations. Specifically, these authors contended that emerging markets can be classified as those economies that are experiencing significant economic growth, or are expected to witness significant economic growth in the near future, and have increasingly opened up to direct foreign investment in the present, which is expected to continue in the future. Additionally, Rahman and Bhattacharyya (2003) noted that, compared to typical developed economies, the institutional infrastructure of emerging markets still lacks the efficiency and effectiveness of a typical developed market.

External factors such as economic development and market conditions greatly impact the context within which marketing processes take place (Dolan, 2000; Swerdlow & Blessios, 1993). Certainly, advertising is no exception. In fact, through decades of research, theoretical frameworks that explicate the economic role of advertising have been widely accepted (Borden, 1942a). Specifically, it has been established that the effect of advertising varies based on the nature of the market and the maturity of the industry/category being advertised (Borden, 1942b). In particular, in an expanding or new market, advertising is likely to have the greatest impact on demand, thus exhibiting a positive relationship with economic growth. This is due to the fact that, as an economy develops, companies operating within that economy tend to use advertising, promotions, and other marketing communications tactics to increase their market share in a growing market (Chang & Chan-Olmsted, 2005; Belch & Belch, 2009). For this reason, it is obvious that the level of economic development of a given country is an important factor in understanding advertising practices and media patterns. In fact, Wurff, Bakker, and Picard (2008) noted that increased economic growth is associated with increased advertising activity and media expenditures. Additionally, economic boom is generally associated with increased urbanization and industrialization—both of which are important drivers of the advertising industry (Dimmick, 1997).

In the case of emerging markets in which consumers are faced with an influx of foreign and national brands as well as increased purchasing power, advertising is an important source of market information about new products and brands. For instance, in a study about television advertising in China, Tai and Pae (2002) found that Chinese consumers viewed advertising as an important instrument in obtaining information about foreign brands. But this is not the only reason why advertising can be considered an important tool in emerging markets. Past researchers have also noted that advertising is a potent source of social meaning that provides context and familiarizes audiences with their growing role as consumers and as a global consumer culture (Cleveland, Laroche, & Papadopoulos, 2009; Cleveland & Laroche, 2006).

At the same time, the adoption of the holding group structure within the advertising industry has resulted in concentrated ownership of advertising agencies (Belch & Belch, 2009). Thus, while the number of advertising agencies worldwide has increased steadily (particularly in emerging markets), it is estimated that approximately 80% of the world's advertising is produced by agencies within the leading global holding companies, namely Interpublic Group of Companies, Omnicom Group, Publicis Groupe, and WPP Group (Advertising Age, 2010; Greenway & Nadeau, 2009). However, while these international holding groups control international agency brands as well as small-to-regional agencies across global markets, they may not be involved in day-to-day marketing communication activities and processes (Melewar, Turnbull, & Balabanis, 2000). Because many advertising-related decisions and systems are implemented on a market basis, there is room for discrepancies or inequalities that are "lost in translation," which obviously raises concerns with respect to ethical practices in these advertising markets. Given the industry adoption of the global holding group networks, this is a pertinent issue to agency management. Additionally, due to the variance in socio-cultural factors as well as economic and institutional frameworks, standardized codes of ethics of advertising holding groups may not be easily understood or adaptable within the emerging market context. This becomes a very crucial area of research, which has implications for practice, as many of the tactical decisions dealing with advertising are acted upon within a local context.

Advertising Ethics Research in the U.S.

Research on the topic of advertising ethics continues to be an area of growing interest for scholars in the U.S. Since the late 1980s, several notable studies marked the beginning of empirical analysis into areas related to advertising ethics. Topics have included the ethicality of advertisers' choice of appeals, such as exploitive, fear, and sexual appeals (e.g., LaTour & Henthorne, 1994; Crisp, 1987); the ethicality of advertising for professional services advertising (e.g., Bullard & Snizek, 1988; Mangold, 1987; Stafford, 1988); ethical issues in advertising for political candidates (e.g., Waller, 2002); and advertising for vice products such as tobacco (e.g., Pomeroy, Castellano, Becker, Johnson, & Brown, 1992). Others have examined unfair targeting practices by advertisers, particularly those targeting children (e.g., Hyman, Tansley, & Clark, 1994) and minority groups (Kinsey, 1987; Treise, Weigold, Conna, & Garrison, 1994). Yet another set of studies has brought to light important issues, such as the use of stereotyped images in advertising (e.g., Green, 1993), as well as the sexual portrayal of females and sexual content in ads (e.g., Schneider & Schneider, 1979). Additionally, Spence and Van Heereken (2005) explored prevailing issues regarding ethics in advertising, spanning topics such as continuing concerns related to stereotyping, targeted advertising, and consumer privacy. More recently, scholars have looked into student perceptions of advertising ethics (e.g., Burnett, Keith, & Pettijohn, 2003; Beard, 2003), as well as practitioner views of ethics in advertising (e.g., Drumwright & Murphy, 2004, 2009).

However, the aforementioned studies have focused on western countries, particularly in North America (e.g., Burnett, Keith, & Pettijohn, 2003; Drumwright & Murphy, 2004, 2009; Castelberry, French, & Carlin, 1993). To date, limited internationally focused studies have examined advertising ethics (Zinkhan, 1994), particularly within the Middle East (Mostafa, 2011).

Business and Marketing Communication Research in the Middle East

In an effort to develop a research agenda, the following section provides a review of past studies that have explored the topic of ethics or related factors in marketing communications and business in general within the Middle East, an important region for emerging markets.

The Role of Socio-cultural Factors

A recent study by Mostafa (2011) examined consumers' attitudes toward ethical issues in advertising among college students in Egypt. The author noted that, in general, advertising has a poor perception in Egypt, which can be ascribed to the "unholy trinity" (p. 43): 1) advertisers, 2) clients, and 3) media organizations—all of which do not want to accept their role and responsibility to increase the ethical bar of the industry. Based on survey results, the author concluded that respondents' gender and religion (Muslim or Non-Muslim) affected their attitudes toward ethical issues in advertising. Results from this study suggested that international adaption strategy, in which international campaigns from foreign markets are adapted for the Middle Eastern market, may not be applicable, given the varied attitudes of consumers. Further, it was suggested that consumer attitudes toward ethical issues in advertising have an impact on the overall perception of the advertising industry, as well as on the efficiency of marketing communication tools (Pollay & Mittal, 1993). Mostafa (2011) concluded that additional research is needed to explore this issue further, particularly in the Pan Arab region and especially with non-student samples.

Another study by Marta, Singhapakdi, Attia, and Vitell (2004) approached the topic of ethics from the marketer's perspective. Specifically, these scholars examined the perceived intentions and the importance of ethical values among marketers in three Middle Eastern markets, namely Saudi Arabia, Egypt, and Jordan. Results from a self-administered questionnaire indicated that the perception of an ethical problem had a positive impact on the intention of Middle Eastern marketers to act ethically. Additionally, the authors noted a positive relationship between the perceived importance of ethics and the intention to behave ethically. While this study examined the topic of ethics from a marketer's perspective, no specific attention was given to ethical issues with respect to advertising. Yet causes of breakdowns in international marketing communications tactics such as advertising have typically been associated with the neglect of cultural attitudes within foreign countries (Jeannet & Hennessey, 2004).

The Role of Multinational Home Offices (Client and Agency Side)

In their examination of advertising strategies and decision-making processes of multinational corporations (MNC) in the Middle East, Melewar et al. (2000) found that the majority of MNCs develop their product positioning strategy and campaign theme at corporate headquarters, while decisions on target segment, media strategy, budget decisions, and creative execution are handled locally. Therefore, local partners in the marketing communication process—advertising agencies, media organizations, and collateral service providers—have an important stake in the advertising process. It has been noted that that multinational clients and holding groups may not be involved in day-to-day marketing communication activities and processes, such as target segment selection, creative tactics, media planning, and budget decisions (Melewar et al., 2000). Thus, these findings emphasize the importance of local partners in developing ethically responsible marketing communications content and procedures for conducting business. Indeed, many of the ethical concerns correspond to the functional areas of advertising practice that are handled on the ground in local markets, such as deceptive or misleading ads (e.g., puffery, exaggeration); promotion of undesirable values (e.g., materialism); promotion of unnecessary or risky products/services (e.g., vice products); targeting vulnerable populations (e.g., children, minorities); stereotypical portrayals that are offensive; and privacy concerns (e.g., using consumers' personal information for commercial purposes without their permission).

The Role of Regulation

Fast-developing regions within emerging markets continue to grow in importance as regional commercial hubs, benchmarking remarkable, growing economic development rates. In light of this development, recent empirical studies have sought to understand factors impacting pro-social practices of businesses in emerging economies, such as the Middle East. Overall, these studies underscored that the daily business operations of international firms operating in the Middle East are best understood within the local socio-cultural framework. For example, recently, Rettab, Brik, and Mellahi (2009) found that firms operating in emerging economies are "embedded in different business systems" (p. 371) as compared to those of developed economies, particularly in terms of institutional legal frameworks (or the lack thereof). These authors found that, due to the emphasis on competitiveness and economic growth in emerging markets, practitioners give higher priority to economic outcomes than to other organizational goals of higher moral content (e.g., corporate social responsibility initiatives).

Indeed, Carrigan, Marinova, and Szmigin (2005) noted that ethical issues are increasingly becoming an important issue related to international marketing. Specifically, the authors indicated that, in developed markets, improved legislation has raised the bar with respect to consumer expectations of marketing behavior and consumer rights, yet emerging markets may be more vulnerable to unethical marketing practices due to their "economic potential, low bargaining power, lack of legal framework" (p. 486). In fact, many times in an effort to reposition or extend the product lifecycle of their products, MNCs have infringed on ethical boundaries of marketing practices, particularly with vice products such as tobacco (Carrigan et al., 2005).

The Transient Worker

Due to the limited talent pool, fast-developing emerging markets rely heavily on expatriate employees with short-term contracts to fill the talent gap (Kamal & Drumright, 2012). This practice greatly limits the long-run perspective or sense of ownership and responsibility of employees with respect to business practices. Budhwar and Mellahi (2007) stated that this issue is further pronounced because such markets often do not provide a "safety net or alternative economic or social provision" for employees. Thus, employee welfare relies heavily on the goodwill of employers, which may cause employees to comply with, mitigate, or obstruct controversial issues with their employers—this raises a red flag with respect to employee decisions regarding ethics at all functional levels of business, including marketing and advertising operations.

The Role of Religion

The role of religion with respect to ethical practices in business (including marketing communications) has received attention from a few scholars. While Islamic doctrine permeates much of the socio-cultural scene in the Middle East, there are functional differences in Middle Eastern countries in terms of advertising regulation due to the variance in economic, political, social, and educational status (Melewar et al., 2000). A handful of studies have examined advertising ethics through the perspective of Islam, most of which focus on the implications of Islam for advertising content and development. Notably, Rice and Al-Mossawi (2002) considered the implications of Islam for advertising messages within the Middle Eastern context. Specifically, these authors stated that religion impacts the execution of marketing communication efforts and that advertisers must understand these differences in order to effectively target Muslim consumers, who continue to increase in size and purchasing power. They also noted that many Muslim countries are witnessing a return to stronger religious commitment among these consumers—underscoring the importance of this issue.

Rice (1999) stated that Islam and Quranic teachings are not in opposition to advertising, provided that it is used to promote products, services, and faith. Recently, Kamal and Drumwright (2012) noted the rise of the "new Islamic consumer"—a new segment within the Muslim consumer market that seeks out brands and products that appeal to their religious views. The authors noted that these consumers do not see their faith in opposition with advertising, promotions, and marketing activities, and they hold a positive view toward them. Yet, research in markets such as Saudi Arabia has suggested that consumers often view advertising as a threat to Islamic culture (Keenan & Shoreh, 2000). This finding has been attributed to the fact that consumers believe advertising neglects Arab cultural norms and beliefs (including religious beliefs). Not surprisingly, Michell and Al-Mossawi (1999) found that ads that go against Islamic principles prompted negative consumer attitudes and poor recall among religiously strict Muslims compared to those Muslims who were not religiously conservative. This has ramifications for brands and advertisers, suggesting that ads that do not take into consideration the religious values of their targets may prompt negative consumer responses toward advertising efforts and the brand itself, as well as negatively affect sales. Rice and Al-Mossawi (2002) stated that religious values of Islam influence consumer acceptance of advertising depictions, including gender roles, body parts, characterization of models used in ads, and the use of certain animals. Additionally, Islamic teachings promote directness and honesty in all communication (Rice, 1999; Rice & Al-Mossawi, 2002); therefore, exaggeration and hyperbole are considered offensive to many Muslim consumers.

On the other hand, others have noted that there may be more commonalities than differences among religious groups in perceptions of advertising ethics. For example, in a study examining consumer perceptions of advertising ethics among Muslim and Christian communities in Cyprus, Gibbs, Ilkan, and Pouloukas (2007) reported a high level of commonality between Muslim and Christian respondents. Further, these authors noted that the majority of respondents from both faiths rejected ethically questionable practices, including the secularization of advertising content, unfair targeting, and stereotyped images. Interestingly, the author noted that religious intensity was a strong indicator of how offensive the respondents found advertising practices. Others have also mentioned that cultural diversity might impact what is deemed as acceptable in advertising, despite religious affiliations. For example, in a study about the advertising of controversial products, Waller, Fam, and Erdogan (2005) found that countries with higher levels of multicultural groups tended to be more flexible and open toward advertising of different types of products (some of which may be considered controversial) due to a high level of diversity in societal beliefs and the desire to maintain social harmony. With respect to the Middle East, this may explain why certain markets within the region with greater outside influences, such as Lebanon and UAE, are more open to advertising content as compared to markets that are more insulated from foreign influence, such as Saudi Arabia.

The Road Ahead: Building a Research Agenda

Because of factors such as the lack of regulation, large youth populations, and lower levels of literacy, emerging markets present marketers
and advertisers with a unique context (Kamal & Drumright, 2012). In
light of the review of literature, the following section provides a discussion of several areas of investigation related to advertising ethics that
merit future research.

As international holding groups acquire local and regional partners
to develop a presence in emerging markets, several important questions
arise. First, how do international marketing communication partners,
particularly advertising agencies, approach the issue of ethics with respect
to the emerging region within which they are entering? Are there differences among international, regional, and local organizations? How do
multinational agencies communicate their ethical standards to local and
regional partners and insure that they are implemented? Generally speaking, more research is needed to understand how multinational agencies
approach the issue of ethics with respect to the regions in which they operate. Future research should explore how these practitioners who work for
multinational agencies uphold ethical standards on the ground in these
emerging markets. For example, what are the functional areas or issues
that best practices should cover in advertising ethics, particularly vis-à-vis
emerging markets? This is of particular importance as local and regional
agencies within multinational agency networks may operate under different management styles and procedures and in different socio-cultural
environments that impact business functions.

Second, in light of the unique socioeconomic and cultural aspects of
emerging markets, are ethical practices adapted to fit better with the local
culture, and if so, how; and what is the effect of the adaptation? MNCs
have typically viewed markets within emerging regions as one mono-
lithic group; for example, the Middle East region has long been regarded
by MNCs as a "single regional market" (Melewar et al., 2000). Future
research may benefit from exploring differences between emerging markets regionally given the variance in cultural and religious tendencies as
these are likely to play a role in the implementation of ethical practices in
advertising. For example, with respect to the Middle East, markets such
as UAE may vary greatly from those of KSA, although economically both
countries may be classified as quite similar.

Additionally, differences of economic growth rates between markets
within the region may result in systematic differences in terms of business
environment and management practices (Carrigan et al., 2005). It can
be deduced that firms operating in fast-developing regions of emerging
markets, such as Dubai, Hong Kong, and Singapore, have a profound
impact and role to play in shaping business practices in the region because

they serve as a base for regional economic activity. For example, the UAE has witnessed rapid economic and infrastructural development, making it a vital business hub within the Middle East region (Business Monitor International, 2009). As advertising expenditures and development tend to closely follow economic growth (Telser, 1971), it is no surprise that the UAE has witnessed a blossoming of its advertising industry (Dubai Press Club, 2009). From the industry perspective, the UAE is regarded as a prime locality within the Middle East, particularly in the Gulf Cooperation Council (GCC) nations, with respect to advertising practices (Barkho, 2007). Therefore, future research should consider the role of regional hubs in setting in place practices with respect to advertising ethics, as they are likely to have an impact on the functional practices across the region.

It has been found that government regulations impact the level of standardization of advertising practices and content. Little is known about how these regulations stack up market to market within emerging economies. Certainly, analysis is needed to understand the broader context of the region, as most of the advertising campaigns that are executed use a regional approach (Belch & Belch, 2009). However, the Middle East is an interesting example of a scenario in which many markets are highly regulated, while others have limited, if any, regulation. This is an issue of great importance to policy-makers. With respect to the Middle East, past research has indicated that advertising and media restrictions in spot markets within the region pose difficulties in trying to execute regional advertising tactics (Melewar et al., 2000). Thus, it would be fruitful for future research to include an analysis of government regulations across markets in the Middle East region to understand market similarities and differences. Furthermore, future research efforts can also explore the degree to which advertising regulations across the regions are understood by participants in the marketing communications process.

Additionally, the markets from which multinational agencies' ethics policies originate have well-accepted regulatory bodies and a history of self-regulation. Thus the question arises: Are international ethics codes applicable across markets of varying economic, cultural, and infrastructural milieus? These issues are critical to practice to better understand and ensure that holding group operations are above board, as well as important for policy in terms of assuring consumer protection across economic conditions.

Future research should consider issues related to advertising content development in the context of emerging markets. An area of concern that is important to policy-makers involves tactical decisions such as creative executions and appeals, as well as media and targeting strategies. More research is needed to understand how regulation should address the unique market characteristics of emerging markets, e.g., consumers with less familiarity with marketing communications practices, low levels of market regulation, less educated populations, and large youth market segments. Specifically, particular emphasis should be given to areas that raise ethical concerns, such as the development of advertising content (i.e., appeals, characterization, and message development) as well as the targeting of vulnerable populations, such as children, and undereducated and lower-income consumers. Undoubtedly, such research would make a significant contribution to practitioners and policy-makers in establishing more systematic and robust regional regulation. In particular, a question that needs further consideration is the following: Do the concerns related to advertising regulation and ethics in emerging markets differ from those in the west and in developed markets?

It also appears that market labor polices and strategies may have an effect on the approach and decision-making process in terms of ethical conduct in marketing communications practices. Emerging markets characteristically rely on short-term and expatriate workers due to limitations in the education, training, and availability of talent. Past research has also noted that the transience of expatriate careers and the perceived lack of employee protection in emerging markets may cause employees to focus unduly on revenue gains over pro-social behavior (Budhwar & Mellahi, 2007). Future research may explore how this issue is being handled within the advertising industry. Specifically, what mechanisms are in place to uphold or support ethical behavior among transient employees? Certainly, such an examination would help to broaden the scope of the research literature and our understanding of the advertising ethics literature. Of particular interest is how foreign talent is trained to understand local market factors, as well as how agencies can encourage a long-term and pro-social approach among transient workers.

One of the emergent themes is the role of religion in understanding advertising ethics. As Muslim populations across the globe grow in size and purchasing power (Rice, 1999), this becomes a more critical question that warrants future research consideration. Undoubtedly, such an understanding can contribute to practice as well as research. Several studies have brought to light the role of religion in the development of advertising content within the Middle East region (Rice, 1999; Rice & Al-Mossawi, 2002). While these studies have examined the implications of Islam on the production of advertising content, more emphasis is needed on how religion may impact the process of conducting the advertising business. Additionally, it would be beneficial to industry practitioners and the research literature to further understand how advertising professionals perceive the role of religion in the practice of advertising. For example, do practitioners see any functional areas in advertising (e.g., creative executions, copy writing, media placement, promotional efforts) that may be in discord with Islamic tenants? It would also be interesting to explore whether advertising professionals believe Islamic values can contribute to more ethical practices in advertising in the Middle East, and if so, how? Yet another avenue for future exploration involves the standardization of advertising practices for markets across regions based on religious tenants. For example, is there a standardized approach that can be applied across predominantly Muslim markets (e.g., Malaysia, Indonesia, Pakistan, Kingdom of Saudi Arabia, Eygpt, Tanzania)? Furthermore, are such practices suitable for communities that host large Muslim market segments across regions (e.g., India, Canada, France, Turkey, Germany)? A testament to such an approach is the growing popularity of Islamic banking within the global financial industry. More research is needed to understand the applicability of this model within the advertising industry and its impact on the development of ethical frameworks.

Conclusion

Overall, while some past research has examined ethical issues in marketing in cross-cultural settings (Singhapakdi, Rawwas, Marta, & Ahmed, 1999; Rawwas, Patzer, & Klassen, 1995), further research is needed to better understand ethical issues related to specific marketing practices, such as advertising, within emerging markets. The current chapter contextualized the topic of advertising ethics within the scope of the Middle East, an emerging market region that has experienced economic growth and expansion of its media and advertising industries. In doing so, this chapter provided a review of the related research literature in an effort to identify key themes that have emerged from previous research.

From the review of research, it is clear that there are a number of important areas of investigation yet to be explored. While these areas have been discussed with regard to the Middle East region, many are applicable across emerging markets. On one hand, these are untapped, emerging markets presenting attractive growth opportunities; on the other hand, they are vulnerable because they lack mechanisms that take into consideration the unique characteristics of these markets. This chapter raises a number of questions for future research in an effort to prompt researchers, policy-makers, and the industry at large to consider solutions that will lead to a more ethical business environment with respect to advertising in emerging markets (the Middle East being an example of such a market). It is hoped that through self-reflection and future research, the ethical pitfalls that the advertising industry has faced in developed markets can be avoided.

References

Advertising Age (2010). *Top 50 Marketing Groups Worldwide in 2010 by Revenues*. New York: Ad Age Data Center.

Barkho, L. (2007). Advertising resources in oil rich Arab Gulf states—implications for international marketers. *International Journal of Business Studies*, 19 (2), 1–24.

Beard, F. K. (2003). College student attitudes toward advertising's ethical, economic, and social consequences. *Journal of Business Ethics*, 48 (3), 217–228.

Beeston, A. (1974) *The Arab Language Today*. London: Hutchinson and Co. Ltd.

Belch, G., & Belch, M. B. (2009). *Advertising and Promotion: An Integrated Marketing Communications Perspective*. New York: McGraw-Hill/Irwin.

Borden, N. H. (1942a). *The Economic Effects of Advertising*. Chicago: Richard Irwin, Inc.

Borden, N. H. (1942b). Findings of the Harvard study on the economic effects of advertising. *Journal of Marketing*, 6 (4), 89–99.

Budhwar, P. S., & Mellahi, K. (2007). Introduction: Human resource management in the Middle East. *International Journal of Human Resource Management*, 18, 1–10.

Bullard, J. H., & Snizek, W. E. (1988). Factors affecting the acceptability of advertisements among professionals. *Journal of the Academy of Marketing Science*, 16 (Summer), 57–63.

Burnett, M., Keith, N., & Pettijohn, C. (2003). An empirical analysis of factors influencing student reactions to ethical advertising dilemmas: Educational experience, work experience, ethical philosophy, and demographics. *Marketing Education Review*, 13 (Spring), 33–46.

Business Monitor International (2009). *United Arab Emirates Business Forecast Report*. London: Business Monitor International.

Carrigan, M., Marinova, S., & Szmigin, I. (2005). Ethics and international marketing: Research background and challenges. *International Marketing Review*, 22 (5), 481–493.

Castleberry, S. B., French, W. A., & Carlin, B. A. (1993). The ethical framework of advertising and marketing research practitioners: A moral development perspective. *Journal of Advertising*, 22 (June), 39–46.

Chang, B. H., & Chan-Olmsted, S. M. (2005). Relative constancy of advertising spending: A cross-national examination of advertising expenditures and their determinants. *Gazette*, 67 (4), 339–357.

Cleveland, M., & Laroche, M. (2006). Acculturation to the global consumer culture: Scale development and research paradigm. *Journal of Business Research*, 60(3), 249–260.

Cleveland, M., Laroche, M., & Papadopoulos, N. (2009), Cosmopolitanism, consumer ethnocentrism, and materialism: An eight-country study of antecedents and outcomes. *Journal of International Marketing*, 17 (1), 116–146.

Cleveland, W. L. (1964). *A History of the Modern Middle East*. Boulder, CO: Westview Press.

Crisp, R. (1987). Persuasive advertising, autonomy, and the creation of desire. *Journal of Business Ethics*, 6 (July), 413–418.

Dimmick, J. (1997). The theory of the niche and spending on mass media: The case of the video revolution. *Journal of Media Economics*, 10 (3), 33–43.

Dolan, R. J. (2000). *Note on Marketing Strategy*. Boston, MA: Harvard Business School Publishing.

Drumwright, M. E., & Murphy, P. E. (2004). How advertising practitioners view ethics: Moral muteness, moral myopia and moral imagination. *Journal of Advertising*, 33 (2), 7–24.

Drumwright, M. E., & Murphy, P. E. (2009). The current state of advertising ethics: Industry and academic perspectives. *Journal of Advertising*, 38 (1), 83–108.

Dubai Press Club (2009). *Arab Media Outlook 2009–2013: Inspiring Local Content*. Dubai: Dubai Press Club. Retrieved April 25, 2013 from www.fas.org/irp/eprint/arabmedia.pdf.

Gibbs, P., Ilkan, M., & Pouloukas, S. (2007). The ethics of marketing in Muslim and Christian communities: Insights for global marketing. *Equal Opportunities International*, 26 (7), 678–693.

Green, M. K. (1993). Images of Native Americans in advertising: Some moral issues. *Journal of Business Ethics*, 12 (4), 323–330.

Greenway, J., & Nadeau, M. (2009). *Art and Copy [Documentary]*. New York: The One Club for Art and Copy.

Hyman, M. R., Tansley, R., & Clark, J. W. (1994). Research on advertising ethics: Past, present, and future. *Journal of Advertising*, 23 (September), 5–15.

Jeannet, J., & Hennessey, H. D. (2004). *Global Marketing Strategies*. Boston, MA: Houghton Mifflin Company.

Kamal, S., & Drumwright, M. E. (2012). *Advertising Ethics in the Middle East: Industry Perspectives*. Accepted for presentation at the 2012 Marketing and Public Policy Conference (MPPC), Atlanta, GA (June 7–9).

Karande, K., Almurshide, K. A., & Al-Olayan, F. (2006). Advertising standardization in culturally similar markets: Can we standardize all components? *International Journal of Advertising*, 25 (4), 489–511.

Keenan, K. L., & Shoreh, B. (2000). How advertising is covered in the Egyptian press: A longitudinal examination of content. *International Journal of Advertising*, 19 (2), 245–258.

Kinsey, J. (1987). The use of children in advertising and the impact of advertising aimed at children. *International Journal of Advertising*, 6 (2), 169–177.

LaTour, M. S., & Henthorne, T. L. (1994). Ethical judgments of sexual appeals in print advertising. *Journal of Advertising*, 23 (3), 81–90.

Mahajan, V., Banga, K., & Gunther, R. (2005). *The 86 Percent Solution: How to Succeed in the Biggest Market Opportunity of the Next 50 Years*. Upper Saddle River, NJ: Wharton School Publishing.

Mangold, W. G. (1987). Use of commercial sources of information in the purchase of professional services: What the literature tells us. *Journal of Professional Services Marketing*, 3 (1,2), 5–17.

Marta, J. K., Singhapakdi, A., Attia, A., & Vitell, S. J. (2004). Some important factors underlying ethical decisions of Middle-Eastern marketers. *International Marketing Review*, 21 (1), 53–76.

Melewar, T. C., Turnbull, S., & Balabanis, G. (2000). International advertising strategies of multinational enterprises in the Middle East. *International Journal of Advertising*, 19, 529–547.

Michell, P., & Al-Mossawi, M. (1999). Religious commitment related to message contentiousness. *Journal of Advertising*, 18 (4), 427–443.

Mostafa, M. M. (2011). An investigation of Egyptian consumers' attitudes toward ethical issues in advertising. *Journal of Promotion Management*, 17 (1), 42–60.

Pan Arabian Research Center (2011). *Advertising Markets Y2010: Markets Ranking and Media Contribution.* Retrieved February 20, 2012 from http://arabiandemographics.iniquus.com/KnowledgeBase.aspx.

Pew Research (2011, January 27). *The Future of the Global Muslim Population: Projections for 2010–2030.* Retrieved February 20, 2012 from http://pewresearch.org/pubs/1872/muslim-population-projections-worldwide-fast-growth.

Pollay, R., & Mittal, B. (1993). Here's the beef: Factors, determinants, and segments in consumer criticism of advertising. *Journal of Marketing*, 57 (3), 99–114.

Pomeroy, H. J., Castellano, J. P., Becker, J. G., Johnson, E. M., & Brown Jr., J. W. (1992). Distilling the truth about alcohol ads. *Business and Society Review*, 83 (Fall), 12–17.

Prahalad, C. K. (2004). *The Fortune at the Bottom of the Pyramid: Eradicating Poverty Through Profit.* Upper Saddle River, NJ: Wharton School Publishing.

Rahman, Z., & Bhattacharyya, S. K. (2003). Sources of first-mover advantages in emerging markets: An Indian perspective. *European Business Review*, 15 (6), 361–371.

Rawwas, M., Patzer, G. L., & Klassen, M. L. (1995). Consumer ethics in cross-cultural settings: Entrepreneurial implications. *European Journal of Marketing*, 29 (7), 62–79.

Rettab, B., Brik, A. B., & Mellahi, K. (2009). Study of management perceptions of the impact of corporate social responsibility on organisational performance in emerging economies: The case of Dubai. *Journal of Business Ethics*, 89, 371–390.

Rice, G. (1999). Islamic ethics and the implications for business. *Journal of Business Ethics*, 18 (4), 345–358.

Rice, G., & Al-Mossawi, M. (2002). The implications of Islam for advertising messages: The Middle Eastern context. *Journal of Euromarketing*, 11 (3), 71–96.

Samli, A. C. (2004). *Entering and Succeeding in Emerging Countries: Marketing to the Forgotten Majority.* Mason, OH: Thomson Southwest.

Schneider, K. C., & Schneider, S. B. (1979). Trends in sex roles in television commercials. *The Journal of Marketing*, 43 (3), 79–84.

Singhapakdi, A., Rawwas, M., Marta, J., & Ahmed, M. (1999). A cross-cultural study of consumer perceptions about marketing ethics. *Journal of Consumer Marketing*, 16 (3), 257–272.

Spence, E., & Van Heereken, B. (2005). *Advertising Ethics.* Upper Saddle River, NJ: Pearson Prentice Hall.

Stafford, D. C. (1988). Advertising in the professions: A review of the literature. *International Journal of Advertising*, 7 (3), 189–220.

Swerdlow, R. A., & Blessios, V. I. (1993). A model for predicting advertising expenditures: An inter-industry comparison. *International Journal of Advertising*, 12 (2), 143–153.

Tai, S. H. C., & Pae, J. H. (2002). Effects of TV advertising on Chienese consumers: Local versus foreign-sourced commericals. *Journal of Marketing Management*, 18 (1–2), 49–72.

Taylor, C. (2005). Moving international advertising research forward: A new research agenda. *Journal of Advertising*, 34 (1), 7–16.

Telser, L. G. (1971), *Advertising and Competition*, Bobbs-Merrill reprint series in economics, ECON-305. Indianapolis, IN: Bobbs-Merrill.

Treise, D., Weigold, M., Conna, J., & Garrison, H. (1994). Ethics in advertising: Ideological correlates of consumer perceptions. *Journal of Advertising*, 23 (3), 59–69.

Waller, D. S. (2002). Advertising agency–client attitudes towards ethical issues in political advertising. *Journal of Business Ethics*, 36 (1), 347–354.

Waller, D. S., Fam, K. S., & Erdogan, B. Z. (2005). Advertising of controversial products: A cross-cultural study. *Journal of Consumer Marketing*, 22 (1), 6–13.

Wurff, R. G., Bakker, P., & Picard, R. (2008). Economic growth and advertising expenditures in different media in different countries. *Journal of Media Economics*, 21 (1), 28–52.

Zinkhan, G. M. (1994). Advertising ethics: Emerging methods and trends. *Journal of Advertising*, 23 (3), 1–5.

Index